DAILY LITURGICAL PRAYER

D0705776

Tracing the origins of daily prayer from the New Testament and patristic period, through the Reformation and Renaissance to the present, this book examines the development of daily rites across a broad range of traditions including: pre-Crusades Constantinopolitan, East and West Syrian, Coptic and Ethiopian, non-Roman and Roman Western. Structure, texts and ceremonial are examined, and contemporary scholarship surveyed. Concluding with a critique of the present tenor of liturgical revision, the author raises key questions for current liturgical change, suggests to whom these questions should be addressed, and proposes that the daily office might be the springboard for an authentic baptismal spirituality.

Exploring the origins, early development and contemporary forms of services of daily prayer, this book focuses particularly on morning and evening offices to highlight a common underlying theology at work across the traditional orders of prayer. Even where irreducibly different ritual forms of daily office exist, Woolfenden examines how prayer and poetic texts indicate that the thrust of the ancient offices was a movement from night to morning – from death to resurrection.

LITURGY, WORSHIP AND SOCIETY

SERIES EDITORS

Dave Leal, Brasenose College, Oxford, UK
Bryan Spinks, Yale Divinity School, USA
Paul Bradshaw, University of Notre Dame, UK and USA
Gregory W. Woolfenden, Ripon College, Cuddesdon, Oxford, UK
Phillip Tovey, Diocese of Oxford and Oxford Brookes University, UK

This new series comes at a time of great change in liturgy and much debate concerning traditional and new forms of worship, the suitability and use of places of worship, and wider issues concerning the interaction of liturgy, worship and contemporary society. Offering a thorough grounding in the historical and theological foundations of liturgy, books in the series explore and challenge many key issues of worship and liturgical theology which are currently in hot debate – issues set to make a significant impact on the place of the Church in contemporary society. Presenting an ecumenical range of books, comparing and contrasting liturgical practices and concerns within various traditions and faiths, this series will appeal to those in university and theological colleges; adult education colleges; those on other ministry or lay ministry training courses; and practitioners and those involved in worship in churches across a broad ecumenical range.

Other titles in the series include

Death Liturgy and Ritual
Volume I: A Pastoral and Liturgical Theology
Volume II: A Commentary on Liturgical Texts
Paul P.J. Sheppy

West Syrian Liturgical Theology
Baby Varghese

Rituals and Theologies of Christian Baptism:
Beyond the Jordan
Bryan D. Spinks

Inculturation of Christian Worship:
Exploring the Eucharist
Phillip Tovey

Daily Liturgical Prayer

Origins and Theology

GREGORY W. WOOLFENDEN

ASHGATE

© Gregory W. Woolfenden, 2004

All rights reserved. No part of this publication may be reproduced, stored in a retrieval system, or transmitted in any form or by any means, electronic, mechanical, photocopied, recorded, or otherwise without the prior permission of the publisher.

The author has asserted his moral right under the Copyright, Designs and Patents Act, 1988, to be identified as the author of this work.

Published by

Ashgate Publishing Limited
Gower House
Croft Road
Aldershot
Hants GU11 3HR
England

Ashgate Publishing Company
Suite 420
101 Cherry Street
Burlington, VT 05401-4405
USA

Ashgate website: http://www.ashgate.com

British Library Cataloguing in Publication Data
Woolfenden, Gregory W.
Daily liturgical prayer: origins and theology. – (Liturgy, worship and society)
1. Divine office 2. Prayer – Christianity – History 3. Liturgics
I. Title
264.1′5

Library of Congress Cataloging-in-Publication Data
Woolfenden, Gregory W., 1947–
Daily liturgical prayer : origins and theology. / Gregory W. Woolfenden.
p. cm. – (Liturgy, worship and society series)
Includes bibliographical references (p.) and index.
ISBN 0-7546-1600-2 (alk. paper) – ISBN 0-7546-1601-0 (pbk. : alk. paper)
1. Divine office – Texts – History and criticism. I. Title. II. Series.

BV199.D3W66 2004
264′.15′09 – dc22 2003063708

ISBN 0 7546 1600 2 (Hbk)
ISBN 0 7546 1601 0 (Pbk)

Printed on acid-free paper

Typeset by Tradespools, Frome, Somerset
Printed and bound in Great Britain by Antony Rowe Ltd, Chippenham, Wilts

To the staff and students of Ripon College, Cuddesdon, Oxford
since 1989, for their patience and support

Contents

A List of the Tables of Services in this Book

Preface

In recent years, a number of major scholarly works have tackled the origins of the Divine Office. It may well be asked why there needs to be another. It should become apparent to the reader that I owe much in both content and inspiration to Robert Taft's widely read and very helpful book *The Liturgy of the Hours in East and West*, published in 1986. Taft's work will remain standard for many aspects of daily liturgical prayer, for example his limpid summary of the controverted origins of the office of Prime. However I believe that there is a need for a study that takes up Taft's 'prolegomena' to a theology of the Divine Office, and this is mainly what this book sets out to do.

In trying to establish what might be a theology of daily prayer, I have attempted to let the liturgical rites speak for themselves as much as possible, hence the large number of examples of prayers and hymnody, in addition to studies of the psalms and other scriptures employed. Inevitably there will be some revisiting of the historical material, taking account of the most recent scholarship. This book will also try to give a more complete account of some traditions of daily prayer that were not given in much detail by Taft or by other authors. For example, the so-called 'chanted office' of Constantinople.

Although the historical material is summarized so far as possible, the principal focus is upon the meaning that authors have given to the services of daily prayer, and which can be found in the structures and texts of those rites of prayer. Another author who has been of great influence on me is Paul Bradshaw, who has shown that we have little concrete evidence for what we would now recognize as a daily office before the fourth century. For that reason, although more ancient works will be cited, they will be treated with caution. However, it seems fair to identify themes in the fragmentary pre-Nicene authors and documents that can be found to be significantly similar to the later, developed forms that we can describe with more confidence.

It should not be thought that I am concerned only with ancient and medieval rites. It is possible that the study may be carried forward in another volume to deal with the Reformation and Counter-Reformation offices and their history to modern times. This will involve consideration of how far a different and contrasting theology of daily prayer may be said to have developed so as to characterize most modern understandings of this form of liturgical prayer.

This book started out as a PhD thesis for Heythrop College in the University of London, but has been considerably revised and re-focused. This then would seem to be the right place to acknowledge the help and support of my supervisors, the late Dr Edward Yarnold SJ, and Dr Francis Laishley SJ. The long-standing inspiration of Archimandrite Robert Taft SJ has been alluded to, and I must also record the valuable criticisms and observations of Professor Paul Bradshaw. Many people who have given me valuable insights are mentioned in the endnotes, but I should record particular thanks to my successive College Principals, the Rt Revd John Garton, Bishop of Plymouth, and the Revd Canon John Clarke, for time and understanding. My good friends, Higoumen Andrew (Wade) and the Revd Phillip Tovey have made interesting and helpful observations and often given me much needed encouragement. This last is true as well of my spiritual father, the Rt Revd Bishop Basil (Osbourne) of Sergievo, who also has given permission for me to quote the liturgical texts produced by the Orthodox diocese of Sourozh.

Throughout the book, the psalms are normally cited according to the Septuagist numberings.

Gregory Woolfenden
Ripon College
Cuddesdon
Oxford

CHAPTER 1

Introduction and Survey of Research

The introduction to the section on the Divine Office in the most recent edition of *The Study of Liturgy*[1] has a definition of the office that neatly encapsulates present-day understanding of this liturgical form. It says: 'The divine office ... may be defined as a pattern of non-sacramental services to be celebrated or recited at intervals during the day (and night)'. This seemingly unexceptional statement begs the questions as to whether (a) the exclusion of any concept of sacramentality, and (b) the obvious bias towards what has been called the 'sanctification of the day', can leave us with a correct hermeneutical principle for understanding the concept of prayer at set times of day and night.

The modern Western, and to a certain extent, Eastern, concept of sacramentality has tended to narrow it down to seven, or even only two, ecclesial acts. This medieval development grew out of a desire to make ever more precise distinctions between 'the sacraments of the new covenant and the broad "sacramental realm" of natural sacraments, Old Testament sacraments, consecrations resembling sacraments, and blessings'.[2] An older understanding of sacraments was much broader; Hugh of St Victor (+ 1142) even included the sign of the cross and the 'opening of the hands in charity' as sacraments, and, unsurprisingly, concluded that the sacraments were too many to number.[3] God is not tied to certain specific acts but rather there are many potential ways in which 'ritual activity symbolizes the presence and activity of God in the faith of the Church'.[4]

The narrowing tendency has never taken over completely in the Christian East, as Bishop Kallistos (Ware) has said: 'we must never isolate these seven from the many other actions in the Church which also possess a sacramental character'.[5] Similarly, Christos Yannaras points out that 'The whole life of the faithful, every turn of his life, is a preparation for participation in or an event of participation in the gifts of the Holy Spirit, in the refashioning of life.'[6] Alexander Schmemann

---

[1] Eds Cheslyn Jones, Geoffrey Wainwright, Edward Yarnold SJ and Paul Bradshaw (London: SPCK, 1992), p. 399.

[2] H. Vorgrimler, *Sacramental Theology* (Collegeville, MN: Liturgical Press, 1992), p. 52.

[3] See my 'The Sacraments and Evangelisation', *The Month*, **CCLIV**, #1503, 2nd ns **26**, #3 (March, 1993), 121–25, quoting *PL* 176, col. 475.

[4] John Baldovin, 'Liturgical Presidency: The Sacramental question', in Baldovin, *Worship: City, Church and Renewal* (Washington, DC: Pastoral Press, 1991), pp. 115–34, 121.

[5] Timothy Ware, *The Orthodox Church* (new edn, London: Penguin, 1993), p. 276.

[6] *Elements of Faith* (Edinburgh: T. & T. Clark, 1991), p. 133.

was anxious not to reduce the whole of liturgical life to the Eucharist, nor to extend the concept of sacrament too widely,[7] but while respecting his concern, we shall maintain that there is, in liturgical forms at evening and morning, an *act* which is at least quasi-sacramental. Most recently, Bishop Hilarion (Alfeyev) has shown how, as late as the thirteenth century, Eastern theological thought was unconcerned about the number of the sacraments.[8]

This leads to the second presupposition, that the offices are more or less arbitrary attempts to Christianize day and night, whereas we shall try to show that the rhythm of day and night, or rather, night followed by day, is fundamental to the whole concept of prayer at particular hours.

The daily symbols of night and day are basic to any symbolic understanding of reality. The cycles of birth and death, winter and summer may be encapsulated in the daily passage from light to darkness, through that darkness, and back again to light. Mircea Eliade, speaking of initiatory symbolism said: 'initiatory death is often symbolized, for example, by cosmic night, by the telluric womb, the hut, the belly of a monster'.[9]

Symbols were essential to the expression of Christianity from its very beginning, and symbols are recognized rather than created: 'They grow out of the individual or collective unconscious and cannot function without being accepted by the unconscious dimension of our being.'[10] Human beings symbolize their relationships with each other, the task of those who explore symbolism is to identify the symbolic ways, not to invent them. Symbolic phenomena interpret context, and not the other way round; symbols in fact throw light by which we may discern the true nature of reality.[11]

We shall stress the dynamic of the office from the beginning of the night to the full light of day, because it ensures that the celebration of daily prayer enables participation in the paschal mystery of Christ's death and resurrection. In the chapters on the traditions of daily prayer, we will first explain their structure, then examine the scriptures they use and how they use them, and finally how the meaning of these services is explicitated in hymn and prayer texts. This method demonstrates the interplay between ritual, visual action, the scriptural proclamation and the *lex orandi*, and is inspired by the work of David Power on sacraments.[12]

---

[7] *Introduction to Liturgical Theology* (London: Faith Press, 1966), p. 34.

[8] *The Mystery of Faith* (Eng. trans., London: DLT, 2002), p. 131.

[9] *Rites and Symbols of Initiation* (Eng. trans. W.F. Trask, New York: Harper & Row, 1958), pp. 14–15.

[10] Dan Sperber, *Rethinking Symbolism* (Cambridge: Cambridge University Press, 1974), p. 49.

[11] Ibid., p. 117.

[12] David Power, *Sacrament: The Language of God's Giving* (New York: Crossroad, 1999), pp. 99–100.

Research on the Subject

A number of books have examined the history of the daily office in recent years, and have advanced the discussion well beyond the works of older scholars. One of the earlier scholars, Batiffol concluded that the order of evening, night and morning offices was the origin of daily prayer,[13] a vigilial form that spread from weekly to festal, and ultimately to daily, use. Jules Baudot[14] and Suitbert Bäumer[15] again also mainly examined Western, and particularly Roman, forms in a similar way.

A major development in the understanding of the Divine Office and its history was Anton Baumstark's positing of the now common distinction between the 'cathedral' and 'monastic' offices.[16] For Baumstark, the cathedral rite comprised only two services, at morning and evening, with a vigil on Saturday to Sunday night. These services used only a small number of psalms, chosen for their suitability for the time of day; whilst monastic prayer became characterized by the use of the whole psalter in course, from 1 to 150, in some set period of time, most often, a week. Monastic offices were multiple; Terce, Sext and None became communal, and forms of prayer late at night, midnight (distinct from the pre-dawn vigil) and at the first hour (Prime), became part of the daily *cursus*.[17]

Baumstark's principles of comparative liturgy became the framework for modern scholars, a first wave of whom included Juan Mateos,[18] whose findings became widely influential. Mateos summed up his view of the nature of the office in an English-language article. Emphasizing the popular nature of the 'cathedral office', he enumerated the now familiar elements: a typical morning office of cathedral type had psalm 50 to open it, then psalm 62, an Old Testament canticle, hymn, a New Testament canticle accompanied by incense, the praise psalms and prayer. The evening office comprised a lamp-lighting ritual, evening psalm or psalms, evening incense and prayer.[19]

---

[13] Pierre Batiffol, *Histoire du Bréviaire Romain* (Paris: 1893), Eng. trans. Atwell Baylay (London: 1898), p. 36.

[14] *The Roman Breviary: Its Sources and History* (Eng. trans., London: 1909), see esp. pp. 27–9.

[15] Suitbert Bäumer OSB, *Histoire du Bréviaire*, 2 vols (Paris: 1905) [translation of *Geschichte des Breviers* (Freiburg, 1895)], pp. 52–3.

[16] French edn 1940, Eng. trans. *Comparative Liturgy* (London: Mowbrays, 1958).

[17] Ibid., pp. 112–15.

[18] E.g., J. Mateos, 'L'office du soir: ancienne structure et realisations concretes', *Revue du clergé Africain*, **19** (1964), 3–25; 'L'office dominical de la Résurrection', *Revue du clergé Africain*, **19** (1964), 263–88; and 'Quelques aspects Théologiques de l'Office du matin', *Revue du clergé Africain*, **20** (1965), 335–49.

[19] J. Mateos, 'The Morning and Evening Office', *Worship*, **42** (1968), 31–47.

Mateos' popular articles of the 1960s accompanied a time of liturgical change everywhere, but he did not convince the revisers of the Roman offices in 1964.[20] They, and many others, followed the path of what Stanislaus Campbell has called 'eclectic traditionalism' which justified reforms by isolated precedents;[21] and clearly distrusted liturgical scholarship.

The Orthodox scholar Alexander Schmemann alerted the West to the findings of older Russian scholarship and was convinced that Vespers and Matins were commonly celebrated in the third century and did not have a monastic origin.[22] Other writers also popularized these views about the origin of and importance for the modern church of the ancient cathedral office.[23]

It was increasingly recognized that prayer at the beginning and end of the day is common to most religious traditions, including Judaism, and as with other Christian acts of worship, such as baptism and the Eucharist, many efforts were made to try and establish Jewish origins for Christian daily prayer.[24] However the idea that we can trace a direct line between synagogue worship and that of the early church is now largely abandoned.[25] Jewish scholars also were increasingly pointing out the dearth of evidence for a recognizeable synagogue service at the time of Christ.[26] The tradition of twice daily prayer in Christianity does not seem to have direct Jewish roots.[27]

---

[20] Stanislaus Campbell, FSC, *From Breviary to Liturgy of the Hours* (Collegeville, MN: Liturgical Press, 1995), pp. 79ff.

[21] Ibid., p. 251. Use of the Mozarabic rite to justify New Testament canticles, but see my *Daily Prayer in Christian Spain* (London: Alcuin / SPCK, 2000), ch. 11.

[22] *Introduction to Liturgical Theology*, op. cit., p. 66.

[23] See e.g., William G. Storey, 'Public Worship: The Liturgy of the Hours', *Worship*, **49** (1975), 2–12; idem, 'The Liturgy of the Hours: Cathedral versus Monastery', *Worship*, **50** (1976), 50–70. A good summary of the two kinds of office is George Guiver, *Company of Voices* (London: SPCK, 1988), p. 56.

[24] E.g., C.W. Dugmore, *The Influence of the Synagogue upon the Divine Office* (London: Alcuin Club / Faith Press, 1964), and R. Beckwith, *Daily and Weekly Worship: Jewish to Christian* (Bramcote: Alcuin / GROW Liturgical Study 1, 1987), esp. pp. 35–8.

[25] See e.g., W. McKinnon, 'On the Question of Psalmody in the Ancient Synagogue', in *Early Music History*, **VI** (Cambridge, 1986), 159–91.

[26] See e.g., Paul F. Bradshaw and L.A. Hoffman (eds), *The Making of Jewish and Christian Worship* (Notre Dame: University of Notre Dame Press, 1991), esp. Stefan C. Reif, 'The Early History of Jewish Worship' on pp. 109–36. Heather A. McKay, *Sabbath and Synagogue* (Leiden: E.J. Brill, 1994) presents the evidence against there being any form of Synagogue worship service in the first centuries of the Common Era.

[27] Paul Bradshaw, in *The Search for the Origins of Christian Worship* (London: SPCK, 2002) sums up modern Jewish and Christian scholarship on the subject, esp. pp. 23–46.

There has, as in the definition quoted at the beginning of this Introduction, been a tendency to define daily offices as simply times of prayer, rather along the lines of an ascetic exercise, twice daily.[28] Baumstark's distinction between 'cathedral' and 'monastic' offices now only seems supportable from the fourth century, the earliest stage from which we have much evidence for the existence of twice-daily public prayer. Paul Bradshaw summarized evidence from an earlier period for prayer three times during the day and once during the night, which may well have been private or at least domestic. For the first two or three centuries the apostolic injunction to pray without ceasing (1 Thess. 5.17) seems to have been influential, but possibly in a largely domestic context.[29] Bradshaw concluded by suggesting that the twice daily pattern may have arisen from practical convenience, or as a conscious desire to replicate the practice of the Temple, and notes that previous examination had tended to ignore the importance of prayer in the night for many Fathers.[30]

In his recently revised work, *The Search for the Origins of Christian Worship*, Bradshaw seems even less willing to go beyond stating a number of features that do seem to be common at morning and evening prayer services; for example, psalms 148–50 and the *Benedicite* in the morning, and a hymn of light, such as Φως 'ιλαρόν, and either psalm 140 or 103. He sums up the daily cathedral office as 'the Church gathered for prayer, exercising the royal priesthood by offering a sacrifice of praise and thanksgiving on behalf of all creation and interceding for the salvation of the world'.[31] The question that Bradshaw asks and which remains unanswered, is how it happened that a scheme of three, probably domestic, prayers in the day and one at night became almost universally two major public services, vespers and matins, in the early or mid-fourth century.[32]

Robert Taft's contribution to this debate has taken the theology of daily prayer seriously as a constituent element of the offices, as he says: 'Evening and morning, at the setting and rising of the sun, the Church is reminded of Jesus' passover from death to life.'[33] He does, however, still seem to see morning and evening as more or less arbitrary times for prayer. He concludes:

> Per se there is no special mystical significance about morning and evening as times of prayer. They are the beginning and end of the day, and so it was

---

[28] E.g., L. Duchesne, *Christian Worship: Its Origin and Evolution* (London: SPCK, 1927), pp. 448–9.

[29] In *Daily Prayer in the Early Church* (London: Alcuin / SPCK, 1981), pp. 47, 50–1.

[30] Ibid., pp. 150–1.

[31] Ibid., pp. 171–8.

[32] Ibid., pp. 175–6.

[33] R. Taft, *The Liturgy of the Hours in East and West* (Collegeville: Liturgical Press, 1986), p. 28.

> perfectly natural to select them as the 'symbolic moments' in which we express what ought to be the quality of the whole day.[34]

From what has been said above, it should be clear that the present author feels that there *is* a particular significance to the 'hinge moments' of the day, a significance recognized, rather than arbitrarily selected.

Taft sums up much of what can be known of the evolution of the structures of the offices both in East and West. He has also established the structures that undergird the still extant traditions, but we are still left unclear as to why *these* structures, and no others, have survived or have been discovered.

Taft ended his work with an attempt to establish a theology of daily prayer.[35] He stressed the transformation of time into event, the daily victory of light over darkness, and suggested some ways in which that is symbolized. However, Evensong in this seems only a thanksgiving after work at which light gives way to darkness and penance, with little sign of eschatological hope that comes only next morning.

A number of recent authors have examined the divine office from a more philosophical or theological point of view.[36] Andrea Grillo speaks of a sacramental ethos and sacramental ethics in connection with the Liturgy of Time, but seems more concerned with rhythm in Christian life than the rhythm of time itself.[37] Renato de Zan emphasizes the evening to evening thrust of Jewish prayer being replaced by that of Roman secular society.[38] This collection shows how wide the discussion is, but does not greatly advance the argument.

Taft concentrated on the morning and evening offices, and did not include the vigil in his structure, perhaps seeing it as either purely monastic, or as an event of the cathedral office tied to Sundays and feasts, and in both cases rather separate from the basic morning and evening structure. He went a long way towards demonstrating that daily offices are liturgical acts of prayer, but is somewhat vague as to just how this is so.

The tendency to treat the morning and evening offices as the hinges of the day, in accordance with the documents of Vatican II, often seems to lead commentators to attempt to fit those services into a single ideal shape of introduction, Word of God, and prayers.[39] The problem with

---

[34] Ibid., pp. 347–8.

[35] 'Towards a Theology of the Liturgy of the Hours', ibid., pp. 331–65.

[36] E.g., in *Liturgia delle Ore: tempo e rito* (*BEL Subsidia 75*, Roma: Edizioni Liturgiche, 1994).

[37] 'Problematiche attuali della preghiera nel ritmi del tempo', ibid., pp. 45–88.

[38] 'Il tempo della preghiera nel Nuovo Testamento', ibid., pp. 89–106, 103.

[39] See introduction to the Society of St. Francis, *Celebrating Common Prayer* (London: Mowbray, 1992), p. 11.

this shape is not that it is false so much as misleading, for it suggests that the two 'hinge offices' function in more or less the same way as each other, but at different points of the day. The edificatory element of the Word of God tends to dominate the core of this type of daily prayer, leaving little room for either service to function as a genuine liturgical act. Just as there is a rite involving a water-bath at the centre of baptism, and another involving a simple meal of bread, the staple of temperate climes, and wine, a sign of festivity, at the centre of the Eucharist; then, we contend, there are the moments of sunset and sunrise which are at the centre of the *acts* of evening and morning prayer. It is the ritualization of these moments that gives rise to forms of evening and morning prayer, which need then to be conceived as actions of at least a quasi-sacramental nature.

How this Book Will Approach the Subject

In the chapters that follow we will first briefly examine the biblical and patristic evidence for the symbolic importance of light and darkness, and for prayer at night. No one disputes that daily prayer was called for by the Bible and the Fathers, and the authors already mentioned have marshalled the evidence succinctly and completely.[40] Here we intend only to explore whether any special importance is given to prayer in the night, and further, the centrality of the theme of light overcoming the darkness.

The next chapter will examine the Church Orders, and, after a brief survey to set the historical context, the following six chapters will examine the offices of the Christian East, noting the common structures and theological outlook that they can be said to share. Three chapters will then examine the Western offices and see how far they share the same concerns.

The conclusion will examine whether there is a function or moment that is being ritualized in evening and morning prayer, and whether this provides an hermeneutical principle for comprehending the liturgy of daily worship. This conclusion will suggest that Batiffol's proposal of the primacy of vigil prayer in the development of the daily office was fundamentally sound. From this it will follow that the thrust of daily prayer is from night to morning and not from morning to night. 'First Vespers' is in fact the evening service that begins the liturgical day – as remains the case in the liturgical practices of all the Eastern churches. The watch for, and in anticipation of, the Lord's return is the fundamental rationale of the daily office.

[40] See e.g., Bradshaw, *Daily Prayer*, op. cit., pp. 1–46, and Taft, op. cit., pp. 3–11.

Finally, as regards nomenclature, the concept of 'vigil' implies being awake and on watch, not sleeping,[41] as does the Greek αγρυπνία.[42] Carlo Marcora described several kinds of vigil,[43] some lasted all night, but most were for a part of the night, very often the early morning before light. In general, we will use the word 'vigil' for any service or part of a service celebrated after Vespers and before Matins. We will always speak of Vespers as a service intended for sundown, while Matins is at sunrise or thereabouts.

[41] See e.g., Lewis and Short, *A Latin Dictionary* (Oxford: Clarendon, 1896).

[42] E.g., G.W.H. Lampe (ed.), *A Patristic Greek Lexicon* (Oxford: Clarendon, 1961).

[43] *La Vigilia nella Liturgia* (Milan: *Archivio Ambrosiano VI*, Milan, 1954), esp. p. 62.

CHAPTER 2

From Evening to Morning: Biblical and Patristic Symbolism

The Old Testament and Early Rabbinic Judaism

The first scriptural text in which the symbolism of night and day illustrates our argument is Genesis 1.5: 'God called the light Day, and the darkness he called Night. And there was evening and there was morning, the first day.' It is the creation of light and dark that allows for the creation of day, itself created out of darkness. As Von Rad puts it:

> Every night, when the created world of forms flows together into formlessness, chaos regains a certain power over what has been created. (Many of our evening hymns know how to express impressively the creaturely feeling of dread toward the night.) And every morning ... , something of God's first creation is repeated.[1]

There is a difference between Genesis and 'the accepted Jewish practice of connecting the day-time with the previous night, that is the custom of regarding sunset as the starting-point of the day'.[2]

The cultic law commands a light to be kept burning through the night:

> You shall further command the Israelites to bring you pure oil of beaten olives for the light, so that a lamp may be set up to burn regularly. In the tent of meeting, outside the curtain that is before the covenant, Aaron and his sons shall tend it from evening to morning before the Lord. It shall be a perpetual ordinance to be observed throughout their generations by the Israelites.
> (Exodus 27.20–21)

The concern that the light be kept burning, actively tended by the Aaronic priesthood, throughout the night, may be seen as a form of vigil. The command is repeated in Leviticus 24.2–3:

> Command the people of Israel to bring you pure oil of beaten olives for the lamp, that a light may be kept burning regularly. Aaron shall set it up in the

---

[1] G. von Rad, *Genesis: A Commentary* (London: SCM Press, rev. edn, 1972), pp. 52–3.

[2] Umberto Cassuto, *Commentary on Genesis, vol. I* (Eng. trans., Jerusalem: Hebrew University, 1961), p. 28.

> tent of meeting, outside the curtain of the covenant, to burn from evening to morning before the Lord regularly; it shall be a statute forever throughout your generations.

Sacrifice was to be offered daily, morning and evening:

> Now this is what you shall offer on the altar: two lambs a year old regularly each day. One lamb you shall offer in the morning, and the other lamb you shall offer in the evening ... And the other lamb you shall offer in the evening, and shall offer with it a grain offering and its drink offering, as in the morning, for a pleasing odour, an offering by fire to the Lord.
>
> (Exodus 29.38–9, 41)

In addition to this twice-daily animal sacrifice there was to be a daily offering of incense:

> You shall make an altar on which to offer incense; you shall make it of acacia wood ... Aaron shall offer fragrant incense on it; every morning when he dresses the lamps he shall offer it, and when Aaron sets up the lamps in the evening, he shall offer it, a regular incense offering before the Lord throughout your generations.
>
> (Exodus 30.1, 7–8)

Bearing in mind the subsequent history of daily prayer in the Christian church, it is interesting that this offering of incense is connected with the dressing of lamps in the morning, and again at night.

The daily sacrifice was organized on the basis of reckoning the day from morning to morning, but as Cassuto pointed out, regulations that connect the night to the preceding day, 'offer no difficulty to our hypothesis. On the contrary, they tally with our explanation, for all the laws relating to the sacrifices were framed to accord specifically with the conditions obtaining in the Land of Canaan.'[3] So which is the earlier? Reckoning the day to start in the morning, or at night?

H.R. Stroes summed up the biblical evidence in an article in 1966,[4] and tentatively concluded that the civil reckoning of pre-exilic Israel was from morning to night, and the cultic from evening to evening. Other scholars argue strongly for a pre-exilic morning to morning reckoning. The custom of the Sabbath light on the evening preceding the Sabbath, presumed old by the Mishnah, has no biblical origin. Also, the light was perhaps lit the night before to avoid kindling a light on the Sabbath and thereby infringing the

[3] Ibid., p. 30.

[4] 'Does the Day begin in the Evening or the Morning?', *Vetus Testamentum*, **16** (1966), 460–75.

day of rest.[5] The Mishnah is however clear that, e.g., 'The *one day* spoken of in the law of *It and its young* means the day together with the night that went before.'[6] Similarly, tractate Berakoth asks about the time of recitation of the evening *Shema*' and goes on to ask the same question of the morning recitation,[7] implying that evening comes first.

The New Testament

New Testament evidence for services of prayer is hard to come by, let alone considerations as to how the day was conceived to begin and end. Geoffrey Cuming examined the evidence and wondered whether there was worship every day, or only on Sundays. He tried to identify some elements of early Christian prayer as found in the letters of Paul; psalms, hymns and spiritual songs. He also noted that 'It is clear that much prayer took place at night, sometimes taking the form of an all-night vigil.' However, content and structure remain entirely obscure and, he says; 'Certainly there is no hint of a night office.'[8]

Taft's overview of New Testament texts on prayer mostly refers to private prayer, but he also mentions the Christian habit of imitating Jesus' practice of praying at night, and the idea of watching for the coming bridegroom that was implied in such practices[9]. A classical text for prayer at night is Acts 16.25: 'About midnight Paul and Silas were praying and singing hymns to God, and the prisoners were listening to them.' This accords with staying awake to watch in Mark 13.35: 'Therefore, keep awake, for you do not know when the master of the house will come, in the evening, or at midnight, or at cockcrow, or at dawn.' Remaining awake and watchful is a theme in Matthew, e.g., 24.42; 'Keep awake therefore, for you do not know on what day your Lord is coming.'

The eschatological theme is illustrated by the parable of the wise and foolish virgins: Matthew 25.6: 'But at midnight there was a shout, 'Look! Here is the bridegroom! Come out to meet him.'' and 25.13: 'Keep awake therefore, for you know neither the day nor the hour.' The bridegroom's midnight arrival becomes a commonplace of early Christianity; waking and praying, or staying awake, in order to watch for the coming Messianic bridegroom. We note the

---

[5] J.Z. Lauterback, 'The sabbath in Jewish Ritual and Folklore', in *Rabbinic Essays* (Cincinnati, 1951), pp. 437–70.

[6] *The Mishnah*, trans. Herbert Danby (Oxford: Oxford University Press: 1933, reprinted 1991), p. 522, Hullin 5.5.

[7] Ibid., p. 2, Berakoth 1 & 2.

[8] 'The New Testament Foundations for Common Prayer', *SL*, 10, (1974), 88–105.

[9] Taft, Op.cit., 5–11.

eschatological interest again in the garden of Gethsemane: Matthew 26.40–41: 'Then he came to the disciples and found them sleeping; and he said to Peter, 'So, could you not stay awake with me one hour? Stay awake and pray that you may not come into the time of trial; the spirit indeed is willing, but the flesh is weak.' There appears to be an apocalyptic side to this exhortation, not just a concern for the avoidance of sleep.[10] The importance of the night watch cannot be doubted and it cannot be limited to an annual Easter observance.

The night watch was part of the eschatological outlook of early Christians. On the other hand there must have been nights when a vigil would have been impossible because of work or other commitments. For example; 'On the first day of the week, when we met to break bread, Paul was holding a discussion with them; since he intended to leave the next day, he continued speaking until midnight' (Acts 20.7). On this occasion, quite possibly because of the incident involving Eutyches' fall from the window, the assembly is prolonged: 'Then Paul went upstairs, and after he had broken bread and eaten, he continued to converse with them until dawn; then he left' (Acts 20.11). It is possible that Eutyches' survival galvanized all present into a watchful night of thanks and eschatological expectation, for life had overcome death.

Perhaps the best New Testament example of a symbolic treatment of light and darkness is the prologue of John's Gospel; e.g., 1.4–5: 'in him was life, and the life was the light of all people. The light shines in the darkness, and the darkness did not overcome it.' We need not see a sort of Zoroastrian dualism here, the symbolism is used to illustrate an ethical dualism, similar to the struggle between children of light and of darkness spoken of in the Dead Sea scrolls.[11] Symbols have a great evocative power and a multi-facetedness that invites participation. The watch in the night, the natural passage into and out of darkness may illustrate basic Christian truths. This then may be the starting-point for understanding the nature and purpose of Christian daily prayer.

Patristic Symbolism

Around 96 CE, Clement of Rome, in chapter 24 of his first letter to the Corinthians, said, 'Day and night declare to us a resurrection. The night sinks to sleep and the day arises; the day [again] departs, and the night comes on.'[12] From the natural phenomenon of the sun's rising and setting, its dying and

[10] E.g., David Hill, *The Gospel of Matthew* (New Century Bible Commentary, Grand Rapids Eerdmans / London: & Marshall, Morgan & Scott, 1972), p. 342.

[11] J.N. Sanders and B.A. Mastin, *The Gospel according to John* (London: A. & C. Black, 1968), p. 74.

[12] (Ante-Nicene Christian Library I, Edinburgh: 1867), pp. 25–6; hereafter ANCL.

coming to life, Clement argues for the reasonableness of the death and resurrection of Christ. The sun and daylight are symbols of life, and the night a symbol of death, or even, as in another author, of ignorance.[13]

Ignatius of Antioch (c. 117) spoke to the Romans of his coming martyrdom as the path to resurrection life in Christ, which he calls 'pure light'.[14] Around 131 the *Epistle of Barnabas* described the Christian ethical way of life as 'The Way of Light'.[15] Clearly it was common for early Christians to describe the redemptive work of Christ, and its working out in the world, in the imagery of light and darkness.

Other second-century authors used similar imagery. Justin Martyr in his dialogue with Trypho (100.4) spoke of Christ as the day,[16] and Melito of Sardis, in his *On Pascha* uses such imagery a good deal. Melito's sermon was for an integrated celebration of the passion, death and resurrection of Christ, probably a Quartodeciman Passover. He makes great use of the contrast between light and dark, life and death; in stanza 68 Christ is 'he that delivered us from slavery to liberty, from darkness to light, from death to life'[17] and this he was able to do for 'he is the first-born of God, ... who tinted the light, who lit up the day, who divided off the darkness'. The mention of the first-born recalls the death of the Egyptian first-born described earlier by Melito, in a passage that makes much of the plague of darkness, 'a darkness that could be grasped and death grasping'. Into this darkness of death Christ goes 'sacrificed at evening and buried at night' but he emerges declaring: 'I am your life, I am your light, I am your salvation.'

Melito was active around 160–170 and it is clear that for him, the symbolism of light and life, darkness and death, evoked meaning. David Power cites Susanne Langer saying that the primary purpose of symbols is in their 'power of formulating experience, and presenting it objectively for contemplation, logical intuition, recognition, understanding'.[18] Natural symbols such as day and night have undeniable power, as is obvious in the writings of such as Melito, because the symbolism provided the formulation of experience of which Langer speaks.

In a fragmentary sermon on baptism Melito described the sun as 'baptized' each day. For the sun sets, as if into the waters, and rises in glory: 'Though one

[13] Hermas, *The Shepherd* (ANCL I, Edinburgh, 1867), pp. 414–15.

[14] *Epistle to the Romans* (ANCL I), p. 215.

[15] (ANCL I), p. 131.

[16] See *PG* 6, 709.

[17] All quotes from S.G. Hall (ed.), *On Pascha* (Oxford: Oxford University Press, 1979).

[18] D.N. Power, *Unsearchable Riches: The Symbolic Nature of Liturgy* (New York: Pueblo, 1984), p. 68.

and the same, he rises for men as a new sun, tempered from the deep, purified from the bath; he has driven off the nocturnal darkness, and has begotten bright day.'[19] Melito again draws upon natural symbols to order reality and to enter into its significance. Further, whereas in *On Pascha* he dealt with light and darkness as symbolic of the resurrection of Christ at Easter, in this fragment he appears to speak of a daily experience of renewal of the sun's rays, and of the risen life of Christ in his people. A people who enter that life by baptism once, but live it every day.

Third-century writers are better known and more numerous, and also provide many examples of the imagery of light and life, darkness and death. Origen, in first half of the third century, is an important exponent of the theme, identifying the Sun of Righteousness in Malachi 1.2 with Christ who is a new day for believers.[20] In his treatment of Sunday, the Lord's Day, Origen spoke of Christians feeding on the 'flesh of the Word' which was their Passover, the old Passover having been eaten not only in the evening but in 'the evening of the world that you might nourish yourselves on the flesh of His Word, you who are always evening until the morning comes ... so, too, you shall rejoice and be glad in the morning, that is in the world to come'.[21] The imagery has taken on a new and more complex aspect, Origen extends the darkness theme to include Christians waiting in the darkened evening of this world for the glorious light of the world to come, called elsewhere 'spiritual day'.[22]

Clement of Alexandria described dawn as an image of the day of birth, which was a reason for turning east to pray, to greet the sun as a natural symbol of the new life of the risen Christ in which his people are to share.[23] In the *Stromata* Clement also described Christ as the day,[24] and in the *Paedogogus*, night is a metaphor for ignorance.[25] Sleep does not exclude watchfulness, 'Wherefore we ought often to rise by night and bless God. For blessed are they who watch for him, ... '.[26] Enlightenment was, for Clement, the gift that brought one from the darkness of ignorance of Christ to His glorious light. The Divine Light could be reached through baptism,[27] a light attained when turning from the darkness of death and sin, and rejecting

[19] Fragment 8b, *On Pascha*, op. cit., p. 73.

[20] Homily on Exodus VII, *PG* 12, 347.

[21] On Genesis, Homily X, *PG* 12, 218.

[22] Lampe, op. cit., *hemera* (John 32.2), p. 606.

[23] *Stromata* VII.7, in *PG* 9, 461.

[24] 6.16, *PG* 7, 376–7.

[25] *Paed.* I.6, *PG* 8, 280ff.; II.9, *PG* 8, 489ff.

[26] *PG* 8, 492–3, English, ANCL I, p. 241.

[27] *Protrep.* 12, *PG* 8, 240–1, C. Mondésert (ed.), *Le Protreptique* (*SCH 2*, Paris: 1949).

Satan.[28] These writers clearly saw the primordial symbols of light and darkness as ways by which the reality of the Christian's passage from death to life in baptism, and in other aspects of ecclesial life, was actually communicated.

The *Acts of Judas Thomas*, early third century, exists in two recensions, Greek and Syriac, and it is impossible to establish how much of the text is original, and how far the group which produced it was part of mainstream Christianity of the time.[29] The apostle Thomas is depicted as baptizing at night and breaking the bread of the Eucharist when the morning light comes. The imagery of light over darkness is a feature of the work, e.g.: 'Come out from the darkness, that the light may receive you!'[30] Not a particularly helpful document on its own, it does show that pattern nocturnal baptism and morning Eucharist, possibly on a Sunday, were known to its compilers. For the present study, light in the night, and longing for the eternal day are the themes to be borne in mind.

The Fathers of the fourth century on are very numerous and so only a small selection of their writings on these topics will be instanced. Basil (c.330–379), in the *Hexaemeron*, was concerned to avoid any suggestion that talk of light and darkness could admit a sub-Christian dualism of the type found in many of the Gnostic writers. He vigorously opposed any suggestion that darkness was a self-contained evil power in permanent mortal combat with the power of Good, identified with God. In these catechetical homilies on the first chapters of Genesis, Basil said: 'The first word of God created the nature of light; it made darkness vanish, dispelled gloom, illuminated the world and gave to all beings at the same time a sweet and gracious aspect.' He then stressed the natures of light and darkness, day and night, as incapable of mixing, and quoted Genesis that there was evening and morning, the first day; evening being the boundary common to day and night.[31]

Basil regarded both day and night as created by God, primordial darkness was simply the absence of God's light. At the end of the homily on Genesis, Basil, carried away by his own eloquence, hastened to conclude with prayer:

> But, while I am conversing with you about the first evening of the world, evening takes me by surprise, and puts an end to my discourse. May the Father of the true light, Who has adorned day with celestial light, Who has made the fire to shine which illumines us during the night, Who reserves for us in the peace of a future age a spiritual and everlasting light, enlighten your hearts in the knowledge of truth, keep you from stumbling, and grant that '... you may walk honestly as in the day.' Thus shall you shine as the

[28] *Paed.* I.6, *PG* 8, 280ff.

[29] Bradshaw, *The Search*, op. cit., pp. 107–8.

[30] See e.g., W. Schneemelcher and E. Hennecke (eds), *The New Testament Apocrypha* (London: Lutterworth, 1965), pp. 456–8.

[31] Basil, *Hexaemeron*, trans. Blomfield Jackson (Oxford: 1895), pp. 51–107, Homilies II.7 & 8.

> sun in the midst of the glory of the saints, and I shall glory in you in the day of Christ, to Whom belong all glory and power for ever and ever. Amen.[32]

The prayer sums up the symbolism outlined above. The darkness approaches but the 'fire' (perhaps a lamp or lamps?) remains to symbolize the presence of Christ whose power can and will overcome the darkness of sin and death. The prayer of thanks for the light is also prayer for protection throughout the threatening darkness of the night, in which God's faithful people are to walk honestly as if in the day. The faithful may always look beyond the oncoming night to the new day symbolizing the everlasting day.

The imagery of light and darkness is also found in Basil's treatise *On the Holy Spirit*. As, for example, in Clement of Rome and Clement of Alexandria, darkness may symbolize ignorance: 'Those that are confined in the darkness of ignorance He enlightens: for this reason He is true light.' The Spirit is 'light perceptible to the mind' supplying light for the search for truth. The Spirit is the only power enabling us to see the brightness of God. We again find the idea of God's eternal day, the spiritual day mentioned by Origen, recurring in Basil who speaks of: 'the day which knows no waning or eventide, and no successor, that age which endeth not nor groweth old'.[33]

The writer known as Denys the Areopagite, appears to have flourished in Syria about the turn of the fifth / sixth centuries.[34] We shall use the translated edition of his works by Colm Luibheid and Paul Rorem.[35] The contrast between darkness and light is very important to this influential author, and although he did not comment explicitly on Vespers and Matins, the ideas expressed throughout his works allow us to see something of the importance of light and darkness in his theology.

De Divinis Nominibus often expresses knowledge of the divine in terms of light or illumination. Light is a sign of the divine goodness and beneficent enlightenment; 'Light comes from the Good, and light is an image of the archetypal Good.' In this, the sun symbolizes the divine goodness, and the light of God enlightens the mind and expels dark error and ignorance: 'It clears away the fog of ignorance from the eyes of the mind and it stirs and unwraps those covered over by the burden of darkness.' And further on: 'But light itself is always light and illuminates the darkness.'[36]

---

[32] Ibid.

[33] Ibid., 2–50, VIII.19, IX.22, XXVI.64, XXVII.66.

[34] A. Louth, *Denys the Areopagite* (London: Chapman, 1989), p. 14.

[35] *Pseudo-Dionysius: The Complete Works* (New York / Mahwah: Paulist Press, 1987).

[36] 4.4, 4.5, 4.24 in ibid., pp. 74, 75, 91–2.

In the *Mystical Theology* a song to the Trinity sings of the overwhelming light of the mystery of God's word being poured out;[37] and in the Celestial Hierarchy light makes known mysteries by symbols because God is truly light, the cause of being and seeing.[38] Not surprisingly, baptism is understood in part as a passage from darkness to light; the candidate avoids the 'dark pits of ignorance', is immersed to represent Christ's three days and nights in the tomb, and then 'clothed' in light; in fact baptism is the gift of illumination.[39]

While Denys makes no explicit reference to liturgical celebrations of time, he employs the image of the growing morning light to illustrate the natural round of the day and night as fundamental symbols; symbols by which the Christian may enter into the mystery of Christ, and come to true illumination and the face to face knowledge of God who is light, the light that banishes darkness.

Eastern Fathers seem to demonstrate a greater willingness to envisage the world in symbolic terms. Baptism is often referred to as 'enlightenment', and the newly baptized are described as 'lights in the world' by Gregory Nazianzen, for they are witnesses in all they do to the light of Christ.[40] However, Western authors are not lacking who describe the rationale for daily prayer in similar terms. Ambrose speaks of the light / dark, death / life symbolism:

> let us anticipate the sunrise, let us hasten to its beginning beforehand, let us say: behold, here I am. The Sun of Justice wishes and waits to be anticipated
>
> ... Be sure to anticipate this sun which you see ... If you anticipate this sun before it rises, you receive Christ the giver of light.

Ambrose uses the same imagery as employed elsewhere; the new Sun of Righteousness from Malachi, night as a time to have hope in Christ the light, Christ himself as symbolized by the light of the new day. In the same work Ambrose speaks of the morning light shining in times of darkness for those who meditate on the words of God.[41]

The wide use of the light and life, darkness and death pairs of symbols has its most obvious place in the sermons and writings of the Fathers that refer to some form of daily prayer. But even where no such references exist, there is still a consistent use of symbolic language and concepts over a period of some three hundred years, often in places far apart from each other. This language is, not

---

[37] 1; ibid., p. 135.

[38] 1 and 13, ibid., pp. 145–6, 178.

[39] 2.III, and 3.I, ibid., pp. 206–8, 210.

[40] *Oration on the Holy Lights XX*, trans. C.G. Brown and J.E. Swallow (Oxford: 1894), pp. 352–9.

[41] *Expositio ps.118, 19, 22, 30, 32* cited in Taft, *Liturgy of the Hours*, op. cit., p. 142.

surprisingly, closely associated with Easter and with baptism, but is also used more widely.

Patristic and Other Testimony to the Existence of Prayer Services in the Evening and in the Morning

Some of the earliest mentions of liturgical worship are associated with the night, especially Easter night. Very early evidence for evening worship combined with a meal, may also be found. Pliny's famous letter to the Emperor Trajan, c.112, lists the following activities by Christians: on a particular day (we may reasonably assume Sunday) they met before daybreak to sing a hymn to Christ as to a god, and to bind themselves to ethical behaviour by an oath. After this they met again to share ordinary food, and this latter practice was given up by Pliny's command.[42] It seems unlikely that Christians would forego the Eucharist, which may have been included in the morning assembly that started before it was light. The common meal may have taken place in the evening of the same day, but that is not explicitly stated. Since Pliny is extremely vague over times, he may not have known when this evening assembly for a common meal took place – it could have as easily preceded as followed the Sunday morning assembly. One must, however, stress that this is pure hypothesis.

Many early mentions of daily worship, or worship at particular times are to do with various kinds of nocturnal vigils. Most citations of this kind have been made available through the works of Carlo Marcora, Robert Taft and Paul Bradshaw. No attempt at greater detail will follow as so much has already been done, but we will attempt to identify some salient features.

A possible early piece of evidence for prayer at night may be found in the *Shepherd of Hermas*, in which the seer finds himself spending a night sustained by the word of God; clearly a reference to a night spent in prayer.[43] Tertullian, who seems to have regarded prayer in the night as the normal act of a good Christian,[44] describes what appears to be a Christian version of the 'symposium'. This was a meeting for prayer and food in the evening: 'After the washing of hand and the lights, some person may stand up in the midst and sing to God some scripture or hymn of their own devising.'[45] The context also makes clear that participants return home that night, so this is not an all-night

[42] Pliny (the Younger), *Epp. X (ad Traj.)*, xcvi; in H. Bettenson, *Documents of the Christian Church* (London: Oxford University Press, 1943), pp. 4–5.

[43] Op.cit. (fn.13), ibid.

[44] *Apologeticum* in *ANCL XI* (1869), p. 121.

[45] *PL* 1, 477.

vigil. Clement of Alexandria says that 'He who has the light watches',[46] and requires turning to the east in prayer 'since the dawn is an image of the day of birth'.[47] These various early Christian practices can all be explained by the pervasive symbolism of light / life as opposed to darkness / death.

An important practical result of this imagery is the frequency with which we encounter night vigils. Some examples are clearly intended to refer to private devotional practices, but others such as the Easter or baptismal vigils mentioned above, are obviously public, congregational acts of the whole church in a particular place.

Cyprian said: 'let us who are always in Christ, that is, in the light, not cease praying even in the night. Let us, most beloved brethren, who are always in the light of the Lord ... compute the night as day'.[48] These words could be referring to private prayer, but could equally well refer to public acts of worship.

Bradshaw quoted Origen's *de Oratione* 12 concerning prayer at morning, midday, evening, and night, and observed that the reference to evening prayer quotes psalm 140.2, the psalm verse that was to prove most influential in the development of the evening office of the next century.[49] This reference may possibly be to a public assembly, but the context does not seem to indicate this; the reference to night prayer appears to be to a pious custom of rising in the night for private prayer rather than repairing to church.

John Chrysostom (c.347–407) frequently commented on liturgical matters. Around 390 he taught his Catechumens a rationale for daily prayer:

> Be very diligent in coming here early in the morning (*orthron*) to bring prayers and praises (εξομολογησεις) to the God of all, and to give thanks for the benefits already received, ... and so pass the time of day as one obliged to return here in the evening to give the master an account of the entire day and to ask pardon for failures ... Then we must pass the time of the night in sobriety and thus be ready to present ourselves again at the morning praise (εηξομολγησιν).[50]

We note the prayer for forgiveness of sins in the evening, the exhortation to pass the night in sobriety (but not necessarily in prayer), and the greater emphasis on thanksgiving and praise in the morning. Another catechism names

---

[46] *Paedogogus 2.9* in ANCL I (1867), pp. 240–3.

[47] *Stromata VII.7*, in *PG* 8, 461.

[48] *PL* 4, 542 and T.K. Carroll and T. Halton, *Liturgical Practice in the Fathers* (Wilmington, DW: Glazier, 1988), p. 10.

[49] Bradshaw, *Daily Prayer*, op. cit., pp. 48–9.

[50] Taft, *The Liturgy of the Hours*, p. 42, cf. A. Wenger (ed.), *Jean Chrysostome, Huit Catéchèses Baptismales inédites* (Paris: Cerf, *Sources Chrétiennes* 50, 1970), pp. 256–7.

the evening and morning stars in that order, and sees the morning light as embracing the light of all others, including the evening.[51]

In his commentary on psalm 140, Chrysostom says that it is chanted daily in the evening; 'as a salutary medicine and forgiveness of sins', and, referring to verse 2, the evening sacrifice is seen as fulfilling a Levitical precept to worship at the beginning and the end of the day. There is no indication that incense or lights were used ceremonially at this time.

Chrysostom also commented on psalm 62: in the morning 'it kindles the desire for God, and arouses the soul and greatly inflames it, and fills it with great goodness and love'. He quotes the first words and explains the psalm as the words of a soul on fire for God, and says: 'Where there is love of God, all evil departs; where there is remembrance of God there is oblivion of sin and destruction of evil . . .'.[52] This fits in well with what we find later in Syrian sources, an explanation of this psalm that does not actually stress keeping vigil so much as thirsting for God.

Although Chrysostom mentions only one evening and one morning psalm, there is no explicit statement that those were the only psalms or canticles used at these services; perhaps these were amongst the few elements that were stable at this early stage. Another stable element was some kind of intercession. Chrysostom, in his commentary on 1 Timothy 2.1, talks of daily worship and daily supplications to be offered evening and morning.[53]

Bishop of Cyr, east of Antioch, Theodoret was an historian and native of Antioch who flourished in the mid fifth century. Night vigils are mentioned as existing in the mid fourth century in his *Church History* II.24, while in the *Philothean History* 30.1 there is clear indication that the Cathedral service of Morning Prayer began at cockcrow,[54] and evening services exist as well. In his *Questions on Exodus* 28, Theodoret mentions the offering of incense and the lighting of the lamps, so ceremonial use of incense now seems to be common. Taft notes that Ephrem may also refer to the ceremonial use of incense when speaking of 'an oblation of incense' in his *Carmina Nisibena* 17.4,[55] but Ephrem may be more connected to the emergent East Syrian tradition (see later).

The argument as to whether the prayer practices were private or not is, to an extent, beside the point, which is that prayer at various points of the day and the night was a desirable thing for devout Christians to do. The rationale behind this practice of prayer was closely connected with the light / life, death / darkness motifs. Rising in the night to pray is easily the most difficult thing to

---

[51] III.4, Wenger, 152.

[52] Taft, op. cit., pp. 42–3.

[53] Ibid., p. 44, *PG* 62, col. 530.

[54] All references from Taft, *Liturgy of the Hours*, pp. 47–8.

[55] Ibid., p. 48.

do, but is seen to be important as it is a way of proclaiming the reality of Christ as the eternal light and day, whose power can never be overcome by darkness and sin.

At the end of the fourth century and at the beginning of the fifth, we find Jerome strongly recommending the practice of nocturnal prayer, even two or three times a night. He seems to be counseling private vigils, which are, as he says, normal amongst the Egyptian monks, in addition to their communal services of prayer. However, not only were such communal services known to take place in monasteries, they are probably alluded to as taking place in non-monastic churches as well. Jerome also knew of occasional public vigils. Unfortunately abuses were now connected with this practice, and some wished to abolish such vigils or confine them to Easter. This all may be in Jerome's attack on Vigilantius who, in spite of his name, as Jerome was quick to point out, was obviously opposed to these celebrations.[56]

That vigils were common and widely accepted is shown by Eusebius of Caesarea's history, written earlier in the fourth century. When he came across Philo's description of ascetics spending part of the night in prayer, he believed him to be describing all early Christians. That this is unlikely is not so important as the fact that Eusebius saw this as a normal thing for Christians to do, to meet together for prayer at night.[57] Athanasius in his *Apologia pro fuga sua 34* described the intrusion of hostile Arian soldiers at a vigil he was celebrating with his people;[58] this would appear to have been the normal prelude to a 'Synaxis', probably a Sunday or Festal Eucharist.

Vigils were also common in Neo-Caesarea at the time of Basil; though it seems that he, or somebody close to him, must have introduced changes which he had to defend to some of the clergy. They were probably rejecting innovations in the liturgy itself, rather than the actual concept of a vigil.[59] The most important vigil was of course that of Easter, when as Gregory Nazianzen said, the candles of the newly baptized were 'illuminating the night with our crowded fires, formed after the fashion of that great light'[60] (i.e., the Trinity from which all light derives its being). This shows that the original symbolic rationale for praying at night, seeing the night as turned to day by the light of Christ, had not been lost. Gregory Nazianzen also knew other kinds of vigil, he referred in another oration to 'nightlong stations'.[61] His best-known expression

[56] *Letters 22, 107 and 109*, trans. W.H. Fremantle (Oxford: 1893), pp. 37–8, 193, 213.

[57] *PG* 20, 180–184.

[58] *Historical Tracts of St Athanasius, Library of the Fathers* (Oxford: 1873), p. 206.

[59] *Letter 207, to the Clergy of Neo-Caesarea* (in Wace and Schaff, Nicene and Post-Nicene Fathers 8, Oxford and New York, 1895, pp. 246–8).

[60] *Oration 45.2* (Nicene and Post-Nicene Fathers 7, p. 423).

[61] *Oration 42.26* (ibid., p. 394).

of the rationale is probably that found in the funeral oration for his father, in which he speaks of 'Easter, the queen of days, the brilliant night which dissipates the darkness of sin, upon which with abundant light we keep the feast of our salvation'.[62]

At a later date, between 513 and 518, we have the evidence of Severus of Antioch.[63] He mentions the evening office in passing in homily 37, and also in hymn 319: 'To thee, O Christ, I offer a sacrifice of praise at the hour of evening.' There are fifteen hymn texts for the evenings. The first contains the words 'direct my steps in thy paths and guide me' (quoting psalm 72.2), the tenth 'repenting at the hour of evening', and the next 'Our spiritual sacrifice we offer to thee, Christ at the hour of evening.' The twelfth contains 'Direct and guide us Lord [that we may] with pure heart present an acceptable sacrifice of thanksgiving'. The themes are typically vesperal, repentance, evening offering of prayer (possibly connected with incense),[64] and prayer for divine guidance and protection.

The night office is mentioned in homily 41, as held before cockcrow, and the more devout laity might attend. Severus may have introduced a Sunday night gospel reading, he mentions it in homily 77, and he also wrote hymns to accompany the Gospel. The Sunday night must refer to Saturday to Sunday, and the reference to introducing gospel readings at the weekly resurrection vigil (perhaps in imitation of Jerusalem) may suggest that there was no such gospel reading in the vigil of Apostolic Constitutions, a probably Antiochene document.

Of 23 morning hymns in *PO* 7, the eighth contains the words: 'Lord in the morning I sing to thee, and ask for life'. The next reads: 'In the nights I have lifted up the hands to the heights of thy sanctuaries ... But now also in the day admit me, O God my saviour, to walk in the glorious light of thy holy commandments'. The eleventh appears to see the morning service as a sacramental act: 'The bright ray of the service has washed me well from my iniquity... and rendered dark night a glorious day of light in my mind'. We might especially note in this last, the recollection of psalm 50, as well as the clear theme of new light freeing from the darkness of sin and death.

Jean Tabet supports the likelihood of Jerusalem influence on Severus, and quotes some of his verses. For example, 'You who honour the light and holy night of the Resurrection by vigil and fortitude, ... you are sons of the light ...' and 'In the night of the holy Sunday of resurrection, clothed and

---

[62] *Oration 18* (in *PG* 35, 1017).

[63] For all that follows on Severus see G. Cuming, 'The Liturgy of Antioch at the Time of Severus (513–518)', in J. Neil Alexander (ed.), *Time and Community: In Honor of Thomas Julian Talley* (Washington, DC: Pastoral Press, 1990), pp. 83–103. Texts of Homilies in *PO* 4, 8, 12, 16, 20, 22, 23, 25, 26, 29, 35–8 (Paris: 1908–), Hymns in *PO* 6, 7 (Paris: 1911).

[64] The fourth prayer cites psalm 140.2.

enlivened in light, I awake from sleep'.[65] Another strophe 'Our spirit arises early . . . Be among us as we early honour Thy Resurrection', alludes to the Isaiah 26.9 canticle: 'My soul yearns for thee in the night', the beginning of a canticle frequently used in the night offices of East and West. Coupled with this is Severus' idea that the resurrection takes place when the light begins to appear, and thus, at cockcrow, the overnight fast ends and the paschal joy of Sunday begins.[66]

Another practice at the offices is found in Severus' Homily 32: 'That is why, every Sunday, we lead you to the baptistery with a celebration, praise, prayer, and supplication, so as to recall these covenants made with God.' The baptismal procession was to remind people of their status as 'sons of light' who must live as such. This visit may have been controversial, since Severus criticizes those who say that the baptistery should only be open once a year, for baptism. When it took place is not clear, but it is an interesting ritual reinforcement of the baptismal theme, perhaps to stir up and inspire a people now mostly baptized in infancy. Visits to the baptistery in connection with evening and morning offices become more common as we shall see.

Conclusions

From the biblical material adduced above we may conclude:

1 The reckoning of the day from evening to evening (in, e.g., Leviticus 23.32) is a very early tradition, upheld by the Mishnah and exemplified by the ancient (non-biblical) tradition of the Sabbath eve lights. It is found in the account of Paul at Troas (Acts 20), and in the complex discussions about the passion and the observance of Passover.

2 A nocturnal watch was known to the Jewish priesthood for the purpose of tending the lights (Exodus and Leviticus). The New Testament took this much further and prayer at night was popular (Acts 16 and Acts 20). This pattern of praying at night is associated with eschatological readiness (e.g., the wise and foolish bridesmaids in Matthew 25), and resonates with the powerful imagery of the prologue to John's Gospel. The light burning through the night may well be a distant ancestor of Christian evening light ceremonies.

---

[65] *L'Office Commun Maronite* (Kaslik, Lebanon: Bibliothèque de L'Université Saint-Esprit, 1972), pp. 217–23.

[66] Ibid., p. 222.

3 The Temple had twice-daily sacrifices at morning and evening, but no clear shape, other than a preference for praying at night, can be discerned in the New Testament.

Patristic writings show that:

1 The symbolism of light overcoming darkness was a powerful image of the risen Christ in, e.g., Melito, Origen and Clement of Alexandria.
2 In Basil this symbolism is closely tied to the hour at which he preaches, and he uses the coming of night to exhort the people to see God's light guiding them into the eternal light. In Basil and other writers, it is clear that the symbolism of light overcoming darkness is not just confined to Easter.
3 Some of the earliest evidence for Christians gathering for prayer is connected with the night. Tertullian spoke of an assembly late at night, and Cyprian stressed the importance of praying at night though he may have had private prayer in mind.
4 By the late fourth century, John Chrysostom expected twice-daily public services of prayer at morning and evening. When commenting on psalm 62 he spoke of that longing for God which is characteristic of vigil prayer.
5 Chrysostom and Severus both gave a rationale for evening and morning prayer; evening prayer is concerned with repentance and the evening offering, also with seeking divine protection. The morning office moves from longing for God to thanksgiving for the presence of the risen Lord at sunrise.
6 The most frequent kind of vigil appears to have been celebrated at cockcrow, as a watchful preparation for the rising sun representing the risen Christ.

CHAPTER 3

The Church Orders

Church Orders, common in the first five centuries, were mutually interrelated documents often circulated in collections and in which material tended to appear in the same order, but perhaps, further elaborated according to need.[1] Bradshaw has referred to them as 'living literature'.[2] The earliest, the *Didache*, the *Didascalia* and the *Apostolic Church Order*, covered matters of Christian life as a whole; liturgical directions were almost tangential to the whole exercise. Later came an increasing tendency to prescribe practice while disguising this prescription as description. Material no longer relevant was progressively omitted, and works like the *Apostolic Tradition* became more popular because they provided the beginnings of liturgical rubrics and canon law; they in their turn ceased to be of importance when councils and synods produced collections of canons.[3] When we examine these documents then, we should be aware that they are probably not describing current practice, but reflect what is perceived as the best practice. We must also note that different versions of texts may well indicate adaptation to the concrete situation of a particular local church.[4]

The Didache

The latest tentative attempt at dating this very early work places it around 110–120 CE, most probably originating in Syria/Palestine.[5] The only references to daily prayer are to the Lord's Prayer said three times daily in *Didache* 8.3, there is no mention of prayer at night but the three times daily is in line with Clement of Alexandria and Origen.[6]

---

[1] Paul Bradshaw, ch. 4; *The Search*, op. cit., pp. 73–97.

[2] Paul Bradshaw and B. Spinks (eds), *Liturgy in Dialogue* (London: 1994), pp. 138–53.

[3] Bradshaw, *The Search*, pp. 93–7.

[4] Ibid., p. 91.

[5] Kurt Niederwimmer, *The Didache* (Minneapolis: Fortress *Hermeneia* series, 1998), pp. 52–4.

[6] Bradshaw, *Daily Prayer*, op. cit., p. 26; *The Search*, p. 175.

The Didascalia

Originally composed in Greek, this work was probably compiled in Syria in the first half of the third century, perhaps around 230.[7] Again it is largely concerned with practical Christian living and good order.[8] In chapter 11 we read that 'It is required of a man to pray diligently at all times'.[9] Chapter 13 exhorts people to regular church attendance, seemingly referring to the Sunday Eucharist, but a comparison is made with pagans worshipping daily, which might suggest that there were poorly attended Christian daily services.[10]

The image of light conquering darkness is found in the chapter on the Resurrection of the dead (20); martyrdom is to be crowned by being raised up in glorious light. Also the light of resurrection is compared with that of creation, a light shining where there was darkness. Eschatological light is also promised to those who remain faithful.[11] All this might provide justification for night vigil services.

Chapter 21 refers to the Paschal vigil: 'You shall assemble together and watch and keep vigil all night with prayers and intercessions, and with the reading of the Prophets, and with the Gospel and with the Psalms, ... until the third hour in the night after the Sabbath; And then break your fasts.'[12] This Paschal vigil commemorates the Lord's passion and three days in the tomb, and heedless Christians are reminded that they have seen a great light; a similar passage concluded: '[you] have long since believed and been baptized in Him: and *a great light has dawned upon you*'.[13]

The Good Friday fast is a fasting of repentance rather than a preparation for baptism. The lengthy section treating of the Friday to Saturday fast concludes:

> Therefore the fast of the Friday and Saturday is especially required of you. And also the vigil and watching of the Saturday, and the reading of the Scriptures, and Psalms, and prayers and intercession for those who have sinned, and the expectation and hope of the resurrection of our Lord Jesus, until the third hour in the night after the Sabbath. And then offer your

[7] F.X. Funk (ed.), *Didascalia et Apostolarum Constitiones Apostolicae* (Paderborn: 1906); Sebastian Brock and Michael Vasey (eds), *The Liturgical Portions of the Didascalia* (Grove Liturgical Study 29, Bramcote: 1982), p. 5; Bradshaw, *The Search*, pp. 78–80.

[8] A. Vööbus, *The Didascalia Apostolorum in Syriac*, 2 vols (CSCO 175, 176, 179, 180, Louvain: 1979).

[9] Vööbus, vol. II, p. 127.

[10] Vööbus, vol. II, p. 136; Brock and Vasey, op. cit., pp. 17–18.

[11] Vööbus, vol. II, p. 175, line 25–176, line 7.

[12] Ibid., vol. II, p. 199, lines 3–7.

[13] Ibid., vol. II, p. 196, lines 1–15.

> oblations. And after this eat and enjoy yourselves, and rejoice and be glad, because the earnest of our resurrection, Christ, is risen.[14]

There is some discussion of the symbolism of the seven days of the week, regarding both creation and resurrection/new creation; and the eschatological eternal day: 'A day thus is to be revealed when the sun will stand indeed in its midcourse, ... For he said: *Behold, I make the first things as the last, and the last as the first*.'[15]

We conclude that those who compiled *Didascalia* may have known a custom of praying three times daily, and a Paschal vigil to which all should come. Finally it witnesses to a strong imagery of darkness and light, leading to the *eschaton* in which all is light.

The Apostolic Constitutions

Probably originating in Syria and originally composed in Greek, Bradshaw dates this work to about 375–380 CE.[16] Books 1–6 are a re-working of the *Didascalia*, while book 7 is a version of the *Didache*. Book 8 elaborates the *Apostolic Tradition*, adding more liturgical material.

Since Funk edited the text, W. Jardine Grisbrooke has produced an English edition of the liturgical material.[17] Book 5 envisages a Paschal vigil lasting until the early hours of Easter Sunday morning, at which catechumens are to be baptized:

> On the sabbath, keep awake from evening until cockcrow, as it begins to dawn towards the first day of the week, and, assembled in church, keep vigil, praying and entreating God, and reading the Law, the Prophets, and the Psalms until cockcrow; then, having baptised your catechumens ...[18]

There is an inconsistency in the material grouped by Grisbrooke under the heading of 'The Divine Office'. *Didache*'s requirement of the Lord's Prayer three times daily is found here.[19] There is also (in book 8.34) a call for prayer six times a day: namely, in the morning, at the Third Hour, the Sixth Hour, the

---

[14] Ibid., vol. II, pp. 199, line 22–200, line 1.

[15] Ibid., vol. II, p. 234, lines 8–11.

[16] Bradshaw, *The Search*, p. 84.

[17] Funk, op. cit.; W. Jardine Grisbrooke, *The Liturgical Portions of the Apostolic Constitutions: A Text for Students* (Bramcote: Alcuin/GROW Liturgical Study 13–14, 1990). References to latter source.

[18] 5.19; ibid., p. 48.

[19] 8.24.2; ibid., pp. 52–3.

Ninth Hour, in the evening, and at cockcrow; a rationale being given for each of these times; the order appears to be referring only to private prayer.[20]

More detailed legislation for public prayer twice a day, morning and evening, is found in book 2.59:

> In your teaching, o bishop, command and exhort the people to come constantly to church, morning and evening every day, ...assemble yourselves together every day, morning and evening, singing and praying in the house of the Lord, saying in the morning the sixty-second psalm, and in the evening the one hundred and fortieth.[21]

This is one of the earliest indications of a twice-daily gathering for prayer, distinct from the *private* custom of praying three, or even six, times a day. There is nothing similar in the earlier documents.

The same passage provides an interesting sentence about Sunday commemoration of the resurrection; 'we offer three prayers in thankful memory of him who rose on the third day; we read from the prophets, we proclaim the Gospel, we offer the sacrifice, and we receive the gift of the holy food'. Some commentators think that the three prayers might be the cathedral Sunday resurrection vigil.[22] The 'prayers' could be psalms or canticles, and 'the prophets' might be the Old Testament canticles, as we find in several later orders for the cathedral Sunday vigil. The order of Gospel, sacrifice, and participation in holy food might well indicate the Sunday Eucharist; however, earlier in Book 2 there is a fuller description of the eucharistic liturgy of the word which mentions an epistle or Acts reading not found here.[23] This passage may refer to a Sunday resurrection vigil.

After chapter 8.34 has prescribed prayers at selected times of the day, morning to evening, there follow the chapters that describe evening and morning offices in greater detail, and in that order, evening first and then morning.[24] Here we have a mismatch between the two systems that shows clearly how these documents, as 'living literature', continued to grow, change and evolve even down to the fourth century. The document resists attempts to harmonize the different strata, and may well be telling only part of the story. With these cautions in mind, we turn to examine its forms of evening and Morning Prayer.

---

[20] 8.34; ibid., pp. 52–3.

[21] Ibid., pp. 53–4.

[22] Ibid., 2.59.4, and p. 54, n. 5; Taft, *The Liturgy of the Hours in East and West*, p. 53.

[23] Book 2, see e.g., Grisbrooke, op. cit., p. 15.

[24] 8.35.1–8.38.5; in ibid., pp. 58–61. J.M. Joncas, 'Daily Prayer in the Apostolic Constitutions', *EL*, **107** (1993) 113–35, 116, notes the different systems of reckoning the day.

Evening Prayer

The bishop is to gather the people for prayer in the evening, 'and after the recitation of the psalm at the lighting of the lamps, the deacon shall bid prayers'.[25] This sentence gives all the structural information available; the bishop presides over an evening assembly, and after the psalm at the lighting of lamps, there are prayers. There is no mention of which psalm is sung at the lighting of the lamps, though book 2.59 calls for psalm 140 to be sung in the evening, as we have seen. Contrary to what Grisbrooke and others have suggested, we cannot link the two passages together too readily.[26] Book 2 does not explicitly associate psalm 140 with lamp-lighting; besides, the psalm is a prayer for acceptance of the evening sacrifice and protection in the night that makes no mention of lights.

The lack of explicit mention in book 8.35 of psalm 140, only of the 'psalm at the lighting of the lamps', may indicate that the document is attempting to standardize variant practices. If we pose the hypothetical question, 'Which psalms should we use in the evening and morning?' Book 2.59 answers, *at least* psalm 62 in the morning and psalm 140 in the evening. Book 8.35 answers the different question, 'At what point of the service do we pray at evening prayer?' with 'after the recitation of the psalm at the lighting of the lamps'. Both answers could establish a basis for common practice.

This argument follows Bradshaw's principles for interpreting early Christian liturgical evidence.[27] Church Orders are not always what they seem; for example, an authoritative-sounding statement may not always be genuinely authoritative. We should beware of a too facile assumption that everything that needs to be said is here, for usually only controverted practices are mentioned. This supports the present author's hypothesis of an attempt to standardize differing customs. On the other hand, Bradshaw also reminds us that the 'Constantinian revolution' intensified existing trends as well as initiating new ones.[28] Constantinian practice may be embedded in these almost contradictory, and certainly rather diffuse sets of liturgical directives.

We can say that psalm 140 was among those used in the evening, and after the final psalm at the lighting of the lamps, there were prayers.[29] Book 8 gives more detail of the prayers to follow the lamp-lighting ceremony. Book 8.36 summarizes a litany that is recognizably similar to that known in the Byzantine liturgy as the *aitesis*. The deacon is to pray for an 'angel of peace', for 'a

[25] 8.35.2; Grisbrooke, op. cit., p. 58.

[26] 8.35.1–2; ibid., p. 58, n.1.

[27] Bradshaw, *The Search*, ch. 1, pp. 14–20.

[28] Ibid., p. 212.

[29] Joncas, op. cit., 128 comes to a similar conclusion.

Christian end', 'for an evening and a night of peace and free from sin', and ends with mutual commendation of those present to God through Christ. This litany is eminently suited to evening prayer, connecting evening and night with a Christian's end, that is, death; and the angel of peace petitions may be seen as prayers for protection in the night. Of other petitions that preceded this, no details are given and an almost exactly similar passage is found in the description of Morning Prayer with the addition, in the reference to the *aitesis*, of a prayer that God be merciful and gracious.[30]

A prayer over the catechumens at the Eucharist in book 8.6[31] appears to be the original form of the *aitesis*, that, at this time of crisis, they will be protected against the powers of darkness. The *aitesis*, as a suitable prayer for catechumens, goes on to cover the passage from the liturgy to life. Its suitability at this point of Evening and Morning Prayer may be readily appreciated.

The bishop's concluding prayer follows the litany,[32] in it he prays to God

> who created the day for works of light and [the] night for rest, given our weakness: for 'the day is yours, the night also is yours: you have fashioned the light and the sun': Do you now O Lord . . . favourably accept this our evening thanksgiving. You who have led us through the length of the day, and brought us to the beginnings of the night, guard us through your Christ, grant us a peaceful evening and a night free from sin and from evil dreams, . . .

The psalm quoted, 73, is not known as an evening prayer, but exhorts the Lord to remember his covenant (v. 20), and: 'Arise, O God, and defend your cause!' (v. 22). The prayer is for the acceptance of the evening thanksgiving, and the time is clearly the beginning of the night, so it is a time to pray for a peaceful evening and a sinless night. Finally the bishop prays that God will cause his face to shine on his servants, and bless those enlightened with the light of knowledge by Christ who has revealed God to the world. The evening light imagery is quite clear; the light of Christ enlightens God's people with knowledge of him that they may depart fearlessly into the night.

Morning Prayer

In this office the 'morning psalm' has often been taken to be psalm 62; but, recalling the mismatch between books 2 and 8, it could just as easily refer to some other psalm as *the* morning psalm. Psalm 62 is really more suited to the

[30] Full text in Grisbrooke, op. cit., pp. 58–60.

[31] 8.6.8ff.; ibid., pp. 22–3.

[32] 8.37.2ff.; ibid., pp. 58–9.

time before the full light of day, and the phrase does not exclude there being other psalms or canticles as well, of which one might be selected to celebrate the rising sun as symbol of the light of the risen Jesus Christ.[33]

The litanies following the 'morning psalm' are similar to those at Vespers. The bishop's Morning Prayer prays to God:

> who gives the sun to govern the day, and the moon and the stars to govern the night; do you yourself look down upon us with kindly eyes, and receive our morning thanksgivings, and have mercy upon us, for we have not spread out our hands to another God: ... but you [alone], the eternal and unending, who have granted us being through Christ ... Make us worthy also of eternal life through him ...[34]

This prayer acknowledges God as author of the day, and implores new creation in Christ. The prayer over the people asks that they be preserved in 'godliness and righteousness' and be judged worthy of eternal life.[35] These prayers treat morning as representing the morning of creation, and as the pre-existent Christ was instrumental in creation, so is he prayed to as the means by which his people enter upon new and eternal life.

The order of the offices in book 8 (evening first and then morning) may well be significant. At the beginning of the night there is an assembly for prayer, perhaps with ceremonial lighting of the lamps, a psalm or psalms are used, and prayer is made that the light of God will illumine the darkness. Then in the morning, after the psalmody, and, specifically after the 'morning psalm', prayer is made to the giver of life that he may lead his people into eternal life, symbolized by the new day.

Book 8.34 gives a rationale for morning and evening prayer.[36] 'In the morning, we pray because light has been sent to chase away the night; in the evening that we may rest from the labours of the day, while at cockcrow, we may once more prepare for a new day in which the works of light may be performed.' While the passage seems mainly concerned with private prayer, nothing in it is at odds with the character of the evening and Morning Prayers of the following chapters. Book 2 provides no rationale for the services, and mentions psalms 140 and 62 without implying that these were the only psalms sung at those services. A rationale is provided for what seems to be the resurrection vigil (see above). Finally, book 7 provides an appendix of morning and evening hymns, the former of which is an early version of the Great

---

[33] Joncas, op. cit., 121 comes to a similar conclusion.

[34] 8.38.4ff.; Grisbrooke, op. cit., p. 60.

[35] 8.39.3ff.; ibid., p. 61.

[36] 8.34.7; ibid., pp. 53–7.

Doxology or *Gloria in Excelsis*, frequently found in Morning Prayer services throughout the East (and also in medieval Milan).

Even if book 2 and book 8 are probably from different sources, and the hymns in book 7 from yet another, it is possible that at least some places had established services of daily evening and Morning Prayer prior to the late fourth century. These were services that celebrated the victory of light over darkness.

The Apostolic Tradition (AT)

The case for Roman origin of this well-known document relies largely on Hippolytus being the author, which is doubtful. If he were not, then the dating of c.215 CE falls as well. Even if it does not represent Roman liturgical practice in the early third century, it was, however, influential in places other than Italy, for example upon *Apostolic Constitutions*, the Syrian *Testamentum Domini* and the Egyptian *Canons of Hippolytus*.[37]

The source of chapter 41, *De tempore quo oportet orare*,[38] is a Sahidic Coptic manuscript of 1006.[39] Hanssens dated the translation to around 700.[40] The chapter has recently been studied by L. Edward Phillips. We will summarize his conclusions here.[41] Phillips noted that there is a different rationale for the Hours of prayer from *Apostolic Constitutions*, and he concludes that the longer horarium of the Sahidic text is a substantial witness to the earlier text.

The faithful are called upon to wash upon rising and pray – But if there is an assembly for prayer and instruction, go and pray there – so the First Hour is instructional. The chapter continues with Third, Sixth and Ninth Hours; because at the third Christ was nailed to the cross (Mark 15.25), at the Sixth darkness covered the earth (Mark 12.33), and at the ninth Christ died (Mark 15.34). However, in an additional warrant for the Hours of prayer, the Third has an interesting reference to the Temple sacrifices. There is in fact a large concentration of biblical imagery in the description of the Third Hour prayer.

At the Sixth Hour, the theme of darkness covering the earth gives a penitential emphasis, whereas the Third and Ninth Hours have a theme of

---

[37] Bradshaw, *The Search*, pp. 89–91; P. E. Bradshaw, Maxwell E. Johnson and J. Edwards Phillips (eds), *The Apostolic Tradition: A Commentary* (*Hermeneia*, Minneapolis: Fortress, 2002), pp. 6–11.

[38] B. Botte, OSB (ed.), *La Tradition Apostolique de Saint Hippolyte* (Münster: Aschendorff, 1963), pp. 88–97.

[39] Ibid., p. xxi.

[40] G. Cuming, *Hippolytus: A Text for Students* (Bramcote: Grove Liturgical Study 8, 1976), p. 6.

[41] 'Daily Prayer in the Apostolic Tradition of Hippolytus', *Journal of Theological Studies* ns, **40**, 1989, 389–400. See also Bradshaw et al., op. cit., pp. 194–215.

thanksgiving. The service at the Ninth Hour is to be one of intense prayer and blessing of God. Christ's death is associated with the new day that commences with the evening: the piercing of Christ's side brings light, the darkness of the Sixth Hour is lifted, and at Christ's falling asleep there is a new day, a type of the resurrection. As at the Third Hour, evocative images are piled up: God's faithfulness, Christ's sacrifice, light, and new day beginning at evening and leading to resurrection day. Phillips shows how the Third and Ninth Hours are associated with the morning and evening sacrifices of the Temple.

One cannot stress too much the images of light and the new day that are associated with the Ninth Hour here. These references are taken up in the *Canons of Hippolytus* and the *Testamentum Domini* (see below), neither of which quotes the next short sentence, 'Ora etiam antequam corpus cubile requiescat' ('Also the hour before which the body rests in bed'). This short statement is very different from the more elaborate warrant for the Third, Ninth and even the Sixth Hours. Phillips thus argues that the Third, Sixth and Ninth Hours are the morning, noon and evening prayers, providing something similar to the Alexandrine pattern known to Clement and Origen.

Paul Bradshaw argued for a similar pattern of thrice-daily prayer with prayer at midnight, and no distinction in importance between the various Hours of prayer, and accepts much of what Phillips suggests.[42] Phillips however, also noted the greater stress on thanksgiving at the Third and Ninth Hours, and the larger number of biblical images as warrants for these times of prayer. The compiler of AT also has a long passage in which he promotes the practice of rising in the night for prayer. There are even indications that washing on rising in the night might well be associated with baptism, and there is a clear concern for watchfulness, illustrated by the parable of the wise and foolish bridesmaids: 'Behold the bridegroom comes, go out and meet him.'[43] What is not clear is whether any of these times of prayer, with the exception of the occasional assembly for instruction, was in any sense a communal exercise.

It is possible that prayer at cockcrow might be a later addition to the document, so Phillips and Bradshaw suggest four times of prayer: morning, noon, evening, and the night – in some regions Morning Prayer was near dawn, in others, such as Alexandria and wherever AT originated, it may have been at the Third Hour. The evening prayer was offered at sunset in some places, and at the Ninth Hour in others. The conflation of the different traditions leads to the emerging pattern of morning, Third, Sixth and Ninth Hours, evening, and in the night. But all of this could refer to private prayer alone, to the devotional practices of individuals. Did the cathedral offices of morning and evening prayer come into existence only in the fourth century, and if so, why do they

---

[42] Bradshaw, *Daily Prayer*, op. cit., ch. 3; *The Search*, pp. 175–6.

[43] Botte, op. cit., p. 94.

not reflect Bradshaw's suggested ancient pattern of prayer *four* times daily? For our purposes we might note the literal translation of the Sahidic of 41.9: 'Because of this, you also, when you go to sleep, shall begin another day and make the type of the resurrection.' Recent comment on this obscure passage certainly recognizes a connection between times of prayer and death and resurrection typology.[44]

Church Orders tend to deal only with disputed matters. For example, AT has no description of a normal Sunday act of worship. Much that must have been done communally remains unknown to us, and as far as documentary sources go, probably always will. Bearing this caveat in mind, there is one other place in AT where worship at a particular time of day is stipulated; at an evening communal meal, found only in the Ethiopic version, which is the latest but fullest version of the complete order.[45] Botte and Chadwick argued for the genuineness of this section, while allowing for changes in the order of meal lamp-lighting.[46]

The passage begins with the account of an evening assembly, into which the deacon brings a lamp, and the bishop prays in thanksgiving, for the Lord has 'revealed to us the inextinguishable light', also acknowledging the beginning of the night, in which however 'we do not lack the light of evening', so we may give praise and glory to God. The next part is confused, but psalms are to be sung, and there is a requirement for the deacon, at the thanksgiving cup, to say a psalm with Alleluia written in it. The instructions concerning the meal now follow, in spite of a prior direction in chapter 25, 'They shall rise, then, after supper and pray; and the boys and the virgins shall say psalms.'[47] The light ritual is extremely simple, just a thanksgiving prayer at the utilitarian act of bringing in a lamp, but symbolizing the inextinguishable light of Christ. The prayer is a fitting beginning of the service/meal that follows.

Secondly, the psalms 'in which "Alleluia" is written'[48] could refer to the Hallel, psalms 112, 113, 114, 115, 116 and 117. The Septuagint also provides the heading 'Alleluia' for psalms 104–6, 110, 111, and 118, 134, 135, and 145–50, which would give a far wider selection than might otherwise be apparent. Was the so-called Egyptian Hallel already an established use by the third century of the Common Era? It was certainly the usage of the Temple before its destruction, a use connected with the slaughter of the Paschal Lamb, and with

---

[44] Bradshaw et al., op. cit., pp. 198, 209.

[45] Cuming, op. cit., p. 6; Bradshaw et al., pp. 156–60.

[46] Bradshaw, 'Other Acts of Worship', in Geoffrey Cuming (ed.), *Essays on Hippolytus* (Bramcote: Grove Liturgical Study 15, 1978), pp. 61–3 and *Daily Prayer*, pp. 55–7.

[47] Cuming, op. cit., pp. 23–4.

[48] Cuming, op. cit., p. 24. We must exercise caution here, this part of the text may be a later addition, but Tertullian witnesses to a not dissimilar practice, Bradshaw et al., op. cit., pp. 158 9.

the Passover *seder*.[49] In fact in the Temple the same group of psalms was repeated if necessary to cover the ritual butchery.[50] This accords with what we have seen of the rationale for prayer at the Ninth Hour, the sacrificial flowing of blood and water. Another possibility is a fifth cup of wine at Passover, with which is connected psalm 135, 'The Great Hallel', seemingly an optional practice, and that as late as Saadiah Gaon (928–942).[51] We conclude that the Egyptian Hallel may be intended because of its association with sacrifice.

The compiler of this part of AT could have known a supper practice that closely reflected the themes of prayer mentioned for the Ninth Hour: sacrifice, new light, new day, etc. How often the supper was celebrated is not known, but even at an early date there may have been some kind of regular evening observance by some at least of the clergy and faithful.

The Testamentum Domini

This work is a much expanded version of AT of which the original Greek text is now lost. The Syriac version first published by Rahmani is the most used, but significantly different readings in the Ethiopic and Arabic versions may depend upon a lost Coptic original. Most scholars believe that it dates from fifth-century Syria.[52] A recent partial edition by Grant Sperry-White argues for a late-fourth-century date because of internal evidence. He also narrows down the place of origin to Asia Minor because of resemblance to Basil's round of offices in 'urban monasteries', parallels with a fourth-century pseudo-Athanasian work from Cappadocia, and the prominent place accorded to widows.[53]

Testamentum Domini describes the daily services of an ascetic minority within a larger community. First there is an account of rising and washing before prayer in book II.24[54](AT 41). We then find: 'Let all be anxious to pray at the third hour, with mourning and labour, whether at the church or in the house... For this is the hour of the fixing of the Only-begotten to the Cross.' This is an expansion of AT explicitly indicating a church service at the Third

---

[49] Lawrence A. Hoffman, *The Canonization of the Synagogue Service* (Notre Dame, Indiana: University of Notre Dame Press, 1979), pp. 118–19.

[50] *Mishnah, Pesahim*, 5.7, Herbert Danby (ed.), (Oxford: Oxford University Press, 1933), p. 142.

[51] Hoffman, op. cit., pp. 120, 5.

[52] Bradshaw, *The Search*, pp. 86–7.

[53] G. Sperry-White, *The Testamentum Domini: A Text for Students, with Introduction, Translation, and Notes* (Bramcote: Alcuin/Grow Liturgical Study 19, 1991), p. 6; hereafter Sperry-White.

[54] Ibid., pp. 31, 38–9.

Hour. The passage on the Sixth Hour is derived from AT, as is that on the Ninth, which takes up AT's imagery even more explicitly: 'But also at the ninth hour let the prayer be prolonged... For at this hour life was opened to believers, and blood and water poured out from our Lord's side.' The stress on the hymn of praise and the sacrificial and redemptive overtones suit the theory that this is the evening service. However, the *Testamentum* has divided AT's Ninth Hour in two, so that the next sentence might be interpreted as referring to another service: 'But at evening, when it is the beginning of another day, he has caused us to give praise, showing an image of the Resurrection.'[55] Next comes provision for midnight prayer in honour of the resurrection, and dawn is the time when the risen Christ praised the Father while psalms were sung. Evening prayer is seen to begin the new day, and is an image of the resurrection, midnight prayer commemorates the resurrection itself, and dawn prayer praises God in the risen Christ.[56]

The remaining references are scattered through book I;[57] in I.22 we find an instruction addressed to a bishop to pray at the First Hour of the night, midnight 'and early twilight when the star of dawn riseth. Then also in the morning, and the third, sixth and ninth [hours, and the] twelfth hour at the lamp [lighting].'[58] I.26 envisages a service with the bishop at early dawn that finishes at sunrise.[59] The first part of the tri-part prayer refers to the morning, praises God as creator who has 'promised us immortal light', and is 'begetter of light, principle of life, giver of knowledge'. The third part of the prayer refers to God who calms storms that we might walk according to his commandments.

A rubric, 'Let them sing four psalms and hymns of praise: one by Moses and of Solomon and of the other prophets', might well refer to the Old Testament canticles such as the Exodus Song of the Sea. Next there is to be the 'hymn of praise', a prayer that begins with the words: 'O Lord, Father, giver of light' which praises God who has 'made us remove material darkness, and have bestowed immaterial light upon us'. The people's response to this, 'We praise you, we bless you, we confess you, O Lord, and we supplicate you our God', seems to echo the *Gloria in Excelsis*.

These texts are strongly reminiscent of ones that refer to baptism. For example, in II.7, an exorcism speaks of the enlightening of one bound and fixed in darkness.[60] This connection of baptism and the morning celebration of the

---

[55] Ibid., p. 39 and n.

[56] For context: J. Cooper and A.J. Maclean (eds), *The Testament of Our Lord* (Edinburgh: T. & T. Clark, 1902), pp. 136–7.

[57] Sperry-White, p. 31.

[58] Cooper and Maclean, op. cit., p. 68 – not reproduced in Sperry-White (p. 31).

[59] Sperry-White, pp. 32–5.

[60] Ibid., pp. 25–9.

resurrection may be intentional. Finally, the Morning Prayers turn to the praise of God as 'ray of light, lamp which never goes out, the un-eclipsed sun, [not] resting, but always giving light among his holy ones'. This Morning Prayer closes with a brief intercessory passage, and a description of a liturgy of the word with instructions.[61] It appears that the Morning Office is to be followed by the Eucharist with instruction and preaching.[62]

A baptismal thrust is also found in the account of the Presbyters' daily praise.[63] Again tri-part, the first prays to God 'who enlightened our hearts and nullified the darkness of our mind ... who brought error to an end'. In the second, God is praised for Christ 'who set us free from the servitude of slavery', and it is again completed by intercession. A rubric at the end reads: 'At midnight let the sons of priestly service, and those of the people who are more mature give praise by themselves. For also in that hour our Lord praised his Father as he rose.' Finally those who faithfully watch and pray are addressed as 'Sons of light'. It looks as if a night vigil could be expected of the more devout, but otherwise, there is still the Morning Prayer which is a way of declaring before God one's status as baptized and thus a son of light, not of that darkness that is daily overcome. We may conclude that for *Testamentum Domini*, participation in the daily morning worship was a natural corollary of being baptized – it was the way in which one's baptism was daily renewed.

The Epitome or Constitutions of the Holy Apostles through Hippolytus

This appears to be a series of extracts from *Apostolic Constitutions*, also influenced by AT.[64] It calls for prayer in the morning (ορθρου), third, sixth, and ninth hours, and at cockcrow. Thanks are given at evening for the completed day so as to enter upon the night; and cockcrow announces the new day in which the works of light may be done.[65] It is not clear whether this text refers only to private prayer.

---

[61] Ibid., p. 35.

[62] See Coneybeare and Maclean, *Rituale Armenorum* (Oxford: 1905), for probable order of morning service, op. cit., p. 164.

[63] Sperry-White, pp. 37–8.

[64] Bradshaw, *The Search*, p. 86.

[65] Funk, op. cit., vol. II, p. 88, xxiv.1; p. 89, xxiv, 6–7.

The Canons of Hippolytus

This is a collection of thirty-six canons and a sermon in Arabic. It is now believed to be the earliest derivative from AT, and thought to be of Egyptian origin c.336–40. One of very few sources we have for Egyptian church practice at this date, it is related to AT, and is part of the complex history of the Church Orders.[66] In Bradshaw's convenient text the relevant canon, 21, may be found on page 26.[67]

The canon concerns a daily assembly of clergy and people in church at cockcrow, involving prayer, psalms and reading of scripture.[68] Cockcrow seems to be abnormally early for lay people; this assembly may relate to the instruction in AT, or it might be an imitation of monastic practice. However we should recognize that a daily assembly for prayer at cockcrow is either the norm, or a norm to be encouraged, at least somewhere in Egypt.

Conclusions from the Church Orders

Apostolic Constitutions alone clearly describes common prayer at least twice daily, though *Apostolic Tradition* may indeed witness to such a pattern, and the *Testamentum Domini* appears to suggest a pattern of prayer at evening, at night, and in the morning. The *Epitome* and the *Canons of Hippolytus* know of prayer at cockcrow. This is not much, but the following points are important:

1 The imagery of darkness and light in all of these is reminiscent of the Paschal vigil and looking eschatologically for the eternal light.
2 *Apostolic Constitutions* 8 witnesses to the evening to morning order in its description of the services, although another order is found elsewhere. *Testamentum Domini* sees evening as beginning the new day.
3 At Vespers in *Apostolic Constitutions* prayer is for light and to be free of sin, so as to enter upon the night enlightened by Christ. For *Apostolic Tradition* the Ninth Hour is a time of 'illumination', and it celebrates the light at the beginning of an evening meal. The *Testamentum* presents an image of the resurrection at sundown and has a strong baptismal theme. For the latter document the Ninth Hour is also the hour of Christ's sacrifice, the time of redemption.

---

[66] See Bradshaw, *The Search*, pp. 83–4.

[67] *The Canons of Hippolytus* (Bramcote: Alcuin/GROW Liturgical Study 2, 1987). Critical text ed. R. Coquin, *PO* 31.2 (1966), pp. 386–9.

[68] *PO* 31, 386–7, as recommended by 1 Tim. 4.13.

4 The morning office in *Apostolic Constitutions* awaits the new light of day and gives thanks for that light, looking to the eternal light symbolizing new creation. The new creation and the eternal light are strongly linked to baptismal themes in the *Testamentum*'s understanding of Morning Prayer, the time when the risen Christ praises the Father.

5 *Apostolic Constitutions* knows a Sunday vigil, *Apostolic Tradition* values a night watch, and appears to understand sleeping and rising as types of death and resurrection. *Testamentum* thinks of midnight as the hour of resurrection, and associates themes of light with prayer and watching at night. The night prayer commemorates baptismal liberation from slavery to sin, so as to become sons of light.

6 The *Epitome* and the *Canons of Hippolytus* mention prayer at cockcrow, that is, before it is fully light and well before sunrise.

7 Although some of the references may be to private prayer, the rationale remains the same in all cases. Evening and Morning Prayer, or evening prayer, prayer at night/before light, and Morning Prayer in that order, all have to do with the light of Christ overcoming the darkness of sin and death. This nocturnal celebration also appears to have baptismal associations.

CHAPTER 4

A Brief Summary of Historical Developments and Geographical Locations

North and North-West from Palestine

The major early church centres that we encounter in the Church Orders and patristic sources are places like Rome, Alexandria and Antioch. The destruction of Jerusalem in 70 CE, and its reduction to the entirely Roman colony city of *Aelia Capitolina* by the Emperor Hadrian,[1] meant that it had no discernable effect on liturgical development until after 325. From the time of Constantine onwards, the city became an important, even pre-eminent, place of pilgrimage, and developed a liturgical style that pilgrims took note of and then tried to reproduce when they returned home.[2] In spite of invasions by the Persians in 614 and the Arabs in 638, together with a destructive earthquake in 746, and resultant curtailment of the liturgical pattern, there was an extremely influential development of liturgical poetry, mostly associated with the monasteries.

Interest in Jerusalem's liturgy has meant that one of the most important sources for it, a Lectionary, is in Armenian.[3] Armenia was one of the first nations to embrace Christianity, with the conversion of King Tiridates by Gregory the Illuminator in 301. The next year Gregory was consecrated bishop by Archbishop Leontius of Caesarea in Cappadocia.[4] In spite of attempts to subject the Armenian church to Constantinople when Caesarea declined, the Armenians remained strongly independent while remaining in communion with other churches down to the Council of Chalcedon, the teachings of that council only being rejected by an Armenian synod in 506.[5]

Upon the destruction of the old Armenian kingdom, a new state was established in Cilicia, and the church there entered into communion with the

---

[1] John Wilkinson, *Egeria's Travels* (3rd edn, Warminster: Aris & Phillips, 1999), p. 7.

[2] See 'Historicization of Liturgical Time', in John F. Baldovin SJ, *The Urban Character of Christian Worship* (OCA 228, Rome: 1987), pp. 102–4.

[3] *Le Lectionnaire de Jérusalem en Aménie*, ed. C. Renoux, in *PD* 35 Fase. 3 (Turnhout Bofors 1989).

[4] M. Ormanian, *The Church of Armenia* (London: Mowbray, 1912, rev. 1955), p. 11.

[5] R. Roberson, *The Eastern Christian Churches* (Rome: Pontifical Oriental Institute, 1990), p. 6.

Roman Catholic crusaders in the twelfth century. When this union ended because of renewed Arab onslaughts, some relics of Western practice remained in the Armenian liturgy. A small Armenian Catholic church has existed since the eighteenth century.[6]

Besides the later Latin influences, there are considerable resemblances to the rites of Constantinople, however this seems to have been a parallel development as the original liturgical tradition of both appears to have been derived from Caesarea in Cappadocia, the Metropolitan see that originally included Byzantium in its province.[7] We have little direct evidence for the liturgical forms in use in Cappadocia; but Syrian, and later, Jerusalem influences appear to have been operative, and we may be reasonably confident that Cappadocia was a main channel through which liturgical and theological ideas passed into Armenia.

Of all the Eastern liturgical traditions, the Byzantine is the best known in the West, and the most widespread in any case. Constantinople was founded by Constantine in 324. It was built upon the site of Byzantion, a Greek colony city of no great importance but strategically well placed.[8] The growing civil importance of Constantinople led to its being recognized as second only to Rome ecclesiastically by the Council of Constantinople of 381.[9]

The areas of the Patriarchate eventually included Cappadocia, Asia Minor, Cyprus, the Balkans, part of the Crimea, and even parts of southern Italy and Sicily, as well as Greece itself. Missionary expansion outside the Empire eventually encompassed Bulgars, Serbs, Romanians, and from 988, the people know as Rus' (modern Russians, Ukrainians and Belorussians).[10] A tendency to elect Greeks as Patriarchs of Antioch and Alexandria, and to abandon the ancient Syrian rites in order to demonstrate orthodoxy, led to the further spread of the Byzantine tradition (now much influenced by Palestinian monasticism) in the Middle East[11] and Georgia.

This liturgical tradition, and especially the 'chanted office', developed in the cathedral of Hagia Sophia (Holy Wisdom), inaugurated in 360. The present building dates from the Emperor Justinian who had it rebuilt in 537 as the domed basilica that still stands.[12] It was converted into a mosque in 1453, and

---

[6] Ibid., pp. 90–91.

[7] A. Fortescue, *The Lesser Eastern Churches* (London: Catholic Truth Society, 1913), p. 441.

[8] *Oxford Dictionary of Byzantium 1*, p. 508.

[9] Ibid., p. 520.

[10] A good account of the expansion may be found in J.M. Hussey, *The Orthodox Church in the Byzantine Empire* (Oxford: Clarendon, 1986).

[11] See e.g., Archdale A. King, *The Rites of Eastern Christendom II* (London: Burns & Oates, 1947), p. 90.

[12] *Oxford Dictionary of Byzantium 2*, pp. 892–3.

has been a museum since the time of Mustafa Kemal (Atatürk). The rites of daily prayer of Hagia Sophia were to be largely replaced by a predominantly monastic office of Palestinian provenance. A number of studies have described the process by which this took place and will be summarized in the relevant chapter.[13]

The Syrian Orthodox church of Antioch separated from the Byzantine and Roman churches after the Council of Chalcedon in 451. At one time a widespread church it is now very reduced in its heartlands of Syria, Lebanon, Iraq and Southern Turkey. There are, however, sizeable numbers in India, mostly in Kerala. There are corresponding groups of Catholics using the same liturgical tradition, and a more Latinized variant is found among the Maronite Catholics of Lebanon.[14] As well as the closely related Syrian and Maronite rites, there was an important variant, the rite or use of Tikrit (or Tagrit) associated with the see of the Mafrian[15] in Mesopotamia (modern Iraq).[16]

South to Egypt and Ethiopia

The Coptic church of Alexandria, the indigenous church of Egypt, has a long history, the beginnings of which are very obscure.[17] The foundation of the Egyptian church is traditionally ascribed to St Mark. The community was at first predominantly Greek in language and culture. It was also concerned for education, and the Catechetical School at Alexandria is famous for the teaching of Clement and Origen. Egypt was the first cradle of Christian monasticism. Antony, born about 251, took up eremitical life when aged about 20, and continued in this life until his death, reputedly at the age of 105, in 356.[18] Antony and his younger contemporary, Pachom (born c.292) the first founder of community monastic life,[19] were both native Egyptians, in modern terms Copts, a name which derives from a corruption of the Greek αιγύπτιος,

---

[13] See e.g., A. Schmemann, *Introduction to Liturgical Theology* (London: Faith Press, 1966), pp. 116ff.; M. Arranz, 'Les grandes étapes', op. cit., and Robert F. Taft, *The Byzantine Rite: A Short History* (Collegeville, MN: Liturgical Press, 1992), pp. 52–66.

[14] For further details see Roberson, op. cit., and C.P. Mathew and M.M. Thomas, *The Indian Churches of Saint Thomas* (Delhi: ISPCK, 1967), pp. 38–9.

[15] The Mafrian led the Syrian non-Chalcedonians in the Persian Empire (c.7th – c.14th cent.). The post later became a titular dignity – Fortescue, op. cit., pp. 328–9, 340.

[16] See also Taft, *The Liturgy of the Hours*, pp. 239–47.

[17] Barbara Watterson, *Coptic Egypt* (Edinburgh: Scottish Academic Press, 1988), p. 24.

[18] Most information on Antony comes from the biography of him by St Athanasius (328–373); Watterson, op. cit., pp. 56–61.

[19] Ibid., pp. 61ff.

which in Arabic, after 640, became *qibt*, 'copt'.[20] The church numbers around 4,000,000 believers.[21] Since the eighteenth/nineteenth centuries, there has also been a small Coptic Catholic church.

In the early fourth century, or thereabouts, two shipwrecked Egyptian boys became attached to the court of the Ethiopian king. They grew influential, and propagated their own Christian beliefs. Eventually, one of them, Frumentius, was made bishop by Athanasius. Frumentius was known in Ethiopia as Abba Selama (Father of Peace), a title held by all his successors until the middle of the twentieth century. Frumentius' successors were invariably Egyptians, as were any other bishops in the country, until 1929. The church became independent of the Coptic patriarchate only in 1957.[22] Distance, both geographical and cultural, ensured that although Ethiopian liturgical practices may have originated in Egypt, they developed an indigenous style. There are some 16,000,000 Ethiopian Orthodox, and about 120,000 members of the Ethiopian Catholic church, which has been operating since the last century.[23]

Developments Further East

Christians existed in the Persian Empire (modern Iraq and Iran) from about the mid second century.[24] The church in Persia suffered much persecution, but developed fine theological schools at Nisibis and Edessa, and in the fourth century produced the great St Ephrem (+373). The church became independent of Antioch under its own 'Katholikos' at the synod of Markabta in 424. In 431 the Council of Ephesus condemned the christological teachings of Nestorius, and in a reaction hostile to the council, and probably influenced by anti-Roman imperial feelings, Nestorian influenced teachings were made official at a synod at Beth Lapat in 484.[25]

Speaking Syriac/Aramaean, East Syrian Christians tended to be more generally Semitic in their thought forms, but their church spread across Asia, even to China, in the seventh–ninth centuries. After the Mongol invasions of the thirteenth century the church was largely confined to the Mesopotamian

---

[20] Ibid., p. ix. The term exclusively applied to Christian Egyptians by the sixteenth century.

[21] Roberson, op. cit., pp. 10–11.

[22] Colin Battell, 'The Ethiopians', in H. Hill (ed.) *Light from the East* (Toronto: Anglican Book Centre, 1988), pp. 62–81, 63–4.

[23] Roberson, op. cit., pp. 11–13, 93–4.

[24] Ibid., p. 1.

[25] Ibid.; and Donald Attwater, *The Christian Churches of the East, vol. I* (London: Geoffrey Chapman, 1961), pp. 188–9.

highlands and parts of western Iran.[26] There was also a long-standing connection between the Katholikos of the East and Malabar, in the south-west of India.[27] As a consequence, South Indian Christians also used the East Syrian rites in Syriac. The subsequent history of the Church of the East is very complex.[28] Suffice to say that the majority of those now following this liturgical tradition are in communion with Rome, some 3,000,000 somewhat Latinized Syro-Malabar Catholics, in India, and around half a million not so Latinized Chaldeans in Iraq and Iran.[29] The continuing Church of the East numbers about half a million, very few in India.[30]

The Western Roman Empire and Its Successors

We will see that Eastern forms of daily prayer appear to share a common theology rooted in both the cathedral and monastic forms of office. When we turn to the Western offices we find what appear to be very different rites which, with their heavy emphasis on reciting the Psalter and other scriptures, appear to be of a predominantly monastic, meditative and edificatory style. This perception of the offices has deeply affected the expectations that Roman Catholics, Anglicans and other Western Christians have. We shall be examining these traditions to see if they originally had much more in common with the forms of the East.

The rite of the Church of Rome was by no means the most important in the Western Europe of late antiquity.[31] As time passed however, it largely replaced other ancient rites, such as those of Gaul and the Celtic regions, nearly extinguished the Old Spanish tradition, and threatened the integrity of the rite of Milan. Allowing for quite wide regional variants, the daily offices of medieval Western Europe's cathedrals and parish churches followed a basically common pattern that had developed from the monastic offices celebrated in the Roman basilicas. Alongside that, however, we find a development of the same pattern, as adapted by St Benedict, which became the *Breviarium Monasticum* of the Benedictine and Cistercian monks.

---

[26] Useful background in H. Hill, 'The Assyrians: The Church of the East', in Hill, op. cit., pp. 100–121.

[27] See L.W. Brown, *The Indian Christians of St Thomas* (Cambridge: Cambridge University Press, 1956), pp. 45, 59.

[28] An excellent short summary is that of Roberson, op. cit., pp. 2–4; see also Attwater, op. cit., pp. 190–192, 199–203; and Hill, op. cit., pp. 113–21.

[29] Roberson, pp. 86–90.

[30] Ibid., p. 4.

[31] See e.g., discussion in Martin Connell, *Church and Worship in Fifth-Century Rome* (Alcuin/GROW 52, 2002), pp. 3–4.

These two related traditions of daily prayer continued substantially unchanged until modern times.[32] The Roman rite of daily prayer underwent two radical changes in the twentieth century. Pope Pius X's reform of the Roman Breviary in 1911 introduced far-reaching changes which destroyed many ancient features or rendered them opaque. The second Vatican Council decreed further radical changes that tended to make the shape of all the services much the same as each other.[33] The shape of the Benedictine office remained much closer to the ideas outlined in St Benedict's Rule until after Vatican II. Since Vatican II, monasteries have endeavoured to develop an office more suited to new understandings of monastic life and there is now considerable local variation.

The ancient, pre-Visigothic liturgy of Iberia (modern Spain and Portugal), the Old Spanish or Mozarabic rite, had probably attained its developed form by the time of the Moorish invasions of 711–56. As the Christians reconquered the Moorish occupied areas the older rite was suppressed in favour of the Roman, surviving only in a few exempted parishes in Toledo. From these parishes came the resources for a revised rite with printed books under the aegis of Cardinal Ximenez de Cisneros, and edited by Canon Alfonso Ortiz in 1500 and 1502. Ciseneros also endowed a chapel in Toledo Cathedral for the performance of the old rite. The eucharistic rite is being much more widely used today, but this chapel is probably the only place where any of the daily office is now regularly celebrated in public. Some festal and Holy Week services of the Breviary are celebrated in a very few other cathedrals.

The rite of Milan has had a continuous history since the time of Ambrose, and probably from before then. Ambrose (+397) was consecrated on 7 December 374, eight days after his baptism.[34] He is the dominant figure of late-fourth-century Milan, but to what extent he was the originator of the city's liturgical tradition is problematic. He was clear that he did not wish to differ from Roman practice, but in this he may well have been referring only to essential matters of doctrinal orthodoxy; for the rest, he defends local customs.[35]

Scholars have disputed the origins of the Milanese rites,[36] but late-fourth-century Milan was a cosmopolitan city. North African and Spanish influences are possible, but the strongest were probably Gallican. After 774, the city was part of the Carolingian Empire, and the Milanese rite came under especial

[32] A. Baumstark, *Comparative Liturgy* (London: Mowbray, 1958), p. 115.

[33] *Documents of Vatican II*, pp. 164–5, #87–#92.

[34] Archdale A. King, *The Liturgies of the Primatial Sees* (London: Longmans, 1957), pp. 288–90.

[35] Cesare Alzati, *Ambrosianum Mysterium*, 2 vols (Alcuin/GROW, 44, 1999 & 2000), I, pp. 16ff.

[36] Achille M. Triacca, 'La Liturgia Ambrosiana', in S. Marsili et al. (eds), *La Liturgia; Panorama Storico Generale* (Casale: Marietti, 1978), pp. 88–110, p. 91.

pressure, only just escaping complete abolition. The surviving manuscripts show signs of having been reformed in a Franco-Roman direction.[37]

Later reforms aimed at better observance of the rite. The great counter-Reformation Archbishop Charles Borromeo (1560–84) vindicated the primacy of the Sunday office and resisted attempts to change to the Roman rite.[38] Since Vatican II there has been much talk of abolishing the rite, but so far such a move has been strongly resisted.[39] A new Missal was promulgated in Advent 1976, and the first volume of a new Breviary emerged the following year.[40]

We have only a few accounts of the forms of daily prayer used in Gaul and the regions under Gallican influence. There is no documentary evidence. As will be mentioned later, we may hypothesize that Gallican offices had a similar shape to those of Spain and Milan. The same also appears to hold good for the only evidence of the offices we have from a Celtic source, *The Antiphonary of Bangor*. This single source allows us only to speculate that Celtic liturgical practice was probably similar to that of Gaul and Spain, and like that of the former, was progressively replaced by Roman practice from an early date.

---

[37] Ibid., pp. 101–2.

[38] See King, op. cit., pp. 309–11.

[39] Alzati, op. cit., vol. II, ch. 7.

[40] Triacca., op. cit., pp. 107–8.

CHAPTER 5

From Jerusalem and the Palestinian Monastic Traditions to Modern Orthodoxy*

The Evidence of Egeria

The most valuable witness to early liturgical practice in Jerusalem is the Spanish pilgrim Egeria, whose pilgrimage there must have occupied much of the period between 381 and 384.[1] From northern Spain or south-west France, she appears to have been some kind of nun, and her descriptions were written for the edification of her sisters. Egeria passed over common practices that were known to her correspondents, and dwelt upon those that were novel, or peculiar to the Holy City.

Egeria's main account of the daily prayer is found in chapters 24ff.[2] It is well known and widely accessible, so in what follows we will simply draw out saliant features. Egeria first describes an early vigil office that starts before cock-crow and continues until daybreak. This is the province of the *monazontes* and *parthenae*, groups of ascetics living a kind of monastic life in the city.[3] Described as the 'singing of the refrains to the hymns, psalms and antiphons', we may identify this as an office simply composed of psalms and/or responsorial canticles, interspersed with prayers.

At dawn the morning office proper began with the 'Morning Hymns', and the bishop now entered the church with the rest of the clergy. The bishop went into the cave of the Holy Sepulchre, prayed for all, blessed the catechumens and blessed the faithful. The morning psalms were probably selected for their suitability to the hour, hence the distinctive name, whereas the psalms and canticles used before dawn are not said to be especially suited to a particular hour. We may distinguish the daily vigil of psalms and prayers celebrated by the ascetics, the more fervent laity and some appointed clergy, from the

* This chapter was unable to take into account S.S. Froyshov's 2003 Sorbonne thesis on the Sinai Georgian Horologion.

[1] Wilkinson, op. cit., pp. 35–44. For critical edn of Latin: see Pierre Maraval (ed.), *Égérie, Journal du Voyage* (Paris: *SC* 296, Cerf, 1952).

[2] Wilkinson, op. cit., pp. 142 ff.

[3] See J. Mateos, 'La vigile cathédrale chez Egérie', *OCP*, **27** (1961), 281–312, 283.

popular, and more ceremonial, celebration led by the bishop himself which must have covered the period between dawn and sunrise.[4]

Besides services at midday and at 3, there was *Lychnicon* at four o'clock:

> All the people congregate once more in the Anastasis, and the lamps and candles are all lit, which makes it very bright. The fire is brought not from outside, but from the cave – that is from inside the railing – where a lamp is always burning night and day. For some time they have the Lucernare psalms and antiphons; then they send for the bishop who enters and sits in the chief seat. The presbyters also come and sit in their places, and the hymns and antiphons go on.[5]

The bishop does not seem to preside at the actual light ceremony, but is present for at least part of the series of evening psalms. The bishop's entry, further psalmody, and the prayer, may well be the central core of an office that has been lengthened by a series of psalms *preceded* by the *lucernarium*.

Egeria's description stresses that the light is taken from that which burnt in the cave of the sepulchre, not from outside. In either case the symbolism would be the same, the light represents the risen Christ amongst his people at the onset of night, and Jerusalem's possession of the sepulchre of Christ permits a graphic realization of this not possible elsewhere. Most importantly, the ceremony appears to be a daily event of a popular nature, and the connection between light ceremonies in the evening and the ceremonies associated with Easter, would establish even more definitely the nature of evening prayer as a vigil at sunset.

No indication is given as to which psalms are used, but it is possible that those named as 'Morning Hymns' or '*lucernare* psalms' were selected for their suitability to the time of day. Those sung before dawn are not qualified by any adjective of this kind. Egeria also describes a daily procession that followed Vespers: 'Then singing hymns, they take the bishop from the Anastasis to the Cross, and everyone goes with him. On arrival he says one prayer and blesses the catechumens, then another and blesses the faithful.' This is repeated behind the cross.[6] This procession may have influenced many other liturgical traditions, becoming the appendix that often *followed* the concluding formulae.

This round of prayer; a daily, pre-dawn vigil, followed by a 'cathedral' Morning Prayer and a service of similar nature in the evening; together with some lesser services during the day as well, was the weekday worship experienced by Egeria. On Sundays the bishop came to church at cockcrow,

---

[4] Ibid., 284–6.

[5] Wilkinson, op. cit., pp. 143 ff.

[6] Ibid, p. 144.

and all then entered the basilica.[7] Before this however, while the people waited they again sang 'hymns and antiphons' with prayers, a semi-formal 'monastic vigil' preceding the cathedral vigil proper.[8]

The main vigil in the basilica comprised the ceremonial entry of the bishop, three psalms or canticles, each followed by a prayer, then a general commemoration; the church was incensed and the bishop read the gospel account of the passion and resurrection.[9] A procession followed and after the usual individual blessings, the bishop retired to his house. Some people returned home, while others continued to keep vigil until daybreak.[10] This weekly commemoration would recall the myrrh-bearing women's visit to the tomb before it was light, their perfumes evoked by the abundant use of incense. The procession to the cross, that is, to the site of Golgotha, added a graphic reminder of the victory of the cross over sin and death.[11]

This order was followed throughout the year, except on certain special days. Egeria goes on to say: 'the psalms and antiphons they use are always appropriate, whether at night, or in the early morning, at the day prayers at midday or at three o'clock, or at Lucernare. Everything is suitable, appropriate, and relevant to what is being done'.[12] Does this exclude the Psalter in course altogether? Even the psalms at night would appear to be 'suitable, appropriate and relevant'. Was this vigil then a cathedral style of office of selected psalms rather than the Psalter gone through in order?[13] In fact a hard and fast division between cathedral and monastic styles at such an early date may be questionable. It seems that elements of cathedral and monastic practice are to be found alongside each other in Jerusalem at the time of Egeria, and the although the cockcrow vigil may have used a less structured psalmody than Matins and Vespers, it may not yet have been a rigidly current Psalter.

Can any very firm distinction can in fact be maintained between cathedral and monastic offices? Paul Bradshaw noted the existence of conservative, monastic-type communities which continued to use a selective approach to the

[7] Ibid.

[8] Mateos, 'La vigile', 299.

[9] 24.10 in Wilkinson, op. cit., pp. 144–5: 'At the beginning of the reading the whole assembly groans and laments at all the Lord underwent for us, and the way they weep would move even he hardest heart to tears.'

[10] 24.9–12, in ibid.

[11] Mateos, 'La vigile', 291–2. He cites as a parallel, the commemoration of the cross in the old Roman Breviary after Vespers and Lauds in Eastertide (see e.g., *Breviarium Romanum*, Pars Verna (Tournai: Desclée 1894), p. 165).

[12] 25.5; Wilkinson, p. 146.

[13] Taft, *Liturgy of the Hours*, pp. 54–5.

Psalter, especially at morning and evening.[14] Recitation of the entire Psalter may not, at this time, have been important to the concept of daily prayer.

Egeria leaves one in no doubt that the 'sanctification of the night' was of considerable importance to the Jerusalem liturgy of this period. On weekdays the ascetics and others rose at an early hour (whilst still dark) in order to pray together, and this daily pre-dawn vigil became, on Sundays, an almost all-night affair. Similarly, the evening *lucernarium*, though begun rather early, is clearly a service celebrating the light that flows from Christ's sepulchre to brighten the church.[15]

Egeria describes other night vigils, the existence of which only goes to show how much of the Jerusalem liturgy was carried out during the hours of darkness, for example, the additional Friday vigil in Lent, the Holy week services and the vigil of Pentecost.[16] It is clear that a major concern of the daily services in late-fourth-century Jerusalem was to proclaim the victory of light over darkness, of life over death, by praying before dawn and sunrise, or after sunset.

Early Monastic Evidence

From roughly the same period as Egeria, there are interesting accounts of monastic life in Palestine and Egypt left by John Cassian. He and his companion Germanus were living monastic life near Bethlehem in about 382–3. They then moved on to Egypt, and Cassian's *Institutes* were written over thirty years later for new monastic communities founded by him in the area of Marseilles. His account of monastic prayer in Palestine, very detailed but often difficult to interpret, is outlined by Taft.[17]

Seeing in the Last Supper, Christ's sacrifice as the true evening sacrifice, the sacrifice offered 'at the end of the ages', Cassian clearly conceived of the end of the day as symbolizing death, and its beginning as re-commencing life in Christ. The liturgical day begins at Vespers, so that the end of one day begins the process that leads to the new day.

Cassian's account of the morning office is involved with the long disputed question of the origins of the office of Prime (covered in detail by Taft).[18] In

---

[14] Paul Bradshaw, 'Cathedral vs. Monastery: The Only Alternatives for the Liturgy of the Hours?', in J. Neil Alexander (ed.), *Time and Community* (Washington, DC: Pastoral Press, 1990), pp. 123–36, 132.

[15] 24.4; Wilkinson, op. cit., p. 143.

[16] 29.1, ibid., p. 150; 30–38, pp. 151–7; 43, pp. 159–61.

[17] Taft, *Liturgy of the Hours*, pp. 76–7, and see Institutes III.1 (*PL* 49, 111–12).

[18] Ibid., pp. 97–100, 191–209.

Bethlehem the night vigil appears to have finished with psalms 148–50, which was part of the morning office – the office that we now identify as Prime came later on. In Gaul there was a pause between the night office and the morning office which included psalms 148–50.[19] The pattern of a night vigil followed by the morning office without a break is, of course, what we have seen in Egeria. On Fridays the nocturnal office lasted nearly all night, and comprised three antiphons, three responsorial psalms and three lessons, perhaps repeated several times.[20]

A reference to psalm 140 as justifying evening prayer may indicate it's use,[21] and the Eleventh Hour is called that of the *lucernarium*.[22] Cassian further emphasizes night vigils. On some days vigils started in the evening and were prolonged into the night (see above). As with Egeria, these offices are hybrids, composed of monastic and cathedral elements, and neither has completely absorbed the other.[23]

An otherwise important source for the Jerusalem liturgy, the Georgian Lectionary,[24] is not directly helpful for the offices. This document knew of extended vigils at Vespers, and at midnight on the eves of great feasts, for example, Christmas.[25] We simply note that the feast starts at Vespers and the vigil continues through the night. Matins on such feasts finished fairly rapidly after a gospel reading.[26] There are three Vespers readings in Holy Week,[27] as in the present Byzantine rite for eves of feasts, and a Gospel as well.

The next dateable evidence from Palestine is the account of the visit of the Abbas John and Sophronius to Abba Nilus of Sinai, attributed to the late sixth, early seventh centuries.[28] Nilus' visitors were shocked at his omissions; at Vespers there were none of the usual troparia with psalm 140, nor with 'O gladsome light', nor with the prayer 'Vouchsafe, O Lord'. Nilus replied that many of the things his visitors missed required clergy, and such were not

---

[19] Ibid., p. 100, interpreting Institutes III.3–4 (*PL* 49, 125–32).

[20] Institutes III.4, III.8 (*PL* 49, 128, 140).

[21] Institutes III.3, *PL* 49, 123–5.

[22] 'post haec nona, ad extremum undecima, in qua lucernalis [or lucernaris] hora signatur'. Institutes III.3, *PL* 49, 126.

[23] See e.g., Taft, *Liturgy of the Hours*, pp. 79–80 and Bradshaw, op. cit., pp. 99–100.

[24] M. Tarchnischvili (ed.), *Le Grand Lectionnaire de l'Église de Jérusalem (Ve–VIIIe siècles) (CSCO 188, Louvain: 1959–60), 4 fascicles.*

[25] Ibid., Tomus 10, 9ff.

[26] Ibid., 13.

[27] Ibid., 85–90.

[28] A. Longo, 'Il testo integrale della <<Narrazione degli abati Giovanni e Sofronio> > attraverso le <<Hermineiai> > di Nicone' in *Rivista degli Studi Bizantini e Neoellenici*, ns **23** (XII–XIII) (1965–6), 233–67. Also N. Uspensky, *Evening Worship of the Orthodox Church* (Crestwood: St Vladimir's Seminary Press, 1985), pp. 59–61.

normally available in his monasteries, so they kept only the people's parts, and also, usually just biblical material. The only non-biblical pieces were 'O gladsome light', the *Gloria in Excelsis*, the Creed and the numerous *Kyrie eleisons*.[29]

On the psalms, the account says:

> When we came to Vespers, the elder began by singing 'Glory to the Father' and so forth; then we said 'Blessed is the man' and 'Lord I call' without troparia; he then took Φως 'ιλαρόν and 'Vouchsafe, O Lord'; after this we began to say the prayer of St Simeon and the rest.[30]

The first psalm referred to appears to be psalm 1, and may well indicate the group of psalms 1–8, still appointed for modern Byzantine Vespers on Saturday night. In fact the whole service looks very like a skeletal form of the modern office.

The Saturday night vigil began after supper. The Psalter was divided into three lengthy sections of fifty psalms each.[31] The psalms were preceded by the *hexapsalmos*. It is not said which six psalms but the modern six seems likely: psalms 3, 37, 62, 87, 102 and 142.[32] After the psalms came the nine biblical canticles of the modern Byzantine canon, psalms 148–50, the *Gloria in Excelsis* and other features, again showing this to be an ancestor of the present Eastern Orthodox morning office of *orthros*.

This austere monastic office employed the entire Psalter at a weekly vigil, and a large amount of psalmody at other times. Although monastic, it retained cathedral elements, but little or none of the poetry found elsewhere at this date. The general shape is recognizably similar to that described by Egeria, though at Vespers the *lucernarium* (Φως 'ιλαρόν) has moved after the psalmody. A vigil of psalms and readings still precedes the morning office. Prayers and other elements requiring a priest, are replaced by the Lord's Prayer at each *stasis*.[33] This simplification of the Jerusalem hybrid rite for desert monasteries could, no doubt, largely be committed to memory.[34]

---

[29] Longo, op. cit., 251–2. See also M. Arranz, 'Les grandes étapes de la liturgie Byzantine', in *Liturgie de l'église particulière et liturgie de l'église universelle* (=Conférences Saint-Serge 22, Rome: Edizioni Liturgiche, 1976), p. 48.

[30] As translated in Uspensky, op. cit., p. 67.

[31] J. Mateos, 'La psalmodie variable dans l'office Byzantin', *Acta Philosophica et Theologica II* (Rome: Societas Academica Dacroromana, 1964), pp. 327–39, 337.

[32] Taft, *Liturgy of the Hours*, p. 199.

[33] Ibid. A *stasis* here is the group of fifty psalms, in modern use it is a third of a *kathisma* (= session), three psalms or the equivalent.

[34] Uspensky, op. cit., p. 66.

The Palestinian *Horologia*

The next important piece of evidence for the Palestinian monastic office is a ninth- century Sinai manuscript, Gr. 863.[35] With this we can couple a manuscript Syriac Horologion of the twelfth century,[36] which latter starts with *orthros*. The first is a *horologion* (book of hours) for weekdays, and declares that it is according to the rule of the lavra of St Sabas. It provides psalms 1–8, exactly as they are arranged in modern use (i.e., in three *staseis*: 1–3, 4–6, 7–8). Then follow the First, Third, Sixth and Ninth Hours, communion from the reserved sacrament, and Vespers.

The Syriac document begins Vespers with the Trisagion and the invitatory verse 'O come that we may worship and bow down before, Christ the King.' Then the incipit of psalm 102,[37] which appears to be a misreading for psalm 103 which begins in the same way. The incipit of psalm 140 may indicate the group of psalms 140, 141, 129, and 116, at the end of which there is a doxology and a *Theotokion*, a poetic stanza. Φως 'ιλαρόν is itself followed by a troparion and *Theotokion*,[38] these are not found in the *textus receptus*, but, as we have seen, were perceived as missing by Abba Nilus' visitors.[39] There is no sign of the prayer 'Vouchsafe, O Lord' (see below) which might simply be presumed, but troparia for each night of the week are provided, followed by the *Nunc Dimittis*.[40] The troparia reflect devotions for each day of the week: for example, Wednesday and Friday commemorate the cross. The Sunday troparion and *Theotokion* commemorate the resurrection. None of the texts of these troparia appears in a similar place in the present *Paraklitiki*[41] (or book of the eight tones for each day of the week). These troparia clearly see the liturgical day as commencing the evening before, as do similar texts of the current Byzantine rite.

In both documents Vespers largely comprises a series of psalms. The first, 103, is the daily first psalm of the present-day order. In the St Sabbas book, after psalm 103 are read psalms 119–33 in three *staseis*.[42] The Syriac document does not mention the *kathisma*, or indeed any current Psalter, possibly the

---

[35] J. Mateos, 'Un horologion inédit de Saint-Sabas', *Studi e Testi 233* (Rome, Vatican, 1964), 47–76.

[36] M. Black (ed.), *A Christian Palestinian Syriac Horologion (Berlin MS Or. Oct. 1019)* (Cambridge: Cambridge University Press, Texts and Studies I, 1954), p. 3; hereafter Black.

[37] Black, op. cit.

[38] Ibid., p. 85.

[39] Longo, op. cit., 353, line 37.

[40] Black, pp. 85–6.

[41] Παρακλητικη (Αθηναι: εκδοσεις Φως, 1991)

[42] Mateos, 'Un horologion', 56.

relevant portion of the Psalter was inserted after psalm 103, perhaps indicating that other portions than psalms 119–33 might be used.

In the modern Orthodox office, psalms 119–33 are appointed for Vespers daily through some six to seven months of the year, and in the rest of the year they are used only at Friday Vespers.[43] On Saturday night the psalmody is always psalms 1–8 (as above), and on Sunday night there is no recital of the Psalter in course at all. The division of the Psalter into *kathismata* is found in a seventh-century *Kanonarion*, and in a ninth-century Jerusalem Psalter,[44] and appears to have first been used by non-monastic churches in Jerusalem.

The St Sabbas Horologion also provides the normal fixed psalms of Palestinian Vespers. After these psalms and the hymn Φως 'ιλαρόν, there are Alleluia chants with verses for each evening of the week.[45] If this Horologion treats the gradual psalms as fixed psalmody, then the Alleluia verses allow for some daily variety. The final sections of this evening office are the prayer καταξιωσον, the *Nunc Dimittis* and the Trisagion. These all seem to have a Palestinian origin. The first of these elements, a prayer/hymn, 'Vouchsafe, O Lord, to keep us this evening without sin' is very close to the present form. An earlier, shorter, version is found in the *Apostolic Constitutions*,[46] and appears to be taken for granted in the visit of John and Sophronius to Nilos (see above).[47] Poetic material and prayers were omitted by Nilos as priestly, and while this text is not scriptural, it appears to be regarded as roughly on the same level as Φως 'ιλαρόν.[48]

The St Sabas Horologion passes directly from 'Vouchsafe, O Lord' to the *Nunc Dimittis*, as in the *Apostolic Constitutions*,[49] though this document also adds the Trisagion as the final element in the service. This means that there is no *Aposticha*, the processional psalm which Mateos supposes is a remnant of the procession to the cross mentioned by Egeria.[50] The normal weekday *aposticha* psalm nowadays is 122: 'To you have I lifted up my eyes, you who

---

[43] Mateos, 'La psalmodie variable', 327–31, and table of psalms in *Psaltir' na Slavyanskom i Russkom yazykach* (Rome: Vatican Polyglot Press, 1950), pp. 418–40.

[44] Arranz (ed.); Uspensky, op. cit., p. 108.

[45] Mateos, 'Un Horologion', 57–8. these are not in the modern office.

[46] Grisbrooke, *The Liturgical Portions*, p. 57: 'Children, praise the Lord: praise the name of the Lord. We praise you, we hymn you, we bless you on account of your great glory, O Lord [our] King, the Father of Christ, the Immaculate Lamb, who takes away the sin of the world. To you belongs praise, to you belong hymn[s], to you belongs glory, to the God and Father, through the Son, in the Holy Spirit, for ever and ever. Amen. Lord now let your servant depart in peace ...'

[47] Longo, op. cit., 233, lines 7–8.

[48] Helmut Leeb (*Die Gesänge in Gemeindegottesdienst von Jerusalem (vom 5. bis 8. Jahrhundert)* (Vienna = Wiener Beiträge zur Theologie 28, 1979), pp. 176–81.

[49] See Grisbrooke, op. cit.

[50] Mateos, 'Un Horologion', 75–6.

dwell in the heavens.' On Saturday evenings it is 92: 'The Lord is King, with majesty enrobed.' The absence of any text of this kind from the St Sabas Horologion may suggest that monastic use did not provide for processions. The Syriac service finishes with three brief troparia asking the prayers of the saints, similar to those that now conclude Fast day Vespers when there is no Presanctified Liturgy,[51] then 40 *Kyrie eleisons*, 15 prostrations and a final prayer.[52]

The Scriptures at Palestinian Vespers

Described by Cassian as known throughout the world at *duodecima* or Vespers,[53] psalm 103 concludes the day and verses 1–18 praise God in his creation; then the psalm becomes vesperal:

> Thou hast made the moon to mark the seasons; the sun knows the time for its setting. Thou makest darkness, and it is night, ...

The psalm then reflects on the greatness of the God whose spirit fills the earth, and praises his glory. One can well see how this psalm commended itself to early liturgists, the parallel to creation from a formless void in Genesis should also spring to mind. The end of the day is at the same time a new beginning.

In contemporary use the longest recitation of psalmody is on the long winter nights and in Lent, when three *kathismata* are read at *orthros*, the *kathisma* at weekday Vespers being always psalms 119–33. In addition the Psalter should be read twice a week in Lent, so as well as three *kathismata* at *orthros*, there is frequently one at each of the Minor Hours as well.[54] One theory is that psalms 119–33 are connected with the liturgy of the Presanctified Gifts.[55] There is no clear reason why these psalms should be connected with communion from the reserved sacrament, and in the St Sabas Horologion, communion *precedes* Vespers with the gradual psalms.[56] While the Constantinopolitan monastic Typikon of Evergetis spread the Psalter over a three-week period in summer, and weekly only in the winter, but twice a

---

[51] See *Horologion* (Rome, 1937), pp. 231–2.

[52] Black, pp. 86–7.

[53] Sermon 136.1, quoted by Bradshaw, *Daily Prayer*, p. 119 and n. 45.

[54] Mateos, 'La psalmodie variable', 328–30.

[55] Ibid., 330–1.

[56] Mateos, 'Un Horologion', 64–8.

week in Lent, it only used psalms 119–33 at Lenten Vespers when there was *no* Presanctified.[57]

The St Sabbas Horologion appears to exhibit a rite of Vespers at which the normal daily psalms were the gradual psalms plus the evening psalms of the cathedral tradition, 140, etc. Most of the Psalter was reserved for the nocturnal vigil before dawn, a vigil which sometimes may have included the whole Psalter, as did that Abba Nilos.

Egeria's description of Vespers has significant evening psalmody prior to the bishop's entry and further psalmody after it. Possibly psalms 119–34 comprised the regular Vespers psalmody of the ascetics, and then the bishop entered for the evening psalms (140, etc.). This is, of course, only a hypothesis in view of the little documentary information that we have.[57a]

The gradual psalms may have been selected because of their association with pilgrimage to Jerusalem. They also, however, suit the time of day: for example, psalm 119 prays for protection at the hour of distress; psalm 120.4 speaks of God as protector of his people who 'sleeps not nor slumbers'. Psalm 129 'Out of the depths' is obviously vesperal, being recited again later with psalms 140 and 141; psalm 130 is a psalm of trust. Psalm 132 is a prayer for unity, and psalm 133 a prayer at night-time. These last two form a suitable conclusion to this prayer, expressing trust in the God who is with his people in times of danger.

If the gradual psalms express trust in the living God to whom the evening sacrifice of praise is offered, then it is natural that psalm 140 with its reference to that evening sacrifice should follow here. The usual evening psalm grouping associated with this Palestinian tradition, psalms 140, 141, 129 and 116, differs from Syrian use in employing psalm 129 instead of psalm 118.105–17. The Syrian choice may have been influenced by a reference to light,[58] whereas Palestine knew the hymn Φως 'ιλαρόν, and was thus free to use psalm 129 instead, with its references to Jerusalem and to waiting for the light. Psalm 141 takes up the theme of protection: 'You are my refuge, all I have left in the land of the living.' The development of this group of four psalms may have resulted from elaboration of the incense rite, psalm 140 alone being too short to cover the actions. The St Sabas Horologion still has no place for the poetic *stichera* intercalated at a later date.[59]

The Alleluia verses after the evening hymn in the ancient Horologion[60] begin with verses from psalm 92 for Sunday: 'The Lord is king, with majesty

---

[57] Mateos, 'La psalmodie variable', 331–3.

[57a] But see note on Froyshov on page 49.

[58] P.E. Gemayel, 'La structure des Vêpres Maronites', *Orient Syrien*, **9** (1964), 105–34, 116.

[59] Mateos, 'Un Horologion', 70.

[60] Ibid., 57–8.

enrobed; the Lord has robed himself with might, he has girded himself with power...' (Saturday evening *prokeimenon* of modern Byzantine Vespers).[61] On weekdays the verses are from psalms 54 (Monday), 4 (Tuesday), the *Magnificat* on Wednesday, psalm 85 (Thursday), and 88 (Friday). Psalm 92 is well suited to begin Sunday. Psalm 54 is a prayer for help by one praying at 'Evening, morning and at noon' (v. 18); 4 is a prayer at the onset of night – 'I lie down in peace and sleep comes at once' (v. 9); and so on. The verses are appropriate to the evening themes of confident prayer to the God who gives help and strength to his people and guides them through the night. The verses are also similar to the standard weeknight *prokeimena* of modern Byzantine Vespers, which were derived from the old Constantinopolitan office to be described below.

The Early Prayer and Hymn Texts

Evidence for non-scriptural poetry at this early stage is not strong, and Palestinian monastic use appears to have known only *Φως 'ιλαρόν* and *καταξοωσον* at Vespers. *Φως 'ιλαρόν* was known to St Basil (+ 379),[62] but this Horologion provides the first complete, if variant, text.[63] The earliest witness to the present text is the fifth-century Georgian lectionary.[64] The following is a translation from a modern liturgical book:

> O Jesus Christ, thou gentle light of the holy Glory of the immortal, heavenly, holy, blessed Father:
> Now that we have come to the setting of the sun and behold the evening light, We sing in praise to God, Father, Son and Holy Spirit.
> Thou art worthy at all times to be praised by holy voices, O Son of God, giver of life, therefore the world gives thee glory.[65]

The lamp-lighting reveals the glory of God who is praised at the onset of darkness. The hymn is a climax reached through alternating thanksgiving for the day and supplication for continuing protection. After the climax little is left but to conclude and round off this prayer that commences the night.

---

[61] *Horologion*, p. 227.

[62] Taft, *Liturgy of the Hours*, p. 38. Also, Antonia Tripolitis, 'Φως ιλαρόν – Ancient Hymn and Modern Enigma', *Vigiliae Christianae*, **24** (1970), 189–96; she suggests a late 2nd/early 3rd cent. date.

[63] Discussed by Mateos, 'Un Horologion', 70–74.

[64] Taft, 'Phos Hilaron', in Alexander P. Kazhdan (ed.), *The Oxford Dictionary of Byzantium* (New York and Oxford: Oxford University Press, 1991), pp. 1668–9. *Le Grand Lectionnaire* ... op. cit., p. 109, Easter Eve Vespers.

[65] *Vespers and Matins* (Oxford: Diocese of Sourozh, 2001), p. 19.

In modern Byzantine books the text beginning *καταξίωσον* is entitled simply 'prayer'.[66] In monasteries it is usually read by the superior,[67] and in parishes by the reader. In all these cases it is treated as a prayer. By contrast, the Typikon of Saint Sabas, still the basic guide to the service in the Slav churches, requires the prayer to be said by the people;[68] a use preserved today by Ukrainian and Carpatho-Russian Catholics,[69] and in Russian churches on Sundays and Feasts.[70] It would appear then that the piece was originally a hymn.[71] A modern version of the text is as follows:

> Vouchsafe, O Lord, to keep us this evening without sin.
> Blessed art thou, O Lord, God of our fathers, and praised and glorified is thy Name, forever. Amen.
> Let thy mercy, O Lord, be upon us, even as we have set our hope on thee.
> Blessed art thou, O Lord, teach me thy statutes.
> Blessed art thou, O Master, make me to understand thy statutes.
> Blessed art Thou, O Holy One, enlighten me by thy statutes.
> Thy mercy, O Lord, endures for ever; O despise not the work of thy hands.
> To thee belongs praise, to thee belongs song, to thee belongs glory, to the Father, and to the Son, and to the Holy Spirit, now and for ever and to the ages of ages. Amen.[72]

Clearly a prayer for protection at evening, the developed refrain from psalm 118 introduces another element; prayer to keep God's laws and commands with understanding, a theme found elsewhere: for example, Spain.

The Syriac document provides only a single, final prayer, which may have been read even in the absence of a priest:

> We bless thee, O gracious Lord, that thou hast granted us the passing of the day in peace, and hast brought us to evening with praise; and that thou hast deemed us worthy to behold the light of evening. Receive our praises, and free us from all the troubles of the Evil One, and destroy every snare he sets for us. Grant us this night acceptable peace, without suffering or distress or disturbance, that we may pass it peaceably and watchfully. Let us arise, O Lord, to praise and prayer, which is worthy of you at all times. Let us

---

66 *Horologion*, p. 229.

67 See Fr Ephrem (Lash), *The Office of Vespers* (Manchester: St Andrew's Press, 2000), n. 12, p. 25.

68 *PG* 29, CCCXXXVIII – Και ο λαος : Καταξοωσον, Κύριε.

69 E.g., *Chasoslov* – Book of Hours (Zhovkva, Ukraine: 1910), p. 180.

70 See musical settings in e.g., *Obikhod Tserkovnogo Penia* (Moscow: Sretensky Monastery, 1997), pp. 53–7.

71 R. Taft, 'The Byzantine Office in the *Prayerbook* of New Skete: Evaluation of a Proposed Reform', *OCP*, **48** (1982), 336–70, 347.

72 *Vespers and Matins*, op. cit., pp. 26–7.

> glorify thy holy name, with the Father, who is without beginning and unsearchable, and with thy living Spirit, for ever and ever.[73]

This prayer ends the day, even though Compline follows. The traditional evening themes of light and repose at night are there, but the prayer also looks forward to the coming day – it is not just an end, but preparation for a new beginning.

Palestinian Matins

The St Sabbas Horologion is unfortunately incomplete and gives us no information about Matins. The order of Matins/*orthros* in the Syriac document[74] has the Trisagion followed by the same invitatory as at present: namely, the words of Luke 2.14, 'Glory to God in the Highest, and on earth peace; among men of good will' three times, together with psalm 50.15; 'O Lord, open thou my lips; and my mouth shall show forth thy praise.' The six psalms then follow, divided into two groups of three by the Gloria and Alleluia. This group of psalms 3, 37, 62, 87, 102 and 142 is paralleled by the ancient Byzantine use of psalms 3, 62 and 133[75] to begin *orthros*, and the Armenian use of psalms 3, 87, 102 and 142.[76]

In modern Byzantine use the six psalms are followed by a litany, and then 'The Lord is God', verses from psalm 117 mentioned in the account of the visit to Abba Nilos as something that the visitors find lacking.[77] Mateos concluded that the more primitive weekday form at this point was the group of verses from the canticle of Isaiah 26.9–20, with the response Alleluia, nowadays used on Lenten and other fasting weekdays.[78] The Syriac document does not mention the Alleluia and verses from Isaiah 36, nor 'The Lord is God'. Nor does it mention psalm 50 or the Psalter in course that should precede it, instead the document goes directly to the nine canticles, and then to the office of Prime, the First Hour.[79]

Abba Nilos' visitors again remarked on the absence of poetic material at the reading of the Psalter and when the biblical canticles were sung.[80] It may be

---

[73] Black, p. 87.

[74] Black, pp. 73–4.

[75] See e.g., M. Arranz, 'Les prières presbytérales des matines byzantines', *OCP*, **37** (1971), 406–36, 409.

[76] Taft, *Liturgy of the Hours*, p. 221.

[77] Longo, op. cit., 253, line 38.

[78] J. Mateos, 'Quelques problèmes de l'orthros byzantin', *Proche Orient Chrétien*, **11** (1961), 17–35, 201–20; 27–9.

[79] Black, op. cit. 74.

[80] Longo: 'Il testo integrale', 253, lines 38–40.

that in urban monasteries, and in the Palestinian cathedral office, such poetic material had already found a place. After this began the morning part of the office, probably with psalm 50, then the canticles, and the praise psalms (148–50); the Great Doxology and prayer brought the whole office to an end;[81] this is structurally identical to the present Byzantine office.

Psalms and Other Scriptural Elements of Matins

The original opening psalm of the six may have been 3 on its own, seen as the psalm that began the monastic midnight vigil.[82] 'I lay down and slept, – I wake again, for the Lord sustains me' could equally apply to night and to the period before dawn, and the emphasis on the defeat of enemies suits the psalm's resurrection theme. The psalm is well suited to a vigil, be it celebrated just before dawn or at an even earlier hour, as we may see in verse 7: 'On my bed I remember you. On you I muse through the night.'

The middle psalm of the first group, 37, a penitential lament, seems intended to make up the number three, as it comes numerically between 3 and 62 and Psalter order is usually observed scrupulously. It is a psalm of penance well suited to a vigil before light.

Of the second group, psalms 87, 102 and 142; psalm 87 is another lament and verses 7ff. with their emphasis on being laid in 'the depths of the tomb, on places that are dark, in the depths' would appear to have influenced its selection. Psalm 102 sings of life delivered from the grave and the joy of being crowned with God's love and compassion, for 'The Lord has set his sway in heaven and his kingdom is ruling over all' (v. 19). If death and darkness dominate in psalm 87, then in psalm 102 God's power over all things is proved, and it is then not entirely unnatural for the last of the trio, psalm 142, to be the penitential prayer of one who seeks salvation from the God who rules over creation. This group shows a consistent rationale, moving from helplessness to an awareness of God's power. Sunrise still lies ahead, but the Morning Prayer has begun and the power of God is able to overthrow darkness, and to save and forgive sinners.

Verses 9a–b, 9d–10, 11c–d, and 15 of Isaiah 26 now follow, with the refrain 'Alleluia' (the whole of this canticle is one of the nine odes that follow later in the service):

> – My spirit seeks thee early in the morning, O God: for thy commandments are a light upon the earth.

[81] Mateos, 'Quelques problèmes', 31–5.

[82] Ibid., 24–6.

- Learn righteousness: ye that dwell on earth.
- The wrath of God shall fall upon a disobedient people: and fire shall now devour the enemy.
- Bring more evils upon them, O Lord: bring more evils upon them that are glorious on earth.[83]

Although not mentioned in many of the earliest sources, this unit appears to be of the Palestinian monastic tradition, and not of the Constantinopolitan cathedral office, even though one of the prayers of that office (see below) quotes the canticle.[84] Clearly the verses are selected for the time of night – a night enlightened by God's commands that judge the earth, shedding light where the darkness of sin still reigns.

The now more commonly used 'The Lord is God', is made up of verses 1, 10, 17, 22–3 of psalm 117:

- The Lord is God and has appeared unto us: blessed is he that comes in the name of the Lord.
- O give thanks unto the Lord, for he is good: for his mercy endures for ever.
- All the nations compassed me about: but in the name of the Lord have I driven them back.
- I will not die, but live: and declare the works of the Lord.
- The stone which the builders rejected, the same has become the head of the corner: this is the Lord's doing, and it is marvellous in our eyes![85]

The resurrectional verses may indicate that this unit is of festal origin.[86] It is accompanied by proper troparia, and those of Sundays always sing of the resurrection. In the context of an early morning vigil office while still dark these psalm verses express strongly the theme of life overcoming death in Christ's resurrection. Possible antiquity is shown by references in the Georgian *Iadgari* which appears to reflect seventh-century practice in Jerusalem.[87]

When we turn to the canticles, those provided in the Syriac document are those of Exodus 15, 1 Samuel 2 (the canticle of Hannah), Habakkuk 3, Isaiah 26.9–19, Jonah 2, Daniel 3.52ff., Daniel 3.57ff., Luke 1.46ff. (*Magnificat*), and Luke 1.68ff (*Benedictus*). These are the canticles appointed for the modern

---

[83] *Vespers and Matins*, op. cit., pp. 69–70.

[84] Arranz 'Les prières', op. cit., 414.

[85] *Vespers and Matins*, op. cit., pp. 68–9.

[86] Mateos, 'Quelques problèmes', 203.

[87] Peter Jeffrey, 'The Sunday Office of Seventh-Century Jerusalem in the Georgian Chantbook (Iadgari): A Preliminary Report', *SL*, 21 (1991), 52–71; 64.

Byzantine *orthros*, except that the last two are now grouped into a single ode, and Deuteronomy 32.1–43 is inserted after Exodus.[88]

The account of the visit to Nilus of Sinai appears to infer that all nine odes or canticles were used, with pauses for prayer (Our Father and *Kyrie eleison*) after the third and sixth.[89] While part of the text may be later than the rest of the narrative,[90] it is possible that from an early stage it was common in Palestine to use all nine canticles at the same service, at least on Sunday. Weekdays may well have used a selected canticle or canticles.

The canticles have associations with the Paschal vigil, especially the first, the Exodus Song of the Sea, and the second of the two Daniel canticles, ode 8 in the modern reckoning. Both are a part of readings listed for the Paschal vigil of the oldest Jerusalem lectionaries.[91] Both passages have been widely employed as morning canticles, and Baumstark thought them the earliest non-psalmic canticles used in Christian worship.[92]

The present arrangement of three groups of three canticles reveals the following pattern: the Exodus Song of the Sea is followed by the Deuteronomy hymn to God who destroys evil, and the song of Hannah which is also about victory through God's power. The second trio comprises Habakkuk 3, a prayer that God's power be known, Isaiah 26.9ff., a yearning in the night for God to raise the dead, and Jonah 2, his prayer for release from the belly of the great fish (a symbol of the tomb), thus a prayer for divine redemption. The final trio is made up of the two Daniel 3 canticles, hymns of praise sung in the midst of danger and possible suffering; and then the *Magnificat* and *Benedictus* dwelling upon the experience of God's goodness. The first trio says that God is powerful and destroys his enemies, the second prays that therefore he will save his people, and the third rejoices in the experience of God's saving power.

The use of all nine together appears to be a Palestinian custom, and may not always have been the norm. On the weekdays of Lent it was customary to use only three canticles each day, hence the term *Triodion* for the liturgical book which covers the fasting season. At the present time, the canon is normally a series of eight poetic odes, made up of a number of poetic pieces called troparia.

In some places the scriptural odes are still used in Lent, together with a poetic canon, in a quite complicated arrangement which results in a canticle

---

[88] See e.g. *Horologion*, pp. 94–9.

[89] Longo, 252. James Mearns, *The Canticles of the Christian Church Eastern and Western in Early and Medieval Times* (Cambridge: Cambridge University Press, 1914), pp. 7–8, thought the reference was to the nine found in Greek Psalters since 1000, and also in four manuscripts, the oldest being the fifth-century Egyptian Codex Alexandrinus, 9–10.

[90] Taft, *Liturgy of the Hours*, p. 199.

[91] Gabriel Bertonière, *The Historical Development of the Easter Vigil and Related Services in the Greek Church* (*OCA* 193, Rome: 1972), pp. 8–18 and chart A–2 (after page 307).

[92] *Comparative Liturgy*, op. cit., pp. 37–8.

for each day, and daily use of *Benedicite* and the two Lukan canticles.[93] As to the original arrangement of these morning canticles, Mateos proposed that older tradition was to use three canticles on Sunday and one on each day of the week.[94] In a recent study Byron D. Stuhlman has suggested a daily fixed canticle (*Benedicite*) plus a variable one, with the *Magnificat/Benedictus* added later to make up the unit ofthree. The daily use of *Benedicite* would fit with such other traditions as that of Constantinople (see below).[95] We may interpret the canticles as the transition from the monastic vigil to the morning office proper, the first ode becoming a variable, and the Daniel canticles a daily start to the morning office, one or both of the Lukan canticles making a 'third' ode.

We may then suggest the following stages of development:

1 The Jerusalem Paschal vigil has readings from Exodus and Daniel which introduce canticles.
2 The Sunday resurrection vigil of three chants most likely included the canticles of Exodus 15 and Daniel 3.
3 The second Daniel 3 canticle, the *Benedicite*, a hymn to God's glory by all creation, is used daily.
4 Somewhat later the resurrection vigil becomes nine canticles developing the themes noted above, and adding the New Testament as well.
5 On weekdays one of the Sunday canticles is added to the *Benedicite*.
6 To develop into the sacred number three, the present ninth ode is also added on weekdays.
7 In the later medieval development of the poetic canons, the weekday canticles retain their three ode form in Lent, alongside the later eight ode poetic form on other days.

The Poetic and Euchological Evidence

Neither the Alleluia responsory after the six psalms nor the triadic troparia that now accompany it make any mention of fasting or penance, hence Mateos' conclusion that this piece was not originally confined to Lent.[96] The

---

[93] For details see *The Lenten Triodion*, op. cit., 75–7.

[94] Mateos, 'Quelques problèmes', 31–2.

[95] Byron D. Stuhlman, 'The Morning Offices of the Byzantine Rite: Mateos Revisited', *SL*, 19 (1989), 162–78.

[96] Mateos, 'Quelques problèmes', 27–8 & n 32: Evergetis prescribed Alleluia for all but the most important days. A twelfth-century typikon edited by M. Arranz [*Le Typicon du Monastère de Saint-Sauveur à Messine* (*OCA* 185, Rome: 1969)] expects Alleluia on Ferias and 'The Lord is God' on Sundays and Feasts, e.g., p. xxxvi.

triadic troparia also appear to be part of this Palestinian structure, and often exhibit a very simple, and probably primitive form, they also suit the hour, e.g.:

> Rising from sleep, we fall before you in adoration, O Mighty Lord, singing you the hymn the angels offer you ...[97]

The eschatological theme of watching for Christ the coming judge is well expressed in another that Mateos thinks primitive:

> Suddenly the judge will come and all our works will be uncovered! Let us shake off laziness, and filled with awe, let us sing our God the song the angels sing: Holy, ...[98]

Originally undifferentiated troparia were later grouped into the octonal system, and other compositions helped make up the full sets now in the liturgical books.[99]

By the time that the Palestinian office had become that of the Constantinopolitan monasteries, poetic material had become more pervasive. The extremely austere office described in the account of the visit dates from the time immediately prior to the Persian invasions of Palestine in 614. After that crisis there was a great monastic revival, particularly centred on the monastery of St Sabas, and characterized by the creation of a vast body of liturgical poetry. This material was attractive to monastic reformers such as Theodore of Studium (d. 826), for it was all ammunition against heretics.[100]

The poetic compositions have almost entirely displaced the scriptural odes of the canon, though the first troparion, the irmos, of each poetic ode usually contains a reference to the canticle it has replaced.[101] For example:

> In Babylon, the Children, sons of Abraham, once trampled upon the flame of the fiery furnace, and they sang the song of praise: 'O God of our fathers, blessed art Thou'.[102]

---

[97] Tone 1, number 1, *A Prayerbook*, p. 71.

[98] Tone 3, number 3, ibid., p. 72.

[99] Mateos, 'Quelques problèmes', 28 and n. 33.

[100] Taft, 'The *Synaxarion* of Evergetis in the History of Byzantine Liturgy', in Margaret Mullett and Anthony Kirby (eds), *The Theotokos Evergetis and eleventh-century monasticism* (Belfast: Belfast Byzantine Texts and Translations, 6.1, 1994), pp. 274–93; p. 287.

[101] Mother Mary and Archimandrite Kallistos Ware, *The Festal Menaion* (London: Faber & Faber, 1969), pp. 546, 552–3.

[102] Replaces first canticle from Daniel 3, first canon for Transfiguration, ibid., p. 489.

Except in certain more penitential canons, such as that composed by St Andrew of Crete, the second ode, Deuteronomy 32, is omitted, hence the odes are numbered 1, 3, 4, etc.

In the modern Byzantine office the praise psalms are immediately preceded by the Exaposteilarion, or in Lent by the Photogokikon, neither of which are mentioned in the Palestinian sources discussed. The Lenten texts call for Christ to send (εξαποστειλον) his light, while the Sunday texts dwell on the resurrection gospel.[103] (Other texts have little or no connection with morning light.) Those of the Lenten weekdays identified as the oldest (in the 1st, 2nd, 3rd and 8th tones) are well suited to the time of day and not at all Lenten; they greet the sunrise that represents the risen Christ who shines his light on his people. That for Monday in tone 1 reads: 'O Christ who makest light to shine, cleanse my soul from every sin, . . . '.[104]

The last major piece of Matins was the Great Doxology, the *Gloria in Excelsis*, originally a Sunday and festal piece.[105] Ferial use was to employ only *kataxioson* in its morning version, the full Doxology only being used on days when the Eucharist followed.[106] This ecclesiastical canticle, often included with the scriptural ones,[107] was widely used in the Eastern churches to conclude the morning office, and the night office at Milan (see below).

Conclusions on the Palestinian Offices

It is now possible to summarize the schemes of the Palestinian monastic offices later taken over by and fused with the old rite of Constantinople. These services do contain classical cathedral elements, and this is consonant with what we saw of the offices at the time of Egeria – in Palestine, monastic influences never seem to have been far away from the cathedral services.

---

[103] Ibid., pp. 218–19 – Sunday texts composed by the 10th cent. Constantine VIII Porphyrogenitos.

[104] *Lenten Triodion*, op. cit., pp. 662–3.

[105] Mateos, 'Quelques problèmes', 32–4.

[106] Ibid., also Taft, 'The Byzantine Office in the *Prayerbook* of New Skete', *OCP*, **48** (1982), 336–70, 354.

[107] E.g., Codex Alexandrinus (see J. Mearns, *The Canticles of the Christian Church* . . . , op. cit., pp. 9ff.; and in eighth-century Ms Turin Bib. Naz. Bv 11 30 (a Jerusalem source, see J.M. Martin Patino, 'El Breviarium Mozarabe de Ortiz, su valor Documental para la Historia del Oficio Catedralicio Hispanico', *Miscellanea 40 Comillas* (1963), 207–97, p. 229.

Vespers

Introductory

Trisagion
Psalm 103

Psalmody

Psalms (119–33)

Lucernarium

The Evening Psalms (140, 141, 129 and 116) (with poetic verses)
Hail Gladdening Light
(Alleluia/*Prokeimenon*)
Kataxioson

Conclusion

(Psalm at procession)
Nunc Dimittis

(Poetry)
Trisagion – *Kyrie eleison*

Material in brackets does not appear to be part of the more austere monastic observances, and it is not at all clear how euchological material was included in the urban monasteries and cathedrals. On the other hand, the service has a clear structure and progression. From the opening psalm's reflection on creation to end the day, the service passes to the gradual psalms with their expression of joy at the prospect of entering into God's house. The evening psalms and the hymn of light form the core of the office and establish the theme of the presence of Christ the light, the coming Christ, clothed in splendour (psalm 92); it is then natural to pass to prayer for protection in the coming night, chant the *Nunc Dimittis* and draw to a close.

Simplified versions of the schemes of Matins produced by Mateos[108] and repeated, with variations, by Stuhlman,[109] are the basis for that given on pages 72–4, which allows us to discern the features of the modern office that have clear Palestinian origins.

---

108 Mateos, 'Quelques problèmes', 23, 202.
109 Op. cit., 174–8.

The old Constantinopolitan office will be discussed further in chapter 7. We should note certain points that remain unclear. For Mateos, psalm 50 begins the morning office,[110] but although it appears in many ancient offices, it is not explicitly found in the Palestinian sources. The Armenian is the closest to the above scheme, and places that psalm just before the praise psalms, 148–50, which appears to fit in with Byzantine arrangements that require psalm 50 after the sixth ode of the canon, that is, before the last three, the morning canticles *par excellence*.[111] The cathedral vigil also remains unclear, but it looks as though the present office has both Constantinople and Palestinian elements.

General Conclusions

I With regard to structure:

1 In the Palestinian tradition, psalmody is particularly associated with night time.
2 Psalm 103 passes from reflecting on the end of the day to entering upon the night as a time for activity as well as rest. The possible daily use of the gradual psalms suggests an eschatological pilgrimage motif, as well as utilizing psalms that suit the end of the day – in other words the journey does not end with the night.
3 Similarly, the hymn Φως ‘ιλαρόν greets the light of evening as earnest of a new day; an interpretation taken up by some of the *prokeimena* that follow, especially ‘The Lord reigns’.
4 At night, the six psalms, especially the set 87, 102 and 142 appear to indicate a passage from darkness to new light. The Lenten Alleluia verses from Isaiah 26, ‘My soul yearns for you in the night’ reinforce this idea, made more obvious in the ‘God is the Lord’ verses from psalm 117.
5 There is a strong paschal emphasis in the canticles which lead into the hymns of light at sunrise, and the praise psalms.

II Egeria describes the offices starting with the pre-dawn vigil, but we also find:

1 Cassian sees Vespers as beginning the daily round, the end of the day presages a new day. The night is more a time for watchful prayer than for rest.

[110] Mateos, ‘Quelques problèmes’, 31.

[111] Jeffrey, ‘The Sunday Office’, op. cit., 74. Also Arranz, *Le Typicon du Monastère du Saint Sauveur à Messine*, op. cit., p. xxxvii, psalm 50 followed the 6th ode on ordinary days.

2 Vespers are described first in the account of the visit to Nilus of Sinai, and overnight vigils start after supper, to sanctify the night.
3 Although several documents provide the Matins to Vespers order as their basic framework, poetic texts, e.g., in the Horologion edited by Matthew Black, reflect the devotional themes of a particular day as starting the previous night at Vespers.

III The prayer tradition is not well developed but we can point out that:

1 The prayer 'Vouchsafe, O Lord, to keep us this night without sin' also looks to active obedience to God's laws as much as praying for protection at night.
2 Morning troparia of presumed Palestinian origin pray that rising from sleep, we watch for the coming Judge and celebrate the hour of praise.
3 The prayer in Black's Syrian Horologion that completes Vespers, moves from ending the day, through watching at night, to waiting expectantly to greet the glory of God in the new day.

The celebration of the Paschal mystery is obvious in the light-filled Vespers described by Egeria, and the texts mentioned all bear witness to this. The passage from night to morning recalls Christ's rising in the night, to appear to his people in the full light of day as the true sun of justice, and the hope of resurrection light for all.

The Minor Day Hours

Both the St Sabas and Syriac Horologia provide services for the Minor Hours during the day. The latter being very close to those of the contemporary liturgical books. They are schematized on pages 72–4.

The Syriac document also provides *mesoria*, services to come in between each of the hours. These draw some of their psalms from those of the hours in the St Sabas Horologion. *Mesoria* are provided in modern liturgical books and have the same psalms as in the Syriac document.[112] The modern Typicon expects them to be used only in fasting seasons other than Lent, and they are very rarely used anywhere today, so we will not study them at any greater depth.

[112] See *Horologion*, pp. 143ff.

The Bible at the Hours

The psalms selected for the Hours in the Syriac MS are all found in the St Sabas document and are those in the modern-day arrangement of Minor Hours in the Byzantine rite. At the First Hour the early morning time is established, for example: 'In the morning I prepare a sacrifice for thee' (5). At the Third, 'Good and upright is the Lord; therefore he instructs sinners in the way' (24) is a good example of prayer for guidance and forgiveness through the day. Among the psalms of the Sixth Hour, 'He who dwells in the shelter of the most High' (90) is a prayer for rest and refreshment in the middle of the day. At the Ninth Hour, 'How lovely is your dwelling place' (83) and other psalms bring us to the end of the day finding refuge in God's house.

These texts which make up most of the services are simply a progression through the day. The selected verses however, found in both the ancient sources and in the modern books, such as those beginning 'Order my steps in thy word' (from psalms 118 and 70) at the First Hour, are chosen more for that time – this prayer concluding that we might 'sing of thy glory and honour all the day long'. The Third Hour uses verses of psalm 50 (Especially 'Take not thy Holy Spirit from me') with prayer for the Holy Spirit. The Sixth Hour has been much more varied as to which psalm verses accompany prayer commemorating the crucifixion; and the Ninth Hour, commemorating Jesus death on the cross, has used psalm 22 in the St Sabas 'The Lord is my shepherd' and psalm 118[170] 'Deliver me according to thy word' in the Syrian and modern books.

The Prayer and Hymns of the Hours

The modern service has a series of troparia, now only used in Lent, which clearly establish a particular theology of the time of day:

- In the morning hear my voice ...
- O Lord who at the Third Hour did send the Holy Spirit ...
- Thou who at the sixth day and hour did nail to the cross the sin that Adam committed in paradise ...
- Thou who at the Ninth Hour did taste death on the cross for our salvation ...

These hymns are found in the Syriac document and a form of that of the Third Hour is found in St Sabas.[113]

[113] Black, 51, line 10.

The themes seem less fixed in St Sabas, though a version of the prayer to Christ the true light that closes the modern First Hour is found there:[114]

> O Christ the true light who enlightens everyone who comes into the world; let the light of thy countenance be marked upon us, that in it we may see light ineffable ...[115]

A closing prayer at the Third Hour in the Syriac document is much more explicit in praying for the Spirit than the contemporary prayer of St Mardarius:

> O God of grace, who hast compassion on us every hour, by the comfort of the Holy Spirit; we bless Thee that thou hast saved us this hour, in which thou didst pour forth abundantly upon thy pure disciples the grace of the Holy Spirit ...[116]

However, the prayer at the Sixth Hour in the same source is very general, while the modern one speaks of the power of the cross to destroy sin.[117] Similarly, the Syriac document's prayer of the Ninth Hour is to pass the time worthily,[118] while the modern prayer dwells on Christ's hanging upon the cross.[119]

There is then a certain fluidity in the themes that are found at the Day Hours; it is not possible historically, to tie them down to a simple scheme of Christ's condemnation/coming of the Holy Spirit, crucifixion and death. As we shall see, this is true across a wide range of services for the Day Hours, and this contrasts with the more clearly developed and common themes of the major offices of Vespers and Vigils/Matins.

Matins/*orthros*

Ferial	Sunday
I – Night Office	*I – Night Office*
a) **Invitatory**:	a) **Invitatory**:
Psalms 3, 37, 62 & 87, 102 & 142	Psalms 3, 37, 62 and 87, 102, 142
Isaiah 26 canticle	Psalm 117 & Theos Kyrios
b) **Nocturnal Psalmody**:	b) **Nocturnal Psalmody**:
1st section – Troparion – Reading	1st section – Troparion – Reading
2nd section – Troparion – Reading	2nd section – Troparion – Reading

[114] Ibid., 49.

[115] *Horologion.*

[116] Black, p. 78.

[117] *Horologion*, pp. 174–5.

[118] Black, p. 84.

[119] *Horologion*, pp. 211–12.

3rd section – Troparion – Reading	3rd section, replaced by psalm 118 (see below)
Variable canticle (?)	*II – Resurrection Vigil*
II – Morning Office	Gospel and other material
Benedicite	Psalm 50 (?)
[*Magnificat* and *Benedictus* later]	3 then 9 canticles
Psalm 50 (?)	*III – Morning Office*
Photogogikon	[Psalm 50 transposed earlier]
	Exaposteilarion
Psalms 148–50	**Psalms 148–50**
Kataxioson or *Gloria in Excelsis* + Kataxioson	*Gloria*, Kataxioson, Trisagion
Intercessory material	Intercessory material
Concluding prayers	Concluding prayers

St Sabas	**Syriac Horologion**
First Hour	
Opening prayers & Come let us worship	Come let us worship
Verse 'The night having passed . . .'	
Psalms 5, 45, 66, 69, 89, 91, 100, 112	Psalms 5, 89, 100
Alleluia with verses from psalm 142	
Prayer: '(Christ) the true light'	'Christ the true light'
Troparia for the day of the week	In the morning . . . (Ps. 5.1), Theotokion
Psalm 118.133–5 & 70.8	Psalm 118.133–5 & 70.8
Trisagion, Creed, Lord's Prayer	Trisagion & Prostration
	'O Lord God of hosts'
Third Hour	
(Opening prayers)	Opening prayers
Psalms 16, 24, 42, 50, 142, 144, 150	Psalms 16, 24, 50
Alleluia (psalm 50)	
O Lord who at the 3rd Hour	O Lord who at the 3rd Hour, Psalm 50.10–11

Troparia for day	Troparia & 'Thou who didst send …'
Psalm 67.19–21	
Trisagion etc. & Prayer	
Sixth Hour	
(Opening prayers)	Opening prayers
Psalms 53, 54, 68, 69, 90, 145	Psalms 53, 54, 90
Alleluia (Psalm 55)	
O thou who at the 6th Hour …	O thou who at the 6th Hour … / Psalm 54
Troparia for day	Troparia & 'Speedily may thy mercies reach us'
Psalm 78.8–9	
Trisagion …	
Ninth Hour	
(Opening prayers)	Opening prayers
Psalms 83, 84, 85 and Dan. 3.26–56	Psalms 83, 84, 85
Alleluia (psalm 22)	
O thou who at the 9th Hour …	O thou who at the 9th Hour …
Troparia for day	Troparia & "Deliver us not"
Dan. 3.34–5	
Trisagion … [120]	Trisagion etc. & Prayer[121]

[120] Mateos, 'Un Horologion', 48–54.

[121] Black, pp. 74–84.

CHAPTER 6

The Jerusalem Pattern of Prayer in Cappadocia and Armenia

The Evidence for the Cappadocian Offices

Robert Taft has discussed the evidence for a Cappadocian cathedral rite in the writings of Basil the Great, his brother Gregory of Nyssa, and the latter's account of their sister Macrina's death in 379. From this he extracts a hypothetical structure:

Lucernarium with *Phôs hilaron*
Psalm 140
Lessons with homily
Intercessions with 'Angel of Peace' petitions[1]

If Taft's skeleton service of Vespers is correct, then what may have developed in Cappadocia would have been similar to the Palestinian tradition:

Continuous monastic psalmody
Light ritual with hymn of light
Psalm 140 with incense (implied by mention of repentance)
Intercessory prayer

Preparatory recitation of the Psalter leads to the Light ritual and a Thanksgiving for light at the end of the day. The service then passes on to prayer for forgiveness, probably involving psalm 140 and purificatory use of incense, and the day finishes with prayers, including the angel of peace petitions, i.e., prayers for protection through the night.

Some of the earliest testimonies to Φως 'ιλαρόν are from this region. Pagans used acclamations such as 'Hail, good light!' or 'Hail, friendly light!', and Clement of Alexandria suggested greeting God with 'Hail, Light!'. Jewish Sabbath meal practices could also be influential here.[2] In the account of the death of St Macrina we find the words: 'but the chant of the singers called to the thanksgiving for the light and she (Macrina) sent me off to church'. Many

[1] *PG* 46, 981ff.; Taft, *Liturgy of the Hours*, pp. 36–41.

[2] Winkler, 'Über die Kathedralvesper', 60–61.

scholars think that the hymn is the thanksgiving for light mentioned in this account.[3] The pagan phrases seem to be echoed in the wording of the hymn, and it is probably fair to say that the rite emerged in a mix of cultures that placed a good deal of emphasis on the coming of the evening light.

Basil also gives us a rationale for offices at morning, the Third, Sixth and Ninth Hours, in the evening, at the beginning of the night, midnight and so back to dawn.[4] The rationale of Vespers is a time of thanksgiving for the day, with confession for failures, and there is a brief quote from psalm 4.5: 'The things you say in your hearts, be sorry for on your beds'.[5]

If there is little Cappadocian evidence for vespers, then there is even less for the morning offices, but some for vigils. In the *Longer Rules* Basil gives a double justification for the morning office. First that the day may be consecrated to God, and prayer made before any work, and secondly, having already justified prayer in the night, Basil speaks of rising to anticipate the dawn, citing psalm 118.148 'My eyes watch through the night to ponder your promise'. Since both descriptions apply to the time just before dawn they must refer to the same service.[6]

The treatise *de Virginitate*, of a writer close to the Cappadocians, has a longer exposition of Morning Prayer.[7] The text speaks of rising at midnight with a verse from psalm 118, then psalm 50 and psalmody interspersed with prayer for forgiveness. At dawn psalm 62 is said; then at daybreak the *Benedicite*, the *Gloria in Excelsis*, '... and the rest', which might well include psalms 148–50. This appears to be a classic pre-dawn monastic vigil, followed by a morning office of broadly cathedral shape. There may have been more psalmody between psalm 62 and the *Benedicite*, as there could be quite a long gap between dawn and daybreak. This is again similar to the Palestinian pattern of a monastic vigil combined with cathedral-style praise at the beginning of the new day.

The *Longer Rules* mention prayer at bedtime, with the classical Compline psalm, 90; and also a midnight office, so as to pray like Paul and Silas (Acts 16.25). This prayer is also justified by reference to psalm 118.62 'At midnight I will rise and thank you'[8] – a common justification for prayer at this time, and the psalm comes to be associated with the midnight office in the Byzantine tradition.[9]

---

[3] *PG* 46, 985; Taft, *Liturgy of the Hours*, pp. 36–8.

[4] *PG* 31, 1013ff.; and see Taft, *Liturgy of the Hours*, pp. 85–6.

[5] Ibid., 86 – Gk text, *PG* 31, 1013 and J. Mateos, 'L'office monastique à la fin du IVe siècle: Antioche, Palestine, Cappadoce', *Oriens Christianus*, **47** (1963), 53–88, 75.

[6] Taft, *Liturgy of the Hours*, p. 86.

[7] Translation in ibid., p. 88.

[8] Mateos, 'L'office monastique', 78.

[9] *Horologion*, op. cit., 13–30.

The cathedral vigil that Basil commended to the clergy of Neocaesarea (Letter 207) appears to have included:

Vigil	Isaiah 26.9ff.
	Psalm 118
	Antiphonal and responsorial psalmody with prayers
	Readings (?)
Matins	Psalm 50
	Hymns and Canticles
	Intercessions[10]

Isaiah 26.9 'My soul yearns for Thee in the night',[11] possibly derived from the Palestinian monastic vigil, is quoted. A reference to 'reinforcing the study of the scriptural passages'[12] is the probable reason for concluding that there were readings. The morning part of the office starts with the 'psalm of confession',[13] the normal beginning of the morning office that would more generally be attended by the laity;[14] the rest of the outline of the office relying on the presumptions outlined above.

This very tentative reconstruction indicates a vigil that commenced with the Isaiah canticle, and then psalm 118 served as an extended meditation on the law of the Lord. This would lead to a further meditative use of psalmody, scripture and prayer – a classical vigil of waiting in prayer upon the word of God. Hearing the word prepares for the 'psalm of confession' at daybreak, and then, in the presence of the risen Lord represented by the rising sun, God's redeemed people sing confident praise to him in union with all creation as the day proper begins.

The Armenian Vespers

The following schema of Armenian Vespers is drawn from Taft,[15] Coneybeare and Maclean,[16] and Raes.[17] Texts will largely be drawn from Coneybeare and Maclean.

---

[10] Taft, *Liturgy of the Hours*, pp. 40–41.

[11] Mateos, 'L'office monastique', 80 (e).

[12] Taft, *Liturgy of the Hours*, p. 39 and Greek text, Mateos, 'L'office monastique', 80 (h).

[13] 'της ξομολογησως ψαλμον', Mateos, 'L'office monastique', 81 (n).

[14] Ibid., 84–5.

[15] Taft, *Liturgy of the Hours*, 223–4.

[16] *Rituale Armenorum*, ed. F.C. Coneybeare and A.J. Maclean (Oxford, 1905), pp. 443–88 – Vespers, 477–82; hereafter Coneybeare and Maclean.

[17] A. Raes, *Introductio in Liturgiam Orientalem* (Rome: PIO, 1947), op. cit., pp. 191–4, 202–205.

Introductory	Lord's Prayer
	Psalm 54.17–18
	Psalm 85
Lucernarium	Psalms 139–41
	Prayer for blessing of light
	Hymn of Light ('Hail Gladdening Light' on Sunday)
	Evening Proclamation/*kataxioson*
	'Let my prayer come before you like incense'
	Litany (incl. Angel of Peace)
	Prayer
	Prayer of Inclination
Appendix	Trisagion w. prayers
	Psalm 120
	Prayer for those in need
	[Lent: Prayer of Manasseh and proclamation,
	Prayer for repentance]
	Dismissal psalms 90, 122, 53 and prayer
	[Sunday, psalms 133, 137 and 53 and prayer]
	Proclamation of the Cross
	'At church door', psalm 121, prayer
	Return, psalm 99, prayer
	Final Invocation and Lord's Prayer

While there is no recitation of the Psalter in course, the core of the service is similar to Palestinian monastic Vespers: psalms 140–1 with 'Hail Gladdening Light'.[18] Gabriele Winkler proposed the following original scheme:

Psalm 54
Light ritual: prayer, hymn and thanksgiving
Psalm 140
Intercession[19]

This is based on the commentary on the Armenian offices attributed to Catholicos Yovhannes Ojneç'i (fl. early 8th cent.),[20] who states that his predecessor Nerses introduced psalm 85[21] at the beginning of the service.

[18] The author attended an Armenian vespers at which this core was entirely omitted and the censing done during the Trisagion; St Sarkis, London, 28 November 2001.

[19] Winkler, 'Über die Kathedralvesper', 78–80.

[20] Called 'John of Odsun' in Coneybeare and Maclean, p. 448. The commentary may owe much to Step'anos Siwnec'i, information for which I am indebted to Fr Daniel Findikyan, of the Armenian seminary of St Nersess, New York.

[21] Coneybeare and Maclean, pp. 448–501, p. 497.

Between the two Catholicoi named Nerses was Movses (574–604), who famously made disparaging remarks about Constantinopolitan liturgical practices, which makes borrowings from there unlikely.[22] May it be that the use of psalm 85 was a Cappadocian practice which also influenced Byzantine usage? Perhaps Catholicos Nerses wished to introduce the monastic psalmody to Vespers in Armenia, and with it, the introductory psalm 85. If such were indeed the case, then either the psalmody in course at Vespers was rejected and the introductory psalm retained, or the recitation of the Psalter in course soon died out.

The Armenian *lucernarium* psalms are a singular grouping of psalms 139, 140 and 141. The commentary of Yovhannes interprets psalm 139 as a prayer for God to save his suffering people from their sins. The psalm prays for delivery from persecutors, like psalm 54 at the beginning. This fits with Yovhannes' interpretation of Vespers as commemorating him who descended into the tomb so as to grant us life.[23] There is nothing specifically vesperal about this psalm, but neither is there about psalm 141. The idea of evening as the hour of Christ's descent into the tomb may well be behind the choice of both of these psalms; perhaps as a later addition to psalm 140, chosen because of its reference to the evening offering, but itself a prayer for rescue from danger,

> From the trap they have laid for me keep me safe: keep me from the snares of those who do evil. (v. 9)

The prayer for rescue is further emphasized by Yovhannes' citation of psalm 141.8: 'Bring my soul out of this prison and then I shall praise your name'.

Prison serves as a metaphor for this life, so the prayer looks forward to release in the future; it is not just a particular evening that is being celebrated, but the whole of life looking toward the *eschaton*.[24] There is no mention of incensation in the rubrics.

After a prayer, the hymn of light and the evening proclamation, there follow the first two verses of psalm 140, though the second, 'Let my prayer come before you like incense', is said to be used only on Fridays.[25] This doublet of psalm 140 following the hymn of light is in the account of the visit to Nilus of Sinai.[26] This weakens any argument for Byzantine influence, instead arguing

---

[22] See R. Taft, 'Water into Wine: The Twice-Mixed Chalice in the Byzantine Eucharist', *Le Muséon*, **100** (1987), 323–42, 329.

[23] Coneybeare and Maclean, p. 493.

[24] Ibid., p. 494.

[25] Ibid.

[26] Longo, op. cit., 253, lines 37–8.

Palestinian provenance.[27] As we saw above, Cappadocian Vespers may actually have been quite close in shape to Winkler's supposed old Armenian pattern: Light ritual, psalm 140 and prayer. If this was the cathedral order, at least in outline, then the monks may have put their psalmody before it, where we now find psalms 139–41. Possibly these psalms, emphasizing death and the tomb, and hence a prelude to the central light theme of ancient vesperal services, replaced the monastic psalmody. This gives a pattern of thanksgiving for light, prayer of evening offering, prayer for the church, and prayer for protection in the night.

The psalms are followed by a lamp-lighting prayer:

> Blessed Lord, who dwellest on high, and praised is the glory of thy majesty; who establishedst the luminaries on high, and sentest forth light from heaven over all the world of mankind. Thou madest the sun to give light by day, and the moon and the stars to give light by night, and the light of the candle. Thou art light laudable, holy and primal light. From thee doth the darkness flee. And do thou, Christ, send forth thy living light into our hearts. And let us with one accord say, Blessed is the name of thy holy glory. And to thee we sing a hymn of praise and glory to Father and Son.[28]

This prayer clearly expresses the ideas of thankfulness and grateful hope with which the evening light could be greeted as a sign of the risen Christ, who overcomes the darkness and bestows light and life upon his people. Yovhannes, having spoken of the descent into the tomb, now speaks of the material light as a symbol of the light that leads to everlasting life.[29] The prayer can stand on its own as a prayer of thanksgiving for the light, it does not require the psalms before it in order to be intelligible as a liturgical unit. It does however lead naturally into the lamp-lighting hymn, which on Sunday (i.e., Saturday night)[30] is 'Hail Gladdening Light'.

The hymn of light is followed by a prayer that sums up Vespers as the hour of thanksgiving for the day past, and prays that we may share in the angelic praise:

> We are all come hither at eventide; and uplifting our hands, we glorify thee, Lord our God. Who hast vouchsafed unto us to pass the day in peace, and attain to the hour of evening ...[31]

---

[27] Taft, *Liturgy of the Hours*, p. 224.

[28] Translation from Coneybeare and Maclean, p. 477.

[29] Ibid., p. 494.

[30] Ibid., p. 478, n. a; Kosrow Andsevatzi says explicitly: 'we sing it (the hymn) the eve of each Sunday'.

[31] Ibid.

The presence of phrases similar to those in the (probably) Palestinian *kataxioson* may be clues to the prayer's ancestry.

The next unit is intercessory prayer; there is a litany which prays for the church, for civil needs, for preservation in peace and a quiet night, and also appears to require the 'Angel of Peace' petitions. It concludes with a prayer that commends the evening sacrifice in the following terms:

> Hear our voices, O Lord our God: accept our prayers and the lifting up of our hands and the words of our prayers; hallowing our evening sacrifice of fragrance, and making it ready for thy approval ...[32]

These opening words so take up the theme of psalm 140 that the prayer could almost be called a psalm collect, the rest of the prayer is a general one for grace and mercy. There then follows a blessing:

> Thee we worship and adore, O Lord our God. We thank thee for granting that in peace we should pass the length of day. Grant us, Lord, we pray thee, to pass this evening and the night which lies before us without sin and without stumbling. That we may stand firm and abide in faith, in hope, ... We entreat for the peace of the whole world, and also for the establishing of thy holy church ... To the end that, receiving from thee all we ask, we may for ever send up on high meet and fitting hymns of glory ...[33]

This blessing looks forward to both the night of repose, and at the same time stands firm in the keeping of God's commands, a frequently found petition at Vespers. These petitions and those for the church imply a time of day when work has ended but the time for sleep is not yet come. The prayers also look beyond this moment to the future that lies with the God who is worshipped in songs of praise – in other words, it can be said to look forward to the coming day.

The remainder of the office appears to have originated as a devotional appendix to the office. First the Trisagion is followed by brief invocations, and then psalm 120 'I lift up my eyes to the mountains: from where shall come my help'.[34] The reference to the Lord's guarding of his people is most appropriate to the evening hour. The psalm prayer requests that God might 'accept the supplications of thy servants in this evening hour' and for mercy on the afflicted, travellers, etc.[35] The prayer attributed to King Mannasseh and its

---

[32] Ibid.

[33] Ibid.

[34] Coneybeare and Maclean, p. 480, refers to psalm 121 but clearly intends 'I lift up my eyes', also cited by Raes (*Introductio*, op. cit., p. 193), so the reference in Taft (*Liturgy of the Hours*, p. 223) to psalm 121 must be a misprint.

[35] Coneybeare and Maclean, ibid.

prayer or 'proclamation' are penitential elements omitted outside of Lent.[36] The psalms of dismissal given by Coneybeare as 90, 122, and 53[37] convey once again the classical themes of the last prayer of the day, protection from evils that threaten, while looking forward to the heavenly rest. Yovhannes expands further and brings in psalm 122, especially the opening words, 'To you have I lifted up my eyes'. He sees this as a prayer that this night may be without sin so that in the morning the sacrifice may be offered.[38] Psalm 53 is also a cry for God's help. On Sundays (i.e., Saturday night) psalms 133, 137 and 53 are used instead; 133 is frequently found beginning night vigils, 137 is a thanksgiving for God's protection,'You stretch out your hand and save me'.[39]

The 'Proclamation of the Cross'[40] involves a prayer for defence, seemingly a procession to the church door with psalm 121 'I rejoiced when I heard them say, let us go to God's house', and prayers which make particular mention of Christ's resurrection,[41] followed by a return procession singing psalm 99 'Cry out with joy to the Lord' and concluded by the prayer:

> Let us praise the Lord God, Father of our Lord Jesus Christ, who hath made us worthy to live in the place of his glorifying, and to sing spiritual hymns. Almighty Lord our God, quicken and have mercy.[42]

Yovhannes made it clear that Vespers finished with the Trisagion and the 'psalm of repose',[43] which, as Raes says, without doubt refers to psalm 90, and after this the people ask the priest to pray for each individual briefly.[44] First found in a fifteenth-century codex, the final procession is similar to the Byzantine festal *litia*.

Coneybeare prints a blessing before a meal after Vespers, and then 'The Hour of Peace' and 'The Hour of Rest'.[45] The Hour of Peace commences with part of psalm 33 'I will bless the Lord at all times', then a 'canon' of six psalms (the first three of which, 4, 6 and 12, are found in modern Byzantine Great Compline), plus plenty of material suitable for late night prayer. The second uses various psalms and canticles, including large sections of psalm 118 (see the

[36] Raes, op. cit., p. 193

[37] Coneybeare and Maclean, p. 481 (numbering altered to LXX).

[38] Ibid.

[39] Coneybeare and Maclean, ibid.; Raes, p. 193.

[40] Coneybeare and Maclean, ibid.

[41] Ibid., p. 482: '... Thy holy wondrous and victorious Resurrection we do laud'.

[42] Ibid.

[43] Ibid., p. 497.

[44] Raes, op. cit., p. 193.

[45] Coneybeare and Maclean, pp. 482–8.

modern Byzantine midnight office for weekdays). These may be related to the Byzantine monastic offices of Great Compline and Midnight. Yovhannes does not mention these additional services in the eighth century; while another commentator, Khosrov, in the tenth century, describes them and knows no distinction between them.[46] We may conclude that the ancient Armenian 'Compline' was the conclusion of Vespers, rather than a separate office. Of the additional material, the oldest stratum appears to be psalms 120 and 90, and a rite of saying 'goodnight' – natural enough additions to Vespers in a 'cathedral' or urban monastic setting; they focus on protection through the night in preparation for God's new day.

The Armenian Night and Morning Offices

At present the Armenians celebrate the night and morning offices together, often daily.[47] Gabriele Winkler has studied the night office in depth.[48] The Morning Office is outlined by Taft,[49] and a translation of both offices is found in Coneybeare and Maclean.[50] From these sources a schema can be created:

The Night Office

Opening

Doxology and Lord's Prayer

Invitatory

Psalm 50.17 and Doxology
Psalms 3, 87, 102 and 142
Hymn, brief supplication, and hymn(s)
Prayer

Psalmody

'Canon' of psalmody and Canticle
Hymnody
Intercessions and Prayers

[46] Ibid., pp. 502–7, esp. p. 506.

[47] Taft, *Liturgy of the Hours*, p. 224.

[48] G. Winkler, 'The Armenian Night Office I', *Journal of the Society for Armenian Studies I* (1984), 93–112 and 'The Armenian Night Office II', *Révue des études arméniennes*, n.s. **17** (1983), 471–551, hereafter *Night Office I* and *Night Office II*, respectively. (Particular thanks to Professor R.W. Thomson of Oxford University for a copy of the former article.)

[49] *Liturgy of the Hours*, 222–3.

[50] Coneybeare and Maclean, pp. 447–64.

The Morning Office

Opening

Psalm 89.14–17 and Doxology

Canticles

Daniel 3 canticles and anthems
Biddings
Magnificat, Benedictus, Nunc Dimittis
Litany and collect
[*Cathedral Vigil – Sunday*
psalms 112.1–3/43.26, 24/145.10,
1 Gospel and Anthem, Biddings]
Psalm 50 and Anthem
Biddings
Psalms 148–50 and Anthem
Gloria in Excelsis
Kataxioson
Anthem of Resurrection
Intercesssions: Litany and collect
Angel of Peace, petitions and collect
Prayer of Blessing
Trisagion

Devotional Appendix

Bidding
Responsory
Gospel of healing and Anthem
Bidding and Blessing

The opening doxology[51] and Lord's Prayer are not mentioned by Coneybeare and Maclean, who pass directly to the twice repeated 'Lord, if thou wilt open my lips, my mouth shall sing thy praises'.[52] A Trinitarian doxology follows, 'Blessed be the consubstantial and unitary holy Trinity, indivisible Father and Son and Holy Spirit, now and ever'.[53] The first, Christological, doxology may have been the original beginning, leading directly to the *psalmodia currens*. Psalms 50.17 and 3 may have been in place by the late fifth century, with the addition of two more psalms and the insertion of the Trinitarian doxology between then and the late seventh century.[54]

---

[51] *Night Office I*, 94.

[52] Coneybeare and Maclean, p. 447.

[53] Ibid.

[54] *Night Office I*, 106.

The group of invitatory psalms bears close similarity to the Byzantine/ Sabaite six psalms described above (chapter 4). Most of the rest of the night part of the office is the psalmody in course and the canticle(s). Refrains to the canticles eventually became poetic troparia, and these troparia followed each canticle on Sundays and feasts by late 6th/early 7th centuries, were used daily by the late 7th/early 8th, and from the 12th/13th centuries poetic material has taken over almost completely.[55] The oldest troparia in the Armenian offices are thought to be those associated with the canticles, and with psalm 50 and the praise psalms (148–50) at Morning Prayer.[56]

Coneybeare and Maclean conclude the night office with a Christological doxology: 'Blessed be our Lord and Saviour, Jesus Christ, Amen.' This may actually be intended to begin the morning office,[57] rather than conclude the night vigil; the two have followed one another without a break for centuries.

In the morning office proper we find several elements of probably primitive origin; the canticles of Daniel 3, psalm 50, the praise psalms (148–50), the Great Doxology and the intercessory material. It may be that a three canticle vigil (reinforced by troparia and a suitable Gospel reading)[58] followed the night psalmody on Sundays, and lead into the dawn praise of the resurrection. The three canticles may well have been Daniel 3 in two parts (vv. 26–45 and vv. 52–88) plus Exodus 15.[59] The early shape would then be:

Night: Psalm 3, *Psalmodia currens*
Vigil: 3 Canticles with troparia, Gospel
Morning: Psalm 50 and Troparion, Psalms 148–50 and Troparia;
Great Doxology

At a later stage the desire for daily canticles with the night psalmody causes Exodus 15 to migrate and other canticles to be added. To make up a trio *Magnificat* is added to the two halves of the *Benedicite*[60] (*Benedictus* and *Nunc Dimittis* being added after the 13th century).[61] The early commentator, Movses K'ertolahayr (fl. 640s), graphically describes the *Benedicite* as the song of those

[55] *Night Office II*, 508–35, 548–50.

[56] Ibid., 535.

[57] See *Night Office I*, 100.

[58] Coneybeare and Maclean, pp. 493ff.

[59] Ibid., p. 500.

[60] Ibid., p. 505, the latter probably still new in the 7th cent.

[61] This possible progression is outlined by Winkler, *Night Office II*, 548–50. The *Benedictus* and *Nunc Dimittis* are not mentioned by Yovhannes Ojneç'i: Coneybeare and Maclean, pp. 489–90.

in prison, being followed by the praise of the redeemed.[62] There is indeed a progression in this structure, from night watch, through resurrection vigil, to morning praise of the risen Lord, and it is very similar to ancient Jerusalem.

Armenian use of Scripture at Nocturns and Matins

Psalm 3 is common to the different systems in Armenia, old Constantinople and Palestine and was also known in the West Syrian tradition of Tikrit.[63] The second triad (discussed in the previous chapter) may perhaps have been imported from Palestine.[64] The greater part of the nocturnal section is a vigil of current psalmody, and the only service in the Armenian daily office that has a recitation of the psalms in course: 'the Armenians restricted the meditative recitation of the psalms to the night office, thus keeping the original features of the cathedral offices of (morning) and (evening) intact'.[65] Yovhannes spoke of the importance of keeping vigil in expectation of Christ's second coming,[66] and Khosrov stressed the seriousness with which this psalmody must be taken.[67]

For the *psalmodia currens* the Armenians divided the Psalter into eight 'canons':

Canon 1: Psalms 1–17	Canon 2: Psalms 18–35
Canon 3: Psalms 36–54	Canon 4: Psalms 55–71
Canon 5: Psalms 72–88	Canon 6: Psalms 89–105
Canon 7: Psalms 106–18	Canon 8: Psalms 119–47

Each canon was followed by an Old Testament canticle: Exodus 15, Deuteronomy 32 (in two sections), the canticle of Anna, Isaiah 26 ('My soul yearns for thee in the night'), Isaiah 38 (the prayer of Hezekiah), Isaiah 42 ('Sing to the Lord a new song') together with Jonah 2, and Habakkuk 3. In modern usage only the last section of each canon survives, and the canticles have been replaced by hymns.[68]

---

[62] Charles Renoux, 'Les commentaires liturgiques arméniens', in A.M. Triacca and A. Pistoia *Mystagogie: pensée liturgique d'aujourd'hui et liturgie ancienne* (Rome: Edizioni Liturgiche, 1993), pp. 277–308, p. 291.

[63] Mateos, 'Les matines chaldéennes, maronites et syriennes', *OCP*, **26** (1960), 51–73.

[64] *Night Office I*, 105.

[65] Ibid., 94.

[66] Coneybeare and Maclean, p. 496.

[67] *Night Office II*, 498, 503.

[68] Ibid., 475–6.

The daily vigil was originally made up simply of the psalms, but the Sunday vigil brought the canticles into the regular offices, from where they passed into the daily vigil, perhaps as specifically paschal elements to add to the Psalter in course.[69] With the disintegration of the Armenian resurrection vigil of Sundays, the canticles were not only attached to the psalms but increased in number,[70] but the Armenians do keep elements of the Sunday vigil in the daily office. The daily vigil of the seventh–eighth centuries, as explained by Winkler, covered the second half of the night, and was already a combination of monastic vigil, cathedral vigil and morning office.[71] It is then unwise to try and make too great a distinction between these offices.

The canticles mentioned have been met before, with the addition of those from Isaiah 38 and 42. The first, the prayer of Hezekiah (Isaiah 38.10–20), 'I said, in the noontide of my days, I must depart', is made by the king when he recovers from mortal sickness, thus, returning to life, and so an appropriate vigil canticle. Isaiah 42.10–13 and 45.8 is combined with Jonah 2, and is a song of the powerful God who goes out against his enemies, the words of 45.8 seem to be the bridge to the Jonah canticle: 'Shower, O heavens, from above, and let the skies rain down righteousness', perhaps as an assurance of God's power that hears Jonah crying out even from 'the belly of Sheol' (2.2). Then follow the Daniel canticles and their troparia. The three New Testament canticles, while later additions to the structure, are commented on by Yovhannes, who saw the *Benedicite* as prefiguring salvation, while the *Magnificat* stands for salvation made present.[72]

Some general biddings are followed by more remnants of the Sunday vigil.[73] These include a series of verses from psalms 112 (vv. 1–3 'From the rising of the sun to its setting praised be the name of the Lord!'), 43 (vv. 26 and 24, 'Awake, O Lord, why do you sleep? Arise, do not reject us for ever'), and 145 (vv. 10 and 1, 'The Lord will reign for ever'), together with a Gospel reading and anthem, and further biddings. The psalm verses are clearly chosen to celebrate the resurrection in mind and Peter Jeffrey suggests that they reflect the three psalms of the vigil mentioned by Egeria.[74] The Gospel citations given by

---

[69] Ibid., 486, see also Baumstark, *Comparative Liturgy*, op. cit., pp. 36–7. However, C. Renoux, 'A propos de G. Winkler, "The Armenian Night Office II" dans *Révue des études Arméniennes* ns t.XVII (1983), p. 471–551' in *Révue des études Arméniennes*, **18** (1984), 593–8, questions Winkler's assumption that the Easter Vigil of the Armenian Lectionary had canticles in the later sense.

[70] *Night Office II*, 488–90.

[71] Ibid., 494–5, Winkler cites the 7th/8th century Zenob Glak, who mentions Daniel 3 as a canticle of the *night* office, ibid., 496, n. 125.

[72] Coneybeare and Maclean, p. 489.

[73] Placed here by Taft (see *Liturgy of the Hours*, p. 222), Coneybeare and Maclean refer to the unit only in part at p. 461.

[74] 'The Sunday Office of Seventh-Century Jerusalem', op. cit., 65–7.

Coneybeare and Maclean[75] relate the empty tomb and the 'myrrh-bearing women'. The anthem that follows the Gospel, 'Rejoicing with great joy, because of the glad tidings of our Lord's resurrection' is entitled 'Gospel of the Balm-bearers'.[76]

Prayer and Hymn Texts at the Night and Morning Office

The poetic material of the night office is late, hymns are attributed to the twelfth-century Nerses Shnorhali. The intercessions possibly date from the period of John Mandakuni in the late fifth century. The latter may once have concluded the office.[77] The text of the prayers attributed to Mandakuni is given by Coneybeare and Maclean, they are clearly to be said on rising from sleep to praise God, 'Aroused all from the repose of sleep', to keep prayerful vigil in the night; 'Let us, in fear and trembling, stand in prayer before him, and give thanks to him in this hour of the night', asking forgiveness of sin; 'With faith let us ask of him forgiveness and remission of our trespasses', with a view to having a place in the coming kingdom; 'And may we become worthy of the eternal and heavenly tents'.[78] A further prayer is given by Coneybeare and Maclean at this point:

> Unto thee do we render thanks, Lord our God, who hast vouchsafed us the repose of peaceful sleep; and awakening us, hast caused us to rise betimes for adoration …[79]

It also introduces the early morning vigil; whilst the one that follows, 'Look down, O Lord' prays 'that we, having served thee, our Lord, in a godly and worthy manner during this life, may at last attain to thy everlasting kingdom of heaven'.[80] This latter prayer could equally end the day.

Each canon of the Psalter was followed by a unit of prayer, and each of these comprised a litany, a prayer and a prayer of inclination.[81] The litanies are quite general in their petitions, though a concern with forgiveness and remission of sins is found, and there is some emphasis on preparing for judgement. This last

[75] Coneybeare and Maclean, p. 455. Matthew 28.1–20; Mark 15.42–16.8; Luke 23.50–24.12; John 19.38–20.18.

[76] Coneybeare and MacLean, p. 455.

[77] *Night Office I*, 108.

[78] Coneybeare and Maclean, pp. 447–8.

[79] Ibid., p. 448.

[80] Ibid., p. 449.

[81] Ibid., pp. 449–52.

theme is exemplified by such petitions as: 'That we may in no wise be found among the rejected in the day of reckoning'[82] and 'That we may stand pure and blameless before the dread tribunal of Christ.'[83] These petitions, and those for protection and forgiveness, are what one might expect of a vigil that waits in hope for the coming of the Just Judge.

Following the first litany is a midnight prayer:

> Howbeit thou hast now aroused us and opened our mouths to set forth the praises ... Accept even now our prayers, ... ever to rise betimes to this same service of thy worship, ...[84]

And again, after the litany of the third Proclamation: 'Vouchsafe unto us, O Lord, reverently ever and always to rise betimes for thy service.'[85] The fourth is perhaps the fullest expression of the theology of the night office:

> We thank thee, Lord our God, who hast aroused us from the repose of sleep through the grace of thy mercy. Awaken our minds through righteousness unto thee, Lord our God; that our eyes may behold thy salvation. May thy Godhead come and dwell with us, and may thy mercy become a shelter and a safeguard over thy ministers. And make us thy servants worthy, by day and by night, and in every hour, to meditate ever in the love of thy commandments, and with thanksgiving to glorify Father, Son and Holy Spirit.[86]

The prayers over the people are similar, praying to stand firm in the divine commandments,[87] and to be awake and ready for the hour of dawn which would by now be breaking; e.g.:

> Power that quickenest, well-spring of immortality, thou art Christ God our Saviour; who hast vouchsafed to us in this midnight to arise and make acknowledgement unto thee as touching thy judgements and righteousness. Now therefore, we pray thee, Lord our God, make us to be awake and ready in the hour of dawn together with thy saints; ...[88]

These prayers are likely to be amongst the oldest elements of the night office, and they appear to presume a vigil begun in the night, and prolonged until

---

82 Ibid., p. 449, Proclamation of first canon.

83 Ibid., p. 450, Proclamation of second canon.

84 Ibid., p. 449.

85 Ibid., p. 451.

86 Ibid., p. 452.

87 Ibid., pp. 449–50, First Proclamation.

88 Ibid., p. 452, Fourth Proclamation.

dawn and the morning office. Thus the fusion of night and morning offices took place at an early date amongst the Armenians.

After the Daniel canticle in the morning part of the office comes another 'Proclamation':

> Having come all of us into the holy catholic and apostolic church, let us pray to the only-begotten Son of God, our Lord and Saviour Jesus Christ, who descended in glory of the Father into the midst of the furnace, and saved the three children from the Chaldeans ... But may we become worthy to keep his commandments; to receive the crown of light and life in ourselves, ... May the Lord almighty quicken us and have mercy.[89]

The idea of being saved from life-threatening danger, coupled with the prayer for the 'crown of light and life' makes this a prayer that sums up much of the theology of Morning Prayer as reflecting a weekly, or even daily, paschal experience.

The primitive core of the Armenian morning office is psalm 50, the *Miserere*, and the praise psalms (148–50), with the Great Doxology.[90] Here we clearly have the archaic structure of cathedral Morning Prayer.[91] Psalm 50 has a troparion, and a bidding follows:

> We do adore thee, O Lord our God, who have passed through the length of the night; and we are come betimes to the place of acknowledgement, and do offer up our Morning Prayer ... to thee we give thanks, who hast made us worthy to pass the night in peace and reach the hour of dawn ...[92]

This is another excellent example of a Morning Prayer that indicates the time of day marked out by prayer. The bidding links the penitence of psalm 50 to the outpouring of praise in psalms 148–50 and the Great Doxology. This latter is followed by a version of the prayer *kataxioson*:

> ... O Lord, make this day to be worthy in peace; and keep us without sin. Blessed art thou, Lord God of our Fathers, praised and glorified is thy holy name unto eternity, Amen.

---

89 Ibid., p. 453. An alternative for Lent includes the words: 'Quench the flame of the furnace of our transgressions; deliver us from the everlasting fire.'

90 Yovhannes' commentary links the cosmic praise of the *Benedicite* to the recognition of how far we fall short of God's goodness in the *Miserere*, and then, as redeemed, sing his praise in psalms 148–50, and with the angels in the Great Doxology, Coneybeare and Maclean, p. 490.

91 G. Winkler, 'New Study of the Early Development of the Office' *Worship*, **56** (1982) 27–35.

92 Coneybeare and Maclean, p. 455.

> Blessed Lord, teach me thy statutes (three times) ... From thee, Lord, floweth the fountain of life; and by the light of thy countenance we behold the light ...[93]

There are troparia with the praise psalms, an anthem of the resurrection and a final ascription of praise:

> O praise, o ye creatures, the creator of all things, Lord, of Lords, King of magnify him, for he is kind and his mercy endureth for ever.[94]

Other prayers are more general while yet others focus on seasonal themes. A Lenten prayer of repentance at dawn is followed by a collect:

> We thank thee, Lord our God, who with thy dawning light hast gladdened all thy creatures, yea, and with the ideal light of thy commandments hast illuminated all who have believed in thee ...[95]

We note the use of the image of light and illumination at the dawn of the new day, nicely balancing the light theme at Vespers. The collect sums up what Yovhannes says of the morning hour as looking forward to the resurrection of all in the coming of Christ, the true Sun of Justice.[96]

A prayer of Blessing, or Inclination, follows which expresses the idea that each day is a foretaste of the eternal day; the gift of the Holy Spirit being given to form God's people into his dwelling-place, as they prepare to leave church and embark upon the business of the day. This part of the service concludes with the Trisagion.[97]

The remaining complex material is another devotional appendix.[98] Most of the texts are not relevant to Morning Prayer so they will not be examined. Coneybeare and Maclean make no mention of a 'Gospel of Healing' with anthem,[99] but do provide a text that sums up the connection of morning light with resurrection praise:

> Unto thy all-powerful and wondrous resurrection Christ our God, do the hosts of angels offer homage. For thou alone hast immortality and dwellest in light unapproachable. And we thy creatures made of dust in lowly awe

---

[93] Ibid., p. 456.

[94] Ibid., p. 453.

[95] Ibid., pp. 459–60.

[96] Ibid., p. 492.

[97] Ibid.

[98] Ibid., pp. 461–4; Taft, *Liturgy of the Hours*, pp. 222–3.

[99] Coneybeare and Maclean, pp. 462–3.

do thee homage, and glorify thy wondrous and victorious resurrection. And to thee with the heavenly hosts we offer praise and glory, with Father and Holy Spirit, now and ever.[100]

Conclusions

1 The Armenian offices display a similar shape to that presumed in Cappadocia, perhaps also relating to Jerusalem.
2 The group of psalms 139–41 prays for a saving from sin and danger, and is seen as representing Christ's descent into the tomb.
3 The lamp-lighting prayer speaks of the light from which darkness flees, gives thanks for the day so that the night may be spent in praise and not just rest, and the prayer of blessing prays for the establishing of the church and looks to the new day.
4 The nocturnal recitation of the Psalter was a watching for Christ's coming according to the commentaries, we pray that we may watch and look to the eternal day. The canticles keep a paschal reference running throughout.
5 If Vespers prayed for deliverance from the grave, then at the night to morning office, the Lord is looked for to come again, that we may behold salvation, and so praise the risen Lord and saviour in the morning.
6 The *Benedicite* and *Magnificat* are interpreted respectively as prefiguring salvation and recognizing the presence of that salvation. Prayers give thanks for being led from darkness to the light of the true sun Jesus Christ.
7 There is once again to be a night to morning dynamic, which culminates in celebrating the new day as prefiguring the eternal day, this is dramatically depicted by some commentators who suggest e.g., that morning birdsong signifies the resurrection of mankind from the tomb.[101]

[100] Ibid., p. 464.

[101] E.g., Yovhannes Ojnec'i, see Renoux, 'Les commentaires', op. cit., 293.

CHAPTER 7

Vespers and Matins in pre-Crusades Constantinople and Later Developments

The Synthesis of the Offices in Constantinople

A number of studies have described the process by which the Byzantine daily service of cathedral type was eventually replaced by one of Palestinian monastic provenance, so it is only necessary to summarize the process here.[1] The process was in three stages.[2] For the first stage, that of the daily cycle, we have only fragmentary evidence of two different forms seemingly indigenous to Constantinople, that of the church of Hagia Sophia, and that of the 'sleepless' monks (see below) on the other. The second stage, following on the revival of Palestinian monastic life after the Persian invasion of 614, saw a considerable increase in the use of poetry in the monastic offices. The great Greek hymnographers were most active in the next century: Andrew of Crete (+720), John Damascene (+780), Cosmas of Maium (787).[3] The monastic reformer, Theodore, moved to the capital in c.798 and revived the former 'sleepless' monastery of Stoudion.[4] He imported monks from the Palestinian monastery of St Sabas, who brought with them their growing *corpus* of hymnody. The Palestinian or Sabaite offices were grafted onto the litanies and prayers of the existing office of the Great Church, thus establishing what became the modern Byzantine office. In due course, the Sabaite *typika* were taken to Kievan Rus' and Muscovy. The third stage saw the formation of the monthly cycles and need not concern us here, as we are dealing with the overall shape of the offices and their function in the sanctification of time.

---

[1] See e.g., A. Schmemann, *Introduction to Liturgical Theology* (London: Faith Press, 1966), especially ch. 4, pp. 116ff.; M. Arranz, 'Les grandes étapes', op. cit.; and Robert F. Taft, *The Byzantine Rite: A Short History* (Collegeville, MN: Liturgical Press, 1992), especially ch. 5, pp. 52–66.

[2] Arranz, 'Les grandes étapes', 45–6.

[3] Ibid., 53–4.

[4] *Oxford Dictionary of Byzantium*, pp. 2044–5; Taft, *The Byzantine Rite*, p. 52, n. 4 and Gilbert Dagron, 'Les moines et la ville: la monachisme à Constantinople jusqu'au concile de Chalcedoine (451)', *Travaux et Mémoires*, **4** (1970), 229–76, 236, n. 46. The Studite reform is conveniently summarized in Thomas Pott, *La reforme liturgique byzantine* (Roma: Edizioni Liturgiche, 2000), pp. 99–129.

The Office of the 'Sleepless' Monks

The monastery of the *Akoimetoi*, or 'sleepless ones', was reputedly founded in 405. The office was conceived as uninterrupted praise of God, carried out by three choirs of monks in turn, each doing an eight-hour shift of duty. At its height, the monastery itself had several hundred monks. Mentioned by Anthony of Novgorod (1200),[5] they had declined after the Iconoclast crisis of the eighth/ninth centuries, and are not mentioned after the sack of Constantinople in 1204.[6]

Each hour of the office was more or less structurally identical, but with proper psalms and prayers. A Greek text was edited for publication by Fountoulis in 1977, and Fr Denis Guillaume's French translation will be used for our explanation of this office.[7]

The basic shape common to all the offices is as follows:

1 Invariable initial prayers
2 Psalm or psalms
3 'Trisagion prayers'[8]
4 [Creed at First Hour only]
5 *Kathisma*[9] in one of the eight tones
6 *Kyrie eleison* (15 times, 60 at First Hour)
7 'O God, cleanse me a sinner' (15 or 60 times)
8 Concluding Prayer

There is no indication of the Psalter in course, but the source is a *Horologion*, perhaps intended to be used with a Psalter. The fixed psalms selected for each office convey the theological meaning of each hour. For example: the First Hour[10] has three psalms: 69, 'O God make haste to my rescue'; 8, 'How great is your name, O Lord our God' and 50, 'Have mercy on me, God, in your kindness', seemingly chosen with the morning in mind.

At the First Hour of the Night psalm 74 prayed to God as judge, at the Second 'The Lord is my light and my help' (psalm 26), and at the Third, confidence in God is expressed (psalm 55). Drawing closer to dawn, at the

[5] D. Guillaume, *Horologe des Veilleurs: Les 24 Heures des Acémètes* (Rome: Diaconie Apostolique, 1990), p. 9.

[6] *Oxford Dictionary of Byzantium*, p. 46.

[7] Guillaume, op. cit., p. 9, n. 5.

[8] I.e., the set of prayers including the Trisagion ('Holy God, Holy and strong'), the prayer 'All-Holy Trinity have mercy', and the Lord's Prayer.

[9] I.e., 'session' = a poetic stanza.

[10] Guillaume, op. cit., pp. 11–18.

Ninth Hour, we proclaim 'God's love in the morning' (psalm 91), while at the Eleventh Hour God is praised for coming to rule the earth (psalm 95). The night ends with psalm 56 expressing readiness to give morning praise to the God who 'rises above the heavens'.[11]

From the need for light at evening, the service progresses through prayers for confidence, renewal and protection, to the growing expression of a resurrection faith, finally issuing in praise of the Creator at sunrise. The Day Hours express Paschal joy at the beginning of the day, progress through prayer for guidance as the day wears on, and finally at sunset give thanks, and ask for mercy and forgiveness once more. Once again, the night is never merely for rest, but to be turned into day, and thus a powerful symbol of God in Christ conquering sin and death.

Some of the concluding prayers at night support this interpretation. That of the First Hour of the Night,[12] 'Lord our God, Father of the true light', prays for light of the heart after the light of day, and that of the Second[13] speaks of the day turning to night. As day approaches, for example, at the Tenth Hour, the prayer is 'We bless Thee, O Christ, Word of very God, Light of Light without beginning',[14] speaking of the light of creation. The prayer of the Twelfth Hour of the Night,[15] 'Lord my God, in you I place my trust', prays to God who is both day and night, and who chases away the darkness of sin.

The office of the 'sleepless' reflected the same concern as the name implied; to, as it were, deny victory to the darkness of sin/night by means of this act of praise, going on all night as well as all day.

The Asmatiki Akolouthia

The ancient office of Hagia Sophia was known as the 'chanted/sung office', the *asmatiki akolouthia*, a term employed, for example, by the fifteenth-century liturgical commentator, St Symeon of Thessaloniki (+1429). Symeon spoke of the *sung* office, to distinguish it from the Palestinian monastic office, much of which was monotoned by a single voice. He understood the singing of the psalms of the office to be the ancient tradition, and he devotes a large part of *de Sacra Precatione*[16] to describing and defending the office, by then largely confined to Thessaloniki, which did not survive the Turkish conquest of that city in 1430.

[11] Ibid., pp. 54–94.

[12] Ibid., p. 56.

[13] Ibid., p. 59.

[14] Ibid., pp. 86–7.

[15] Ibid., pp. 90–94.

[16] *PG* 155, 624ff, especially chapter 345.

In addition to Vespers and Matins, *hesperinos* and *orthros*; there was a special Lenten service, *tritoekti* ('Tersext') which replaced the eucharistic liturgy on weekdays; a midnight office, a vigil called *pannychis*; and, according to Arranz, the Third, Sixth and Ninth Day Hours.[17] Many of the prayers and rubrics of this office have survived in *euchologia* (priests' service books) and have been incorporated, not always happily, into the Palestinian monastic office, and thus form part of the modern Orthodox daily service. The offices were formed of 'antiphons' of the Psalter, interspersed with litanies and prayers; there was a restrained use of ecclesiastical poetry. We shall mainly concentrate on Vespers and Matins, little will be said of the Day Hours, but the midnight office and the *pannychis* will be examined more closely. The prayers have been edited by Miguel Arranz,[18] following upon the work of Mateos,[19] and also that of the musicologist Oliver Strunk on the antiphons and their role.[20] We also note the work of Priestmonk Nilo Borgia in the 1920s,[21] and the more recent work of Alexander Lingas.[22] From these various sources it is possible to construct schemata for the services of Vespers and Matins:

Vespers	Matins
Introduction (in Narthex)	**Introduction (in Narthex)**
Blessed is the kingdom...	Blessed is the kingdom...
Great Synapte	
Prayer 1	Prayer 1
Antiphon I – Psalm 85	Antiphon 1 – psalms 3, 62, 133
Prayer 2 – 2nd Antiphon	Prayer 2 – 2nd Antiphon

---

17 Arranz, 'Les grandes étapes', 50.

18 (Underlining will signify the abbreviations to be used henceforth) 'Les prières sacerdotales des vêpres byzantines' *OCP*, **37** (1971), 85–124; 'Les prières prebytérales des matines byzantines' *OCP*, **37** (1971), 404–36 & *OCP*, **38** (1972), 64–115; 'Les prières presbytérales des Petites Heures dans l'ancien Euchologe byzantin' *OCP*, **39** (1973), 29–82; 'Les prières presbytérales de la 'Pannychis' de l'ancien Euchologe byzantin et la 'Panikhida' des défunts' *OCP*, **40** (1974), 314–43 & *OCP*, **41** (1975), 119–39; 'Les prières presbytérales de la Tritoekti de l'ancien Euchologe byzantin' *OCP*, **43** (1977), 70–93 & 335–54; 'L'office de l'Asmatikos Hesperinos ('vêpres chantées') de l'ancien Euchologe byzantin' *OCP*, **44** (1978), 107–30 & 391–419; 'L'office de l'Asmatikos Orthros ('matines chantées') de l'ancien Euchologe byzantin' *OCP*, **47** (1981), 122–57. See also his *Kak molilis' Bogu drevnie bizantitsy* (Leningrad Theological Academy, 1979).

19 J. Mateos, 'La Psalmodie ' and 'Quelques problèmes', op. cit.; and 'La synaxe monastique des vêpres byzantines' *OCP*, **36** (1970), 248–72.

20 Oliver Strunk, 'The Byzantine Office at Hagia Sophia' in *DOP*, **9/10** (1955–6), 177–202, reprinted in his *Essays on Music in the Byzantine World* (New York: Norton, 1977), pp. 112–42. We cite the later edition.

21 N. Borgia, ΩΡΟΛΟΓΙΟΝ: *'Diurno' delle Chiese di Rito Bizantino (Orientalia Christiana xvi–2, Rome: PIO, 1929)*, see reconstruction of Asmatikos Hesperinos, pp. 232–53.

22 E.g., 'Festal Cathedral Vespers in Late Byzantium' in *OCP*, **63** (1997), 421–48.

Prayer 3 – 3rd Antiphon	Prayer 3 – 3rd Antiphon
Prayer 4 – 4th Antiphon	Prayer 4 – 4th Antiphon
Prayer V – 5th Antiphon	Prayer 5 – 5th Antiphon
Prayer 5 – 6th Antiphon	Prayer 6 – 6th Antiphon
Prayer 6 – 7th Antiphon	Prayer 7– 7th Antiphon
Prayer 8 – 8th Antiphon and *Kekragarion* (psalm 140)	Prayer 8 – 8th Antiphon and *Benedicite*
(Entry into Nave)	(Entry into Nave)
Central Part of Office (in Nave)	**Office in the Nave**
Introit	Prayer 10, psalm 50 and Hymns of day*
Prokeimenon	
Ektene/*Great Kyrie eleison*	Prayer 11 and psalms 148–50
Prayer IX and psalm 114	
Prayer X and psalm 115	*Benedictus*
Prayer XI and psalm 116	Great Doxology (feasts)
Litany and Prayer for Catechumens (XII)	Trisagion and entry into Sanctuary on feasts
2 Litanies and Prayers of Faithful (XIII, XIV)	**Office in Sanctuary**
Aitesis and Prayer 7	*Prokeimenon*
Inclination Prayer (9)	Prayer 9 and Gospel
	Litany and Prayer for Catechumens (XII)
Processional appendix	
	2 Litanies and Prayers of Faithful (XIII, XIV)
Litany, prayer (XVIII) and Inclination (XIX) – Sacristy	*Aitesis* and Prayer 12
Prayer (XX) and Inclination (XXI) in Baptistery	Inclination Prayer 13 Dismissal
Last Dismissal Prayer (XXII)	
	[NB The weekday service did not enter the sanctuary and the litanies appear to have been taken in the Nave.]

* Hymns of the day following psalm 50 appear to sometimes include the *Kontakion*,[23] a lengthy poem of many stanzas.

[23] Arranz, *Kak molilis' Bogu*, op. cit., pp. 277ff.

These services were conceived as a progress or procession. This is obvious in the description of Anthony of Novgorod (1200):

> When they sing Lauds at Hagia Sophia, they sing first in the narthex before the royal doors; then they enter and sing in the middle of the church; then the gates of Paradise are opened and they sing a third time before the altar.[24]

The similarity of structure between the two services is more apparent than real, and only holds for the chanting of the antiphons of psalmody in the narthex. The central core of Vespers, taken in the nave, with its three 'little antiphons' of selected psalms, contrasts with the central core of Matins, with its three rather different elements: psalm 50, the Praise psalms and the Great Doxology. Another difference is that part of the morning office is in the sanctuary, at least on Sundays and Feasts; while the evening office has a processional appendix, only found in certain manuscripts[25] and not included in Borgia's reconstruction.[26] There is also a similarity of structure with the developed eucharistic rite in which the public service opens with a service of three antiphons and prayers and then, after the entry with the Gospel book, moves into the celebration of the Word. This parallelism is most obvious in Vespers.

Like the office by Egeria, the services begin with lengthy psalmody, mainly attended by monks, nuns and some devout laity.[27] This may be an 'urban monastic' characteristic, and would probably last in Constantinople as long as monks took an active part in the offices of the Great Church.[28]

After the psalmody in the narthex, the major ceremonial moment of the entry from narthex to nave began the central part of the service, as described by St Symeon.[29] The eighth antiphon, psalm 140 with refrains, accompanied the entrance.[30] At some point prayer 8 was said, still the prayer of the entrance in the modern Vespers, and with lights and incense the clergy led the congregation into church, where at the ambo, on a Saturday night, hymns of the resurrection were sung.[31] The refrains of the psalm were often based loosely on the psalm

---

[24] Translation from Strunk, op. cit., 112, perhaps implying that this form of office was forgotten in Russia.

[25] Arranz, 'Asmatikos Hesperinos', 117.

[26] Nor in a recent reconstruction celebrated liturgically in the chapel of St Peter's College, Oxford (26 May 2001), arranged by Dr Alexander Lingas (now of the University of Arizona).

[27] Borgia, marginal notes, op. cit., pp. 236ff. and Uspensky, *Evening Worship*, op. cit., pp. 27–57 & 109–10.

[28] Suggested by Arranz, 'Asmatikos Hesperinos', 410.

[29] In *PG* 155, 629, 631.

[30] Strunk, op. cit., 134.

[31] Summarised in Arranz, 'Asmatikos Hesperinos', 411.

itself; for example, 'Let my prayer come before you, o Saviour of the world'.[32] There is no reference to incense in the psalm refrains,[33] it is more a sign of eschatological glory than of propitiatory sacrifice.[34] Symeon saw incense at the entry into the Holy of Holies with the risen Lord Jesus as our being made holy by him who brings about our salvation, a clear baptismal symbol.

After the entry on Saturday was the *prokeimenon* from psalm 92, 'The Lord is King with majesty enrobed'.[35] The evening *prokeimena* remain today as survivals of the 'chanted office', found more or less as they are now in the tenth-century Hagios-Stavros 40 *Typikon*.[36] Unlike those of the Liturgy, the weekday *prokeimena* do not necessarily precede readings, and, unlike those used at Matins, which are festal or proper to the tone of the week, they are rarely replaced except in Lent. The *prokeimenon* was followed by a litany know as the *ektene*. This is probably a late addition to the offices.[37]

The central core of 'chanted Vespers' were three 'little antiphons'with prayers.[38] First, four verses of psalm 114 with the refrain 'By the prayers of the Mother of God, O Saviour save us'. Secondly, psalm 115 with the refrain 'O Son of God, risen from the dead, save us who sing to you',[39] together with the hymn, 'Only-begotten son and Word of the Father'; and thirdly, psalm 116 with Trisagion as refrain.[40] It is the opinion of some scholars that festal readings would have taken place at this point.[41]

The remainder of the central core was largely intercessory. A litany and prayer for the catechumens (XII), two litanies of the faithful (as in the eucharistic Liturgy) with prayers (XIII and XIV), the *aitesis* with a prayer still used (7), and the final prayer over the people, also still used (9). Prayer XIII again gives thanks for protection through the day, and, now that we

---

[32] Wednesday of 2nd week, Strunk, op. cit., 141.

[33] The Liturgy of the Presanctified preserves an incensation during verses 1–4a, with verse 2 as a reponse, see Janeras, 'La partie vespérale de la Liturgie byzantine des Présanctifiés', *OCP*, **30** (1964), 193–222, 207–9.

[34] Winkler, 'Über die Kathedralvesper', op. cit., 73.

[35] 'Asmatikos Hesperinos', 411 – A *prokeimenon* is a responsorial psalm chant. A refrain is intoned and repeated, after a verse the refrain is repeated, and after the cantor has intoned the first, the singers sing the second half of the refrain. Few *prokeimena* now have more than one verse.

[36] Mateos, 'Le Typikon', 178–81.

[37] Stefano Parenti, 'L'Ektenê della Liturgia di Crisostomo nell'Eucologio St.Peterburg Gr.226 (X secolo).' in E. Carr, S. Parenti, A-A. Thiermayer and E. Velkovska (eds), *ΕΥΛΟΓ ΗΜΑ: Studies in Honor of Robert Taft, SJ* (Studia Anselmiana 110, Rome: 1993), 295–318.

[38] Borgia, op. cit., pp. 243–5.

[39] Arranz, 'Asmatikos Hesperinos', 412.

[40] 'Asmatikos Hesperinos', ibid.

[41] Personal communication from Archimandrite Ephrem (Lash), May 2001.

have been led to the light of evening, for protection from the passions of the flesh.[42]

The Proclamation of Scripture

The Psalter in course may have originated amongst the sleepless monks.[43] The first antiphon at Vespers comprised only psalm 85, and at Matins, psalms 3, 62 and 133,[44] but for the current psalmody the Psalter was divided into 68 antiphons of roughly equal length, each comprising one to six psalms. The even numbered antiphons were provided with short refrains, the odd numbered with the response 'Alleluia'.[45] A typical complement might be six variable antiphons, preceded and followed by fixed antiphons, making eight in all. A 10th-century *typikon*[46] directs the number of antiphons to be sung at Matins and Vespers at certain seasons, so that the number of psalms was lessened in the evenings and increased in the mornings after the summer solstice. At the autumn equinox the number of antiphons was almost equal. In other words the greater burden of psalmody was in the morning on the shortest winter days, and at evening on long summer evenings.[47] This remarkably logical arrangement appears to have been unique to Constantinople.

This system might demand 24 antiphons per day, suggesting a reading of the Psalter twice a week with no strict attachment of antiphons to specific days. (Psalms recited elsewhere in the offices are omitted from the antiphons.) Saturday and Sunday were exceptions; the antiphons of the former were seven canticles, and the latter, psalm 118.[48] The canticles were a unique arrangement:

1 The Exodus 15 Song of the Sea
2 Deuteronomy 32

[42] Text in J. Duncan (ed.), *Euchologe de la Grande Eglise (MS Coislin 213)* (Rome: PIO, 1978), pp. 86–7; hereafter Duncan. French translation in Arranz, 'Asmatikos Hesperinos', 124.

[43] Diane Touliatos-Banker, 'The "Chanted" Vespers Service', *Κληρονομια*, **8** (Thessaloniki: Moni Vlatadon) (1976), 107–18, 115.

[44] Strunk, op. cit., 120–21.

[45] Ibid. 122. Citing MS Athens 2061 of 14th/early 15th cent., giving music for psalms and canticles.

[46] J. Mateos (ed.), *Le Typicon de la Grande Église (Ms Sainte Croix n. 40, Xe siècle)* (*OCA* 165–6, Rome: 1962–3) (H–S 40).

[47] Op. cit., 129. See also Arranz, 'Asmatikos Hesperinos', 406, for table of the antiphons in H–S 40.

[48] Strunk, op. cit., 131. The present *typikon* requires psalm 118 to follow the normal *kathismata* (2 & 3) on certain Sundays (see e.g., *The Liturgikon* (Englewood Cliffs, NJ: Antiochian Orthodox Christian Archdiocese of North America, 1989, pp. 140–41).

3 Habakkuk 3
4 Isaiah 26.9ff. + Jonah 2
5 Hannah (1 Sam. 2) + *Magnificat*
6 Prayer of Hezekiah (Isaiah 38.10ff.) + Manasseh
7 First canticle from Daniel 3[49]

The short refrains alternating with Alleluia, such as 'Save us, O Lord' or 'Remember me, O Lord',[50] often have no connection with the psalms that they accompany. Being easily remembered, they would help keep the interest of those who did not know the Psalter by heart.[51] Later arrangements standardized the number of antiphons at morning and evening and paid no concern to the length of time over which the Psalter was recited.[52] It also became customary to reduce the number of antiphons at Vespers when there were to be readings: for example, on feasts and Lent weekdays.[53]

The Vespers *prokeimena* may represent a very ancient use of a psalm selected for its suitability to the time of day. For example, the *prokeimenon* for Saturday night, from psalm 92, 'The Lord is king, and has put on glorious apparel',[54] is well suited to the celebration of Sunday as an anticipated entry into the Lord's kingdom.

As in Egeria's Jerusalem, the Byzantine cathedral Vespers had two series of psalms interspersed with prayers, and interrupted by an entry with incensation. The three 'little antiphons' (psalms 114, 115 and 116) may witness to a more primitive trio of psalms and prayers following psalm 140. It is probably not accidental that the three are drawn from the *Hallel*, which, it seems likely, were the psalms intended to accompany the solemn evening meal in *Apostolic Tradition* (see chapter 3 above). The cathedral part of Vespers took place in the nave, while the preceding part, predominantly of the urban monastics was in the narthex. The three psalms: 'I loved because the Lord will hear the voice of my supplication', 'I believed, therefore I spoke' and 'Praise the Lord, all you nations', may be said to express trust in the God who delivers his people.[55]

---

[49] So Schneider, outlined in Strunk, op. cit., 132.

[50] Strunk, ibid., 140.

[51] The Palestinian absence of refrains may indicate use of whole Psalter by heart; see my 'The Use of the Psalter by Early Monastic Communities', *Studia Patristica*, **26** (1993), 88–94.

[52] Athens Ms 2061, see Arranz, 'Asmatikos Hesperinos', 393–9 and *Kak molilis' Bogu*, op. cit., 276–83.

[53] Arranz, 'Asmatikos Hesperinos', 399.

[54] *Vespers and Matins*. (Oxford: St. Stephens Press, 2001), p. 21.

[55] Uspensky (op. cit., pp. 54–5) suggested that the three little antiphons were originally psalms 140, 141 and 129, which seems unlikely.

The Witness of Prayer

The numbering of the prayers in the schema (pp. 96–7 above) is derived from Arranz.[56] Prayers with Arabic numerals are found in the *present* liturgical books, they also indicate the order in which they are used. Prayers 1 to 7 are now recited quietly by the priest during the recitation of the opening psalm, 103;[57] number 8 is said at the entrance, before 'Hail Gladsome light', and number 9 is still a prayer of inclination, said towards the end of the service. The prayers with Roman numerals are those only found in older *euchologia*.[58]

The first prayer is a psalm prayer that accompanied the fixed first antiphon, Psalm 85. The prayer is really a catena of psalm verses:[59]

> O Lord, compassionate and merciful, long-suffering and of great mercy (v. 15), give ear to our prayer, and attend to the voice of our supplication (v. 6). Work upon us a sign for good (v. 17a). Guide us in thy way, that we may walk in thy truth. Make glad our hearts, that we may fear thy holy Name (v. 11); ...[60]

The end of the day is a time to experience God's gracious, saving power, and to pray to him with confidence for continued guidance as night falls.

The next six prayers (including V) are quite general, and would have suited any group of psalms. Prayer 5 (of the sixth antiphon) is more obviously vesperal:

> Visit us in thy goodness, and grant that, for the remainder of the present day, by thy grace we may avoid the manifold snares of the evil one, and preserve our life unassailed, ...[61]

Forgiveness and guidance are the themes of this prayer. Prayer 6 (of the seventh antiphon) is also a general evening prayer, giving thanks for gifts received, especially the pledge of the future kingdom, and

> that we may complete what remains of this day without reproach before thy holy glory, and hymn thee, our God, who alone art good, ...[62]

---

[56] Arranz, 'Les prières sacerdotales', 117–18.

[57] An eighth prayer, V, is found in some recensions; e.g. *Liturgikon, siest Sluzhebnik* (Rome: Vatican Polyglot Press, 1952), pp. 14–15.

[58] E.g. Barberini, 336, S. Parenti and E. Velkovska (eds), *L'Eucologio Barbarini gr. 336* (Rome: C.L.V., 1995), and Coislin, Duncan, op. cit., above. 8th and 11th cents. respectively.

[59] Arranz, 'Les prières sacerdotales', 89.

[60] *Vespers and Matins*, p. 6.

[61] Ibid., p. 9.

[62] Ibid., p. 10.

The prayers may then be general but several pray that God will grant us grace to face the night in confidence and trust.

The prayer of the entrance quotes psalm 140 and other scriptural passages:[63]

> In the evening, in the morning and at noonday we praise thee, we bless thee, we give thanks to thee, Master of all and loving Lord: Direct our prayer in thy sight as incense (v. 2a), and incline not our hearts to words or thoughts of wickedness(v. 4); but deliver us from all who seek after our souls (v. 9). For to thee Lord, O Lord, we lift up our eyes and in thee have we put our hope (vv. 8a, 8b). Put us not to shame, O our God. For to thee belongs all glory, honour and worship ...[64]

In this prayer incense primarily symbolizes prayer in which we petition for delivery from danger as we place our hope on God.

Prayer IX at the first little antiphon is a prayer for the end of the day that has survived at Sunday evening Vespers of Pentecost, following the first of the so-called kneeling prayers:

> Blessed art thou, O Lord, Master Almighty, who hast lightened the day with the light of the sun and hast illuminated the night with flashes of fire, who hast vouchsafed us to pass through the length of the day and to draw near to the beginning of the night; ... Grant us also that the present evening with the coming night and all the days of life may be perfect, holy, peaceful...[65]

We pray for the Lord's continued compassion and guidance, not simply to complete the day, but to let the evening and night begin the rest of life.

Vespers on the *evening* of Pentecost Sunday begin Monday. This accords with canon 20 of the Council of Nicaea, which decreed that prayer on Sundays and in Paschaltide be offered standing. In other words, the first service of a liturgical day is Vespers, and this is made abundantly clear by the striking change in atmosphere when kneeling is resumed after the Vespers entrance on Pentecost evening, as decreed by canon 90 of the Quinisext council of 691.

The prayer that accompanies the second little antiphon quotes two classic evening psalms:

> O Lord, Lord, who deliverest us from every arrow that flieth by day (Ps 90.5), deliver us also from everything that walketh in darkness (Ps 90.6). Receive the lifting up of our hands as an evening sacrifice (Ps 140.2).

---

[63] See Arranz, 'Les prières sacerdotales', 98–9.

[64] *Vespers and Matins*, pp. 17–18.

[65] *Liturgikon*, p. 410. The kneeling prayers are not found in the earliest sources, such as HS 40, and may have come into 'chanted vespers' from elsewhere, see M. Arranz, 'Les prières de la Gonyklisia ou Génuflexion', *OCP*, **48** (1982), 92–123.

> Vouchsafe us also to pass without reproach the course of the night untempted of evil things, ...[66]

The prayer of the third little antiphon, psalm 116,[67] is much longer in the modern liturgical books than in the sources. It is a prayer that praises the glory of God:

> O God, ... who hast vouchsafed us also to stand at this hour before thine unapproachable glory, that we might hymn and praise thy wonders: Be gracious to us, thine unworthy servants, and grant us grace that ... we may offer thee the thrice-holy glorification ... Remember, O Lord our infirmity, and destroy us not ... that, fleeing from the darkness of sin, we may walk in the day of righteousness ...[68]

Arranz emphasizes the vesperal themes of the antiphons: sunset, advancing night, divine protection, etc.,[69] and might have added 'and looking forward in eschatological hope'.

The progression towards darkness is characteristic of prayer 7, which in the 'chanted office' accompanied the more personal *aitesis* litany. We pray to God who lives in light unapproachable, who has divided light from darkness and brought his people together to offer evening praise, that he will accept the evening offering of incense.[70] It closely parallels that of *Apostolic Constitutions 8* (37) (see above), as Uspensky demonstrates.[71] Both prayers petition for a peaceful and sinless night, and for salvation. Prayer 7 continues:

> that, enlightened by meditation on thy commandments, we may rise up in joyfulness of soul to glorify thy goodness ...[72]

We note that the confident hope that all shall rise again, argues powerfully in favour of the vigil nature of Vespers.

Prayer XIV prays that God, who lives in inaccessible light and has called us to evening praise, may

> protect us from the darkness of sin, illumine the eyes of our souls, so that remaining always in thy fear, and walking in thy light, we may contemplate thy marvels, and glorify thee in all things ...[73]

---

[66] *Liturgikon*, p. 414.

[67] Arranz, 'Les prières de la Gonyklisia', 105.

[68] *Liturgikon*, pp. 417–19.

[69] Arranz, 'Asmatikos Hesperinos', 417.

[70] *Vespers and Matins*, pp. 11–12.

[71] Uspensky, pp. 25–6.

[72] *Vespers and Matins*, ibid.

[73] Duncan, p. 87; Arranz, 'Asmatikos Hesperinos', 124–5.

The prayer over the people, number 9, used in the modern office, is a night prayer of blessing:

> Guard them at all times, both during this present evening and in the approaching night, ...[74]

Borgia inserts a dismissal prayer which recapitulates some of the themes,[75] and closes the office with 'Go forth in peace',[76] as does St Symeon.[77]

A *lucernarium* ceremony?

Throughout Lent the contemporary office has a series of Vespers readings from Genesis and Proverbs, each preceded by a *prokeimenon*. When the Liturgy of the Presanctified Gifts is celebrated, after the second *prokeimenon*, the celebrant turns to the people with a lighted candle and the thurible, exclaiming 'The light of Christ illumineth all'[78] and the people prostrate. This ceremony recalls Egeria's account of light being brought out from the Holy Sepulchre, represented by the sanctuary. Janeras thinks that it is possible to detect a primitive order of reading, light acclamation/*lucernarium*, and the Lenten form of psalm 140.[79] The earliest Constantinopolitan Vespers may have commenced in darkness,[80] and after the light ceremony there followed the evening psalm. This rite may have been preceded in Lent by the readings of catechumenal instruction,[81] prolonged until the time of the lamp-lighting, according to a commentary of Chrysostom quoted by Uspensky.[82] With the disappearance of the catechumenate and the growth of the antiphons of the distributed psalter in the narthex, the readings and the light

---

[74] *Vespers and Matins*, p. 30.

[75] Borgia, 250–51, the source is a Grottafferata MS not mentioned by other authors.

[76] Ibid., 251: ΠΡΟΕΛΘΕΤΕ ΕΝ ΕΙΡΗΝΗ (sic), also Arranz, 'Asmatikos Hesperinos', 125, and Duncan, op. cit., 88.

[77] *PG* 155, 636 and Uspensky, op. cit., pp. 50–51.

[78] *Liturgikon*, 346–7.

[79] V. Janeras, 'La partie vespérale de la liturgie byzantine des Présanctifiés', *OCP*, **30** (1964), 193–222.

[80] Uspensky, op. cit., p. 137.

[81] Ibid., pp. 130–32. The present system is found in HS 40 (see Mateos, *Le Typicon*, II, op. cit.) and see G. Winkler, 'Der Geschichtliche Hintergrund der Präsanktifikatenvesper', in *Oriens Christianus*, **56** (1972), 184–206, 192–3, quoting Chrysostom in *PG* 54, 597.

[82] Uspensky, p. 132. Commenting on the Presanctified in St Symeon (*PG* 155, 653), Arranz says that no lamps were lit before the prophetic readings, 'La Liturgie de Présanctifiés de l'ancien Euchologe byzantin', in *OCP*, **47** (1981), 332–88, 371.

ceremony were displaced. The ceremony appears to have been part of the ancient cathedral rite.[83]

The Processional Appendix to Vespers

As in many other places, Constantinople's 'chanted Vespers' acquired a processional coda. Some traditions, including the modern Byzantine, extend this procession, or at least its material, from feasts to every day, and duplicate it at the end of Matins. The old rite of Hagia Sophia, by contrast, appears to have had this procession only on certain days at Vespers. As a result, some of the oldest manuscripts make no mention of the prayers that appear to have accompanied the procession, and St Symeon did not refer to it in his commentary.

The prayers appear to be quite late additions to the service.[84] The first prays that God, the giver of all good things, will regard the lowliness of his people, that they may serve him as sanctified vessels,[85] and that he may be for his people, the guide to go with them on their way in hope of the eternal kingdom.[86] Although said in the sacristy, the *skeuophylakion*, the prayer is vaguely baptismal. The next station was at the Great Baptistery on the opposite side to the sacristy.[87] Here was said a prayer of thanks for admission into the company of the saints in light. This was clearly a prayer that takes up the baptismal theme of passage from darkness and death to the light of God's face, in hope of the resurrection life. There was a further prayer of inclination that the baptized might remain faithful to the grace given, and that they be illumined with the knowledge of God's truth.[88] Clearly the idea of baptism as a passage from darkness to light, from death to life, remained an important aspect of evening worship as late as the eleventh century. This baptismal aspect of Vespers is also emphasized by Uspensky.[89]

---

[83] Janeras, op. cit., 221–2. Winkler, op. cit., 199–206, felt that Antiochian Vespers centred on the 'Light of Christ' and psalm 140, and that there was neither light ritual nor incensation in 11th cent. Constantinople.

[84] 11th century sources, see Arranz, 'Asmatikos Hesperinos', 125–9.

[85] Duncan, p. 89.

[86] Arranz, 'Asmatikos Hesperinos', 126; Duncan, p. 89.

[87] Arranz, 'Asmatikos Hesperinos', 127, n. 55.

[88] Duncan, p. 90.

[89] Uspensky, 50–54.

The 'Chanted Matins' of Hagia Sophia

The opening part of the 'chanted Matins' also took place in the narthex. After a blessing came the fixed first antiphon of psalms 3, 62 and 133, preceded by a prayer. Then came the antiphons of the Psalter for the day with prayers. The final antiphon was the *Benedicite* from Daniel 3, a very commonly found morning canticle, where the whole of creation is called to give praise to God. Creation thus rejoicing in the new creation brought about by Christ's resurrection.

The Sunday Psalter was evidently psalm 118.[90] Symeon sees the assembly in the narthex before the closed royal doors (i.e., the central doors of the church), as betokening the exclusion of sinners from the ancient paradise.[91] The priest carried out an initial incensation during the first section of the Psalter, entering the nave by a side door and returning with a cross. When the last few verses of psalm 118 were reached, the doors having been completely opened at verse 170, 'Let my pleading come before you; save me by your promise'. An introit was sung and the remaining verses of the psalm were sung in the nave. During this entry, the cross, with three lighted candles upon it, was taken to stand upon the ambo. The psalm was followed immediately by *Benedicite*. Symeon speaks of the power of the cross to open the doors to heaven and reveal the Triune God.[92]

The Central Part of Matins

According to Symeon, the *synaxarion* (a reading on the sufferings of Christ, or the life of a saint) was read at this point.[93] This was probably a medieval monastic addition. The *ektene* followed, and then psalm 50 with a refrain.

The *Benedicite* and psalm 50 are frequently found elements in early forms of Morning Prayer, though their position relative to one another can vary, in modern Byzantine use psalm 50 precedes the canticle. As already mentioned, the scriptural canticles without *Benedicite* were sung as the Saturday psalmody.[94] We may then conclude that the *Benedicite* was one of the elements that began the morning part of the office,[95] probably as a reminder of

---

[90] *PG* 155, 636–7, see Arranz, 'Les prières des matines', 103. The reading of Psalm 118 was divided into the same three parts (vv. 1–72, 73–131, 132–76) as in contemporary use.

[91] *PG* 155, 636: 'παλαι παραδεισον', also 641–5.

[92] Ibid., 640.

[93] Ibid., 645.

[94] Strunk, op. cit., 134–5.

[95] A possible survival in the modern office may be the incensation at ode 8 (replacing *Benedicite*) and the *Magnificat*, perhaps to prepare to enter the Nave, as at Vespers.

the Paschal vigil where it has a major role.[96] The somewhat abrupt juxtaposition of a song of cosmic praise followed by a prayer of penance (psalm 50) might conceivably be explained by the fact that the creation gives praise first, and human beings are moved to repentance so that they too might sing God's praises.

If the core of 'chanted Vespers' was the little antiphons and prayer, then that of 'chanted Matins' was psalms 50 and 148–50, with prayer, then the *Benedictus*[97] and the Great Doxology which, as today,[98] concluded with the solemn singing of the Trisagion, and, on Sundays, one of two resurrection troparia.[99] Meanwhile the clergy went in procession from the ambo in the nave to the sanctuary.[100] As Anthony of Novgorod said: 'then the gates of Paradise are opened and they sing a third time before the altar'.[101] A powerful sense of movement is one of the most striking features of this Constantinopolitan rite, but the weekday office was concluded in the nave.

The Office in the Sanctuary included the Sunday resurrection gospel, which in many places was inserted between the night and morning parts of the office, as in contemporary Byzantine practice. The resurrection gospel has also been placed after the reading of the Psalter (Egeria), after the ninth ode of the canon, after the Lauds psalms (148–50), or after the Great Doxology.[102]

The remainder of 'chanted Matins' comprised the same group of litanies as at Vespers; for the catechumens, two for the faithful, and the *aitesis*, all accompanied by appropriate prayers; an inclination prayer and the dismissal. The service ended with a dismissal and later devotional or processional elements.

The Psalms and Other Scriptures of the Morning

The psalms that began the office clearly indicated the hour of celebration. We have already commented on psalms 3 and 62 in chapter 4, and psalm 133 with its call to 'Lift up your hands to the holy place and bless the Lord through the night' surely urges and inspires prayer at this pre-dawn vigil.

Though we need not comment further on the 'distributed Psalter', the Sunday use of psalm 118 is of interest. This psalm was traditionally recited at

---

[96] See e.g., Bertonière, op. cit., 186.

[97] Mentioned by St Symeon, *PG* 155, 648.

[98] See *Horologion*, p. 127.

[99] Ibid., p. 133.

[100] *PG* 155, 649; Arranz 'Les prières des matines', 105.

[101] Strunk, op. cit., 112.

[102] Ibid., 215.

night/early morning in the Christian East. In the modern Orthodox Matins it is appointed for Saturdays and for Sundays in Lent[103] (also daily, Monday to Friday, at the midnight office).[104] This highly didactic wisdom psalm appears to have had no defined liturgical use in Judaism, but has been widely used by Christians. In modern use the psalmody in course is followed on Sunday by the *Evlogitaria* of the Resurrection, named from the refrain from psalm 118 sung between these verses that sing of the myrrh-bearing women coming to the tomb of Christ, 'Blessed art Thou, O Lord, teach me thy statutes'.[105] During this a general incensation of the church is made.

The incense rite may be associated with the psalm being the Sunday psalmody of the cathedral rite.[106] We may see the verses as extending psalm 118's theme of obedience to God's will, to Christ's total obedience to death, so leading us to his transforming resurrection. The same idea may be operative in the modern office's further use of *Evlogitaria* in services celebrated for the departed.[107] The use of this psalm on Saturday may have been influenced by its use at services for the departed; Saturday, especially Holy Saturday, being seen as the day commemorating Christ in the tomb. This recalls the theme of death being overcome by life that we believe is constitutive of prayer in the night. Again, on Holy Saturday the 176 verses of the psalm are intercalated with the verses known in Greek as the *εγκωμια* or *Θρηνοι*. The poetry is late, but the theme of the descent to the place of the dead is, of course, much older.[108]

The canticle *Benedicite* and the praise psalms have been discussed elsewhere, so we pass directly to the Sunday gospel readings, which, since at least the tenth century, are a series of eleven resurrection accounts, read in rotation, and referred to in Greek as the 'dawn gospels'.[109] They are virtually identical with, and in the same order as, those in HS 40.[110] In 'chanted Matins' the Gospel was the climax of the service, making clear the progress of the service from darkness to light, from death to resurrection. The Gospel is preceded by one of eight *prokeimena* in the tone of the week. They are also in

---

[103] *Festal Menaion*, op. cit., 533–4. Psalm 118 is now often replaced by *polyeleos* (see below) or omitted.

[104] Ibid., 74.

[105] *ευλογητος ει, Κυριε, διδαξον με τα δικαιωματα σου6.*

[106] Diane H. Touliatos-Banker, *The Byzantine Amomos Chant of the 14th and 15th Centuries* (Analecta Vlatadon 46, Thessaloniki: Patriarchal Institute for Patristic Studies, 1984), p. 54.

[107] Ibid., pp. 88–90.

[108] See Sebastià Janeras, *Le Vendredi-Saint dans la tradition liturgique Byzantine* (Studia Anselmiana 99, Rome: 1988), pp. 395–402.

[109] E.g., ΠΑΡΑΚΛΗΤΙΚΗ, op. cit., 30, 'ΕΩΘΙΝΟΝ Α''.

[110] *Typicon de la Grande Église*, II, op. cit., pp. 172–5, and see table in Hapgood, *Service Book* ... (Englewood, NJ: 1975), op. cit., xxiii.

HS 40,[111] and may contribute to our understanding of the theology of Matins.

The first (psalm 11) is 'I myself will arise, says the Lord'. The second is from psalm 7, 'My God awake, you will give judgement'. Numbers three, 'Proclaim to the nations, God is King' (psalm 95), and four, 'Stand up and come to our help' (psalm 43), renew a strongly eschatological theme. Psalm 9.33, 'Arise then, Lord, lift up your hand!' is the fifth, and similar to the seventh, also from psalm 9. The sixth (psalm 79), 'O Lord rouse up your might, O Lord come to our help' is more a prayer for divine vindication. The eighth (psalm 145), 'The Lord will reign for ever, Sion's God from age to age', serves as an expression of faith in the risen Lord. The psalm texts are chosen to celebrate the resurrection as both a present and an eschatological reality in the lives of those present, and form a fitting prelude to the resurrection gospel.

The Prayers of Matins

That the office began before dawn is stated all the more forcibly not only by the prayer of the first antiphon, but also by the prayers accompanying the antiphons of the Psalter. The prayers have survived into the modern office as the first eight of a group of twelve said quietly by the priest during the reading of the *hexapsalmos*.[112] The designation εωθινον (early in the morning) is found before the prayers in some MSS.[113]

The prayer of the invitatory psalms (1) is an excellent example of early Morning Prayer:

> We thank thee, O Lord our God, who hast raised us from our beds and hast put into our mouths a word of praise, that we may venerate and call upon thy holy name . . .[114]

The prayers of the antiphons extend the theme of praying to God through the small hours. The second begins:

> From the night our spirit rises early towards thee, our God, for thy commandments are a light upon the earth . . .[115]

---

[111] Mateos, *Le Typicon*, 170–73.

[112] Psalms 3, 37, 62, 87, 102 and 142, see chapter 4.

[113] E.g., *Coislin 213*, Duncan, pp. 96ff. (Goar, *Ευχολογιον sive Rituale Graecorum*, ed. J Goar (Paris: 1647; repr. Graz: 1960), 39–45).

[114] *Vespers and Matins*, p. 52.

[115] Ibid., p. 53, Quoting the canticle of Isaiah 26.9ff.

This becomes a prayer for church, state and all people. Prayer 3:

> From the night our spirit rises early towards thee, our God; for thy commandments are a light ... Enlighten the eyes of our understanding, lest we sleep for ever in our sins unto death. Drive away all darkness from our hearts. Favour us with the Sun of Righteousness and preserve our life without injury, ... Grant us to see the dawn and the day with joyfulness, that we may raise our Morning Prayers to thee.[116]

The prayers move from a simple statement that we have risen from our beds, through general prayer for both church and world, to more specific needs. Sleep, darkness and death are connected with sin; while the light to be shed by the sun of righteousness will bring us into the glorious light of God's new day.

Prayer 4 continues the themes, God calling the light to shine out of the darkness, but sleep bringing refreshment. Prayers 5 and 6 are similar, and prayer 7 again states that those praying have been raised from their beds, and continues:

> Give us grace in the opening of our mouth, and according to our strength accept our thanksgiving; and teach us thy statutes.[117]

It concludes by asking forgiveness of sins in preparation for the approaching dawn, symbol of the coming Christ. This is the celebration of the baptismal new life in Christ renewed every day in his faithful people, who may thus pray for protection and guidance in the coming day.

The prayer at the canticle *Benedicite* so sums up the morning themes that it is worth quoting in full:

> O Lord our God, who hast banished from us the sluggishness of sleep and hast convened us together by a holy calling, that we may lift up our hands even in the night, and acknowledge before thee thy righteous judgements: Accept our prayers, petitions, thanksgivings and night-time worship; and grant us, O God, faith unashamed, steadfast hope and sincere love. Bless our coming in and going out, our deeds and works, our words and thoughts; And grant us to arrive at the beginning of the day, praising, singing and blessing the goodness of thine ineffable kindness.[118]

While the prayer accompanies the canticle it only cites psalm 133, more suited to the beginning of the office. The mention of 'our coming in and going out' may have attracted the prayer to the entry, but equally it may have been

[116] Ibid., p. 54.

[117] Ibid., pp. 58–9.

[118] Ibid., p. 60.

composed for the beginning of a night to morning vigil office.[119] Whatever its provenance, it explicitly reflects the vigil marking the passage from darkness to light; from sleep that stands for death, to waking praise that stands for life in God who makes all things new.

Psalm 50 was accompanied by Prayer 10, which is a true psalm prayer and thus a prayer of penance:

> O Lord our God, who hast granted unto men pardon through repentance and has set for us the repentance of the prophet David as an example of the acknowledgement of sin and of confession which is unto forgiveness: Do thou thyself, O Master, have mercy on us according to thy great mercy, ... But inasmuch as thou art good and lovest mankind, graciously vouchsafe that even until our uttermost breath, we may offer unto thee the sacrifice of righteousness and an oblation upon thy holy altar.[120]

Repentance leads to the offering of a new sacrifice of praise to God, and the prayer well expresses the ancient idea of the morning as a time to be forgiven so as to give praise.[121]

Psalms 148–50 were preceded by the current prayer 11:

> O God, our God, who hast brought into being by thy will all the powers endowed with speech and reason, we pray thee and supplicate thee: Receive our praise, which together with all thy creatures we offer according to our strength, and reward us with the rich gifts of thy goodness...[122]

This prayer commenced the morning praise, that is, psalms 148–50 and the *Benedictus* together with the Great Doxology on Sundays and feasts.[123] We note that, being brought into creation as rational creatures, we give thanks with the rest of creation for this 're-making'.

The troparia of the Great Doxology on entry to the sanctuary are probably of great antiquity:

> To-day is salvation come into the world. Let us sing praise unto him who rose from the grave, the Author of our life: For in that by death he hath destroyed Death, he hath given unto us the victory and great mercy.[124]

---

[119] Arranz, 'Les prières des matines', 424–5.

[120] *Vespers and Matins*, pp. 62–3.

[121] See also Arranz, 'Les prières des matines', 427.

[122] *Vespers and Matins*, pp. 62–3.

[123] Arranz, 'Les prières des matines', 429.

[124] Tr. Hapgood, *Service Book*, op. cit., 35.

> When thou hadst risen again from the tomb, and hadst burst the bonds of hell, thou didst loose the condemnation of death, O Lord, redeeming all men from the snares of the enemy...[125]

The texts are for Sunday but well express the resurrection character of all morning offices.

The first prayer of the faithful (XIII) was clearly matinal:

> Lord, Lord, yours is the day and yours is the night, you have formed the light and the sun, ... deliver us from darkness and the shadow of death, ...[126]

The twelfth prayer, of the *aitesis* litany, is now the last of those said during the six psalms:

> We praise thee, we hymn thee, we bless thee, we give thanks unto thee, O God of our fathers, that thou hast brought us in safety through the shades of night and hast shown unto us once again the light of day ... Illumine our hearts with the true sun of thy righteousness; ... that walking uprightly as in the day, in the way of thy commandments, we may attain unto life eternal, ... and may graciously be vouchsafed to come unto the fruition of the light unapproachable.[127]

Inappropriate in its present position, this text sums up Morning Prayer,[128] giving thanks for protection through the possible threats of the night, and praying for the gift of new light, also asking God's guidance through the day, whilst yet looking beyond it to the eternal day of God's unending light. The dynamic that began the evening before at Vespers has been reinforced and brought to its climax in the full light of another new day, God's gift to his people.

The final prayer, 13, is still the prayer of inclination in the present rite and corresponds to prayers in the *Apostolic Constitutions*.[129] It is not a particularly matinal prayer, except in so far as it prays to God the Lord of all creation very much a morning theme:

> O holy Lord, who dwellest in the highest, who regardest the humble, and with thine all-seeing eye dost behold all creation, to thee have we bowed ...[130]

---

[125] Ibid.

[126] Ibid., 103, ll 3–7.

[127] *Vespers and Matins*, pp. 64–5.

[128] Also Arranz' opinion, 'Les prières des matines', 435.

[129] See chapter 3 above.

[130] *Vespers and Matins*, pp. 89–90.

The Other Services of the Constantinopolitan Cathedral Office

It was formerly thought that the daily office of Hagia Sophia comprised only Vespers and Matins, together with the *tritoekti* in place of the Divine Liturgy in Lent.[131] However the cathedral office did also possess Minor Hours of Midnight, Terce, Sext and None.[132] Somewhat different from the modern monastic forms, these each comprised three antiphons with presbyteral prayers, a dismissal prayer, and one of inclination. The daily round (in e.g., Barbarini 336 of the eighth century) comprised Vespers, Midnight office, Matins, First, Third, Sixth and Ninth Hours. In addition there was *tritoekti* in Lent and the *pannychis* (a popular night vigil) for particular occasions, when it probably replaced the Midnight office.

The Midnight office, like the Day Hours, had five prayers,[133] which are clearly intended for the middle of the night. The first, for example, quotes psalm 118.62: 'At midnight I will rise and thank you for your just decrees', and prays for fidelity at the coming day of judgement. The concluding prayer over the people sums up the office neatly, praying that we may reach the dawn prayers enlightened by the true light of the knowledge of God's will. In these prayers vigil is kept as an eschatological sign, protection from the powers of darkness is sought, and there is an awareness of the creative power of God which only appears to be dormant at night, and prayer that we may reach the dawn of true enlightenment.

The prayers of the *pannychis*[134] are found in many old *euchologia*.[135] They are not seasonal and reflect an antique spirituality more concerned with celebrating the hours of the day and the night than of seasons or annual commemorations.[136] Arranz' reconstruction of this office has the following shape:[137]

Psalm 90 and entrance into church
Three prayers with litanies, interspersed with
Three antiphons comprising psalms 119, 120 and 121
Psalm 50 (perhaps part of 3rd antiphon)
[*Prokeimenon* and Gospel in some sources]
Final Prayer and Inclination Prayer
Repeated *Kyrie eleison*, with or without *ektene*

[131] Mateos, *Le Typicon*, xxiv, and Arranz, 'Tritoekti', op. cit., esp. 335–6, 353–4.

[132] Arranz, 'Les prières presbytérales', 30. Prime appears in some later mss; ibid., 38.

[133] Ibid., 31–4, *L'eucologio*, 61–4.

[134] Arranz, 'Pannychis', 330–9. In HS 40 (Mateos, *Le Typikon*) after Vespers on 17 days.

[135] Ibid., 325–40, *L'eucologio*, 133–7.

[136] Arranz, 'Pannychis', 137.

[137] See Arranz, 'Pannychis', 336, and 341–3.

Kontakia are also mentioned in some sources, and canons would seem to be the latest additions.[138] The service appears to have been a genuinely popular 'cathedral' observance.

Psalm 90 is a prayer for protection.[139] The psalms of the antiphons, 119, 120 and 121 are three of the 'gradual' or pilgrimage psalms. The general theme is joy in going to worship God in his holy place. *Pannychis* for the first week of Lent and the first half of Holy Week in the Dresden document had a fixed *prokeimenon* (psalm 28, 'The Lord will give strength to his people') and a Gospel reading from Luke 21.8 ff.: 'Watch out that you are not deceived'.

The antiphon prayers are suited to the hour.[140] The first asks for the continuation of divine light to illumine the people. In the second, God is the light that replaces that of the day. The third also stresses immaterial light and concludes with a petition for delivery from the darkness of sin so as to behold the light of God's face. Clearly this vigil of prayer turns the darkness of the night into a time to spiritually perceive the true light. The concluding prayer prays to the Father of light for delivery from the darkness of sin, so as to be illumined instead by the divine light of God's only son, the true sun of justice, who lights the way for those who keep vigil. Attributed to St Germanus I of Constantinople (+ 733), the prayers soberly and concisely sum up the ideal of the vigil.[141] The *pannychis*, with poetic elements from the Sabaite Matins such as canons and *kontakia*, later became the basis of the funeral and memorial services; the latter known to Russians as the *panikhida*.[142]

The Day Hours had the same structure of three antiphons with prayers, prayer of dismissal and prayer of inclination (The First Hour is supplied with only two prayers in Barberini 336, for cleansing and for guidance on the way of truth).[143] The Third Hour clearly commemorates the sending of the Spirit,[144] while the Sixth recalls Christ's cross and Peter praying at the Sixth Hour (Acts 10.9).[145] The Ninth Hour speaks of Peter and John going to the Temple at the ninth hour (Acts 3.1), and of remaining constant and watchful in prayer.[146] We should note that these services do not always reflect the themes of the Spirit/betrayal, crucifixion and the death on the cross, characteristic of the Palestinian monastic hours used today.

---

[138] Ibid., 342.

[139] Also at midday, see Sixth Hour in *Horologion*, pp. 169–70.

[140] For details and texts see Arranz, 'Pannychis', 316–24, & *L'eucologio*, ibid.

[141] See, Arranz, 'Pannychis', 321–2.

[142] Ibid., 314–15.

[143] *L'Eucologio Barbarini*, 77–8.

[144] Ibid., 78–81, especially 1st & 2nd prayers.

[145] Ibid., 81–4.

[146] Ibid., 84–7.

Excursus A: The Later Development of the Byzantine Vigil

While the older service came to be replaced by the present, largely Palestinian, hybrid office, there was a continuing tradition of Vespers and Matins being services that sanctify the night. These themes are particularly prominent in the All-Night Vigil, *agrypnia* or *vsenoshchnoe bdenie*.

The origins of the present vigil may best be traced back to that of Nilus of Sinai (see chapter 4 above). The Studite *typikon* did not have this kind of *agrypnia* or vigil, but Vespers were followed by Compline, *mesonyktikon* (midnight office) and *orthros*, all served separately.[147] As the *typikon* of St Sabas became more popular, it replaced Studite practice with that of the *agrypnia*, still celebrated in full in the monasteries of the Holy Mountain (Athos); where Vespers, Matins and Liturgy one after another can still last for some twelve to fifteen hours.[148]

N.D. Uspensky wrote an important study of the vigil, first published in Russian and edited, with comments, by Miguel Arranz.[149] According to the *typicon* the vigil should start just after sunset and finish at sunrise. Not surprisingly modern use, in both parishes and most monasteries, is to abridge it quite radically, in Russia to between two and three hours. The earliest sources of the modern form date from the twelfth–thirteenth centuries,[150] and many elements foreign to the 'chanted office' found their way in to this vigil.[151]

The group of psalms 134–5 (sometimes replaced by psalm 118) known as the *polyeleos*, now precedes the gradual hymns and Gospel. In some uses, psalm 136 'By the waters of Babylon' is added on the three Sundays that immediately precede Lent.[152] It does not seem possible to simply identify this part of the service (*pace* Taft and Mateos) with the vigil described by Egeria.[153]

Uspensky's summary of the Palestinian *agrypnia*[154] shows it to have been the same shape as Vespers and Matins today, the bread and wine blessed at the end of Vespers serving for light sustenance between the services and during which

---

[147] Robert E. Taft, 'Mount Athos: A Late Chapter in the History of the Byzantine Rite', *DOP*, **42** (1988), 179–194, 186.

[148] Archimandrite Ephrem (Lash), Review of Taft's *Liturgy of the Hours...*, *Sobornost*, **11** (1989), 102–5, 103.

[149] *OCP*, **42** (1976), 117–55, 402–25; *St Vladimir's Theological Quarterly*, **24** (1980), 83–113, 169–95.

[150] Ibid., 107.

[151] *PG 99*, 1705, and see Taft, 'Evergetis in the History of Byzantine Liturgy' in Mullet and Kirby, op. cit., *The Theotokos Evergetis and Eleventh Century Byzantine Monasticism*, 288, fn 37; and Taft, 'Mount Athos', op. cit., 182–4.

[152] Mateos, 'Quelques problèmes', 205, n. 12; *Festal Menaion*, 556.

[153] Taft, *The Liturgy of the Hours*, pp. 288–9; Mateos, 'Quelques problèmes', 205.

[154] Arranz, 'N. D. Uspensky', 176–8.

there was reading. At the end there was a short break and all returned later for the Eucharist. In Russia, by the sixteenth/seventeenth centuries the vigil was starting much later, perhaps midnight.[155] More was sung than nowadays and the Vespers entrance was very solemn, all available clergy taking part, possibly a continuing tradition of the 'chanted service'. At Matins the *polyeleos* was accompanied by great solemnity, and the canon continued to have scriptural verses as well as troparia. Another relic of the 'chanted Matins' was an entry into the sanctuary before the Great Doxology, and there seems to have been a second Gospel reading in this, the original Constantinopolitan position.

The 1682 *Typikon of Jerusalem* shortened the vigil to six–seven hours in winter, four–five in summer. Eventually city churches had the vigil at dusk on Saturday, and villages, early on Sunday morning; by now, the 'all-night vigil' lasted no more than three hours. The Russians had, however, transformed the monastic vigil into a popular office,[156] and in spite of Nikon's reforms[157] and later decadence, it remains a way of devoting at least a part of the night to prayerful vigil. A vigil that was enlightened by faith in the resurrection that overcomes the powers of death and darkness.

Excursus B: The Poetic Canons

The latter part of the modern Byzantine Matins is dominated by the canon, originally the set of nine scriptural canticles or odes (see chapter 4). The refrains of the canticles grew into troparia, of which the first, the *eirmos*, usually reflected the theme of the scriptural canticle. The poetic odes largely replaced the scriptural ones except for *Magnificat*, except in Lent.[158] The second ode, the long canticle of Deuteronomy, tended to be dropped altogether, hence most poetic canons have only eight odes.

St Andrew of Crete (c.660–740) is credited with being the main creator of the canon as a genre,[159] and his most famous composition, the Great Canon of Penance, is sung at Matins of the Fifth Thursday of Lent. This long work is worthy of at least cursory examination, as one of the earliest canons it still

[155] What follows summarizes Arranz, 'N. D. Uspensky', pp. 178–93.

[156] Moscow's Epiphany Cathedral has 'All–Night Vigil' on Saturday and Vespers and Matins daily at 5 p.m., V.A. Sudarikov and S.V. Chapnin, *Pravoslavnaya Moskva* (Moscow: Brotherhood of St Tikhon, 1993), p. 16.

[157] Cyril Korolevsky described an Old Believer vigil of Vespers and Matins from midnight to about 5 a.m.; 'Chez les Starovères de Bucovine' in *Stoudion*, **IV** (1927), 123–37. A modern Old Believer Vigil attended by the author in August 2002 lasted from 4 to 9 p.m. (Pokrov Cathedral at the Rogozhsky Cemetery in Moscow).

[158] See rubrics in *Lenten Triodion*, pp. 75–9.

[159] *Oxford Dictionary of Byzantium*, pp. 92–3.

reflects the older use of the canticles; and Andrew did compose an ode for the Deuteronomy canticle.[160]

The first *eirmos* refers to God as Helper and Protector, alluding to the Exodus 15 canticle. The troparia reflect on Adam and Eve and the sinner's helplessness. The second *eirmos* quotes the first words of the biblical ode 'Attend, O heaven', and continues to catalogue sinfulness, referring to Cain and Abel, and Noah. The fourth *eirmos* recalls the first verse of the Habakkuk 3 canticle, 'Lord, I have heard of your fame', and meditates on Jacob and Job. The fifth directly quotes the canticle of Isaiah 26.9–20, 'From the night I seek thee early', and the first troparion continues:

> In night have I passed all my life: For the night of sin has covered me with darkness and thick mist. But make me, Saviour, a son of the day.

The sixth canticle, Jonah 2, is a type of the resurrection, reflected by the *eirmos*:

> With my whole heart I cried to the all-compassionate God: and he heard me from the lowest depths of hell, and brought my life out of corruption.

In the seventh ode from Daniel 3, the *eirmos* addresses God 'O God of our fathers'. The troparia recall the confessions of Old Testament fathers such as David, Solomon and Manasseh. Ode 8, the Song of the Three Children, uses the refrain in the *eirmos*:

> let everything that hath breath and all creation praise Him, bless Him, and exalt Him above all for ever.

The poetry reflects a universality that well suits the *Benedicite*, a song of all creation to God. The final ode, *Magnificat* and *Benedictus*, is introduced by the *eirmos*:

> Conception without seed; nativity past understanding, from a Mother who never knew a man; childbearing undefiled ...

Then is recalled how the Old Testament has led to the New; as the light of day advances, examples of sin and forgiveness from the New Testament are adduced.

The canon moves from Genesis, through the patriarchs, kings and prophets to the New Testament. The interconnecting themes would argue that the use of the whole nine odes was normal practice at this date. The dynamic from creation to new creation, from old beginnings to new hope, nicely mirrors the

[160] Trans. in *Lenten Triodion*, pp. 378–415.

themes we have seen so often in Matins, and indeed in the whole overnight movement of prayer from evening to morning.

Conclusions

I *From the office of the 'sleepless' monks*

1 The hours of night as celebrated by these monks followed a progression reflected in the psalms. At the First Hour, God is the judge (psalm 74), at the Second the Lord is said to be 'my light' (psalm 26), and so on until we reach morning praise (psalm 56).
2 Several prayers of the office reflect this theme as well, praying for light at the onset of night at the First Hour; and at the Tenth, that new light is perceived coming to fruition. This progression of night to day and back again is a constant anamnesis of the Christian life entered at baptism.

II *The 'chanted Vespers'*

1 The structures of the evening and morning offices express their theological meaning.
2 As in Egeria, Vespers has two major section of psalmody divided by an entry.
3 The light brought from within the sanctuary in the Presanctified Liturgy, clearly symbolizes the Christ who lives beyond the tomb.
4 Psalm 140 is associated with the movement from narthex to nave, and the incense and procession represent eschatological glory.
5 The *prokeimena*, especially on Saturday, also look to the new day; for example, 'The Lord is King'.
6 The texts of the processional appendix of Vespers speak of movement from darkness to light.
7 Evening prayers often speak of guidance in the way as well as protection for the night. They look beyond mere repose.
8 Other prayers, for example, at the little antiphons, often reflect the idea of night opening up to life.

III *The 'chanted Matins'*

1 The progression from narthex, to nave, to sanctuary (on Sundays and feasts) dramatically emphasized the movement of the office from darkness to light.
2 The vigil before the sunrise was begun with the appropriate psalms 3, 62 and 133, and continued as a waiting for the light until the *Benedicite*.

3 The incensation and entry into church, led by a cross with three candles, was the passage from darkness to light, from exclusion from the old paradise to inclusion in the new.
4 The central core of the morning office, psalm 50 praying for forgiveness, with the meditative *kontakion*, and then the praise psalms leading to the Great Doxology, were the praise of the new day.
5 Finally the service in the sanctuary on Sundays proclaimed the resurrection.
6 The prayers of the pre-dawn vigil speak of being 'raised from the bed', watching so as to behold the dawn because we are the sons of light not of darkness.
7 After the processional entry at *Benedicite*, the prayers stressed the praise of God, and one of the final prayers looks for illumination by the true sun of righteousness. We move from the sunrise to contemplate the eschatological sun.
8 Antony of Novgorod's mention of the doors of paradise opening at the Matins entrance is reflected in Simeon of Thessalonica's seeing the service in the narthex as representing the exclusion from paradise.
9 The doors of paradise are opened by the cross as entry to the true paradise, paving the way for the Sunday celebration of the resurrection as both a present and an eschatological reality.

IV *From other sources*

1 The *pannychis* is another example of prayer at night as an eschatological sign, an affirmation that night/death is to be denied victory.
2 The poetic canons also reflect the night to morning dynamic, the triadic structure of the nine odes moves from confession of sin, through hope of new life, to the new light of Christ who redeems his people.
3 Other prayers continue these themes of redeeming the time, rather than simply recalling past events, such as the passion and death of Christ. This is an office that sanctifies the whole of life by the Paschal mystery.

CHAPTER 8

The East Syrian/Chaldean Tradition

Many aspects of East Syrian liturgical practice display signs of considerable antiquity, not least the daily services of Vespers and Matins. Juan Mateos has made a detailed study of the night and morning offices, *Lelya-Sapra*.[1] An English translation of the East Syrian offices was edited by A.J. Maclean at the end of the nineteenth century.[2] He had been a member of the Archbishop of Canterbury's Mission to the Assyrian Church, and was one of the editors of the revised and corrected liturgical books for that church.[3] Since it is fairly widely available, most quotations will be from Maclean's edition, *ESDO*. The evening office, *ramsha*, has not been studied in as much detail, but two Indian scholars, Jacob Vellian[4] and Sylvester Pudichery,[5] have provided useful studies. Overall we know little of the original shape of these offices, the present norms for the daily cathedral offices of Matins and Vespers were established by Katholikos Isho'yahb III in 650/1. Monastic Day Hours had largely disappeared by the ninth century, perhaps partially absorbed by Vespers and Matins.[6]

East Syrian Vespers

The Syriac word for Vespers, r*amsha*, is derived from a word meaning sunset.[7] The opening prayers with the farced Lord's Prayer are a common opening for all East Syrian services and are attributed to the ninth-century patriarch Timothy I (+816).[8] There then follows a prayer to introduce the two *marmyatha* (sing. *marmitha*), or sections of the Psalter. In the commentary of

[1] Juan Mateos, *Lelya-Sapra: Les Offices Chaldéens de la Nuit et du Matin* (OCA 156, Rome: 1972), based on Paul Bedjan's Breviary (Paris: 1886–7, repr. Rome: 1938) with reference to manuscripts; hereafter *Lelya-Sapra*.

[2] A.J. Maclean, *East Syrian Daily Offices* (London: Rivington, Percival, 1894); hereafter *ESDO*.

[3] See J.F. Coakley, *The Church of the East and the Church of England* (Oxford: Clarendon Press, 1992), passim.

[4] Jacob Vellian, *East Syrian Evening Services* (Kottayam: Indian Institute for Eastern Churches, 1971).

[5] Sylvester Pudicherry, *Ramsha: An Analysis and Interpretation of The Chaldean Vespers* (Bangalore: Dhamaram College Studies 9, 1972).

[6] Taft, *Liturgy of the Hours*, pp. 225–7.

[7] Pudichery, op. cit., p. 17.

[8] Ibid., p. 19, n. 8; Vellian, op. cit., p. 6.

Gabriel Qatraya (c.615),[9] the sanctuary veil remained closed during the *marmyatha*, and after the psalms the veil was drawn back (leaving that concealing the altar closed). This may mean that the cathedral office began at this point. The eucharistic liturgy also opens with a *marmitha*, after which the sanctuary curtain is drawn open for a procession (as was also the case at Vespers).[10]

Sundays and Festal Vespers	**Weekday Vespers**
The Pre-Cathedral Service	
Introductory Prayers and Psalmody	Introductory Prayers and Psalmody
Incensing and Light ceremony, Vesperal Psalms and Anthems	
Incense Hymn (*ayk etra*)	
Hymn, *Laku Mara*	Hymn, *Laku Mara*
Alleluiatic psalm and anthem	Alleluliatic psalm and anthem
Vesperal Psalms, 140 etc.	Vesperal Psalms
Alleluiatic psalm and anthem	Alleluiatic psalm and anthem
Intercession and Conclusion	
Litany and Petitions (*karozutha* and *ba'utha*)	Litany and Petitions
Trisagion and Inclination	Trisagion and Inclination
Processional Material	
	Anthem of Vespers
Procession and anthem	
Alleluiatic psalm (3rd)	Alleluiatic psalm (3rd), anthem
Our Father, conclusion	*Suba'a*, Our Father, conclusion

It is thought by some that the *marmyatha* at Vespers may be relics of None, and that at the Eucharist, of Terce.[11] However, the *marmyatha* are current psalmody, whereas almost all known forms of Minor Hours employ a small group of fixed psalms. The commentary attributed to George of Arbela (ninth/tenth century) mentions Hours and Compline, but no trace of this monastic office, other than Compline, remains in the modern

[9] Sarhad Hermiz Jammo, 'L' office du soir Chaldéen au temps de Gabriel Qatraya', *L' Orient Syrien*, **12** (1967), 187–210, 188.

[10] Ibid., 204.

[11] Juan Mateos, 'Les différentes espèces de vigiles dans le rite Chaldéen', *OCP*, **27** (1961) 46–63, 47 n. 3; and also P. Yousif, 'The Divine Liturgy According to the Rite of Assyro-Chaldean Church', in J. Madey (ed.), *The Eucharistic Liturgy in the Christian Orient* (Kottayam: Publisher, 1982), pp. 175–237, 198–9.

books.[12] A Lenten form of Third Hour, integral to Matins, *qutta'a*,[13] has one *hullala* (group of psalms), and *ESDO* provides a form with three *hullala* for noon in the fast,[14] which may be a form of Sixth Hour. If the division of the Psalter into *marmyatha* is older than into *hullale*,[15] then one or two *marmyata* (not *hullale*) at ordinary weekday *ramsha*, attested as early as Qatraya, might: (a) pre-date a fuller organization of the Psalter in course, (b) reflect an urban monastic arrangement. Most ancient forms of Vespers have some kind of psalmody before the central cathedral rite. The *marmyatha* might be an early arrangement of such psalms.

According to Qatraya, the core of the service began with the opening of the veil and a procession from the sanctuary to the *bema*. The *bema* was an enclosed platform in the centre of the church with seats for the clergy and lecterns for scripture readings. It fell out of use from about the fourteenth century, but the chants that accompanied the processions remained.[16] Qatraya describes the procession of the bishop with lights, incense, and a prayer as 'containing the doctrine of the manifestation of Christ, which we express in figure'.[17] The procession may have been accompanied by the hymn of incense, *ayk'etra* (which was omitted on weekdays when the bishop did not process). Vellian also links the hymn to the bishop's entry, and the incensation following at this point, or during the hymn *Laku Mara* that comes next.[18]

Qatraya speaks of a light taken from that kept burning in the sanctuary and used to light a lamp in the church, and symbolizing the communication of the light of Christ to his church.[19] This relatively simple but dramatic ceremony eventually became more complex, as we see in pseudo-George of Arbela, who speaks of many lamps being lit, and then cross, gospel-book and clergy come forth. The interpretation however remains the same, thus Abraham bar Lipheh: 'the appearance of the lights symbolizes the mystery of the Divine Rising, that is, of that great Sun of Justice';[20] and Qatraya: 'Light which has

---

[12] Gabriele Winkler, 'Das Offizium am Ende des 4. Jahrhunderts und das heutige Chaldäische Offizium', *Ostkirchliche Studien*, **19** (1970), 289–311, 305.

[13] *Lelya-Sapra*, pp. 161, 171; Winkler, 'Das Offizium', 306.

[14] *ESDO*, p. 224.

[15] Winkler, 'Das Offizium', 309, n. 113.

[16] R. Taft SJ, 'On the Use of the Bema in the East Syrian Liturgy', *Eastern Churches Review*, **3** (1970), 30–39. A modern Chaldean *bema* in Paris was described by P. Yousef at the 1993 congress of *Societas Liturgica*, Fribourg, Switzerland.

[17] Jammo, op. cit., 188.

[18] Vellian, op. cit., p. 8.

[19] Jammo, op. cit., 189.

[20] Vellian, op. cit., p. 9.

appeared on earth, to whose appearing the peoples will flock, the great sun of justice, who destroyed the power of darkness.'[21]

While the lamp ceremony and procession disappeared,[22] the incense ceremony survived. Although the medieval forms were greatly elaborated, the same themes were celebrated. The service started in a darkened church with the psalmody, emphasizing worship in the holy place with humility and yet with hope. Then came the dramatic moment of the opening of the veil and further lighting of lamps, accompanied by a hymn declaring the presence of the risen Lord Jesus made manifest to his people. Greater emphasis on the evening incense, and perhaps the moving of the service into the afternoon, as in many other places, would all serve to downplay the significance of the light service, but not all trace has been lost.

Having celebrated the advent of Christ to his people, the faithful turn to address their evening thanksgiving to God. They pray for their daily, spiritual and material needs: 'evening and morning constitute the course of the ages (= the days) through which we are drawn, we must, henceforward, give thanks for the passing of the hours and petition for that which is necessary'.[23]

To summarize the first part of the service: before the opening of the veil and the lamp-lighting rite, we await Christ's coming. The procession of lamps and incense represents the advent of Christ, and in the selected psalms or psalm verses that come next, confident prayer is made. The Evening Psalms sum up the evening thank-offering, ask pardon of God, and look for a greater manifestation of life.

The cathedral psalmody, psalm 140 etc., with its surrounding complex of *shurraye* and *onyata*, is followed by intercession in the form of three litanies.[24] The first is called *ba'utha* (supplication), the second *karozutha* (proclamation), and the third has no specific name but commences with a petition praying God to send the 'angel of peace'.[25] At this point the deacon should put on stole and girdle, whereas for the rest of the service no special vestments are used.[26] The three litanies existed at the time of Qatraya who expected the people to rise for the third part of the intercessions for 'this shows our resurrection from the fall into sin, and signifies the acceptance of our prayers'.[27] A phrase more redolent of a ritual renewal of the baptismal covenant one could not hope to find! The

[21] Jammo, op. cit., 189.

[22] Pudichery, op. cit., p. 194.

[23] Jammo, op. cit., 191.

[24] In Lent readings are inserted here.

[25] Vellian, op. cit., pp. 12–13.

[26] *ESDO*, p. 6; Pudichery, op. cit., p. 53, n. 25.

[27] Jammo, ibid.

same litanies are found at the Eucharist[28] and baptism,[29] while entirely different litanies, *karozwata*, are appointed for the night office, for the festal vigil, and also for the Lenten weekday Morning Prayer.

The Trisagion and prayer of inclination probably concluded the ancient service. The complex appendix that now follows may have its origin in a Constantinopolitan procession from church to the palace in honour of Constantine's victory,[30] though perhaps a more likely source, since the procession is in honour of the cross, is Jerusalem. On weekdays instead of the processional *onita d-basaliqe* there is the *onita d-ramsha*, possibly connected with communion at Vespers on days when the Eucharist was not celebrated.[31]

The office of Vespers concludes with a series of prayers for help. Twenty-three such prayers are given in *ESDO*, but Maclean indicates that the practice was for each priest present to say one, and in most cases a large number would have been omitted.[32]

Psalms and Other Scriptures at Vespers

The recitation of the Psalter at Vespers does not correspond to that of *lelya*, the night office. For *lelya* the Psalter is divided into 20 divisions called *hullale* (Alleluia), a 21st *hullala* comprising three Old Testament canticles.[33] This recitation of the Psalter in course was to be completed twice a week during the night office.[34] The following are the psalms of the vesperal *marmyatha*:

Monday:	10, 11, 12, 13;
	14, 15, 16
Tuesday:	24, 25, 26;
	27, 28, 29
Wednesday:	61, 62, 63;
	64, 65, 66

28 Brightman, *LEW*, 262–66.

29 J.A. Assemani, *Codex Liturgicus Ecclesiae Universae*, vol. 1, *De Catechumenis* (Rome: 1749), p. 190; G.P. Badger, *The Nestorians and their Rituals* (London: 1862), p. 202.

30 So Qatraya, Jammo, op. cit., 193 and see Pudichery, op. cit., p. 194; Vellian, op. cit., pp. 14–15.

31 Vellian, op. cit., pp. 28–9 – e.g., *ESDO*, p. 11: 'The body of Christ and his precious blood are on the holy altar. In fear and love let us approach to it, and with the angels chant to him; Holy, holy, holy, Lord God.'

32 *ESDO*, p. 16, n. 1; Pudichery, op. cit., p. 44.

33 Mateos, *Lelya-Sapra*, 448–9.

34 See *ESDO*, p. 86.

Thursday: 95, 96, 97;
98, 99, 100
Friday: 84, 85;
86, 87
Saturday: 144, 145, 146;
147, 148, 149, 150

On feasts the *marmyatha* are:

Sunday (i.e. Saturday night):
Advent to Epiphany: 86, 87
Other Sundays: 64, 65, 66
Memorials:
on Fridays: 84, 85
on other days: 14, 15, 16[35]

This semi-continuous psalmody appears to show some principle of selectivity. The normal *marmitha* for the eve of Sunday comprises psalm 64 ('Praise is due to thee, O God, in Zion...To thee shall all flesh come on account of sins ... O God of our salvation who art the hope of all the ends of the earth'), psalm 65 ('Make a joyful noise to God, all the earth ... I will come into thy house with burnt offerings; ... Blessed be God, because he has not rejected my prayer') and psalm 66 ('May God be gracious to us and bless us and make his face to shine upon us'). These psalms call upon sinners to have the confidence to praise God who does great things for his people, and who shines the light of his grace upon them – themes eminently suited to the liturgical beginning of Sunday.[36]

Something similar may be seen on a weekday, for example the group of psalms 24–9 set for Tuesday: 'To thee, O Lord, I lift up my soul' (24); 'Prove me O Lord, and try me' (25); 'The Lord in my light and my salvation; whom shall I fear?' (26)'; 'To thee, O Lord, I call; ... lest, if thou be silent to me, I become like those who go down to the Pit' (27); 'May the Lord give strength to his people! May the Lord bless his people with peace!' (28); and 'I will extol thee, O Lord, for thou hast drawn me up, ...Thou hast turned for me my mourning into dancing; ... O Lord my God, I will give thanks to thee for ever' (29).

The grouping of cathedral psalms 140, 141, 118.105–13 and 116 is found in the other Syrian rites, which argues for antiquity.[37] Qatraya mentions psalm

[35] For consistency LXX numbering is used. East Syrian books use the Peshitto, see table in Pudichery, op. cit., p. 12, n. 29.

[36] Similar themes are explored in ibid., p. 21.

[37] See e.g., P.E. Gemayel, 'La structure des Vêpres Maronites', *Orient Syrien*, (1964), 105–34.

140 and the verses from psalm 118,[38] chosen because of the words: 'Your word is a lamp for my steps and a light for my path'. Pseudo-George of Arbela saw the four evening psalms as representing the whole economy of salvation, from the Fall in the first verses of psalm 140, to Pentecost in the song of all nations praising God which is psalm 116.[39] Psalm 140 is clearly an evening psalm of incense, 141 speaks of dependence upon God and psalm 118.105–13 of light, while psalm 116 expresses praise for the mercies of God.[40] These are the evening prayer themes that we find, in one way or another, almost everywhere in traditional evening offices. The psalms had short responses with variants on great feasts.[41] They do not seem to have had any direct connection with the incense ceremony as was general elsewhere.

The evening psalms are preceded and followed by a psalm called *shurraya*,[42] with the *onita da-qdam*[43] before, and the *onita d-batar*[44] after. In the cycle of *shurraye* for ordinary Sundays in *ESDO* and Pudichery,[45] the selected verses are more or less appropriate. God's power is sung in psalms 46 and 92; his protecting mercy in 88 and 124; singing his praises in 64 and 48.[46] A similar weekday system extends over a fortnight, the weeks 'before' and 'after'.[47]

Qatraya says of the Sunday *shurraye*:

> on the sabbath day, the evening that precedes the night of the Lord, in which is portrayed the figure of the resurrection of all, these *shurraye* are said and in the middle of them 'Lord I have cried', as on other days, although we know that the resurrection was only accomplished at the fourth vigil of the night.[48]

The passage is clear that, from Vespers on, Sunday night was devoted to celebrating the resurrection.

The Sunday *shurraye d'aqdam* sing of thanksgiving for God's protection, often emphasizing victory over enemies.[49] The weekday *shurraye* after the vesperal psalms again show some systematization, with a separate cycle of

---

38 Jammo, op. cit., 191.

39 Vellian, op. cit., p. 12.

40 Pudicherry, op. cit., p. 30, n. 36.

41 Ibid., p. 31. Also *ESDO*, pp. 5, 72–3.

42 Meaning 'beginning'; Pudichery, op. cit., p. 26, n. 26.

43 I.e., 'response before'; ibid., p. 28, a psalm verse and poetic strophe.

44 I.e., 'response after', ibid.

45 *ESDO*, p. 70, and Pudicherry, op. cit., 27.

46 Pudichery, ibid.

47 Ibid., p. 50.

48 Ibid.

49 Ibid., p. 32.

three Fridays.[50] They emphasize the confidence given to those who walk in the right way, that they may know God's protection: for example, the blameless one walking in God's ways (14), the pure one ascends on high (23), and so on.

The *shurraya* following the processional chant at the end of Vespers is usually a portion of psalm 118, and it is interesting to note that this psalm of meditation on the blessedness of keeping God's law[51] occurs in vesperal offices elsewhere. It may have served as didactic reinforcement of the obligation to live the Christian life into which those present have been baptized.

Prayer and Hymnody

The opening prayers are fairly general expressions of adoration. For example:

> Let us confess, O my Lord, thy Godhead, and worship thy Majesty, and lift up perpetual praise without ceasing to thy glorious Trinity, at all times, Lord of all, Father, Son, and Holy Ghost, for ever.[52]

A similar prayer comes at end of the psalms.[53] A common feature of these prayers is the spirit of thanksgiving for the end of the day, facing the night by promising to lift up perpetual prayer to God.

The 'hymn of incense' On Sundays is:

> As the fragrance of sweet incense, and the smell of a pleasant censer, receive, O Christ our Saviour, the request and prayer of your servants.[54]

Psalm verses are sung between repeats of this anthem, on Sundays and Feasts from psalm 83, 'How lovely is thy dwelling place, O Lord of hosts'. In the prayer that follows incense is a symbol of offering, and not just of prayer:

> O Christ, who didst accept the blood of the martyrs in the day when they were killed, accept this incense from the hands of my feebleness in the loving kindness of thy compassion, for ever.[55]

Qatraya, a very early witness to the use of incense at Vespers, quotes a prayer no longer used:

---

[50] Ibid., p. 52.

[51] Cf. ibid., p. 56, n. 30.

[52] *ESDO*, p. 2.

[53] Ibid., p. 69, for Sundays and festivals.

[54] Ibid., p. 69.

[55] Ibid.

> With the diffusion to us of the pleasing sweet odour of your love, we hasten to meet your heavenly manifestation.[56]

Here incense adds solemnity to a ceremony that draws most of its symbolism from the revealing of light. As Gabriele Winkler summarizes: 'The light is the symbol of the first and second comings of Christ, and the incense symbolises the love of God.'[57]

The hymn *Laku Mara* is one of the most widely known East Syrian compositions:

> Thee, Lord of all, we confess. And thee, Jesus Christ, we glorify. For thou art the Quickener of our bodies. And thou art the Saviour of our souls.[58]

It is repeated with psalm verses from psalm 121, 'I was glad when they said to me, "Let us go to the house of the Lord!"' Jammo describes this chant as the centre of the lamp-lighting ceremony[59] which expresses the coming of Christ, the accompanying incensation symbolizing the sweetness of the love of Christ.[60]

There is a prayer of thanksgiving and adoration before psalms 140 etc., in which God's care and protection of his people is a motive for giving thanks. The prayer after the vesperal psalms:

> Hear, O our Lord and our God, the prayer of thy servants in thy compassion, and receive the petition of thy worshippers in thy mercy; and have compassion on our sinfulness in thy loving- kindness and mercies, O Physician of our bodies, and good Hope to our souls, Lord of all ...[61]

The inclusion of a reference to having mercy on sinners leads naturally to the intercessions that follow the *shurraya* and *onita d-batar*; which may indicate the greater antiquity of the prayers. The relatively late poetic *onyata* do not help establish the liturgical-theological meaning of *ramsha*. The final section of the intercessory material is what is called in the Byzantine rite the *aitesis*.[62]

Qatraya's Vespers was completed by the Trisagion,[63] preceded by a prayer still used:

---

[56] Jammo, op. cit., 190, 203.

[57] Winkler, 'Über die Kathedralvesper in der verschiedenen Riten des Ostens und Westens', *Archiv für Liturgiewissenschaft*, **16** (1974), 53–102.

[58] *ESDO*, p. 3.

[59] Jammo, op. cit., p. 190.

[60] Jammo, op. cit., 205.

[61] Ibid.

[62] *ESDO*, p. 10.

[63] Jammo, op. cit., 193.

> To thee, O Lord, mighty God, we entrust our bodies and souls; and of thee, O our Lord and our God, we ask forgiveness of trespasses and sins ...[64]

Appropriately, this is a prayer for forgiveness when entrusting one's life to God at the hour of rest. The Trisagion is followed by a prayer at the imposition of hands, the former final blessing. The weekday version reads:

> May our souls be perfected in the one complete faith of thy glorious Trinity, and may we all in one union of love be worthy to raise to thee glory and honour, confession and worship, at all times, Lord of all ...[65]

Introduced by what Pudichery refers to as a blessing of the deacon,[66] 'May Christ make thy service glorious in the kingdom of heaven',[67] these formulae look for united perfection in the eschatological kingdom, and accord with the vesperal themes identified above.

The first strophe of the processional *onite d-basaliqe* is proper to the Sunday or feast.[68] The second is seasonal, and the prayer that introduces the procession is one for divine assistance and that God will reveal himself to save his people.[69] In some places the day's Gospel is read after the *onita*, making the appendix a form of vigil of preparation for the Sunday or feast.[70] A further processional chant, the *onita d-sahde*, in praise of the martyrs, was probably connected with a procession to the place where the relics were kept.[71] The relics may have been in a separate building some distance away, for directions for the reception of a sixth-century Nestorian bishop visiting a town require him to venerate the place of the martyrs, 'if he finds one at the gate of the city', by offering incense there.[72]

The prayers that complete the office are for the pardon of sins and assistance as the people enter upon the night. For example:

> May the blessing of him who blesseth all, and the peace of him who make all things peaceful, and the compassion of him who hath compassion on all, and the guardianship of our adorable God, be with us and among us and

---

[64] *ESDO*, p. 10.

[65] Ibid., p. 11.

[66] Pudichery, op. cit., p. 39.

[67] *ESDO*, p. 77.

[68] Pudichery, op. cit., p. 170.

[69] *ESDO*, pp. 78–80.

[70] Pudichery, op. cit., p. 42.

[71] Ibid., p. 57; Vellian, op. cit., pp. 18–19.

[72] L. Larson-Miller, 'A Return to the Liturgical Architecture of Northern Syria', *SL*, **24** (1994), 71–83, 78–80.

> around us, and keep us from the Evil one and his hosts, at all seasons and times, Lord of all ...[73]

Then, taking the hand cross, the presiding priest gives the concluding blessing or *huttamo*, nine alternatives being given in *ESDO*;[74] for example, the first: 'pardon our sins and forgive our offences, deliver us from our afflictions, answer our requests and bring us to the excellent light, and deliver us by thy living sign from all harm, hidden and open'.[75] Forgiveness of sin, protection, but above all, the new light that lies always ahead, are all themes consonant with what we have seen above. All this is sealed by the exchange of a kiss of peace, and among the Chaldeans and Nestorians by the reciting of the Nicene Creed.[76]

Qatraya's discussion of the *onita d-basaliqe* includes this interesting remark: 'every evening, *which is the beginning of the day*';[77] elsewhere he says that kneeling ceases at Vespers on Saturday night.[78] Clearly the earliest extant commentator on the East Syrian office saw Vespers as the beginning of the new day, a new daily entry into the economy of the salvation won by Christ.

Lelya-sapra: the East Syrian Morning Office

Lelya, originally a monastic night office, is now more often celebrated today immediately before the morning office, *sapra*.[79] A visitor to the Chaldean monasteries of Iraq in the 1950s reported that the night office had been brought forward to sunrise, and that daily service commenced at about 4.30 a.m. with the night office.[80] In parishes *lelya* probably always precedes *sapra* without a break, except on Sundays and feasts when the cathedral vigil, *qale d-shahra*, comes between the two.[81]

---

[73] *ESDO*, pp. 16–17.

[74] Ibid., pp. 20–22.

[75] Ibid., p. 20.

[76] Ibid., pp. 22–3; Pudichery, op. cit., pp. 44–5.

[77] Jammo, op. cit., 194.

[78] Ibid., 195.

[79] Maclean in *ESDO*, p. xvii.

[80] Jules Leroy, *Monks and Monasteries of the Near East* (English edition, London: Harrap, 1963), pp. 169–70.

[81] Taft, *The Liturgy of the Hours*, p. 237.

Schemes of the Night and Morning Offices[82]

Lelya (Festal)	Ferial
Initial Prayer	Initial Prayer
3 Hullale	3 Hullale
qalta and psalms	
'onyata d 'mawtba	*'onyata d'mawtba*
qanona and teshbohta	*shubbaha and teshbohta*
karozutha	*karozutha*
madrasha	
suyyake (2 Hull.)	
Qale d-shahra	
3 psalms (*3 marmyata*)	
'onita d-lelya	
qanona (*shubbaha*) and *teshbohta*	
karozutha	
Sapra	
Morning psalms (99, 90, 103.1–16a, 112, 92, 148–50 and 116)	Morning psalms (99 etc.)
'onita d-sapra	
hymns of light	*Laku Mara*
Benedicite with refrain	Psalm 50 (vv. 1–19) with refrain and peace prayer
teshbohta, Teshbohta	
Trisagion	Trisagion
(Lord's Prayer)/Dismissal prayers	(Lord'sPrayer)/Dismissal prayers

Lelya has, especially on weekdays, a very simple structure. The service mainly comprises psalms but also some ecclesiastical poetry (*'onyata d-mawtba*), the *qanona*, a selected psalm with refrain and followed by the hymn called *teshbohta* and prayer, a *karozutha*. The *madrasha*, a lengthy doctrinal poem is only found on some feasts and Sundays, and the *suyyake* on a Sunday are two *hullale* that begin the vigil, *qale d-shahra*.[83]

On weekdays the proper *qalta* and *'onyata d'mawtba* after the psalms, are then followed by the *shubbaha*, a selected psalm with refrain. After this psalm comes the *teshbohta* for the day of the week, a hymn which again takes up

[82] After *Lelya-Sapra*, pp. 102–3, seasonal material (or forms to which seasonal material is attached) in italics.

[83] Ibid., pp. 41–2.

similar themes: prayer for forgiveness and healing, that the prayer of God's people may be heard and they be made worthy to praise him.

A litany, the *karozutha*, concludes the weekday *lelya*. There appears to be only the one litany of this form, the petitions of which ask mercy of God who created men and women in the image of his glory, who promised good things to the faithful, who foreknew the need for redemption, and who dwells in light. The prayer that is placed by Maclean at the beginning of the ferial *sapra*, 'O Compassionate, Merciful, and Pitiful one', concludes the ferial night office.[84]

Festal *lelya* has a more complex conclusion; a proper didactic poem called *madrasha*[85] (not used on the lightest summer nights). On Sundays there is another group of psalms, the *suyyake*. After a very general prayer,[86] there are extra psalms that appear to be part of an ancient recitation of the Psalter in course over Saturday–Sunday night.[87]

The Psalms and Other Scriptures at *lelya-sapra*

ESDO provides for recitation of the Psalter twice a week, dividing it into 20 *hullale* (the 21st is a group of Old Testament canticles). Maclean's rubrics indicate monotone recitation with Alleluia at the end of each *hullala*,[88] which are distributed thus:

Monday and Thursday	1–7
Tuesday and Friday	8–14
Wednesday and Saturday	15–21[89]

On Sundays, *hullali* 5–11 would alternate with 12–18,[90] these would be farced with responses on festivals, and a prayer would be said at each subdivision or *marmitha*.[91]

Parishes may have used seven, ten or even three *hullali* on a Sunday.[92] These sizeable portions of psalmody originated as monastic night-time vigils, and an all-night vigil comprising the entire Psalter is described by pseudo-George for

[84] *ESDO*, pp. 101–3; *Lelya-Sapra*, p. 93.

[85] *Lelya-Sapra*, pp. 53–4.

[86] *ESDO*, p. 159.

[87] Ibid., p. 160.

[88] *Lelya-Sapra*, p. 86, hence the name, *hullala*, Alleluia.

[89] Ibid.

[90] Ibid., p. 46.

[91] *ESDO*, p. 152.

[92] *Lelya-Sapra*, pp. 395–8.

feasts of the Lord.[93] Even after the disappearance of monastic life, the main daily psalmody continued to be recited at this nocturnal vigil of monastic type. So, as we find elsewhere, the bulk of the Psalter is recited at night, or in the night part of the morning office, with no consideration of the suitability of particular psalms to the hour.

The selected psalm verses or *qalta* for the Sundays include verses such as: 'Turn your ear, O Lord, and give answer' (85) (a prayer for protection in adversity); 'I lift up my eyes to the mountains: from where shall come my help?' (120) (which sings of the Lord's unsleeping watchfulness).[94] The same themes – protection, salvation from threatening peril, and above all from death – run through the psalms selected for the Sundays and feasts.[95]

The *shubbaha* psalms are selected for each day of the week: Monday, psalm 12, 'How long, O Lord, will you forget me?'; Tuesday, psalm 27, 'To you, O Lord, I call, my rock, hear me'; Wednesday, psalm 66, 'O God, be gracious and bless us'; and so on.[96]

Nocturnal Prayer and Hymnody

The introductory prayers clearly indicate that this is a nocturnal vigil before dawn. For example:

> Strengthen, O our Lord and our God, our weakness in thy compassion, and comfort and help the wants of our soul in thy loving kindness; waken the sleep of our thoughts and lighten the weight of our limbs; wash and cleanse the filth of our trespasses and of our sins. Illumine the darkness of our minds, and stretch forth (thine arm) and confirm us, and give us strength and a helping hand, that thereby we may arise and confess thee and glorify thee, without ceasing all the days of our life, Lord of all ...[97]

A similar prayer precedes the group of three on Sundays and feasts ('Let us arise, O Lord, in the hidden power of thy Godhead').[98]

Each *hullala* has a prayer, and so does each of the smaller divisions, the *marmyatha*. They are psalm collects but do not cover the whole Psalter, only the first psalm of each *marmitha* is reflected in the prayer.[99] The entire series of

---

[93] Ibid., 403.

[94] *ESDO*, p. 156.

[95] *Lelya-Sapra*, p. 50.

[96] *ESDO*, pp. 97–8; *Lelya-Sapra*, p. 91.

[97] *ESDO*, pp. 85–6.

[98] Ibid., p. 151.

[99] *Lelya-Sapra*, p. 309.

prayers is given by Maclean in *ESDO*.[100] As examples, the prayer of the second *marmitha* of *hullala* 2 (psalms 14, 15 and 16) begins with this prayer:

> Make us worthy, O our Lord and God, with consciences pure and sanctified by thy truth, to dwell in thy holy tabernacle, and to walk in thy way blameless, all the days of our life, Lord of all ...[101]

The prayer takes up the first words of psalm 14: 'Lord, who shall dwell in thy tabernacle':

> Grant us, O my Lord, to confess thy loving kindness, and make us worthy to relate thy wonders; and strengthen us to confess, worship, and glorify the hidden and glorious strength of thy glorious Trinity, at all times, Lord of all ...[102]

From the first *marmitha* of *hullala* 16 commencing with psalm 105, verse 2 reading: 'Who can express the noble acts of the Lord: or show forth all his praise?' [??] Finally, the first *marmitha* of the last *hullala*, comprising the canticles Exodus 15: 1–22 and Isaiah 42.10–14, highlights the Exodus Song of the Sea:

> Thee, O excellent and magnifical, strong and glorious, mighty and warlike, powerful and full of mercies, great King of glory, etc. ...[103]

The farcings of the psalms, or *qanone*, attributed to Mar Aba (5th/6th centuries) are certainly ancient, judging from their sobriety and brevity,[104] they also often reflect vigil themes. There is a proper *qanona* for each psalm.[105] The most simple of these refrains are but one phrase: for example, 'Thou art my true hope',[106] for psalm 53, 'Have mercy on me God, men crush me'. More obviously theological responses are also present, for example: 'A bridechamber and blessing which passeth not away, hath our Lord promised to his saints',[107] for psalm 133, 'O come bless the Lord, all you who serve the Lord', an explicitly night time psalm awaiting Christ the bridegroom.

---

[100] *ESDO*, pp. 86–95.

[101] Ibid., p. 87.

[102] Ibid., p. 92.

[103] Ibid., p. 94.

[104] *Lelya-Sapra*, pp. 315–16.

[105] Ibid., pp. 316–38; *ESDO*, pp. 236–48.

[106] *ESDO*, p. 239.

[107] Ibid., p. 247.

The *qalta*, singular *qala*, comprise selected psalms or psalm verses preceded by one or more refrains[108] and a prayer:

> For thy nature, which is hidden and incomprehensible, and unbounded by the thought and folly of all creatures, O my Lord, glory is fitting and the sound of praise is right. Worship is seemly and due from all whom thou hast created and formed in heaven and in earth, Lord of all, ...[109]

The *'onyata d'mawtba* are preceded by somewhat general prayers.[110] The term *mawtba* indicates sitting, these chants appear to have been sung originally between the *hullale*.[111] They also appear to serve as introductions to the intercessory prayer of the *karozutha*.[112]

A prayer of praise precedes the *shubbaha*:

> To thee be glory from those on high, and confession from those below; and worship and praise and exaltation from all whom thou hast created and fashioned in heaven and earth, Lord of all ...[113]

A piece with similar themes, the *teshbohta* may be represented by this example for Wednesday (attributed to Mar Abimelek, 6th century):

> May thy mercies be on our trespasses. O Christ, who lovest the voice of the penitent. Hear our requests and heal us, for thou art good. And remove from us the canker of our wickedness, because thou knowest the sufferings of our race ... Let us cleanse our stains according to thy will, and grant us with one accord to confess thy name ...[114]

In the Breviary these hymns are entitled 'Praise of the Night',[115] and are well suited to forming a break in the lengthy monastic psalmody.

---

[108] *Lelya-Sapra*, p. 47.

[109] *ESDO*, p. 95.

[110] E.g., Ibid., p. 156: 'May our prayer, O my Lord, please thee, and may our request come before thee ...'.

[111] *Lelya-Sapra*, pp. 441–2.

[112] *ESDO*, pp. 96–7:

> O merciful God, pity thy people ... Fence us around with thy strong truth ... Give peace to all the world. which is disturbed and confused by its sins ... Make peace between priests and kings ... May the righteous who pleased thee ... beseech thee for our souls. That thou have mercy on us all ...

[113] Ibid., p. 97.

[114] Ibid., p. 99.

[115] *Lelya-Sapra*, p. 92.

The Sunday *teshbohta* is longer and preceded by a refrain called *qanona*.[116] These are often hymns of praise to the risen Christ who brings redemption to the people, who are to be prepared for his coming. For example:

> Glory to thy mercies, which sent thee to us, O Christ the Sun of righteousness; the brightness which shone from the house of David ... and in that hour when thy mercies shine forth, may we go forth to meet thee according to thy will.[117]

We note that this prayer on Sunday night is in expectation of the second coming of Christ.

We can conclude by saying that the Chaldean night office, *lelya*, was a monastic office characterized by recitation of the psalms in course. The long sections of psalmody were interspersed with prayers of a general nature, and poetic chants that stress healing and forgiveness of sins. However the idea of a Christian vigil is never totally lost, it is a night watch in expectation of the morning that will symbolize the second coming of the Saviour.

Vigil Psalmody and Canticles of *qale d-shahra*

On Sundays and Feasts, there is another office, similar in structure to *lelya* but made up of shorter pieces. As at the night office there is psalmody, poetic compositions, a psalm with a refrain, a hymn and a litanic prayer. The name *qale d-shahra* means 'chants of the vigil'.[118]

On Sundays the psalms are now the 14th and 21st *hullale*: psalms 92–100, and the canticles, Exodus 15.1–22 and Isaiah 42.10–14 and 45.8; Deuteronomy 32.1–21a; and Deuteronomy 32.21a–44.[119] On festivals there are three selected psalms rather than a full *hullala*.

The original elements of the Sunday vigil may have been the three canticles, which all have Paschal overtones. Later, with the division of the Psalter into *hullale*, and the alternation of one *hullala* with the canticles, something of the paschal nature of the vigil was lost. The three canticles are most suitable for commemorating the resurrection just before dawn/sunrise. The Exodus 15 canticle is very commonly found at Easter and Sunday vigils. Exodus 15 and the canticle from Isaiah 42.10–14 and 45.8, with phrases such as

---

[116] *ESDO*, pp. 156–9.

[117] Ibid., pp. 157–8.

[118] *Lelya-Sapra*, p. 55.

[119] *ESDO*, p. 160. Maclean did not differentiate this from the rest of the 'Festival Night Service'.

> Sing to the Lord a new song ... The Lord goes forth like a mighty man, ... let the earth open, that salvation may sprout forth, and let it cause righteousness to spring up also,[120]

may be compared with that from Deuteronomy 32:

> Give ear, O heavens, and I will speak, ... A God of faithfulness and without iniquity, just and right is he ... See now that I, even I, am he, and there is no god beside me; I kill and I make alive; ... I will take vengeance on my adversaries.

We again note the eschatological theme of waiting for God to come into his own, for the risen Lord to arise at the last time.

Vigil Prayer and Hymnody

The prayer preceding the *hullale*;[121] 'May the sounds of our Hallelujahs', is for the acceptance of the praise 'we offer to thy glorious Trinity, night and day'. Of the prayers which follow, the second and third refer to the praise of all creation, and the first emphasizes watchfulness:

> Make us worthy, O our Lord and our God, with the watchful ones and the companies of angels, with voices full of confession to sing praise to thy glorious Trinity, night and day, Lord of all ...[122]

Starting with a prayer for acceptance, and then that the congregation may be watchful like the angels, finally there is petition that we may share in the cosmic praise of the Creator, since it is by God's power that the creation emerges from the formless darkness.

The poetic part of this cathedral vigil is represented by the *'onita d-lelya*, the response of the night,[123] This *'onita* is similar in purpose to those of the 'mysteries' at the Eucharist, the *'onita d-basaliqe* at Vespers which we have already discussed, and that of the morning.[124] *'Onyata* represent a very ancient form, though later ones can be long and mediocre.[125] Some concluding strophes are relevant to our theme:

---

[120] Seemingly peculiar to the Chaldean tradition.

[121] *Lelya-Sapra*, pp. 308–9.

[122] *ESDO*, pp. 153–4.

[123] *Lelya–Sapra*, p. 59; 'Night Anthem' in *ESDO*, pp. 154–5.

[124] Ibid., note 1.

[125] Ibid., 426–7.

> O Christ, neglect us not, and be not far from thy worshippers. For in thee, O my Lord, we have taken refuge. Guide us in thy way of life, that we all may sing praise to thee, O Lord God.[126]

God's guidance and protection are suitable vigil themes. Festal verses are similar. For example, this rather mechanical vigil text:

> Come, O my Lord, to the help of thy worshippers, who keep vigil on the festival of N.; and reveal thyself to us in thy mercy, and hearken to the words of our prayers, ...[127]

As at the end of festal *lelya*, a selected psalm with refrain, *qanona*, is followed by a *teshbohta*. The psalm is called *shubbaha* because of its refrain 'Glory to thee, O God' and is preceded by a doxological composition that introduces a chant in the same style:

> Glory to thee from all mouths, and confession from all tongues, and worship and honour and exaltation from all creatures, O secret and glorious Being, who dwellest in the exalted heights, Lord of all ...[128]

The *qanona* was chanted in the sanctuary and the festal psalm, 148, is followed by psalms 150 and 116, a doublet of *sapra* (see below). At Easter the *shubbaha* comprises only psalm 96 'The Lord is King, let earth rejoice',[129] clearly an outpouring of praise, suited to the day, in the sanctuary which represents the heaven into which the worshippers at the vigil are called.

The praise of the risen Lord continues with the *teshbohta*. That proper to Sundays, attributed to Mar Narsai, praises God for redemption and is also used at an office of the baptistery at the end of *sapra* on Monday to Friday in Holy Week, and so may have been part of the ancient preparation for baptism. The hymn dwells on the redeemed life.[130] If originally a baptismal hymn, it would support a baptismal 'undercurrent' in the *qale d-shahra* – the baptized not only praise the resurrection, but celebrate their redemption and resurrection life gained through baptism. The hymn is very beautiful, as may be seen from the following excerpts:

> Praise to him who in his goodness hath made our race free, from the slavery of the Evil one and of death ... Blessed is the Compassionate one, who,

[126] *ESDO*, p. 160 – for the period of Annunciation only in Bedjan, see *Lelya-Sapra*, p. 59.

[127] 'Prayer of 3rd Anthem' in *ESDO*, p. 154.

[128] *ESDO*, p. 161; *Lelya-Sapra*, pp. 60–1.

[129] *Lelya-Sapra*, p. 237.

[130] Ibid., pp. 61–2, 428.

> when we sought him not, came forth to seek us, and rejoiced in giving us life ... It is a thing too great for us and for all creatures; it is a new thing which he hath done to our humanity, that he hath made our body a holy temple ... Come ye earthly and heavenly ones, wonder and be astonished at the greatness of the step by which our race hath come to the great heights ...[131]

The Sunday *karozutha* of *qale d'shahra* is eminently suited to a vigil before it is fully light:

> O thou who didst spend the night in prayer to God for the salvation of our race, we make request,
>
> R. O our Lord, have mercy upon us.
>
> O thou who didst save us from the power of darkness, and hast brought us to the kingdom of thy well-beloved Son, we make request, ...[132]

A diaconal litany is always concluded by a presbyteral prayer, following concluding *qale d-shahra*:

> Make us worthy, O our Lord and our God, ... to serve before thee purely and diligently, wakefully and earnestly, justly and uprightly, honestly and in holiness, and without blame. And may our service, O my Lord, please thee, and our prayer and vigil persuade thee, and our entreaty appease thee ...[133]

This is a prayer for acceptance of the night's vigil, an offering of waking prayer for those present and for all God's people; a fitting close to the vigil now that it is time for the morning office proper.

Excursus: Other Vigil Forms in the Chaldean Tradition

We have already seen that towards the end of Vespers, *ramsha*, there is a group of psalms called *suyyake*. When these occur there is usually a further extension of Vespers, the *subba'a* or Compline. Mateos believed this to be a form of nocturnal vigil that joined Vespers and Compline.[134] Matéos further suggested that there were two kinds of Chaldean vigil for different days, the first commenced with the nocturnal office of *lelya*, a 'nocturnal vigil'. The second

---

[131] *ESDO*, pp. 161–2.

[132] Ibid., p. 162.

[133] Ibid., p. 164.

[134] Mateos, 'Les différentes espèces de vigiles', 47 and n. 3.

prolonged Vespers and then added Compline, a 'vespero-nocturnal vigil' for memorials, Lenten ferias and the feasts of the Lord. Finally, there were a few days on which an all-night vigil was celebrated: on Good Friday, and some solemn feasts when the two basic kinds of vigil were combined into one night-long service.[135]

The vespero-nocturnal vigil might extend Vespers through to midnight, and *lelya* on such days was correspondingly shorter. The ancient psalmody of Friday night was psalms 81–5, 88, and 95–100 (or 98–100). The earlier form of this is represented by the refrain for psalm 133, to be chanted on all Fridays of the year:[136]

> The saints sing Glory by night with the watchful ones, and tens of thousands of the companies on high repeat the glory of the greatness of Jesus our victorious King.[137]

The themes are the classical vigil ones of watchfulness in expectation of the coming kingdom and the judgement.[138]

The second level of development of this vespero-nocturnal vigil was to enrich it with texts commemorating the saints, this became the Friday *qale d-shahra*.[139] In earlier days the Chaldean Friday night vigil had celebrated the mystery of redemption.

The Good Friday vigil extends from Maundy Thursday, and is found elsewhere: for example, Jerusalem at the time of Egeria. On feasts such as Christmas there appears to have been a lengthy procession at the end of Vespers, and the vigil continued through the night.

Texts of *subba'a* that prolongs Vespers show traditional Compline themes:

> Make us worthy, O our Lord and God, of a peaceful evening, and a restful night, and a morning in which good things are proclaimed, and a day of good deeds of righteousness; that thereby we may propitiate thy Godhead, all the days of our life, Lord of all . . .[140]

This prayer looks forward to morning after a time of sleep, and other prayers are similar. It is possible that *subba'a* and even more so, *lelya*, were adapted from the monastic round, because they helped reinforce the idea of sleep and waking as representing death and resurrection.

---

[135] Ibid., 48.

[136] Mateos, 'Les différentes espèces de vigiles', 50–53.

[137] *ESDO*, p. 213.

[138] Mateos, 'Les différentes espèces de vigiles', 53.

[139] Ibid., 54–5.

[140] *ESDO*, p. 82. See also full text of Compline as a separate service, pp. 185–204.

Sapra: Chaldean Morning Prayer

As may be seen from the scheme given on page 132, the Chaldean Matins has a roughly similar shape to *lelya* and *qale d-shahra*: psalmody, hymnody, a canticle and *teshbohta* and prayer. The psalms are the same each day, and include the commonly found 148–50 (together with 116 as a doxology).

Pseudo-George of Arbela indicates that the same psalms were used at *sapra* in his day. The first three, 99, 90 and 103, formed a group sometimes concluded by a prayer. After Psalm 112 the bishop came out of the sanctuary and all the lamps were lit, he said a prayer and intoned psalm 92 and then went to the *bema* with the clergy for the solemn singing of the praise psalms. The rite continued with the *'onita d-sapra*, opening of the veil and incensation, followed by the hymns of Ephrem and Narsai, the *Benedicite*, the *Gloria in Excelsis* and the conclusion.[141]

The Morning Scriptures

The fixed psalms,[142] accompanied by prayers, include:

Psalm 99, 'Cry out with joy to the Lord', with the refrain: 'Glorify the Lord, all the whole earth. O giver of light, O Lord, we lift up glory to thee.'
Psalm 90, 'He who dwells in the shelter of the most high', the Sunday refrain of which is: 'When the creator established the light the angels wondered at it. And when it shineth forth each morning let them and us give him glory.'
Psalm 112, 'Praise, O servants of the Lord, Praise the name of the Lord!';[143] weekday refrain: 'Glory to him who created the light', and on Sundays: 'Glory becometh thee, O God, for thou art the Creator of the light.'[144]

Psalm 92, 'The Lord is King, with majesty enrobed', is included under the same doxology as psalms 148–50 and 116. The praise psalms have no refrains but conclude with 'Glorify the Lord, all the whole earth. O Giver of light, O Lord, even to thee do we lift up glory.'

The psalms are clearly appropriate to the time, and some are found in other traditions; psalm 99 as a morning psalm in the West, psalm 90 is shared only with the Maronite Sunday *safro*. Psalm 112 is found in the Syrian, Antiochene and (some) Tikritian ferial offices,[145] and psalm 92 in the old Roman Sunday

141 *Lelya-Sapra*, pp. 404–6.

142 See *ESDO*, pp. 103–4, 165–7.

143 Includes 'From the rising of the sun to its setting, praised be the name of the Lord!'

144 *ESDO*, pp. 104, 166.

145 See Mateos, ' Les matines chaldéennes, maronites et syriennes', *OCP*, **26** (1960), 51–73.

Lauds. All this only shows that widely dispersed Christians have often opted for the same themes in the psalms they have picked for particular times of day.

The most ancient part of *sapra* must be psalms 148–50 and 116. Psalm 99 is a sort of invitatory, 90 is difficult to explain but 103 is chosen for its reference to light. The solemn intonation of psalm 92, 'The Lord is King, with majesty enrobed', is obviously resurrectional, but also extended to weekdays.[146] The refrains appear to be very ancient. The order of the psalms has a certain logic. After the invitatory, three psalms in order with the themes of hope in the Creator (90), the light of creation (103), and the majesty of God who is over all (112). Then the resurrection psalm 92 and the praise psalms.

After the *onita d-sapra* and hymn of light, the morning praise continues, on feasts, with the Daniel 3 canticle, *Benedicite*, a Paschal vigil canticle in which all creation praises the Creator. This canticle is one of the oldest parts of *sapra* as is the weekday use of psalm 50, the *Miserere*,[147] a prayer for forgiveness that God's people may offer right worship.

Prayer and Hymnody in the Morning

The prayers that accompany the sunrise psalms have the creation of the light as their common theme. On Sundays the psalms are preceded by a prayer commencing 'Enlighten us, O my Lord, with thy light, and gladden us by thy coming'.[148] The weekday prayer also reflects the theme of creation.[149] The prayer after psalm 99 speaks of 'lifting up glory and praise' on weekdays and the Sunday one refers to God as the light of all creatures.[150] The daily prayer of psalm 90 refers to God as protector, 'Glorious, O my Lord, is the great and confident hope of thy Godhead, and high and exalted is the wondrous refuge of thy Majesty'.[151] One of two prayers follows psalms 103 and 112 on Sunday. For example:

> Thou, O my Lord, art the Creator of light in thy loving kindness, and thou orderest the darkness in thy wisdom, and enlightenest creation with thy glorious light.[152]

[146] *Lelya-Sapra*, pp. 416–17.

[147] Ibid., p. 417.

[148] *ESDO*, p. 164; The first prayer of the morning office, that preceding it concludes the cathedral vigil.

[149] Ibid., p. 103.

[150] Ibid., pp. 103–4, 165.

[151] Ibid., p. 104.

[152] Ibid., p. 166.

On Sundays the psalmody closes with this prayer:

> To thee, O Christ, the true Light, the glorious Brightness who art of the Father, who wast revealed and didst shine forth in the world, for the renewal and salvation of our nature, in the first fruits which are of us, we lift up praise, and honour, and confession, and worship, at all times, Lord of all ...[153]

The weekday prayer, although entitled 'prayer of the *Lakhu Mara*', rounds off the cosmic praise of psalms 148–50 and 116.[154]

The ecclesiastical poetry at *sapra* commences with the *'onita d-sapra*, a poetic piece derived from a psalm response. At *sapra* it only occurs on feasts, on weekdays *Lakhu Mara* is sung instead. The psalm verses used are from psalm 99.[155] Like all *'onyata*, it accompanied a procession from the sanctuary with incense.[156] The most often repeated texts are clearly Morning Prayers:

> At the early dawn of the morning we glorify thee, O Lord, For thou art the saviour of all creatures ... Give us, in thy compassion, that towards which we make our way, that we may arrive according to thy will in peace ...[157]

We note the themes of (a) praise of God by all creatures, and (b) the implied eschatological destination.

One of two hymns of light, *nuhra*, attributed to Mar Ephrem and Mar Narsai, now follow.[158] The psalm verse which opens that of Ephrem (from psalm 96) appears to have been a refrain; 'Light shines forth for the just and joy for the upright of heart'. The hymn is also found in Maronite use, which may indicate a very ancient tradition. Some excerpts are given:

> Jesus our Lord, the Christ, hath shone forth to us from the bosom of his Father. He has come and taken us out of darkness, and hath enlightened us with his excellent light.
>
> The day hath shone forth on the sons of men, and the power of darkness hath fled ... He has caused his glory to shine forth in the world, and hath enlightened the lowest depths.[159]

---

[153] Ibid., p. 167; and see Mateos, *Lelya-Sapra*, 71, n. 1.

[154] *ESDO*, p. 104.

[155] *Lelya-Sapra*, p. 71, n. 2.

[156] Ibid., 375–6.

[157] *ESDO*, pp. 106–7.

[158] *Lelya-Sapra*, pp. 72–5.

[159] *ESDO*, pp. 167–8.

The hymn well expresses the theology of the morning office. Light after darkness represents redemption by Christ whose second coming is awaited in hope. The hymns are preceded by a prayer:

> In the glorious light, O my Lord, of thy revelation, and in the joyful Epiphany of thy coming, which all creatures whom thou hast created look for, and hope for, and expect.[160]

We again note the praise of God by all creation in addition to the other themes listed.

The prayer that concludes the *Benedicite* and precedes the Great Doxology nicely sums up the themes of the former:

> We glorify, and exalt, and sing hallelujahs, and praises to the hidden and sacred Nature, blessed and incomprehensible, of thy glorious Trinity, and thy lovingkindness to our race we are bound to confess, worship, and glorify at all times, Lord of all . . .[161]

These themes of cosmic praise are taken up by the *teshbohta* that follows the psalm, and which is intimately connected with it.[162] The *teshbohta* at this point on feasts is the *Gloria in Excelsis*, another widely found ancient morning hymn, continuing similar themes to those of the *Benedicite*.[163]

As at *ramsha*, the morning service closes with the Trisagion, preceded on weekdays by a prayer for peace.[164] A daily *karozutha* was known to Gabriel Qatraya, who mentioned that such litanies at the evening and morning offices were not used in monasteries because monks were not clergy.[165] The first concluding prayer, 'O Compassionate one, whose name is holy', is the prayer of the Trisagion, and calls on God to make his people holy temples as they prepare for the day,[166] The prayers said by different priests, as at *ramsha*, lead to the *huttama* that commends the needs of the faithful to God.[167]

On weekdays, except in Lent, the office of the martyrs follows the prayer of dismissal. The fixed strophes of the *'onita d-sapra* are then chanted (see above) and the office is brought to a close with the priests's prayers and *huttama*.[168]

---

[160] Ibid., p. 167.

[161] Ibid., p. 170.

[162] *Lelya-Sapra*, pp. 95–6, 379, 419; text: *ESDO*, p. 105.

[163] *Lelya-Sapra*, p. 418.

[164] *ESDO*, p. 106.

[165] *Lelya-Sapra*, pp. 418–23.

[166] Ibid., pp. 78–9; text: *ESDO*, pp. 171–2.

[167] *Lelya-Sapra*, pp. 79–81.

[168] Ibid., pp. 98–100.

The *huttama* given by MacLean is a very suitable ending to the type of office that we have described:

> Bestow, O our Lord and our God, in thy lovingkindness, at this morning time, salvation to the oppressed, release to prisoners ... healing to the sick ... pardon to sinners ...[169]

It is reasonable to associate the idea of emerging from the darkness of night with the risen Christ at sunrise, with prayer that others, in 'darkness' of other kinds, might be given enlightenment and release.

Conclusions

I *The Structures of the Offices*

1 Chaldean Vespers has psalmody in course distinct from the overnight recitation of the whole Psalter.
2 The opening psalmody is carried out with the veil of the sanctuary closed. The opening of the veil and the procession to the *bema* mark the beginning of the cathedral service.
3 As with Egeria and the light ceremony that survives in the Byzantine Liturgy of the Presanctified Gifts, the light comes from within the sanctuary as a triumphal emergence of Christ the true light.
4 The tripartite intercessions at Vespers are those otherwise used only at the Eucharist and at baptisms.
5 The Sunday vigil, *qale d'shahra*, again stresses watchfulness, and uses canticles associated with Easter.
6 The morning office, *sapra*, looks for the new light. It anciently began with a procession to the *bema*, to celebrate the risen Christ.

II *The texts*

1 Opening prayers at Vespers are for compassion to sinners, and victory over enemies. Final prayers look for the coming kingdom.
2 Night prayers seek illumination and to be able to walk blamelessly; with some emphasis on being wakefulness.
3 The morning office praises God the Creator for the light; the fixed psalms reflect these themes and hymns, especially the *nuhra* of Ephrem, sing of meeting the risen Lord in the new light of day.

[169] Full text: *ESDO*, p. 108.

III *The commentator, etc.*

1 For Qatraya and others, the procession at Vespers signifies Christ, the lights represent the first and second comings, and incense the love of God.
2 Qatraya's day is 'evening and morning', for the sun of justice destroys the power of darkness. He speaks of the 'evening that precedes the night of the Lord' who rises at the fourth watch of that night, and also of 'every evening, which is the beginning of the day'.
3 The intercessions are interpreted baptismally, and *qale d'shahra* is all about watchfulness and the coming new creation.

The thrust of the Chaldean office moves into the night at *ramsha*, continues through the night-watch of *lelya*, to celebrate the resurrection at *qale d-shahra*. Finally looking beyond earthly worship to the consummation of all things, it comes to the triumphant climax of *sapra* at sunrise, the morning praise of the Chaldean liturgical tradition.

CHAPTER 9

The West Syrian and Maronite Traditions

Much of our treatment of these traditions will derive from Mateos' comparative study of Matins in these three traditions.[1] We should also note than in spite of Latinization of the eucharistic liturgy, the Maronite offices exhibit characteristics that may well be those of a more ancient stratum of the West Syrian tradition.[2] West Syrian texts below are largely from the edition of the ferial Breviary or *Shimo* edited by Dom Bede Griffiths. The Syriac version of this, *Kthobo Daslutho Shimtho*, is the basic book used in India. The festal material from the *Penqitho* is represented by material from the four-volume work of Francis Acharya which includes many newly composed texts.[3]

Table 1 Syrian/Maronite Vespers

West Syrian	Maronite
Introductory	**Introductory Prayer**
Common Beginning	Common Beginning
Introductory Prayer	Introductory Prayer
Psalm 50 with *enjane* or variable psalm with canon	Alleluia with refrains
	Prayer, psalm 50, hymn
Central Part	
Preparatory Prayer	Preparatory Prayer
Evening psalms (140, 141, 118.105–17 & 116)	Evening psalms (140, 141, 118.105–17 & 116)
Sedro	*Soghito*
Incensation	*Sedro*
1st Qolo	*Qolo of Incense*
Prayer of Incensation	Incensation
'Etro	*'Etro*
2nd Qolo	*2nd Qolo*

[1] J. Mateos, 'Les matines chaldéennes, maronites et syrienne', *OCP*, **26** (1960), 51–73, 66.

[2] Taft, *Liturgy of the Hours*, p. 240.

[3] Bede Griffiths (ed.), *The Book of Common Prayer of the Syrian Church* (Vagamon: Kurisumala Ashram, nd.), henceforth Griffiths; Francis Acharya (ed.), *Prayer with the Harp of the Spirit*, 4 vols. (Kurisumala Ashram, 1983), henceforth Acharya.

Bo'utho	NT Lessons
Hullala	
Gospel	*Bo'utho*
Korozutho	
Prayer	
Concluding Part	
Trisagion	Trisagion
Short Prayer	
Lord's Prayer	Lord's Prayer *et al.*
Huttamo	*Huttamo*

It has been suggested that the original shape of Maronite Vespers was:

Monastic Psalmody (in course)
Cathedral Psalmody (fixed – psalms 140 etc.)
Office of Light
Rite of Incense[4]

Syrian ferial Vespers commences with the *slûto d-sûrôyo*, the introductory prayer to the office. On Sundays and feasts the prayer is variable and is followed by either a psalm with *quqliûn* (a form of responsorial psalm) and *kurôko* (a hymnic verse of two strophes intercalated with the *Gloria Patri*),[5] or by psalm 50 with *'enyôno*. The latter is another poetic refrain, which may have developed from a very simple chanted response.[6] Psalm 50 is found as early as the tenth/eleventh century, and its introduction as a regular penitential beginning to the office may be due to monastic ascetic influences.[7]

A Maronite feature is this Alleluia with refrains before psalm 50:

> Halleluia, Halleluia, Halleluia, Glory to you, O God (x 3).
> Have pity on us and save us, in this world, in the next, and in both!
> Have pity on us! Grant health and expectation to the souls who pray to you with psalms (*mazmûré*), halleluias and prayers ...[8]

[4] P.E. Gemayel, 'La structure des Vêpres Maronite', *Orient Syrien*, **9** (1964), 105–34, 128.

[5] J. Puyade, 'Les Heures canoniales Syriennes et leur composition', *Orient Syrien*, **3** (1958), 401–28, 407–9.

[6] Ibid., 404.

[7] Gemayel, op. cit., 113.

[8] Ibid., 110.

Clearly a conclusion to psalmody just as the prayer that precedes opens that psalmody,[9] it has remained after the recitation of the psalms themselves has vanished. We have then, a clear indication of variable, monastic-style psalmody, in the typical position: that is, prefacing the cathedral office with its fixed psalmody centred on psalm 140.

The central part of this service contains the most ancient strata of material. We note that in both forms the group of fixed evening psalms comprises 140, 141, 118.105–17 and 116. The remainder of the central part is largely made up of the complex of hymnic pieces associated with the rite of incensation. The *Sughitho* is a poetic text composed of a verse of 16 syllables, formed into four groups of four. It often concludes the psalmody and precedes the incense rite at Vespers, the Night Office and Matins.[10]

There is a highly developed rite for the offering of incense.[11] The texts used, the *prooemion* and the *sedro*, are frequently referred to together as *hussoyo* which means expiation. This gives a clear idea as to the purpose of the incense rite, an expiatory offering of the incense. In the oldest extant manuscripts, from the seventh to ninth centuries, the texts are called *sedra d-besme*: that is, *sedro* of perfumes or incense.[12] There is a clear connection between forgiveness of sins and the incense rite.

As time passed, the incense ritual of Vespers took over from that of the lamp, which remained only as semi-hidden reference in some the texts. In fact the Eastern vesperal tradition generally, but especially the West Syrian/ Maronite tradition, becomes dominated by the theme of the evening offering of incense more than thanksgiving for light. The rite of incensation was interpreted as an offering for the remission of sins from an early period. The *sedro* became the prayer for imposition of incense, but before the tenth century[13] there appears to have been a more ancient 'prayer of perfumes' which was displaced until after the incensation.

In a study of Maronite Vespers, Gemayel also stressed the expiatory role of the incense ceremony. In the 1624 *shimta* there was a rubric directing the priest to make a sign of the cross over the faithful at this point saying: 'Peace to you; that your pardon, Lord, may be on our souls, and on the souls of our Fathers'.[14]

Preceding and following the incense rite, the West Syrian/Maronite Vespers has variable pieces called *qôlo* or *qûbôlo*. These are groups of four or five poetic

---

9 Ibid.

10 Ibid., 117–18.

11 Taft, *Liturgy of the Hours*, p. 242.

12 J. Mateos, '*Sedres* et prières connexes dans quelques anciennnes collections', *OCP*, **28** (1962), 239–87, 251.

13 Mateos, '*Sedres*', 274.

14 Gemayel, op. cit., 123–4.

strophes, sometimes interspersed with psalm verses,[15] they often refer to the incense offering of Aaron (Leviticus 16.12) or Zechariah (Luke 1.5ff.),

In this central section of the vesperal office we find a considerable divergence between the West Syrian and Maronite traditions. The former has no readings from scripture except a Gospel reading at festal Vespers, while the Maronite has a series of readings from the Old and New Testaments, preceded by a chant, *mazmuro*, which is a kind of responsorial psalm on the theme of the feast occurring.[16] An Alleluia chant, the *hullolo*, follows the readings in the Maronite and precedes the Gospel in the West Syrian rite.[17]

Another poetic piece, the *bo'utho* or 'supplication' follows the readings in the Maronite use and precedes the Alleluia verse in the West Syrian.[18] In Maronite use, these texts may follow the Gospel reading because that use possesses no litanic prayer of the deacon such as the West Syrian *korûzûtho*.[19] The West Syrian ferial form has no Gospel reading, and so the *bo'utho* is effectively the last text of the service except for the concluding formulae.

Taft tells us that, in West Syrian festal usage, the *korûzûtho* is replaced in Orthodox usage by another poetic chant, a *ma'nito* (responsory) or a *teshmeshto* (gloria chant), the Catholics retaining the litanic form.[20] Griffiths does not give an example of this formula, Francis Acharya supplies a text for Sunday vespers (i.e., Saturday night) which, not surprisingly, emphasizes the resurrection but is otherwise largely a general intercession for the needs of God's people.[21]

Compline (*Soutoro*)[22]

This service is normally attached directly to Vespers and does not use the festal texts of the major offices such as Vespers. The order is as follows:

Initial Prayer
Psalm 4 with strophe (*eqbo*)[23]

---

[15] Puyade, op. cit., 409.

[16] Puyade, op. cit., 408; Gemayel, op. cit., 128–31.

[17] Taft, *Liturgy of the Hours*, pp. 242–3.

[18] Ibid.

[19] Gemayel, op. cit.

[20] Taft, *Liturgy of the Hours*, p. 243.

[21] Acharya, vol. 1, pp. 216–17.

[22] Griffiths, pp. 7–10 and *passim*.

[23] This psalm is mentioned by A. Raes, 'Les complies dans les rites orientaux', *OCP*, **17** (1951), 133–45, 142; not found in Griffiths.

Proemium and *Sedro* of Repentance
Qolo
Bo 'utho
Psalms 90 and 120 with responses
Teshbohta[24]
Conclusion with Creed and blessing

Maronite Compline includes psalm 50 with the initial prayers, psalm 90 is intercalated with verses, and the *proemium, sedro*, etc. follow rather than precede the psalms.[25] The dominant theme of both offices is penitential.

Matins (*lilyo* and *safro*)

Matins of the West Syrian/Maronite tradition has been rather more extensively studied than Vespers, especially in Jean Tabet's study of the Maronite office.[26] Tabet points out that the Maronite *shîmto* differs from the Syrian *shîmo* in that the latter is purely ferial and does not contain a Sunday office.[27] The Maronite book not only possesses a Sunday office, it has not been influenced by the Byzantine cycle of eight tones, the *octoechos*.[28] The Maronite *shîmto* places Vespers (*ramsho*) before Compline (*suttoro*). Then follows *lilyo*, the night office together with *safro*, the morning office; the Lesser Hours are placed after that.[29] Some of these features are found elsewhere, but the Maronite lack of the *octoechos*, its inclusion of a Sunday office in the weekly cycle, and the clear indication that the liturgical day started at Vespers, would all argue that a more primitive tradition was retained.

Schemata of the various forms of the West Syrian morning offices have been compiled by Juan Mateos,[30] the following is an attempt at a simplified synopsis of this:

[24] A poetic arrangement of biblical verses, again only mentioned in Raes.

[25] Raes, 'Les complies'.

[26] Jean Tabet, *L'Office Commune Maronite* (Kaslik, Lebanon: Bibliothèque de l'Université Saint-Esprit, 1972), henceforth Tabet.

[27] Griffiths provides a Sunday office (pp. 311–51) from the Pambakuda (Kerala) edition of the *Penqitho* or festal Breviary (pp. xiv–xv).

[28] Tabet, p. 4. An octonal system exists among the West Syrian but only from around eleventh century, see Aelred Cody, OSB, 'The Early History of the Octoechos in Syria', in N.G. Garsoïan, T.F. Mathews, and R.W. Thomson (eds), *East of Byzantium: Syria and Armenia in the Formative Period* (Washington, DC: Dumbarton Oaks, 1982), pp. 89–113, p. 90.

[29] Tabet, p. 6.

[30] J. Mateos, 'Les matines chaldéennes, maronites et syriennes', *OCP*, **26** (1960), 51–73.

Table 2 Sunday Matins

Maronite	**Antioch**	**Tikrit**
Lilyo		
a) Midnight		
Ps. 133 etc. & verses	Ps. 133 etc. & verses	Ps. 133 etc. & verses
b) Stations *(qawme)*	**Periods *('eddone)***	**Periods *('eddone)***
1. *hussoyo, bo'utho, madrosho*	2 pss. Then *hussoyo, qolo, etc.*	Psalms, 2 Canticles
	poetry, *madrosho*	
2.as above	as above	as above
	Gospel, pss. 148–50, poetry	
3. as above	as above	as above
	Magnificat & ***memro***	
c) Fourth *qawmo*		
Benedicite	*Sedro*	
Sogith	*Magnificat*	
Hussoyo & mazmuro	Ps. 132, *hussoyo*	
Pss. 148–50, 116	Pss. 148–50, 116	
Bo'utho, madrosho	***Bo'utho***	
	Great Doxology	
Safro		
Magnificat		
Pss. 62, 90, 50	Pss. 50, 62, 18	Ps. 50
Nuhro & *Benedicite*	Isaiah cant. & *Magnificat*	Dan cants. & *Magnificat*
Pss. 148–50 & 11	Pss. 148–50 & 116	Pss. 148–50 & 116
Poetry, readings	Beatitudes, *hussoyo*	*hussoyo*, Beatitudes
Bo'utho	*qolo, bo'utho*, Gospel	*hullolo*, Gospel, poetry

Table 3 Weekday Matins

Maronite	**Antioch**	**Tikrit**
Lilyo		
a) Midnight		
as Sunday	as Sunday	as Sunday
b) Stations or Periods		
1. *hussoyo, bo'utho, madrosho*	*'eqbo, hussoyo, bo'utho*	Psalms, Cant. Poetry
2. do.	do.	Ps. 50, poetry, pss. 148 etc.
3. do.	do.	Pss., ps. 62, *hussoyo*, etc.
c) Fourth *qawmo*		
Benedicite & poetry	*Sedro, Magnificat*, Ps 132	*Magnificat*
Pss. 148 etc	Pss. 148 etc.	*hussoyo*, poetry
Bo'utho, madrosho	*Bo'utho*, Great Doxology	Great Doxology
d) Safro		
	Ps. 50	Pss. 5 & 50
		Psalmody
Magnificat	*Magnificat*	Daniel Canticles, *Magnificat*
Ps. 62	Ps. 62	
Nuhro		
Pss. 148–50/116, with strophes	Pss. 112, 148 etc. with strophes	Ps. 112 etc (As Antioch)
Sugitho, hussoyo	*hussoyo, qolo*	*hussoyo*, poetry
Bo'utho	*Bo'utho*	

Common to all these forms is an invitatory service called in Syriac *m'irono* (awakening),[31] and, for convenience, referred to in the schemata as 'midnight'. The normal introductory prayers precede the unit, the core of which is psalm 133.

[31] Tabet, p. 63.

Table 4 Lilyo

Lent	**Advent**
(Ancient Midnight Office)	
1. Pss. 3 etc. (as above)	Pss. 3 etc. (as above)
(Ancient Morning Office)	
2. Periods (*'eddone*)	Periods (*'eddone*)
a) Psalmody, Exodus canticle	Psalmody
Hussoyo, poetry, *madrosho*	
b) Psalmody	
Ps. 50	Ps. 50
Hussoyo, poetry	*Hussoyo*, Poetry
Pss. 148–50/116, *madrosho*	Pss 148–50/116, *madrosho*
(Nocturn and Second Morning Office added from Antioch)	
c) Psalmody	Psalmody
Ps. 62, *hussoyo*, poetry	
Magnificat	*Magnificat*
Hussoyo, poetry	*Hussoyo*, poetry
Great Doxology	Great Doxology
Safro	
Pss. 5 and 50	Ps. 50
Psalmody	Ps. 99
Pss. 112, 148 etc.	Pss. 112, 148 etc.
Hussoyo, poetry	*Hussoyo*, poetry

The major part of *lîlyo* is made up of three units of similar structure called *qawme* (stations), or *'eddone* (periods).[32] In Maronite use these each comprise the complex group of poetic texts known as *hussoyo* (i.e., *prooemium, sedro, qolo* of incense and *'eqbo*), followed by a *bo'utho*, and a *madrosho* (a doctrinal poem).[33] The *hussoyo*, as we have seen, was originally largely concerned with a propitiatory offering of incense, later this becomes linked with prayer for the dead, and the intercession of the saints, hence the title given in the schemata. The rites seem to totally lack psalmody, which appears to have been entirely replaced by these poetic compositions.[34] That these are late appears to be shown by the fact that prior to the fifteenth century, ferial Matins appears to

[32] In the schemata above, Mateos uses *qawme* as the Maronite word, and *'eddone* as that used in the Antiochene festal and Tikrit books; Griffiths however, uses *qawme* for Sundays as well as ferias (e.g., pp. 325, 331).

[33] Mateos, 'Les matines', 55.

[34] Ibid., 57.

have comprised only the *m'irono*, two or three poetic pieces, one or two *qale* and a *bo'utho*.[35] Some of the chants show that the poetic material replaces an ancient psalmody: for example, 'In the middle of the night, David rises to sing (psalms) and says: Have pity on me, Lord God'.[36] The Tikrit rite does show evidence of psalmody, but not necessarily in a tripartite grouping. The differences between the three are the more striking if we compare the Lenten feria given above with an Advent feria:[37]

Tikrit was like the East Syrian rite in inserting a Vigil on Sundays between the night and morning offices (number [1] in the Sunday scheme on page 72, beginning with the Exodus canticle). In the original arrangement the core of the night office was probably lengthy psalmody, replaced at a much later date by the poetic pieces that make up the *qawme/'eddone* groups.[38]

Each Maronite *qawmo* is preceded by a variable prayer that is usually concerned with the night office seen as celebrating the light that shines in the darkness. On the other hand, prayers that once punctuated the psalmody are no longer used, though Mateos has studied some of them (see below).

The final part of *lilyo*, sometimes referred to as the fourth *qawmo*, employs the group of psalms 148–50/116, which are repeated as part of *safro*. These psalms are widely regarded as a most ancient part of daily Morning Prayer,[39] so why is the unit repeated at the end of the night part of the office? The most likely explanation is that *Lilyo* was originally the monastic night office and *safro* the cathedral morning service.[40] The Syrian cursus has always lacked a Prime or First Hour, which may be connected with this.

Tabet concurred and noted that the so-called 'fourth *qawmo*' of the Maronite use included material such as the Daniel 3 canticle *Benedicite*, most often associated with early morning and the Paschal vigil.[41] The uses of Antioch and Tikrit have the *Magnificat* here, and it is repeated in *safro*, while the Maronite *safro* only has it that office.

Groups of poetic texts precede the praise psalms in the Maronite fourth *qawmo*, which includes a morning offering of incense. The praise psalms are normally found as the climax of the morning office, and, as already mentioned, are duplicated in all three forms of the West Syrian complex of *lilyo* and *safro*. The Antiochene and Tikriti orders of *lilyo* add the Great

---

35 Ibid.

36 4th *qawmo* of Wednesday in 1890 Maronite *Shimto*; Mateos, 'Les matines', 62.

37 Ibid., 67.

38 Ibid., 68, 72.

39 See W. Jardine Grisbrooke, 'The Laudate Psalms: A Footnote', *SL*, **20** (1990), 162–84.

40 Mateos, 'Les matines', 58.

41 Tabet, pp. 171–5.

Doxology.[42] Once again it is clear that *lilyo* was originally a monastic Morning Prayer, no doubt starting earlier than that of the secular churches. The duplication may have arisen from the custom of monks becoming bishops and combining a monastic household and its rite with a cathedral order of Morning Prayer.[43] Relics of the two services as separate appear to have survived until the early modern period. Tabet relates the accounts of seventeenth- and eighteenth-century visitors who describe the Maronite people as going to church first in the evening, spending another two hours in church at midnight, and finally returning in the early morning to 'continue the office'.[44]

In *safro* proper the common element is the group of psalms 148–50 and 116. Another constant is their being prefaced by psalm 50, preceded or followed by psalm 62 (though not in Tikrit). The psalms and canticles are followed by various poetic elements, so we have a relatively simple structure of morning vigil psalmody leading to the sunrise praise psalms and hymnody, which latter (especially in the *bo'utho* form) includes intercession. Antioch and Tikrit also include a gospel reading on Sundays, seemingly a resurrection text.[45]

The Word of God

Most of the scriptural texts that we find in the West Syrian offices are psalms and biblical canticles. The Vespers psalms group of 140, 141, 118.105–17 and 116 is also found in the East Syrian rite (see p. 122) which may well be a sign of its antiquity. Psalm 140, the psalm most frequently chosen for evening worship in the Christian East, and said by Chrysostom to be recited every day and known by heart,[46] is followed by psalm 141 as is also the case in Byzantine tradition. The short doxological psalm 116 rounds off this group, but the Syrian traditions differ from the Byzantine by using a stanza of psalm 118 instead of 129. The stanza, comprising verses 105–17, was chosen because of verse 105 'Your word is a lamp for my steps and a light for my path'.[47]

As already mentioned above, not all the Syrian rites of Vespers now provide any other scriptural elements other than short verses with the hymnody. The Maronite lectionary printed at Quzhaya, Lebanon, in 1841, provides six readings in all: three from the Old Testament, two from the New, Acts and

[42] See e.g., Griffiths, pp. 20–21.

[43] See Tabet, p. 174, and Mateos 'Les matines', 58–9.

[44] Tabet, p. 102.

[45] E.g., Acharya, vol. 1, pp. 248–9; John 20.1–18.

[46] Stressed by Puyade, op. cit., 402.

[47] Puyade, op. cit., 403, and Gemayel, op. cit., 115.

Epistles, and, finally, a Gospel reading. But it is not at all clear as to whether this was ever the normal weekday practice. Elsewhere these six readings were found at the eucharistic celebration.[48] Such a group of readings appears to have been a kind of vesperal-vigil. Although West Syrian/Jacobite usage is to read the Gospel of the Sunday at Sunday Vespers,[49] the revised use of Francis Acharya provides an alternative resurrection gospel.[50]

The psalms selected for *soutoro* or Compline are psalm 90, 'He who sits under the protection of the Most High' and psalm 120, 'I have lifted up my eyes to the hills, from whence will come my help'.[51] Both are prayers for the protection of the God who 'neither slumbers nor sleeps'. Psalm 120 is not so widely found elsewhere, but psalm 90 is almost universal. Psalm 4 mentioned by Raes, with its exhortation to 'ponder on your bed and be still' is an obvious choice, frequently found elsewhere. It is not mentioned by Griffiths.

The *m'irono* features psalm 133:

> Bless the Lord, all you servants of the Lord,
> You who stand by night in the house of the Lord,
> Lift up your hands to the holy place and bless the Lord,
> The Lord bless you from Sion, he who made heaven and earth.[52]

This psalm was also used as an invitatory to the nocturnal part of the office in the ancient rite of Constantinople (see pp. 95ff), and, on certain days appeared in the Coptic and Ethiopian offices, it is mentioned by John Chrysostom.[53] The uses of Antioch and Tikrit follow this with the last stanza of psalm 118, and psalm 116 as a doxology. The verses from psalm 118 are full of longing for the Lord's mighty help. The rite of Tikrit also prefaces the whole group of psalms with psalm 3, a very frequently found night invitatory.[54]

Contemporary books say nothing of a recitation of the Psalter in course at any of the offices, even the modern edition of Francis Acharya makes no attempt at wholesale replacement of the poetic texts by such a recital of the Psalter. Evidence of a one-time recitation of the Psalter is found in some manuscripts such as the Maronite ones listed by Gemayel.[55] The following allows for the Psalter to be recited in a day:

---

[48] Gemayel, op. cit., 130–32.

[49] Griffiths, p. 317.

[50] See above.

[51] Griffiths, pp. 7–9.

[52] Translation as given in Griffiths, ibid.

[53] Tabet, p. 63.

[54] In Palestinian *hexapsalmos*, old Byzantine, Benedictine, and, on some days, old Spanish offices.

[55] Gemayel, op. cit, 111.

Safro	*Ramsho*
1st *Marmîtho*; Psalms 1–14	9th *Marmîtho*; Psalms 83–91
2nd *Marmîtho*; Psalms 15–24	10th *Marmîtho*; Psalms 92–103
3rd *Marmîtho*; Psalms 24–36	Compline
Terce	11th *Marmîtho*; Psalms 104–7
4th *Marmîtho*; Psalms 37–44	*Lîlyo*
Sext	12th *Marmîtho*; Psalms 108–17
5th *Marmîtho*; Psalms 45–55	13th *Marmîtho*; Psalms 118–30
6th *Marmîtho*; Psalms 56–67	14th *Marmîtho*; Psalms 131–43
None	15th *Marmîtho*; Psalms 144–50
7th *Marmîtho*; Psalms 68–74	
8th *Marmîtho*; Psalms 75–82	

Bar Hebraeus' arrangement is almost exactly the same,[56] so this may have been quite common. However it must have been largely confined to monasteries, and it is hardly surprising that it was replaced by poetic material. This arrangement places most of the psalmody in the evening, overnight and morning offices. There is the same tendency to complete the Psalter in course at night that we have observed elsewhere.

The Syrian offices also use some of the biblical canticles. The *Benedicite* is common to most of these series and is almost universally used at Matins. The presence of *Benedicite* towards the end of Maronite *lilyo* and at the beginning of Tikrit *safro* argues that it was originally part of the Antiochene service as well, and may well have taken the place of the *Magnificat* at the end of *lilyo* as in the Maronite rite. The Sunday Matins of Tikrit concludes each section of nocturnal psalmody with the canticles of the present Greek canon (except Deuteronomy 32), itself of Palestinian provenance.[57] This arrangement seems to be a later borrowing, but the arrangement of Tikrit Sunday *safro*; psalm 50, Daniel canticles and *Magnificat*, (psalm 18) and the praise psalms, looks like an ancient morning office.

Psalm 62 at *safro* is a psalm of watching for the dawn as we have seen, and the penitential psalm 50 is also common as a beginning of the morning office. Other elements include psalm 90 in Maronite *safro*, psalm 112 in the Antiochene ferial office, Psalm 18 and the canticle of Isaiah 42 on Sundays. The Tikrit use, already mentioned, places the Daniel canticles and the *Magnificat* between psalm 50 and psalm 18, and on weekdays placed psalm 5 before psalm 50. Psalm 112, 'Praise, you servants of the Lord ... from the

[56] Ibid. Bar Hebraeus (+1286), speaks of division of the psalter into 15 *marmyata*, Tabet, p. 106.

[57] Aelred Cody has argued that the canon only entered Syrian use with the ideal of the eight tone system, op. cit., 98–100.

rising of the sun to its setting great is the name of the Lord'[58], is not a common morning psalm but is clearly suitable. Psalm 5 is frequently found in Western offices as a morning psalm, because of the verse;

> It you who I invoke O Lord, in the morning you hear me; in the morning I offer you my prayer, watching and waiting.

It is again a vigil or watching psalm, very appropriate to early morning. Psalm 18, 'The heavens proclaim the glory of God', included in the Sunday orders of Antioch and Tikrit by Mateos, is not mentioned by Griffiths, but seems eminently suited to the Sunday resurrection theme.

Euchology and Other Texts

Gemayel thought the use of psalm 118.105 indicated an ancient service of light, and illustrated this by quoting a prayer from a Syrian Orthodox source of the ninth century, which is entitled 'Prayer at the Lighting of the Lamp at Vespers':

> Thee we adore, o thou our benefactor. Thee we praise O Light of our souls. To thee we pray, O Treasury of our petitions. As thou hast given to us in thy mercy, the lights that pass away, so also do thou grant to us thy light that does not end, so that in both worlds, we may praise, adore and glorify thee O Trinity, Father, Son and Holy Spirit ...[59]

The prayer that precedes the Vespers psalms on weekdays reads:

> Grant us, Lord God, that while our bodies rest from the labours of the day and our souls are released from worldly thoughts, we may stand in your presence with tranquillity at this time of evening and that we may offer you ceaseless praise and uninterrupted thanksgiving; that we may acknowledge your loving kindness by which you direct and rule our lives and protect and save our souls; to you we offer praise and thanksgiving, now and always and for ever.[60]

These are classical vesperal themes; arrival at the end of the day, protection for the coming night and for the whole of life, the evening is also seen as a time to enter upon 'ceaseless praise and uninterrupted thanksgiving'. Puyade gives

---

[58] Griffiths, p. 24.

[59] Gemayel, op. cit., p. 116, translation of MS Brit. Mus. Add. 14.518m, f° 88r. Also quoted by Mateos, '*Sedres*', 273, suggesting that psalm 118.105–17 was an ancient *lucernarium*.

[60] Griffiths, pp. 4–5. A freer version with a more explicit light theme ('our minds turn to you as to the inner light', instead of 'our souls are released from worldly thoughts') is in Acharya, p. 22.

another prayer to precede the evening psalms from the Mosul edition of the Penquitho (or festive Breviary):

> Hear Lord God, and give ear to the words and supplications of your worshippers. Accept our services and our prayers that we present before you as a pleasing sacrifice and pure odour. For the memory of you, set a guard on our mouths and on our lips. Do not let the Evil One dispose us to evil words. Grant instead that our tongues rejoice at all time in psalms of glory; and we will offer to you glorification and acknowledgement, Father, Son and Holy Spirit, now and unto the ages. Amen.[61]

The prayer quotes psalm 140.3–4 in praying for protection against evil and sin, thus emphasizing the other aspects of psalm 140 that commended it to Christian vesperal use from the earliest years.

Gemayel drew attention to the light theme in the *sughitho* or poetic verse that completes the evening fixed psalmody in the Maronite sources:

> Light your lamps, O brethren, for he has arrived, the Bridegroom who must come . . .[62]

> O Beam of Light, it is you who have dissipated from this darkened world the shadows of sin; you have cheered the gloomy faces of creatures so that they might contemplate your teaching. The people who sat in the shadow of death have seen the great light . . .[63]

The latter two examples not only may appear to refer to a lamp-lighting ceremony, but both contain phrases that associate the prayer with psalm 118; 'direct our steps according to your law', and 'that they might contemplate your teaching'.

A *sedro* entitled 'Prayer for the lighting of the lamp at Vespers':

> O Christ our God, through the holy apostles, you have illuminated the whole world with celestial and divine fire, and have burnt and consumed completely the thorns of sin, of error and of ignorance. Lord, shine into our souls the light of your word, and let the sun of justice shine in our hearts, darkened by the shadows of sin, of error and of ignorance; so then as we are taught by the wise teaching of your divine heralds, we may bring forth worthy fruits of penitence, and persevere in their teaching, without being led astray or unsettled, until our last breath . . .[64]

---

[61] Puyade, op. cit., 404–5.

[62] Ibid., p. 116 (Sughitho of Sunday).

[63] Before the evening psalms at Sunday Vespers.

[64] J. Mateos, 'Sedres', p. 263.

Though probably intended for a feast of apostles, it is quite clearly an evening prayer for forgiveness of sins, symbolically burnt away in the evening incense rite, and replaced by the light of Christ.

Some *prooemia* contain references to the theme of light but one of the most interesting clearly expresses absolution of sin. Other tenth- or eleventh-century texts are incense prayers of absolution:

> Glory to the Father and to the Son and to the Holy Spirit, who absolves fault and remits sin, ... we implore your mercy and pray for your goodness, Lord; grant to your servant absolution and remission of sins ...[65]

Clearly there was a long-standing tradition of the incense ceremony as a kind of bloodless sacrifice, though the presence of an intercession would seem to also connect the oblation with the other theme often linked with the use of incense, that of intercessory prayer. The theme of sacrifice is found in the poetic texts called *qolo*:

> Accept, Lord, this incense from our hands like the incense of Aaron which kept death away from the people.
> *Praise Him all you peoples.*
> May incense which your servants have offered for the satisfaction of your mercy be for our pardon and the forgiveness of our sins. etc.[66]

Similarly a Maronite text from Sunday Vespers:

> Lord that this incense offered to your majesty be accepted in the sanctuary as was the incense of Zechariah who beheld the angel who announced John: 'He will be a son for your old age and will announce the Christ.' etc.[67]

The West Syrian *bo'utho* (supplication) of Mar Jacob for Vespers on Monday (i.e., Sunday evening) is a good example of that genre:

> We call upon you, Lord our Lord, come to our help, hear our petition and have mercy on our souls.
> Lord our Lord, Lord of the Watchers and the angels, hear our petition and have mercy on our souls.
> In the evening when the light of their sun sets upon earth, may I be enlightened, Lord, to praise your creation; **may your word be a lamp to my feet**, Son of God, and in place of the sun may it give light to me, **and I will walk by it**.

---

[65] J. Mateos, 'Trois recueils anciens de Prooemia syriens', *OCP*, **33** (1967), 457–82, 462.

[66] Vespers on Tuesday in Griffiths, p. 76.

[67] Gemayel, op. cit., p. 127.

> At the time of evening the priests sang in praise; and the sacrifices (of) Moses were offered in the evening; *evening and morning the law prescribed* that sacrifices should be offered, and the priests were moved to offer praise to your godhead in the evening.
> (...)
> The evening has come upon me and has placed me in the watch of the night; be to me a sun, Lord, in the evening **and I will walk by you.**[68]

The **bold** type indicates words that echo psalm 118, with the reference in verse 105 to the word of God as a lamp and we note the desire to walk in God's commandments. The underlined words emphasize the idea of sacrifice offered evening and morning. As the community enters upon the night of watchfulness, it does so assured of the presence of the light of Christ who instructs his people in the way that they should go, and it confidently prays to watch with the angels during the night.

Gemayel provides an example of a Maronite *bo'utho* from a Sunday Vespers:

> The day is ending and gathering together its beams from the universe. The beautiful disc that gives joy to mankind has been carried off. The night appears; the darkness spreads; the earth is hidden and, with it, all semblance of the day.[69]

These texts may also be seen as versified litanies, similar in theme to the well-known 'Angel of peace' litany. Once again though, the theme of protection for the coming night is dominant, and in this case, in the prayers that effectively conclude the office (the remainder of the Maronite Vespers being the Trisagion, Lord's Prayer, Hail Mary, and Creed, followed by the *hûttômo* or final blessing). For example, in a concluding formula associated with the Trisagion:

> Lord Jesus Christ, do not close the door of your mercy in our faces, Lord; we confess that we are sinners, have mercy on us. Your love made you descend from your place to us, Lord, by whose death our death was ended; have mercy on us.[70]

This final confession of resurrection faith that leads into the invocation of the 'Holy God' expresses Vespers as entry upon a miniature repetition of the Paschal night.

The introductory prayer of Compline preceding the psalmody is for protection, rest and refreshment. The psalms are intercalated with Alleuias and poetic verses that repeat similar themes:

---

[68] Griffiths, pp. 38–9.

[69] Ibid., 132.

[70] Griffiths, p. 7.

> An evening full of peace and a night of holiness, grant us, Christ our Saviour, for you are the king of glory.
>
> Lord, let your mercy protect us and your grace rest upon our faces, and let your cross guard us from the evil one and his powers.[71]

The opening variable prayers of *lilyo* have references to rising from sleep, to being strong in watchfulness and to the night service as being a joining with the never-ending praise of the angelic hosts. This is not so much a tentative struggle to wipe sleep from the eyes, so much as an enthusiastic desire to join in eschatological joy, at least ideally.[72] A prayer with similar thrust is found as a common beginning for *lîlyo* in West Syrian usage:

> Awaken us, Lord, from our sleep in the sloth of sin that we may praise your watchfulness, ... grant us in the glorious company of the angels who praise you in heaven, to praise you and bless you in holiness ...[73]

Maronite *m'irono* has another variable prayer precede the psalms, and then there a series of variable poetic strophes in all three rites. The prayers are appropriate to the hours of darkness before morning: Sunday's prays for the grace of participating at the feast of the bridegroom who is Christ the true light, and that we may thus have our lamps lit in emulation of the wise virgins of Matthew 25.1–13.[74]

The poetic strophes also reflect the theme of watchfulness in the night. In the Maronite Sunday texts this watchfulness is associated with the careful use of that with which one has been entrusted, as in the parable of the talents (Matt. 25.14–30). They then evoke images of calming the storms of evil, for example, by instancing Christ's coming to the disciples on the lake on a stormy night. The weekday strophes tend to be more concerned with penance, while those that refer to the time of the night are likely to be the more ancient. Tuesday's begins 'On my bed I remember you, O friend of men, and in the middle of the night, I rise to give thanks for your bounty'.[75] The first strophe on Friday is found, with variations, in the West Syrian, Tikrit and Chaldean uses:

---

[71] Ibid., 7–10.

[72] Tabet, pp. 59–61.

[73] Griffiths, p. 11.

[74] Tabet, p. 64.

[75] Ibid., pp. 67, 74.

> It is right and just that we come to praise you, O our Saviour, and to re-echo, in company with the angels, the thrice-holy hymn; O God, glory be to you.[76]

Examples of similar West Syrian strophic texts are given by Mateos. For example:

> Let me awake that I may sing with the watchers, a watchful praise to you, O watchful one, who sleep not, and who are served by watchers and angels.[77]

Clearly, in all Syrian traditions, *lîlyo* was an office that once began in the middle of the night, or at least, in the small hours, a time of sleep and rest. The dominant theme is of vigilance, of watchfulness; penitential themes appear to be later, it is nocturnal praise which most characterizes these offices.[78]

Some interesting and illustrative prayers are those that may once have accompanied the psalms of the morning office. Probably once part of a general anthology, they maintain the theme of light overcoming the darkness of the night. For example:

> Gather us into your house, and visit us in your light, and lead us into your kingdom, Father ...[79]

Other prayer texts in the night office include those at the end of each *qawmo*. That of the first *qawmo* of Monday addresses Mary as 'Mother of the Sun of justice' and others pray for place in light for the departed.[80]

Texts associated with the canticle *Benedicite* are often inspired by that text:

> Lord God, you are blessed in the heights of heaven and upon the earth, in the seas and in all the abysses ...

While for Monday we find a reference to:

> Ananias and his young companion, fair and beautiful, in the furnace of ardent fire ...[81]

---

[76] Ibid., pp. 82–3.

[77] Mateos, 'Les matines', 59.

[78] Tabet, pp. 88–9; Mateos, 'Les matines', 72.

[79] J. Mateos, 'Une collection syrienne de "prières entre les marmyata"', *OCP*, **31** (1965), 53–75, 305–35; 74–5.

[80] Tabet, pp. 111–13.

[81] Ibid., pp. 124–5.

Morning strophes are often intercalated in the canticle. For example:

> Grant us, Lord, a morning of peace and a daytime of justice.[82]

Clearly the three youths in the furnace are a type of the resurrection, and the fourth *qawmo* was originally a morning office with its own offering of incense:

> O Christ, propitiatory incense, immolated upon the height of Golgotha, and made incense of expiation for sinful Adam, receive our incense and our prayer, and grant us all your mercies.[83]

When we turn to *safro* we first note the prayers that accompany the praise psalms, the primitive core of this office. Tabet gives the following from a Maronite manuscript:

> We adore you, Lord of the heavenly and earthly beings; we give thanks to you, God of spiritual and corporal beings, for you have multiplied peace in the heavens and glory on the earth ... make us worthy to worship you in spirit and in truth, for in you is our hope and it is upon you that we call, our Lord and God. Glory to you.[84]

This example of celestial praise is also reflected in the strophes accompanying the psalms. For example:

> Come, let us bow down, let us worship, celebrating and exalting our God at all times.[85]

The praise theme on Sundays is explicitly linked to the resurrection, as we see in the following example from Griffiths:

> On Sunday, the great day, God rose from the grave and gave joy to the earth and to heaven by his resurrection from among the dead.[86]

The prayers that accompany the early part of the service reflect the concern to watch in eschatological prayer like the wise virgins:

---

[82] Ibid., p. 127.

[83] Ibid., p. 152.

[84] Ibid., p. 261.

[85] Ibid., p. 269, for Tuesday.

[86] Griffiths, p. 340.

> Make us worthy, Lord God, of your morning which will not pass away, of your light which will not be dimmed and of your kingdom which will have no end, with all the righteous and the holy ones who from morning until evening have tilled your vineyard.[87]

These prayers express a longing for the eternal day symbolized by the new day beginning. The contrast between awaiting in the darkness the new light is well drawn and most attractive as we can see in another West Syrian text:

> Creator of the morning, who drive out the darkness and bring light and joy to the creation; create in us habits of virtue and drive from us all the darkness of sin; give us light and joy by the glorious rays of your grace, Lord our God, for ever.[88]

The most important thing to note is that these texts interpret the morning hour eschatologically; there is concern to express sorrow for sin on emerging from darkness, but a greater concern to see the sunrise as symbolizing the new life in Christ. The spiritual sense of the morning is emphasized in the Maronite *safro* in the hymn of light or *nuhro* attributed to St Ephrem, and similar to a form found in the Chaldean tradition:

> he is come, he takes the shadows away from us and has illuminated us with his joyous light ... our King comes in his great glory; let our lamps be lit and let us go to meet him! ... Brethren, rise, prepare to give thanks to our King and Saviour who will come in his glory and we shall rejoice in the joyful light of his kingdom.[89]

One of the last texts of the *safro*, the *bo'utho*, can be seen as the climax to the series of prayer that began at *ramsho* the previous night:

> Lord have mercy upon us on this passing morning. And on the morning which does not pass away make us to stand at your right hand ... On this morning I will sing praise to you, and on that which is to come I will magnify you; on both mornings glory to you, Lord of the two worlds.[90]

Here, in one of the most ancient forms of Syrian ecclesiastical poetry,[91] is a clear picture of morning as the climax the faithful have waited and prayed for. They sing now with joy, but that joy will be greater in the everlasting day. The

---

87 Tabet, p. 192.

88 Griffiths, p. 22.

89 Ibid., pp. 242–3.

90 Ibid., pp. 112–13, Tuesday.

91 Tabet, pp. 293–4.

Syrian Morning Prayer is complete, but it looks forward, beyond the present day and hour, to the kingdom of God whose fulfilment must always lie in the future.

The Minor Hours

The Syrian Third, Sixth and Ninth Hour services are normally combined with other services. For example, in Jerusalem, the Ninth Hour preceded Vespers and Compline, while the Third and Sixth follow Matins,[92] something similar is common in India. The services are short and now entirely made up of poetic material and prayers. The opening prayer at the Third Hour prays for cleansing through repentance, that at the Sixth prays to continue to walk in the way of God's commandments, and at the Ninth, there is a seeking for rest in the bosom of the patriarchs, Abraham, Isaac and Jacob.[93] The rest of the Third Hour is a *proemium* and *sedro, qolo* and *bo'utho* for the day of the week. Tuesday's *qolo* in Griffiths dwells on parables of watchfulness and readiness to heed the call to the heavenly banquet; watchfulness is also reflected in the *bo'utho*.[94]

The Sixth and Ninth Hours use a common *bo'utho*, the *proemium* and *sedro* and the *qolo* are proper to the day of the week and at the Ninth Hour, are to do with the departed and those of the Sixth Hour often celebrate Mary. These themes are reflected in the common *bo'utho* texts. At the Sixth Hour:

> May the memory of Mary be a blessing to us and may her prayer be a stronghold for our souls.

And at the Ninth Hour:

> Renew full of mercy, your creatures by the resurrection, your servants and your worshipers who slept in your hope.[95]

The themes of these services extend that of watchfulness, and then dwell on following God's will throughout the day, guided and upheld by the prayers of the saints, and especially the Mother of God. As the day begins to draw in, thoughts and prayers turn to the faithful departed, and so the end of all things, and thus into the contrasting of darkness and light that leads us back to

---

[92] Taft, *Liturgy of the Hours*, p. 243.

[93] Griffiths, pp. 25–7.

[94] Ibid., pp. 114–15.

[95] Ibid., pp. 26–7.

ramsho, Vespers. The traditional Western and Byzantine themes of the Holy Spirit at Terce, the cross as Sext and the death of Christ at None are not found in this system.

Conclusions

1 The traces of current psalmody found in this tradition seem to indicate that it was a nocturnal exercise and so connected with *lilyo* and *safro*.
2 The development of the incense rite as a penitential ceremony imparts such a flavour to Vespers.
3 *Lilyo* commenced in the night as a pre-dawn vigil, and was a form of monastic Morning Prayer. This explains the tendency for certain units to be duplicated in the combined *lilyo* and *safro* – which were still celebrated apart in some places as late as the seventeenth and eighteenth centuries.
4 Tikrit, at least, appears to have known a resurrection vigil on Sundays.
5 In spite of relatively late multiplication of poetic and euchological texts, the classic theme of Vespers ending the day so as to enter upon a night of prayer may still be found, as may traces of a light ceremony.
6 We also find the morning office themes of waking to watch in prayer, and giving praise to God for our share in Christ's resurrection life.
7 The morning is a time to hearken to the promise of the eternal day.

CHAPTER 10

The Daily Prayer of the Coptic and Ethiopian Churches

The Offices of the Coptic Monks

Robert Taft has described the very pure type of monastic office still used by the Coptic church.[1] These services are all constructed along the same lines: they concentrate on the recitation of the Psalter in course, and have relatively little material that is directly concerned with the time of day. In the beginning however, the monks, like the secular churches, had two services: at cockcrow, and in the evening. These had exactly the same structure:

Psalmody	12 psalms in Psalter order, with silent prayer and a collect after each
Lessons	Weekdays: Old and New Testament Sundays: Epistle or Acts, and Gospel[2]

These services, at late afternoon and before dawn, corresponded to the 'cathedral office' but the monks began their day earlier. Only on Saturday and Sunday were these services taken in common, and even then, they were really far more meditative than the community services of the peoples' churches. Pachomius called the evening office 'The Office of Six Prayers' and the six pieces of scriptures accompanied by prayers, were not necessarily from the psalms, but could be from any of the scriptures.[3]

John Cassian lived in the wilderness of Scetis between 380 and 399. He indicated that, at that time, there were only the two daily services, and no Day Hours. The monks were called to ceaseless prayer, and the two common synaxes were simply moments of spiritual nourishment. It is not known for certain when the weekday synaxes came to be taken in common, or when the evening and morning synaxes come to be supplemented by Day Hours. Secure evidence for the Day Hours is only found at the end of the ninth century.[4]

---

[1] Taft, *The Liturgy of the Hours*, pp. 249–59 and 'Praise in the Desert: The Coptic Monastic Office Yesterday and Today', *Worship*, **56** (1982), 513–36.

[2] Taft, 'Praise in the Desert', 520–21.

[3] Ibid., 526, and see my: 'The Use of the Psalter by Early Monastic Communities', *Studia Patristica*, **26** (1993), 88–94, 91.

[4] Taft, 'Praise in the Desert', 527–8; *Liturgy of the Hours*, pp. 251–2.

The present Coptic office has eight Hours: Morning, Terce, Sext, None, Eleventh Hour (Vespers) and Compline, and two that seem to be later: 'Prayer of the Veil' before bed, and a Midnight Hour of three Nocturns, and these two repeat psalms already used at the other Hours. Except for the two later services, the structure of these Hours is always the same:

Fixed Initial Prayers
Twelve psalms (ideally)
Gospel lesson
Psali (poetic refrains)
Lord have mercy (41 or 50 times)
Trisagion
Lord's Prayer
Dismissal Prayer of Absolution
Final Prayer

There is little variety, but some proper elements such as the *Gloria in Excelsis* at Morning Prayer are found.

A version of these services in English is to be found in an appendix to *The Coptic Morning Service of the Lord's Day* translated and edited by John, Marquess of Bute.[5] In this arrangement the psalms set for the Hours are as follows (LXX numbering):

Morning: 50, 1–6, 10–12, 14, 15, 18, 24, 26, 62, 66, 69, 112, 142
Terce: 19, 22–3, 25, 28–9, 33, 40, 42, 44–6
Sext: 53–4, 56, 60, 62, 66, 69, 83–6, 90, 92
None: 95–100, 109–12, 114–15
Vespers: 116–17, 119–28
Compline: 129–33, 136–7, 140–1, 145–7
Prayer of the Veil: 4, 6, 12, 24, 26, 66, 85, 90, 116–17, 122, 130–3, 137, 29
Prayer of Midnight: 3, 6, 12, 69, 85, 90, 116–17, 118 (At this office the Vesper psalms are repeated and then those of Compline, thus making a much longer office,[6] providing the three Nocturns mentioned above.)

A modern English-language Book of Hours for lay use, offers the same psalmody and prefixes psalm 50 to the psalms at all the Hours. The Prayer of the Veil is accompanied by a rubric stating that it is said in monasteries

[5] John, Marquess of Bute (trans. and ed.), *The Coptic Morning Service of the Lord's Day* (London, 1882), pp. 119–44, hereafter Bute.

[6] Bute, pp. 141, 142.

between Compline and Midnight, this last varies much more from Bute's version.[7]

Several psalms are ones that are commonly associated with particular times of day: for example, 62 is a constantly found morning psalm, and 142 is the final one of the six psalms that open Byzantine *orthros*. There would certainly appear to be some principle of selection at work here, though later ties with other non-Chalcedonian churches, such as the Syrians,[8] mean that one cannot rule out reciprocal influences. An interesting feature is the use of psalms 119–28 at Vespers and the remaining 'psalms of ascent' at Compline together with the classical evening psalm 140. As we have seen, evening use of the 'gradual psalms' appears to be a widespread phenomenon.

Alongside this office there were orders that provided for the entire Psalter to be recited every day. Two manuscripts at Deir es Suriani are summarized by Zanetti.[9] For example:

Matins, psalms 1–18	Vespers, psalms 116–17 and 119–28
Terce, psalms 19–52	Compline, 129–51[10]
Sext, psalms 53–94	Midnight, 118
None, psalms 95–115	

Vespers in this order is the only service that corresponds in any material way to the normal order. A similar order is attributed by Abu'l Barakat to the monastery of St George at Sadamant.[11] These orders often show some kind of principle of selection in operation, even while trying to provide for the praying of the complete Psalter, however they never replaced the traditional order.[12]

Besides the psalms, the Coptic monastic offices have a number of poetic and euchological texts. Many of the Troparia and Theotokia appear in Greek books, though sometimes in different places from those provided in the Coptic books.[13] The *psali* at the morning office begin with words that commence the concluding prayer of the First Hour in the Byzantine tradition: 'O Thou, the

---

[7] *The Agpeya, being the Coptic Orthodox Book of Hours* (Sts. Athanasius and Cyril of Alexandria Orthodox Publications, n.d.).

[8] E.g., The monastery of Anba Bishoi, known since the eighth century as Deir es Suriani (monastery of the Syrians).

[9] Ugo Zanetti, SJ, 'La distribution des psaumes dans l'horologion copte', *OCP*, **56** (1990), 323–69, 333–7, 357–8.

[10] The use of the apocryphal psalm 151 is common in these medieval orders.

[11] When Vansleb visited in the seventeenth century the whole Psalter was still recited. De Lacey O'Leary, *Daily Office and Theotokia of the Coptic Church* (London, 1911), pp. 35–6.

[12] Zanetti, op. cit., 362–3.

[13] O.H.E. Burmester, 'The Canonical Hours of the Coptic Church', *OCP*, **2** (1936) 78–100, 84.

true Light, Which enlightenest every man that cometh into the world'. The theme of light is continued;

> Let the thoughts of the light abound within us, and let not the darkness of passion cover us, ... In thy goodness, thou hast prepared for us the night; grant unto us this day without sin.

The verses at the Third Hour concentrate on the coming of the Holy Spirit, those at the Sixth on the passion and crucifixion, at the Ninth the focus is on Christ's death on the cross. At Vespers we find the common evening tradition of asking forgiveness of sins: 'Lord, I have sinned in thy sight like the prodigal son, but accept me, O Father for I repent ...', interspersed with verses from psalm 122, which provides the processional appendix, the *aposticha*, in the modern Byzantine rite. At Compline, there are the verses based on Isaiah 8.8ff., 'God is with us', also part of Great Compline in the Byzantine order. The verses at the midnight office stress watchfulness, and refer to the wise and foolish virgins; a very common vigil theme.[14]

The prayers misleadingly called Prayers of Absolution are prayers that 'complete' the office, 'absolve' being used in that sense. At the morning office, the first is in thanksgiving for the sun to enlighten the day, and to God who has enabled the night to be passed in peace. The light of day is prayed for as a guide into purity and truth. The prayers at Terce, Sext and None have the same themes as the *psali* of those hours, with that at None concentrating more on praying for a good death.[15] The prayer of absolution at Vespers is a prayer for rest and sleep.[16] The second, or alternative, 'We give the thanks, O our Lord, the Merciful' thanks God for granting that the people may 'see the light of evening'.[17] This appears to be a version of the Greek prayer of the first Antiphon at Vespers in the Constantinopolitan office.[18] Another prayer that could be of Greek origin is found at Compline, and prays for rest in our sleep.[19] The prayer of absolution at the midnight office, attributed to St Symeon Stylites, is a very general prayer of penance.[20] The prayer which concludes all the offices, 'O Thou, who at every time and

---

[14] For the above, Bute, pp. 121–41.

[15] Ibid., pp. 123–31.

[16] Ibid., 133; 'O my Lord Jesus Christ, my God, give me in my sleep rest for the body, and keep us from the darkness which is the cloud of sin ... Awake us for the hymn of night and morning'.

[17] Ibid., p. 134.

[18] Burmester, op. cit., 94, n. 6.

[19] Bute, pp. 138–9; Burmester, op. cit., 95–6, n. 1.

[20] Bute, pp. 143–4.

every hour art adored and glorified'[21] is also found in the present-day Byzantine Minor Hours.

Vespers retains many of the traditional themes of the evening office as elsewhere: thanksgiving for the day, for the evening light, prayer for forgiveness of sins, and a quiet night. The morning office similarly is a prayer of dawn/sunrise, thanking God for the light and praying that his people may walk in that light. The light is the light of creation re-creating the new day. The midnight office draws upon texts that emphasize watchfulness, but its themes are not nearly so developed as the evening and morning offices. It is highly likely that the original twice-daily offices of the monks were indifferent to the time of day. The later collects and hymns drew out the themes characteristically associated with night and morning: an order of prayer witnessed to by Paphnutius in the second half of the fourth century, speaking of two monks: 'they used to go to the church together daily both evening and morning'.[22]

Ethiopian Monastic Offices

The close connections between the Egyptian and Ethiopian churches implies some considerable similarities between their monastic offices. Ethiopia, however, has other, less known, traditions. The office known as the 'Horologion of the Copts' is a more or less direct translation of the office described above. Its date is not known but there was a 'copticizing' movement in Ethiopia around the fourteenth century.[23] Edited in Ge'ez (the Ethiopian liturgical language) with a translation into Russian,[24] it was discussed in Taft, and will not be examined here. It now seems to have been largely replaced by an order attributed to Abba Gyorgis Saglawi who died c.1426, and which is little more than a series of scripture lessons.[25]

Relics of the Cathedral Office in Egypt

When we turn to the Egyptian cathedral office we are on much more shaky ground, because what has survived is highly fragmented. The principal relics are

---

[21] Ibid., 124.

[22] Burmester, op. cit., 82.

[23] Habtemichael Kidane, *L'Uffico Divino della Chiesa Etiopica* (Rome: *OCA 257*, 1998), pp. 40–1, hereafter Kidane.

[24] B. Turaev, *Chasoslov Efiopskoi Tserkvi* (Saint Petersburg: Imperial Academy of Sciences, 1897).

[25] Taft, *Liturgy of the Hours*, 266–71.

the offices of the Evening and Morning Incense, and the ‘Psalmodia’. These are sung whenever the Eucharist is to be celebrated, and are distinguished by Burmester, precisely as being *sung* and not recited. Burmester outlines the full usage in which these services are combined with the monastic hours in the following manner: on non-fast days: None, Vespers, Compline, Psalmodia, Evening Offering of Incense; then Midnight Prayer, Psalmodia, Morning Prayer, Psalmodia, Morning Offering of Incense, Terce, Sext and Divine Liturgy. On fast days Vespers comes first, with None said before Liturgy. In monasteries the Prayer of the Veil follows Compline.[26] The liturgical day is perceived as running from evening to morning, whether that is from None or from Vespers, while the monastic office runs from morning (psalms beginning with psalm 1) to evening.[27]

The Offerings of Evening and Morning Incense have much the same shape, the following is an attempt to schematize Burmester's description and reconcile it with Bute's text for the Morning Offering. (Our interpretation differs in some respects from that of Taft.)

<table>
<tr><th>Evening Incense</th><th>Morning Incense</th></tr>
<tr><td colspan="2">Fixed introductory prayers</td></tr>
<tr><td colspan="2">Invitatory (according to day of week) with praise of Mary and the saints</td></tr>
<tr><td colspan="2">Putting on of Incense</td></tr>
<tr><td>Evening Prayer of Incense</td><td>Morning Prayer of Incense</td></tr>
<tr><td colspan="2">Incensation of altar, with ‘3 Small Prayers’ and Psalm verse</td></tr>
<tr><td>Prayer for Dead/for Sick</td><td>Prayer for Sick/Travellers (weekdays)
Prayer for Sacrifices (Sundays)</td></tr>
<tr><td>Vouchsafe, O Lord</td><td>Hymn of the Angels</td></tr>
<tr><td colspan="2">Trisagion</td></tr>
<tr><td colspan="2">Lord's Prayer</td></tr>
<tr><td colspan="2">Hail to Thee</td></tr>
<tr><td colspan="2">Preface to Creed</td></tr>
<tr><td colspan="2">Creed</td></tr>
<tr><td colspan="2">Blessing with candles and cross</td></tr>
<tr><td colspan="2">Solemn Kyrie eleison (Litany)</td></tr>
<tr><td></td><td>(OT Lessons on some fast days)</td></tr>
<tr><td colspan="2">Prayer of the Gospel</td></tr>
<tr><td colspan="2">Psalm verse</td></tr>
</table>

[26] O.H.E. KHS-Burmester, *The Egyptian or Coptic Church: A Detailed Description of her Liturgical Services and the Rites and Ceremonies Observed in the Administration of her Sacraments* (Cairo: Publications de la Société d'Archéologie Copte, 1967), p. 32.

[27] The Coptic church in London precedes the liturgy with the evening and morning offerings of incense (personal experience of the author).

Psalm 140.1–2 with Alleluia	Psalms 142.8 and 66.2–3 with Alleluia
Gospel lesson	Gospel lesson
Synaxarium (if no liturgy)	(Homily read on some fast days)
The Three Great Prayers and Incensation	The Three Great Prayers and Incensation
Lord's Prayer	Lord's Prayer
Three Prayers of Absolution	Three Prayers of Absolution
Veneration of cross and Gospel	Veneration of cross and Gospel
Final Blessing	Final Blessing

The fixed introductory prayers are used before all Coptic services. Although the Psalmodia immediately precedes the service, it is only at this point that the sanctuary curtain is drawn back and the altar candles lit.[28] Clearly this is seen as the actual beginning of the cathedral or public office, and we have seen this ceremonial distinction elsewhere: for example, the Chaldean rite (see pp. 123ff.). There is an elaborate ceremony of putting on incense and the prayers for Evening or Morning Incense respectively lead into the incensation. The thirteenth-century Metropolitan Michael described the priest going through the congregation with the smoking thurible, after having offered at the altar, so that they may recollect and repent of their sins, and then he prays that those sins may be forgiven.[29]

There then follow three 'small prayers' (Burmester) for the church universal, for the Patriarch and for the local church, during which the priest censes the altar.[30] Outside the sanctuary, the priest continues incensing saying two psalm verses reflecting the theme of worship in the Temple of God.[31] This is completed by a few verses in honour of Mary.

At the Evening Offering, these are prayers for the departed, travellers or the sick according to season.[32] Burmester says that the people then say 'Vouchsafe,

[28] Burmester, *Egyptian Church*, p. 35, and f.5.

[29] G. Winkler, 'L'aspect pénitentiel dans les offices du soir en Orient et en Occident', in *Liturgie et Rémission des Péchés* (20th Conférence Saint-Serge 1973, Rome: Edizioni Liturgiche, 1975), pp. 272–93, 282.

[30] Burmester, *Egyptian Church*, pp. 37, 324–5.

[31] Psalm 5.8: 'But I through the greatness of your love have access to your house. I bow down before your holy temple, filled with awe.'
Psalm 137.1b–2a: 'In the presence of the angels I will bless you. I will adore before your holy temple.'

[32] Burmester, *Egyptian Church*, pp. 37–8 and n. 7; Bute, pp. 12–14.

Lord, to keep us this day without sin', the well-known evening prayer *kataxioson*, whilst at the morning office, the Hymn of the Angels is appointed: 'Glory be to God in the heights', an ancient morning hymn.

The Trisagion, Lord's Prayer and the hymn to Mary are the same in both. During the Creed the people are incensed, and after a blessing with a cross with (preferably) three candles, there is a solemn *Kyrie eleison* accompanied by cymbals.[33]

At certain fasting times the altar candles are now extinguished, the sanctuary veil closed and prophetic lessons are read.[34] This may be a relic of a public service that had an instruction tacked on it. Unlike many others, the early Egyptian church made ample provision for readings.

The prayer of the gospel and a psalm verse for the day, introduce a procession to read the Gospel. After the Gospel the Synaxarium (a form of martyrology) may follow. A homily is read in the mornings of fast days.[35] 'The Three Great Prayers' are a wide-ranging intercession duplicated at the liturgy.[36] At the end of the prayers, the priest incenses the people, and the clergy; all then say the Lord's Prayer once more.[37] The final prayers of the office are three 'Prayers of Absolution' said inaudibly by the priest. The cross and Gospel book having been venerated, the services close with a blessing, again quoting appropriate psalm verses, from psalms 66.2 and 27.9.[38]

The Scriptural Material

The little now in the services is instructive. The Alleluia chant at the Evening Offering takes its verses from the classical evening psalm, 140.1–2; while at the Morning Offering they are from psalms 142.8 ('In the morning let me know your love') and 66.2–3 ('O God be gracious and bless us').[39] After the Hymn of the Angels some sources have verses from Isaiah 26.9, 'My soul yearns for thee in the night' (a traditional morning canticle, especially in the Greek canon). Others employ psalm 62.7b–8a, 'On you I muse through the night for you have been my help' (Words that are part of the repeat at the Greek

---

[33] Ibid., pp. 38–41.

[34] Ibid., p. 42.

[35] Ibid., pp. 42–5.

[36] Ibid., pp. 44, and 334–6, para. 24; text also in Bute, pp. 24–31.

[37] Ibid., pp. 44–5.

[38] Burmester, *Egyptian Church*, p. 45. For Bute this blessing concludes the eucharistic liturgy, pp. 114–17.

[39] Burmester, *Egyptian Church*, p. 43.

hexapsalmos), and from psalm 5.4, 'In the morning you hear me; in the morning I offer you my prayer, watching and waiting'.[40] This is clearly an early morning vigil.

The Prayers and Hymns at the Offering of Incense

On the last four days of the week there is a common invitatory to the Evening and Morning Offerings, a very general ascription of praise to the Trinity and to the saints. Sunday to Tuesday inclusive, there are different ones for evening and morning.[41] The evening one is as follows:

> Come, let us worship the Lord (x 3). Let us cast ourselves before him day and night. My King and my God! I will hope in Him, that He may forgive us our sins.

We see here the traditional vesperal interest in forgiveness of sins. The morning one is similar but longer and prays that the day be kept free from sin, and concludes:

> The night hath passed. We give thanks to Thee, Lord, and we beseech Thee to guard us this day without sin and save us.

The Prayer of Incense for evening is as follows:

> Christ our God, the great and terrible and true: the Only-begotten Son and Word of God the Father. Thine Holy Name is an ointment poured forth, and in every place shall incense be offered to Thine Holy Name and a pure sacrifice.
> *(Deacon: Pray for our sacrifice which we are presenting.)*
> We pray Thee, our Master, accept our supplications, and let our prayer be set forth before Thee as incense: the lifting up of our hands, (as) an evening sacrifice: for Thou art the true evening sacrifice, Who didst offer thyself up for our sins on the Precious Cross, according to the good-pleasure of Thy good Father, who art ...[42]

It will be apparent that the prayer is a patchwork of scriptural quotes, from the Song of Songs (1.3), Malachi (1.11), and above all from psalm 140.2. The latter psalm may have been connected with the evening office.

---

[40] Ibid., pp. 39 and 325, para. 7.

[41] Ibid., pp. 322–3, paras. 2 and 3.

[42] Ibid., p. 323, para. 4.

The morning Prayer of Incense is much shorter, and evokes, rather than quotes, biblical ideas:

> God, who didst accept the gifts of Abel the just, and the sacrifice of Noah and Abraham, and the incense of Aaron and Zacharias.
> *(Deacon: Pray for our sacrifice which we are presenting.)*
> Accept this incense from our hands, we being sinners, for a sweet odour, for the remission of our sins with the rest of thy people. For blessed and full of glory . . .[43]

The Psalmodia

The Psalmodia is a daily choral service in three forms, the first immediately precedes the Evening Offering of Incense. The second comes between Midnight and Morning Prayer, and the final, extremely short form, between Morning Prayer and the Morning Offering of Incense.[44] The Psalmodia of the Evening has the following order:

Fixed initial prayers with psalm 50
Psalm 116
The 'Fourth Ode' (i.e. psalms 148–50)
Psali (poetic refrains) of season and day
Theotokia (Marian/theological hymns) of the day
Lobsh of the *Theotokia* (another poetic piece)
Difnar (antiphonary) hymn for the day
Conclusion according to day of week[45]

As can be seen, this is little more than a patchwork of poetic pieces following each other with little connection to each other.

The much longer Psalmodia of the night has a strong resurrection theme:

Fixed initial prayers
'Arise ye sons of light' – Invitatory verses
'We see thy resurrection' (Sundays and Eastertide)
Ode 1) Exodus 15.1–21 with poetic verse after
(*Nunc Dimittis* and Hail to thee, Mary – weekdays)
Ode 2) Psalm 135 with poetic verse after
Ode 3) Daniel 3.52–68 with poetic verse after

---

[43] Ibid., pp. 323–4, para. 5.
[44] Ibid., p. 108.
[45] Ibid., also Taft, *Liturgy of the Hours*, p. 255.

('Wherefore we bring a sacrifice' – certain Sundays only and 'We follow Thee')
Intercessions in honour of saints
Doxologies of Feast or day
Ode 4) Psalms 148–50
Psali of feast or day
Theotokia and *Lobsh* of day
Difnar hymn and response (*tarh*)
Conclusion according to day of week
Creed with its preface
Litany and Sanctus
Dismissal Prayer of Absolution[46]

The resurrection theme and the choice of the first three odes from scriptural material frequently employed at Sundays vigils are amongst the considerations that have caused many to think that this is part, at least, of a Sunday resurrection vigil.[47] The case seems very strong; the Exodus Song of the Sea, psalm 135 'O give thanks to the Lord for he is good' (the *polyeleos* of Byzantine tradition), and the *Benedicite*, are all canticles that have been identified with resurrection vigils of one kind or another. The *turuhat* (sing. *tarh*) that follows the first ode read: 'The Lord said to Moses: stretch forth thy rod over the sea of Sari that it may divide in two' and 'Through the prayers of Moses the Archprophet, Lord, grant us the forgiveness of our sins'.[48] Those appointed to follow the second and third odes are similarly general and pray for forgiveness of sins.[49] The so-called fourth ode, the commonly found group of psalms 148–50, may well be the morning praise that follows the resurrection vigil. The *turuhat* to follow these psalms are of a different form to those after the first three. 'Take into your hands the ten strings, the harp of David, the holy psalmodist' and 'We worship thee, O Christ our God, with thy Good Father and the Holy Spirit, for thou hast come and saved us'.[50] The forgiveness prayed for in the first three odes has been granted in the fourth.

While there is no sign of a resurrection gospel, the above might have been a vigil of three antiphons. The now daily Gospel reading at Morning Incense

---

[46] Burmester, *Egyptian Church*, pp. 109–10; Taft, *Liturgy of the Hours*, pp. 255–6; and M. Brogi, *La Santa Salmodia Annuale della Chiesa Copta* (Cairo: Edizioni del Centro Francescano di Studi Orientali Cristiani, 1962).

[47] Taft, 'Praise in the Desert', 532–3.

[48] Burmester, 'The Turuhat of the Coptic Year', *OCP*, **3** (1937), 505–49, 536–7.

[49] Ibid., 538, 1st *tarh* of 2nd ode: 'Let us sing with the hymnodist David, the prophet, the holy psalmodist.' 539, 2nd *tarh* of 3rd ode: 'Pray to the Lord, O Three Holy Children, Sedrach, Misak, Abdenago [that he may forgive us our sins].'

[50] Ibid., 542–3.

may have been displaced from its position in this vigil. This would make some sense of the psalm verses sung with Alleluia during the procession of the Gospel:

> In the morning let me know your love for I put my trust in you. Make me know the way I should walk: to you I lift up my soul. (Ps. 142.8)
> O God, be gracious and bless us and let your face shed its light upon us. So will your ways be known upon earth and all nations learn your saving help. (Ps. 66.2–3)[51]

These are morning psalms that have the theme of walking in God's ways, as personal prayer and as hope for the world. This seems eminently suited to a solemn proclamation of the Gospel of resurrection at sunrise.

In addition, some manuscripts described by O'Leary appear to provide for psalm 50 and selections of the Psalter before the odes,[52] then, if we relate all this to the Offering of Morning Incense as well, it is possible that the original shape may have looked something like this:

'Arise ye sons of the light'
Psalm 50 (and other psalms?)
Odes: 1) Exodus 15 and *turuhat* (?)
  2) Psalm 135 and *turuhat* (?)
  3) Daniel 3 and *turuhat* (?)
Alleluia with psalm verses
Gospel
Psalms 148–50, with *turuhat*
Incense ceremony and Morning Prayer of Incense
Hymn of the Angels, with *turuhat*[53]
Trisagion
Intercession/Litanies
Lord's Prayer
Concluding Prayer
Prayer of Inclination
Conclude with veneration of cross and Gospel

This very tentative reconstruction is envisaged as the Sunday and festal service, culminating in the Gospel and the praise of the risen Lord Jesus

---

[51] Burmester, *Egyptian Church*, p. 43.

[52] O' Leary, op. cit., pp. 73–5, 79.

[53] Burmester, 'The Turuhat of the Coptic Church', 545: 'Glory to God in the high (places), and peace on earth and goodwill among men. We praise thee, we bless thee' and 'And that God became the Son of Man in truth, Jesus Christ the same yesterday, and today, and for ever and ever. Amen.'

symbolized by the newly risen sun, and then concluded with prayer. The weekday morning praise might, if it is true that its relics are found in the Psalmodia of the evening, have looked something like this:

Introduction and psalm 50
A morning psalm with psalm 116 as a doxology (?)
Psalms 148–50
Incense ceremony and Morning Prayer of Incense
Hymn of the Angels
Trisagion
Intercession/Litanies
Lord's Prayer
Concluding Prayer
Prayer of Inclination

If the Psalmodia of the evening is really a morning office, and the Psalmodia of the night a resurrection vigil,[54] all that is left of cathedral Vespers is the Offering of the Evening Incense:

An opening formula
The Evening Prayer of Incense quoting psalm 140
Incensation
Vouchsafe, O Lord to keep us this night...
Trisagion
Intercession/Litanies
Lord's Prayer
Concluding Prayer
Prayer of Inclination
Veneration of cross (?)

This is an even more tentative suggestion than that made above and assumes no Gospel reading at the Evening Offering.[55] The floating Alleluia verse with psalm 140.1–2 may have belonged before or after the evening prayer of incense which quotes it. While psalm 140 may not have had such a privileged position in these offices as it had in most others, there is some evidence of its use in the works of the two great third-century Egyptian teachers, Clement and Origen.

[54] The Psalmodia of the morning comprises but two brief formulae, Burmester, *Egyptian Church*, p. 111; Taft, *Liturgy of the Hours*, p. 256. These may have been part of the opening of Matins.

[55] See Taft, *Liturgy of the Hours*, pp. 31ff., for discussion of readings.

[0] Origen, *de Oratione* 12, 2 (*PG* 11, 451ff.), Clement, *Stromata* VII.7 (*PG* 9, 461ff.) quotes the verse in a context of prayer in general and Morning Prayer in particular!

They quote at least verse 2 of the psalm when speaking of prayer, and in Origen's case, that is certainly evening prayer.[56] At that date we cannot be certain that these teachers are not referring to private prayer only; but even if that were the case, the quotations are surely indicative of a psalm that was to be influential in defining the theology of Vespers.

The Offices in Egypt – Conclusions

1 What most people recognize as the Divine Office is now largely identified in Egypt as being the austere monastic round of more or less fixed services. However these services, especially at night, do appear to follow the night to morning dynamic that we have identified elsewhere.
2 Examining the relics of the cathedral office leads us into largely uncharted territory, but it does seem possible to say that the still important offices of Evening and Morning Incense carry at least some of the ancient Vespers and Matins themes.
3 The Psalmodia also appears to contain traces of an ancient night to morning office.

The Ethiopian Cathedral Office

This is a complex subject in which it is difficult to come to any very clear historical conclusions for research is, as yet, in very early stages. Nevertheless, with the assistance of Bernard Velat's edition of the common of the cathedral office,[57] and the guidance now available from Kidane's study of the Ethiopian cathedral office,[58] it may be possible to draw some tentative conclusions concerning the overall theological trajectory of this tradition of daily prayer.

The liturgical book, the *me'eraf*, provides the ordinary or common of the cathedral office. The *deggua* is the collection of antiphons proper to the feast or season, the *qene* provide variable, poetic elements for these offices. There are thirteen different types of poetic pieces, used only in the main offices: *wazema*,[59] *mawaddes, kestat za-'aryam* and *sebhata naghe*.[60]

The following simplified schemata are derived from *me'eraf*[61] and Kidane:[62]

[57] Bernard Velat, *Etudes sur le Me'eraf* (*PO* 33, Paris: 1966); hereafter, *Me'eraf*.

[58] See note 23, above.

[59] Also the name given to a proper hymn, *Me'eraf*, p. 314.

[60] Ibid., pp. 47–65.

[61] Ibid., pp. 128–39.

[62] Ibid., pp. 315, 330–1.

Wazema – Vespers

Festal	**Ferial** (only in Lent)
Opening Prayer and Hymn (*wazema*)	Opening Prayer and Hymn (*wazema*)
Prayer for Travellers, psalm 23, 1st *qene*	Prayer for travellers, psalm of day
Prayer for rain, psalm 92, 2nd *qene*	Prayer for rain, psalm of day
Prayer for King, psalm 140, 3rd *qene*	Prayer for King, psalm 50
Liton (Evening Thanksgiving)	*Liton* (Evening Prayer)
Readings from Epistles/Acts	Readings from Epistles/Acts
Dan. 3.52–6, 4th *qene*	
Mesbak before, and Gospel	*Mesbak* and Gospel
3 prayers of Evening	3 prayers of Evening
Verses of psalms 101, 84 and antiphons	Verses of psalms 101, 84 and antiphons
Christ Lord have mercy (x 3)	Christ Lord have mercy (x 3)
Prayer of blessing	Prayer of blessing
Doxology, Creed, Our Father, Dismissal	Doxology, Creed, Our Father, Dismissal

It will be readily apparent that the basic structure of *wazema* or Vespers is quite simple. After the opening chant of the Trisagion of the *kidan*, a sequence of supplication, psalm and poetry is repeated three times. Then follow the evening prayer, readings, canticle and poetry, the Gospel, further prayers of evening, and some psalm verses with antiphons; a litany and other suitable pieces bring the office to an end.[63] Kidane tells us that there is only a weekday office in Lent and its structure is identical to the festal version.[64]

The Evening Use of Scriptures

We shall first examine the psalms of the Sunday and festal *wazema*. Psalm 23, 'The Lord's is the earth and its fullness', does not immediately appear to be one which suits the evening. The second, psalm 92, 'The Lord is King with majesty enrobed', with the response Alleluia, is an obvious choice for the weekly

[63] Ibid., p. 300.

[64] Ibid, pp. 327–30.

commemoration of the resurrection. The Sunday commemoration of the resurrection seems to be the controlling reason behind the employment of these two psalms. Psalm 140 which follows them, is the classical evening psalm. Velat gives the first words of a response 'The bush';[65] a probable reference to Mary, for the burning bush that was not burnt up is often taken as a poetic type of Mary. On Lenten weekdays, psalm 140 is replaced by psalm 50.

The psalms that precede psalm 50 in Lent are:

Monday, psalms 1 and 2	Tuesday, psalms 31 and 32
Wednesday, psalms 63 and 64	Thursday, psalms 81 and 82
Friday, psalms 111 and 112	Saturday, psalms 131 and 132[66]

These psalms are the first two of the psalmody in course that is largely completed at Matins in Lent.[67] These psalms may have been selected simply to keep the ancient allotment of three psalms/antiphons.[68]

The climax of the festal service, psalm 140, is continued on Sundays and feasts by singing part of the canticle from Daniel 3, 'Blessed be the Lord, the god of our fathers'.[69] Usually associated with Morning Prayer, where it is also found in the Ethiopian use, this canticle stresses the glory and grandeur of God, and also acts as a response to the Epistle readings inserted between the *liton* and the canticle.

Readings are also found in the weekday office but not the canticle. The readings are from St Paul's letters, one of the Catholic epistles, and Acts. Velat says that only the Gospel reading is chosen for its connection with the day being celebrated.[70] Immediately before the Gospel on both Sundays and weekdays, there is a chant called *mesbak*, psalm verses chosen for their suitability to the feast or season; for example, a *mesbak* appointed for Saturday drawn from psalm 117:[71]

> This day was made by the Lord; we rejoice and are glad. O Lord, grant us salvation, Alleluia! For his love endures for ever. Glory to the Father, to him who rules over the whole world. Glory to the Son, to the Creator of all things, to him who sanctifies the Sabbath. Glory to the Holy Spirit, to this name, to the ages of ages.

---

[65] Ibid., pp. 303–4.

[66] Ibid., pp. 316–26.

[67] Ibid., plan of the Psalter in Lent on p. 140a.

[68] Kidane, p. 332.

[69] *Me'eraf*, p. 305.

[70] Ibid., pp. 298–9.

[71] Ibid., pp. 305–13.

There follow verses from Psalms 101 and 84, with proper antiphons, called *salast* and *salam* respectively. The verses of psalm 101 are as follows:

> O Lord listen to my prayer, Alleluia (x 5);
> and let my cry for help reach you, Alleluia (x 5)!
> And do not hide your face from me,
> In the day of my distress, turn your ear towards me, Alleluia!
> And answer me quickly when I call. Alleluia!
> For ever, and for ever and ever![72]

Both sets of psalm verses pray for protection and salvation, a typically vesperal theme not much in evidence in the office until this point. These texts end most Ethiopian cathedral offices.

Prayer and Hymnody in the Evening

The poetic *qene* are not provided by Velat, and we turn to the prayer that follows these psalms. The *liton* derives its name from Greek but is not litanic.[73] It is a prayer of thanks for being permitted to enter into the dwelling-place of God, where the mystery of God is surrounded by a pleasing aroma (a possible reference to the offering of incense at psalm 140) and it continues to pray for deliverance from evil.[74] This may indicate that the cathedral Vespers had the commonly found emphasis on the sin-offering of incense.[75]

The weekday *liton* has an introduction, 'We supplicate the Lord' and also prays 'Keep us in this holy place so that we may celebrate and sing in psalmodies'. It continues to pray for protection through the night for those who have now come to the 'light of evening'.[76] Psalm 50 may be a later replacement of psalm 140, perhaps from a desire to emphasis the penitential aspect of Lenten weekdays.[77] That there may once have been an entrance ceremony is suggested by the fact that both *liton* prayers thank God that his people may enter into the place of worship.

The prayers interspersed with the psalms are general intercessions for the concerns mentioned above in the schema. The Gospel reading is followed by the three prayers called *kidan* of the evening, which are prefaced by a dialogue similar to that normally associated with the eucharistic prayer, the Anaphora:

---

[72] Ibid., p. 258.

[73] *Me'eraf*, p. 175.

[74] Ibid., p. 181.

[75] Winkler, 'Über die Kathedralvesper', 82–3.

[76] *Me'eraf*, p. 181.

[77] Kidane, p. 333.

Priest: May the grace of the Lord be with you all.
People: With your spirit.
Priest: Let us give thanks to our God.
People: It is right and just!

The first prayer gives thanks for delivery from the darkness of the unredeemed, the second is a joining in the never-ending angelic praise of God who became flesh, and the third a general intercessory prayer for those in special need. The latter also acknowledging that the church has received the power of the Spirit and concludes:

> Praising You without taking rest, without ceasing, we are reproducing in our hearts the image of Your Kingdom, because of You and because of your well-beloved Son, ...[78]

If the *liton* is a prayer of thanksgiving for entry into the holy place, so also does the *kidan* continue the theme of thanksgiving in a similar fashion to the Eucharist. This is the sacrifice of evening praise offered at the altar of God, and hence may be seen as the culmination or climactic moment of Ethiopian Vespers.

After 'O Lord, have mercy on us, O Christ', sung three times, there is a litany for the needs of the people, including petitions for angelic protection at every time and every hour, for pardon of sins, and for continued help and protection. The two pieces called *meltan* that follow the litany continue the same themes, and the service comes to an end with a doxology, the Creed and the Lord's Prayer.[79]

The *wazema*, especially that of Sundays and feasts (prescinding from the opening hymn and the seasonal *qene*) has a clear trajectory. The opening psalms establish motives for praise: the resurrection, the power of the God of light and life, the overcoming of the power of death. Then psalm 140 and the *liton* offer the evening sacrifice of that praise. God's glory is sung in the canticle and the Gospel proclaimed, and the note of unending praise is continued through the *kidan*; the service finishes, naturally enough, with the sort of prayers and supplications that come naturally as the congregation prepare to leave and take their night's rest.

The Ethiopian Vigils

On Sundays and feasts, there is a brief period of repose after Vespers, and then at first cockcrow (about 1 a.m.) the Sunday vigil, *mawaddes*, commences,

[78] *Me'eraf*, p. 174.
[79] Kidane, pp. 314–15.

followed by the morning office and the eucharistic liturgy, without interruption. The whole series of services lasts well into the morning.[80] As with so much of Ethiopian church practice, this could well reflect what was normal among all churches in the earlier centuries. On the thirty greatest feasts, a special vigil called *kestat za-aryam* replaces the other morning offices and is particularly rich in poetic content.

As with *wazema*, the schema of *mawaddes* is derived from *me'eraf*[81] and Kidane.[82]

Mawaddes – Vigil of Sunday	Kestata za-Aryam – Festal Vigil[83]
Opening Prayer, Trisagion, morning *Kidan*	Complete recitation of Psalter
	Psalm 50.16–17, Trisagion, Kidan
Psalms 89, 71 [117], Thanksgiving, *Liton*	Festal psalm verses
Variable Psalmody, *Liton, mazmour* – prayer for sick	Psalms 112.45, 149–50, 3 and 133
	Incense and supplication
Psalms 62, 3 and 5 – prayer for travellers	Psalms 65 or 99, *meqnaye*
Psalms 39–41 – prayer for rain	Canticles with antiphons and hymns
Psalms 42–44 – prayer for fruits of earth	[Exodus 15, Deut. 32, Isaiah 38,
Psalms 45–7 – prayer for rivers	Manasses Jonah 2, Dan. 3 (in 3 parts)]
Psalms 48–50 – prayer for king	Psalms 149–50 and *qene*
Psalms 117, 91 and 92 – prayer for peace Invocation,	[Habakkuk 3, *Magnificat, Benedictus mawase'et, Nunc Dimittis* and *burake*]

Velat divides *mawaddes* into 'periods'; *kestata za-aryam* is more difficult to divide, but we note the role of the canticles. It should be kept in mind that the poetic material, especially at *kestat za-aryam*, is often of considerable length. *Mawaddes* precedes the Morning Praise and Eucharist every Sunday unless one of a few major feasts supervenes.[84]

[80] Taft, *Liturgy of the Hours*, pp. 264–6, 271.

[81] *Me'eraf*, p. 130–2.

[82] Kidane, p. 275.

[83] Ibid., pp. 281–3. Velat appears to duplicate the morning office, so we follow Kidane.

[84] Kidane, p. 274.

The introductory part of *mawaddes* comprises four selections of psalm verses, called *mesbak*, with *litons* after the third and fourth, a *mazmour* (proper hymn) and the prayer for the sick. The first section of *kestata za-aryam* is similar. The verses of psalm 50, 'My tongue shall ring out your goodness. O Lord open my lips and my mouth shall declare your praise', repeated three times, are probably the original beginning of the office. There then follows a catena of psalm verses chosen to suit the feast being celebrated.[85]

Velat's second period of *mawaddes* comprises psalms 62, 3 and 5 (morning psalms suitable for a vigil) and the supplication for travellers.[86] There are then a series of four units (or periods), each comprising a set of three psalms with antiphons and a supplication. The seventh 'period' of *mawaddes* comprises psalms 117, 91 and 92.[87]

The counterpart of psalms 39–50 at *kestata za-aryam* appears to be the recitation of the entire Psalter.[88] Later, before the canticles, there is a unit comprising either psalm 65 or psalm 99, both of which are songs of joy and thanksgiving starting with the words 'Cry out with joy to God all the earth', and hymns called *meqnaye* and *'aboun*. The *meqnaye*, of which there are two forms, continue the theme of joyful glorification of God. The second *'aboun* for feasts of angels commences with the words 'Those who fear the Lord do not neglect to pray to Him at Midnight; for at this moment the stars of heaven, the light of the sun and the moon .... praise Him'.[89]

The canticles make up a great part of *kestata za-aryam*, with *qene* or other poetic material interspersed between them.[90] According to the text in the *me'eraf*, the canticles are actually executed in an abbreviated form. After the tenth canticle the last verse of psalm 149 and psalm 150 are sung with Alleluias, after that comes more poetry and the rest of the canticles.[91] This arrangement ensures that at least part of the group of psalms 148–50 follows the *Benedicite*, as at *mawaddes*; this is likely to be a relic of an ancient morning part of this office.

---

[85] *Me'eraf*, pp. 406–16.

[86] *Me'eraf*, pp. 130, 355–61.

[87] Ibid., pp. 379–84.

[88] Kidane, pp. 281.

[89] *Me'eraf*, pp. 419–21.

[90] Ibid., pp. 339–40. The *qene* are improvised according to set conventions by the *dabtara* or cantors in the course of the celebration and are one of the many unique features of this office, see Kidane, pp. 207–23.

[91] *Me'eraf*, p. 422.

Vigil Scripture

The psalms from which are drawn the introductory chants called *mesbak* are psalm 89, 'O Lord, you have been our refuge from one generation to another', and psalm 71, 'O God give your judgement to the king'. The verses chosen can vary for the season. A further *mesbak* is chosen from psalms that begin with the Ethiopian word *ghenayou* ('Give thanks to the Lord for he is good'), for example, psalm 117; and the verses are again chosen to suit the season. These texts establish the festivity being celebrated, and this is even more true of the next *mesbak*, the psalms of which are chosen to suit the feast or Sunday. For example:

> Lord, do not reprove me in your anger.
> Return, Lord, rescue my soul,
> Save me in your merciful love;
> All my foes will retire in confusion,
> foiled and suddenly confounded.[92]

These verses of psalm 6 are appointed for the 3rd Sunday of Lent, the Sunday of the Paralysed Man.

The psalm verses at *kestata za-aryam* can be from as many as thirty psalms.[93] It is followed by a festal *mesbak* for all times of the year comprising selected verses of psalms 112, 149 and 150:

> From the rising of the sun to its setting, praised be the name of the Lord (3 x). This honour is for all his saints. Praise God in his saints, for all the heavenly hosts glorify you, and to you be glory for ever. Amen.
>
> Alleluia to the Lord! To him who has aided us, we address our praise. To him who has separated the light. He will come to our aid, our God and our Saviour, our God, the God of salvation. Glory to the Father! Glory to the Son! Glory to the Holy Spirit. I give thanks and I glorify and I exalt the King of glory for his word is righteousness, His words are worthy of faith and all his ways are right. His kingdom is eternal and his dominion [will endure] from generation to generation.[94]

This interesting combination of psalms and poetic composition is a form of introduction to the festal vigil.

At the beginning of *mawaddes* we find psalm 62, 'O God, my God, unto thee I rise early at dawn', and psalm 3, both suited to a vigil and to the

---

[92] Ibid., pp. 339, 352.

[93] Ibid., e.g. Lenten season, pp. 407–9.

[94] Ibid., pp. 416–17, translation of the psalms is adapted to LXX readings.

commemoration of the resurrection. Psalm 5, 'Unto my words give ear, O Lord; ... in the morning Thou shalt hear my voice', more frequently occurs as a psalm of the morning, properly so called.[95] A similar group of vigil psalms appears in *kestata za-aryam*. In this latter case the psalms are 50, 3 and 133.[96] Psalm 50 is frequently found at the beginning of the morning offices, and psalm 133 is also of very frequent occurrence at night vigils, as we have seen.

Psalms 39–50 are always used at *mawaddes* and do not appear to be part of any other recitation of the Psalter in course used in the Ethiopian cathedral office. At Lenten Matins there is a group of psalms 33–50 on Tuesday morning which may be in some way connected.[97] The clue may be in the use of psalm 50. The third psalm in each group is sung with the response 'Alleluia', and psalm 50 has an additional antiphon 'Be merciful to us' for all seasons of the year. In addition, before the supplication (in this case for the king), there is another prayer for the king and the realm.[98] This sixth 'period' is followed by one containing typically resurrection and morning psalms, so it is possible that psalm 50 at this position marks the change from the night part of the office to that of the morning. If this is the case, then the group of psalms leading up to psalm 50 are not entirely unsuited to a vigil:

> God is for us a refuge and strength. (psalm 45)
> God goes up with shouts of joy! (psalm 46)
> O God, we ponder your love within your temple. (psalm 47)
> With the morning their outward show vanishes. (psalm 48)
> From the rising of the sun to its setting. (psalm 49)

The psalms of the seventh 'period' of *mawaddes* ('Give thanks to the Lord for he is good... The Lord's right hand has triumphed'/'It is good to give thanks to the Lord'/S'The Lord is King with majesty enrobed') are all suited to a Sunday resurrection vigil, and the antiphon sums up the resurrection vigil theme:

> Isaiah said: Who is this glorious man who comes from Edom?
> Ezekiel said: Adonai will be sent from heaven.
> David said: Blessed is he who will come, who will come from Sion.[99]

---

[95] Ibid., pp. 356–61.

[96] Ibid., p. 417.

[97] Ibid., p. 140a.

[98] Ibid., pp. 378–9.

[99] Ibid., p. 383.

The vigil canticles include those most normally associated with Morning Prayer. Deuteronomy 32 (divided in two), the prayer of Hezekiah from Isaiah 38, the prayer of Manasses and the *Nunc Dimittis* are additional to the Greek odes. Daniel 3 is in three parts rather than two, and the *Benedictus* and *Magnificat* are treated as distinct, whereas in the Greek canon they are treated as one ode. The Exodus Song of the Sea, the canticles of Jonah 2, Isaiah 26, Habakkuk 3 and Daniel 3 are all types of the resurrection, and so associated with the Paschal vigil. The others all suit the hour of morning, except perhaps the very penitential prayer of Manasses and the *Nunc Dimittis*.

There are clear parallels between the two kinds of vigil. After festal invitatories both have series of psalms suited to the night, or very early morning, hour. Then while *mawaddes* has a series of psalms in course until the morning is signalled by psalm 50, the *kestata za-aryam*, having had the entire Psalter first,[100] has selected psalms and the canticles with hymns. In both cases these are vigils that were intended to cover the long wait through to dawn. After the psalms of the vigil, *mawaddes* has the resurrection psalms and canticles, and having reached the sunrise, psalms 148–50.

The Prayers and Hymns of the Vigils

The major part of the opening prayers is the *kidan* of the morning. This commences with a prayer glorifying God as the author of all things, who has promised the light that can never be extinguished. The second prayer, addressed to the God of light, is eminently suited to a service of prayer that declares the power of light over darkness:

> . . . Light before the world, our guardian, incorruptible treasure. By the good pleasure of your Father, you have illuminated for us the accumulation of shadows in which we are, You who have made us to come out of the abyss into the light and who have given to us life by death, . . .[101]

The third prayer of the *kidan* is a supplication, first of all for those undergoing hardships of various kinds, and then that God's faithful people will walk in his ways, all suited for prayer at night.[102]

The *litons* at *mawaddes* are drawn from the collection that is also employed for Vespers and Matins.[103] The preamble for the first speaks of the living name

[100] Kidane, p. 281.

[101] *Me'eraf*, p. 171.

[102] Ibid., pp. 171–2.

[103] Ibid., pp. 177–86.

of God that does not die, the watcher who does not sleep, and a later one prays that we be numbered among the children of the light of God's glory. These prayers may not be a primitive part of the beginning of the vigil, but the choice of them is consistent with the theological themes associated with vigils. The *mazmour* is festal, and the prayer for the sick is similar to the kind of supplication, interspersed through the offices, that we have already examined when discussing *wazema*.

The four supplications that follow the sets of the psalms in course are taken from the same general collection as at *wazema*. They have no necessary connection with the psalms, but seem to be included in order to alternate psalmody and prayer. These supplications are not found in *kestata za-aryam*, which does, however, have a supplication to conclude the opening section of vigil psalmody, which is of two, rather than three, members and makes reference to the hour of celebration:

> . . . For He has protected and helped, sustained and brought us to this hour. We pray and supplicate that he will establish us in complete peace and good health the rest of this night, . . .[104]

This is a prayer that completes and sums up the sentiments of the three psalms at the beginning of the vigil. This supplication is followed, and in a sense, completed by a lengthy blessing.[105]

The *kidan* of the morning comprises prayers drawn from the *Testamentum Domini*, from the prayers to follow the 'Hymn of the Praise of the Seal'.[106] In the first, God the Father of light is praised for removing material darkness and bestowing immaterial light, in the second, the Son is called the lamp which never goes out; and in the third thanks are given that we have been made to conquer the bonds of death. Another proper hymn comes between the *kidan* and the *liton*. This has a preamble that praises God who protected the Patriarchs, helped the people of Israel through the wilderness, and sent the prophets and the apostles to whom was given the Holy Spirit; which Spirit is now supplicated for this community.[107] Once again there is a progression from night to the first signs of morning, the morning that symbolizes Christ's resurrection and new life for all his people.

---

104 Ibid., pp. 198–204.

105 Ibid., pp. 418.

106 Sperry-White, op. cit., pp. 34–5.

107 *Me'eraf*, pp. 172–3, 185–6.

Sebhata Naghe

The morning office *sebhata naghe* has three forms: for Sundays, for ordinary ferias and for Lenten ferias. Once again, the schemata are drawn from *me'eraf*, revised with Kidane.[108]

***Sebhata Naghe* – Matins**

Festal	**Ferial**
Opening Prayer	Opening Prayer
Prayer of Absolution	Prayer of Absolution
Ezl (proper)	*Ezl* (proper)
Liton	Supplication
Psalms 62, 91, 5 and 64	Psalms 62, 91, 5 and 64
Meqnaye and *Qene*	*Meqnaye*
Supplication for Sick	Supplication for Sick
Canticle XV and *qene*	Psalm 50 **or** One of Canticles II, VI, XI, XV, XIII & XIV for feast
Supplication for Travellers	
Canticle IX (Dan.) and *qene*	Canticle IX
Canticle X (Dan.) and *qene*	Canticle X
Psalms 148–50 with Anthems and *qene*	Psalms 148–50 with Anthem
Supplication for King	Supplication for King
'Aboun	*'Aboun*
Mawase'et	
'Esma la-alam	
Mesbak	*Mesbak*
Gospel	Gospel
Kidan	
Psalms 101 and 84 with anthems	Psalms 101 and 84 with anthems
Invocations	Invocations
Creed	Creed
Lord's Prayer	

[108] *Me'eraf*, pp. 136–9 and Kidane, pp. 341, 347–8.

Sebhata Naghe for Lent[109]

Two Marian Hymns

[NB. In the First week of Lent, the conclusion is more complex with verses from psalms, especially from 2 and 84.]

'Ezl

Medgam and *Liton*

Psalm 62

Psalms 3–30 (Mon.), 33–60 (Tues.), 64–80 (Wed.), 83–110 (Thur.), 113–30 (Fri.), 133–47 (Sat.)

Mastagabe of day

Medgam and Supplication for Sick

Meqnaye of psalms (verses)

Supplication for Travellers

Canticle IX and *medgam*

Canticle X, antiphon and *medgam*

Psalms 148–50, antiphon and *medgam*

'Ema la-alam and *medgam* (twice)

Medgam and *'Aboun* (twice)

Isaiah and Synaxarium readings

Mesbak and Gospel (?)

Psalms 101 and 84 with antiphons

Invocations and Marian prayer

Final Prayers

Minor Hours, Monday to Friday only

Terce: Psalms 85–6 and a canticle each day (one of I, IV, VII, X, XIII).

Sext: Psalm 21, one of canticles II, V, VII, XI and XIV, psalm 56

None: Psalm 102, one of canticles VI, IX, XII and XV, psalm 87

109 After *Me'eraf*, revised with Kidane, pp. 348–9.

Morning Psalmody

Psalms and canticles make up the greater part of the morning office. Common to both weekday and Sunday forms are psalms 62, 91, 5 and 64, always treated as a group. Then follow *meqnaye* (select verses of those psalms), the morning praises (psalms 148–50) a concluding groups of verses from psalms 101 and 84, and two canticles from Daniel 3. Another psalm or canticle is chosen for each day, and there are readings of the Synaxarion on many days, and a Gospel every day.[110] This would give the following simplified schema, which can be compared with a similar simplification of Lenten Matins:

Psalms 62, 91, 5 and 64	Psalm 62
Psalm 50 or Canticle of day	Course
Canticles IX and X	Canticles IX and X
Psalms 148–50	Psalms 148–50
(Readings and) Gospel	Readings and Gospel
Verses of psalms 101 and 84	Verses of psalms 101 and 84

The simplified plan is extremely informative. The block of psalms at the beginning of the office contains several classical morning vigil psalms. Psalm 62 with the idea of waiting for dawn, and then psalm 91 singing of how good it is to praise God, and especially 'to proclaim your love in the morning and your truth in the watches of the night'. Psalm 5, 'in the morning I offer you my prayer, watching and waiting', and finally psalm 64, 'Blessed is he whom you chose and call to dwell in your courts'; from vigil to joining in the heavenly worship of God.[111] The *meqnaye* in these psalms reinforce the theme by choosing the verse that most reflect it. For example:

62 O God, my God, unto Thee I rise early at dawn.
(O Thou, be to me a help, be to me a refuge.)
At the dawn I meditated on Thee, for Thou art become my helper.
91 And to chant unto Thy name O Most High,
To proclaim in the morning Thy mercy.

All this exhibits a movement from darkness to the light of God's glory. Having entered into worship, the canticles provide a festal theme. For the feast of the cross, the canticle of Habakkuk –'I considered thy works and I was amazed' – seems apposite, as does the *Magnificat* for minor feasts of Mary.[112] Canticle XV, the *Nunc Dimittis* is suited to Christmas. The Canticles of Daniel 3,

[110] Kidane, p. 341.

[111] For texts, see *Me'eraf*, pp. 441–3.

[112] Ibid., pp. 448–50.

'Blessed are you, Lord God of our Fathers' and 'Bless the Lord, all you works of the Lord', are constantly met with as morning canticles because of their association with Easter. Psalms 148–50, once again, are seen to act as the climax of the praise of the risen Christ at sunrise.

The Lenten Matins also fits the pattern, though the group of four psalms is reduced to psalm 62 alone because of the Psalter in course. The system ensures that the entire Psalter is covered at Vespers and Matins (but overwhelmingly at Matins) from Monday to Saturday inclusive. Once again the time for lengthy psalms in course is before the light, as a lengthening of a much shorter cathedral vigil into the small hours. The rest of Lenten Matins is much the same as any other weekday. After the psalms come the Daniel 3 canticles and psalms 148–50, readings from Isaiah and the Synaxarium, but enriched with poetic material, and lengthened at the end by a form of additional service that invokes God's mercy in time of need.[113]

Kidane says that the biblical reading is now somewhat limited and largely replaced by non-biblical works.[114] The service finishes with the same excerpts from psalms 101 and 84 that we have seen at *wazema*, relatively brief invocations, the Creed and Lord's Prayer.

Morning Poetry and Prayer

The difference between festal and ferial Matins is largely in the amount of hymnody employed. Feasts, not surprisingly, have much more. There are three proper chants at the beginning of festal Matins: *angargari*, *'esma la-alam* and *salam* of the *kidan* (the *kidan* that follows is that of the morning). There is a proper *'ezl* for all days, and then the *liton* of the morning for each day (Mondays appears to be used on feasts). *Qene* are attached to canticles and psalms 148–50 on feasts, but not on weekdays. A coda is added to the praise psalms on Sundays, a few additional verses called *meltam*. Hymns under the title of *'aboun* or *'esma la-alam* are found on all days, and another called *mawase'et* on feasts.[115]

In the morning office, as also at *mawaddes*, the *liton* of the morning always occurs near the beginning of the service. That appointed for Monday prays quite clearly that God's people be enabled to pass from darkness to light, from corruption to incorruption, from ignorance to true knowledge.[116] Wednesday's

[113] Ibid., pp. 493–5.

[114] Kidane, p. 244.

[115] *Me'eraf*, pp. 452–9.

[116] Ibid., pp. 182–5.

is a general supplication for the light of God's face to shine on his people, so that they might rejoice in his goodness. On Saturday the *liton* begins:

> O Jesus Christ, source of grace, power and wisdom of your Father, for you are the Lamb of God who takes away the sins of the world. Be merciful to us for you have come down from heaven in accordance with your Father's wisdom, in order to save your creatures, who you have fashioned, from the death which destroys ...

The selected verses from psalms 101 and 84 draw the offices to a close and introduce the final invocations. They sum up the festal theme at the end of the service.

A characteristic Lenten piece is the *medgam*, of which there are normally nine (12 in the first week). The word indicates a repeat, but is now defined as a text recited in a low voice.[117] That which opens Lenten Matins gives glory to God for having woken the people from sleep, given them light, and allowed them to worship in the holy place. The second and third are more general, the fourth follows canticle X and mentions the three children. The fifth follows psalms 148–50 and is specifically matutinal:

> Each morning, we bless you and we give you glorification and thanksgiving, at all times ...

The sixth, seventh and eighth are general ascriptions of glory to God, and the ninth, 'Give ear to my voice, O Lord', may once have introduced or concluded intercessory prayers.[118]

The *mestagabe* that follow the reading of the Psalter and are proper to the day of the week are centonized verses of the psalms just recited,[119] and if there is a unifying theme, it is a request that God hear the prayer of his people. Every day there is a *meqnaye* of free form that draws upon several psalms, including psalm 62, weaving in texts of ecclesiastical composition. The themes are generally supplicatory and make reference to the time of day: namely, the morning, or early morning.[120]

[117] Ibid., p. 469.

[118] Ibid., pp. 486, 492–3.

[119] Ibid., pp. 222–31.

[120] Text at ibid., pp. 488–9.

The Minor Hours

The Minor Hours occur in the Ethiopian cathedral office in several different forms, briefly outlined in Kidane's treatment of the special 'stational' liturgy, *mehelela*, celebrated on ten occasions in the year.[121]

Psalms 85 and 86 for the Third Hour, 'Turn your ear O Lord, and answer' and 'His city is upon the holy mountain', both appear to expect the nations to come and adore God. Psalms 21 and 56 at the Sixth Hour, 'My God, my God, why have you forsaken me?' and 'Have mercy, on me O God', could be described as prayers for help in time of trouble. Psalms 102 and 87 at the Ninth Hour, 'Bless the Lord, O my soul' and 'O Lord my God, I call for help by day, I cry at night before you', may be seen preparing for the evening, the end of the day. The themes associated with the Day Hours in other systems are not present here. These Hours mark the presence of God's salvation in the progress of the day, more than in the remembrance of the past saving events. There appear to be no forms for the First Hour or for Compline.

The Ethiopian Cathedral Office – Conclusions

1 This office appears to be predominantly festal, lacking even Vespers on ordinary days.
2 The Psalter is again largely executed at night, or in the very early morning. This also applies to the biblical canticles. Those canticles include those we associate with the Paschal vigil.
3 There are broadly two kinds of vigil, a festal one lasting all night with the entire Psalter, and an ordinary one simply starting before light and coming to its climax at sunrise.
4 These conclusions are made in the awareness that this probably very primitive celebration of overnight prayer may well be under threat due to the exigencies of modern life. It is already largely the preserve of a specialist group of liturgical musicians rather than a celebration of the entire church.

[121] Kidane, pp. 288ff.

CHAPTER 11

The Roman and Benedictine Offices

Hitherto we have examined Eastern forms of daily prayer which may be said to share a deeply rooted common theology in both cathedral and monastic forms of office. We will also demonstrate that a similar theology was found in the Old Spanish tradition and, originally, in that of Milan. However, the Roman and Benedictine offices appear to be very different forms which, with their heavy emphasis on reciting the Psalter and other scriptures, may be perceived as having a more monastic and meditative or edificatory style. This perception has deeply affected the expectations that Roman Catholics, Anglicans and other Western Christians have of the daily office. We shall now examine these traditions to see if they originally had more in common with the rites of the East and the non-Roman West.

The Roman rite of daily prayer underwent radical change in the twentieth century. Pope Pius X appointed a Commission to reform the Roman Breviary which, in 1911, introduced far-reaching changes which destroyed many ancient features or rendered them opaque.[1] The second Vatican Council decreed further radical changes, tending to make the shape of all the services much the same as each other.[2] We shall try to establish in this chapter what might have been the original shape and rationale of the Roman office, and also attempt to identify relics of the 'cathedral' form of that office. Using the forms that pre-date the pontificate of Pius X as the basis for our discussion,[3] we shall also use the Sarum Breviary[4] as an example of a pre-Tridentine book.

The shape of the Benedictine office remained quite close to that outlined in St Benedict's rule until after Vatican II. This rite was closely related to the Roman from its very beginnings, the latter being monastic in origin, and it was not directly affected by the 1911–12 reform.[5] Since Vatican II, monasteries have striven to develop offices more suited to new understandings of monastic life and these vary from place to place. We will use a pre-Vatican II monastic

---

[1] See e.g., Baumstark, *Comparative Liturgy*, p. 115.

[2] *Documents of Vatican II*, pp. 164–5, #87–#92.

[3] The Council of Trent made a few revisions which simplified but did not alter the shape of the rite. We use *Breviarium Romanum ex decreto SS. Concilii Tridentini restitutum* ..., 4 vols. (Tournai: Desclée, Lefebvre et cie., 1894); hereafter, *Breviarium Romanum.*

[4] F. Proctor and C. Wordsworth (eds), *Breviarium ad usum Insignis Ecclesiae Sarum*, 3 vols. (Cambridge: 1879–86); hereafter *Sarum.*

[5] Baumstark, op. cit., p. 115.

breviary to illustrate the medieval and later Benedictine office.[6] Obviously the *Breviarium Monasticum* (*BM*) was subject to a good deal of development from the time of St Benedict onward, so we shall often refer to his rule (*RB*).[7]

The Beginnings of Daily Prayer in Rome

The earliest forms of the offices in Rome are not known to us, in fact it is not at all clear whether any recognizable forms existed in which it would be possible to distinguish the 'cathedral' and 'monastic' elements.[8] If *Apostolic Tradition* is not a reliable witness for Roman practice, there are few useful references anywhere else. A letter of St Jerome (Rome, 382–5) possibly refers to the lamps lit at sunset.[9] A similar hint is found in Uranius' letter on the death of Paulinus of Nola (410).[10] This is from an area to the south of Rome.

There is clearer evidence for a morning office. The letter on the death of Paulinus refers to Matins,[11] and Arnobius the Younger, living in Rome in the middle of the fifth century, refers to psalm 148 as sung daily throughout the world at dawn, as the creation's first praise of the Creator.[12] Jerome refers to Morning Prayer in passing.[13] Batiffol and Schuster thought that there was no Vespers before the seventh/eighth century. Callewaert, however, noted Jerome's testimony, and also pointed to the prayers for times of day in the so-called Leonine Sacramentary, and suggested parallels with the Rule of St Benedict.[14] St Benedict's liturgical material in *RB* is of the same family of that of the *Rule of the Master*. The latter being a probably older work which Benedict may have drawn upon,[15] but Benedict declares that he is following the

[6] *Breviarium Monasticum…pro omnibus sub regula S. Patris Benedicti militantibus* (2 volumes), (Bruges: Desclée de Brouwer, 1930); hereafter *Breviarium Monasticum*.

[7] Numerous versions are available, but especially useful is Timothy Fry et al. (eds), *RB 1980: The Rule of St Benedict in Latin and English with Notes* (Collegeville, MN: Liturgical Press, 1981); hereafter *RB*.

[8] Bradshaw, *Daily Prayer*, pp. 111ff. and Taft, *Liturgy of the Hours*, p. 132.

[9] Letter 107.9, to Leta, *PL* 22, 875, and Taft, *Liturgy of the Hours*, pp. 143–4: 'with lamp lit, offer the evening sacrifice'.

[10] 4, *PL* 53, 862: In which, the penultimate phrase may echo verse 29 of psalm 17: 'Quoniam tu illuminas lucernam meam, Domino', a verse often found in non-Roman lucernaria.

[11] Ibid.

[12] *Commentary on psalm 148, PL* 53, 566.

[13] See n. 11, 'mane hymnos canere'.

[14] C. Callewaert, 'Vesperae antiquae in officio praesertim Romano', in *Sacris Erudiri* (Steenbrugge, 1940), pp. 91–117, 97–101, 103–8.

[15] See discussion in Fry, *RB*, pp. 79–83.

Roman church, so, by the early sixth century there must have been a vesperal office in Rome.[16]

The earliest material relating to Vespers and Matins in Rome includes the prayers of the Leonine or Verona Sacramentary (or *libellus missarum*). This document takes us back to the earliest prayer forms of the Roman liturgy and includes prayers to conclude morning and evening prayer. It is possible to date the prayers to between 440 and 560.[17]

There are four morning and three evening prayers.[18] The first evening one may stand for the others: it prays that after the trials of the day, we may be sustained at night and refreshed as the needs of the day require. There is a common theme of protection through the night, and a rather pessimistic contrast between earthly changeability and the unchanging God. These prayers are placed after the four morning ones and appear less negative in outlook if seen as coming before them. The Morning Prayers having a more 'up-beat' feel about them, entering upon the new day as the earnest of that eternal day for which one has been praying since the evening before.

The first Morning Prayer implores God who separates day from night to separate our works from those of darkness, and seeks everlasting light. The second prays that we may rejoice in God's watchful protection, and makes a play on the word for 'vigil' and 'watch'. Being prayers for the early morning, they refer to rising from sleep in spite of human weakness.

The Shape of the Monastic Offices of the Roman Tradition

Paul Bradshaw has outlined the history and background of the Roman monastic office,[19] and Robert Taft noted how little the basic structure changed from the time of St Benedict to Vatican II.[20] This office must have influenced both that of the *Rule of the Master*,[21] as well as that of St Benedict. The shape of this office is dominated by the recitation of the Psalter in course, and this recitation is arranged in a sophisticated way that largely avoids duplicating fixed psalms.

---

[16] Callewaert, op. cit., 117.

[17] C. Vogel et al. (eds), *Medieval Liturgy: An Introduction to the Sources* (Washington, DC: Pastoral Press, 1986), p. 44.

[18] L.C. Mohlberg et al. (eds), *Sacramentarium Veronense* (RED series maior I, Rome: 1956), pp. 75–6.

[19] Bradshaw, op. cit., pp. 124–9.

[20] Taft, *Liturgy of the Hours*, p. 307.

[21] Citations refer to A. de Vogüé (ed.) and Luke Eberle (trans.), *The Rule of the Master* (Kalamazoo, MI: Cistercian Publications, 1977; hereafter *RM*.

The daily round began with Nocturns or Vigils, later known misleadingly as Matins. This, the longest office, was to commence at the Eighth Hour of the night in winter (i.e., a little past midnight) in order to assure digestion![22] Beginning in the small hours,[23] it was followed by a long gap in winter and a very short one in summer, and Lauds (called Matins in *RB*) came after it at daybreak.[24] The Master's choice of time is because: 'cockcrow is the end of the waning light, since night gives birth to day'.[25] In the summer he left no gap between the night and morning offices.[26] Light overcoming the dark is part of the very progression of the offices, and in, spite of the gap, Nocturns and Matins/Lauds were thematically linked.

Following Lauds, Prime was established early on in the Roman daily cycle;[27] there were also Terce, Sext and None; then Vespers, and after that Compline also appears to have already gained a place.

Distribution of the Psalter

The Minor Hours of Prime, Terce, Sext and None in *Breviarium Romanum* are almost entirely composed of sections of psalm 118.[28] Prime had psalm 117 before psalm 118 on Sundays, and, originally, psalm 53 on weekdays.[29] Compline comprised psalms 4, 90 and 133 daily and little else.[30] This fixity is not found in the evening and night/morning offices. Leaving aside Lauds for the moment, we find that the greater part of the psalmody in course was appointed for Vespers and Nocturns:

Sunday, 1st Nocturn, psalms 1–14 (excepting 4 and 5 used elsewhere)
2nd Nocturn, psalms 15–20
3rd Nocturn, psalms 21–6[31]

---

[22] *RB 8.*

[23] J.A. Jungmann, 'The Origin of Matins', in *Pastoral Liturgy* (London: Challoner, 1962, p. 117), suggests 2 a.m.

[24] *RB 8.4.*

[25] *RM 33.4*, p. 195.

[26] *RB 33.7–13*, ibid.

[27] Bradshaw, *Daily Prayer*, p. 138.

[28] Ibid., 11 sections of 16 verses each, the first two for Prime, the next three for Terce, and so on.

[29] Ps. 53 came to precede 117 at Prime on Sundays (*Brev. Rom.(autumnalis)* 25). Further selected psalms from Matins followed 53 daily except Saturday in the medieval books (ibid., 33–37 and *Brev. Sarum II*, 38–42.)

[30] *Brev. Rom.*, 164–6, added psalm 30.

[31] Taft, *Liturgy of the Hours*, p. 136. Probable 5th–6th cent. arrangement.

This was soon modified so that psalms 15–17 formed the second Nocturn and psalms 18–20, the third, giving eighteen psalms in all, instead of twenty-four.[32] Psalms 27–108 (omitting 62, 64, 66 and 99), were divided, twelve psalms each, among the rest of the days of the week.[33] Later adjustments placed psalms 21–5 in Prime, and psalm 26 went to Monday morning. The whole system moving by one until Wednesday morning, which lost psalm 53, also to Prime, and there was another minor adjustment on Saturday.

The structure of Vespers

Sunday	**Weekdays**
Round brackets = omitted from monastic office, square brackets, = additions in monastic office	*(Roman psalms/Monastic)*
Deus in adjutorium	Deus in adjutorium
Psalms 109	e.g., Tuesday, Psalms 121/129
110	122/130
111	123/131
112	124/132
(113) with antiphons	125 with antiphons
Capitulum: Benedictus Deus	*Capitulum: Benedictus Deus*
[Responsory]	[Responsory]
Hymn – e.g., *Lucis Creator*	Hymn – e.g., *Telluris*
Versicle: *Dirigatur*	Versicle: *Dirigatur/Vespertina*
Magnificat with antiphon	*Magnificat* with antiphon
[*Kyrie* and Lord's Prayer]	[*Kyrie* and Lord's Prayer]
	(*Preces Feriales*)
Collect	Collect
Memoriae	*Memoriae*
Benedicamus Domino	*Benedicamus Domino*

[32] See e.g. *Breviarium Romanum*, 11–18.

[33] Taft, *Liturgy of the Hours*, p. 136.

The Structure of Matins-Lauds
Matins

Sunday	**Weekdays**
Domine labia mea aperies	*Domine labia mea aperies*
[Psalm 3]	[Psalm 3]
Psalm 94 with Invit. ant.	Psalm 94 with Invit.
Hymn (e.g., *Nocte surgentes*)	Hymn (e.g., *Somno refectis*)
Nocturn I	Nocturn [I]
12 Psalms, 3 ants./6 Psalms, 3 ants.	12 Psalms, 6 ants./6 Psalms and ants.
Versicle (e.g., *Memor*)	Versicle (e.g., *Domino*)
3/4 Biblical readings and Responsories	3 Biblical readings and Responsories
Nocturn II	[Nocturn II
3 Psalms with ants./6 Psalms, 3 ants.	6 Psalms and ants.
Versicle	*Capitulum* (e.g., *Vigilate*)
3/4 Patristic readings with Responsories	Versicle]
Nocturn III	
3 Psalms with ants./3 Canticles, 1 ant.	
Versicle – *Exaltare*	
3/4 Homiletic Readings with Responsories	
Te Deum Laudamus	
[Gospel and *Te decet laus*]	

Lauds – Sunday	**Weekday**
Deus in adjutorium	*Deus in adjutorium*
[Psalm 66]	[Psalm 66]
Psalms [50]	
[117]	Psalms 50
92	42 –Tuesday
99	62 and 66/ [56 – Tuesday] & ants.
62(and 66) and one [or two] ants.	
Benedicite with ant.	Canticle – Isaiah 38, Tuesday
Psalms 148–50 with ant.	Psalms 148–50 with ant.
Capitulum: Benedictio	*Capitulum*: Nox praecessit
[Responsory]	[Responsory]
Hymn – e.g., *Ecce jam noctis*	Hymn – e.g., *Splendor paternae*

Versicle: Dominus regnavit	Versicle: Repleti
Benedictus with antiphon	*Benedictus* with antiphon
[*Kyrie* and Lord's Prayer]	[*Kyrie* and Lord's Prayer]
	Preces Feriales
Collect	Collect
Memoriae	*Memoriae*
Benedicamus Domino	*Benedicamus Domino*

The Minor Hours (Sunday and Ferial)

Deus in adjutorium
Hymn (e.g. *Jam lucis* at Prime)
Prime, Psalms 53/118.1–32 118.1–32
(Athanasian Creed)
Terce, Psalms 118.33–80/33–56
Sext, Psalms 118.81–128/57–80
None, Psalms 118.129–76/81–104
Little Chapter
(Short Responsary)
Versicle and response
Preces – long at Prime
Fixed or proper Collect
Conclusion
Office in Chapter – Prime

The Order of Vespers

The first part of the order of Vespers is five (or in Benedictine use, four) psalms in course. The *psalterium currens* is largely confined, as we have already seen, to the evening and the early morning. Day Hours and the ancient morning office remained comparatively unchanging.

The following preliminary observations apply to all the offices. (a) There is relatively little differentiation between weekday and Sunday offices.[34] (b) The psalmody leads into the main ceremonial part of the office. (c) The structures

[34] Festal offices have a three Nocturn Vigil of nine psalms and readings and greater use of selected psalms, but do not differ structurally and will not be examined here.

of Vespers and Lauds (on its own) appear to mirror one another, though, as we shall see, this impression is deceptive. The lack of differentiation between the weekday and Sunday offices probably reflects monastic provenance, the office is a vehicle for meditative prayer based on continuous use of the Psalter.[35]

Josef Jungmann drew a parallel between the offices described by Egeria and various statements in canonical collections concerning reading psalms whilst waiting for the 'main' service to begin. He also mentioned a practice still current when he wrote (1950s ?):

> The fact that psalmody, which constitutes the first section of the Hours and Nocturns, was not so highly esteemed as the second section which begins with the lessons is expressed, indeed, by the custom much followed today of simply reciting the psalms at Lauds and Vespers, except on occasions which demand the solemn rite, and only beginning to sing *a capitulo*, thus marking off the latter section in contrast to the first.[36]

When we turn to the similarity of structure between Vespers and Lauds, we first see that the psalms at Vespers are always part of the continuous recitation of the psalms in both the Roman and Benedictine rites. Those at Lauds are selected for the Hour and culminate in the Old Testament canticle and the praise psalms, the 'laudes' that give this part of the Morning Prayer cycle both its name and its traditional character. Though the two offices have tended to assimilate to one another in shape, the psalmody argues a different history and purpose.

The original structure of Roman Vespers may have been five psalms, versicle and response, *Magnificat*, and then the prayers; the Lord's Prayer or a collect.[37] There was neither *capitulum* (Little Chapter) nor Hymn. The central core of the office, after the psalms in course, was then Versicle and Response, *Magnificat* and prayer. The thirteenth-century liturgical commentator, William Durandus, Bishop of Mende, described the incensing of the people taking place during the *Magnificat*, but he still saw the versicle 'Dirigatur . . .' as the moment of offering incense[38] (see next section).

The Roman rite resisted hymns until the twelfth century,[39] even later in some places. *RB* accepted them from the beginning, placed between the Vespers *capitulum* and versicle. However, the *capitulum* (a short reading) is followed in

---

[35] See Adalbert de Vogüé, *La règle de St Benoit* (SC 184–6: 1979), and my 'The Use of the Psalter by Early Monastic Communities', op. cit.

[36] J.A. Jungmann, 'Psalmody as the Introduction to the Hours', in *Pastoral Liturgy*, op. cit., pp. 157–162, 161–2.

[37] Callewaert, op. cit., 117.

[38] *Rationale Divinorum Officiorum, Lib. V. XI, de Vesperis* (Venice: 1599), pp. 161, 162.

[39] *RB*, 'The Liturgical Code in the Rule of St Benedict', 379–414, 400, and Guiver, op. cit., pp. 158–9.

RB by a Responsory.[40] Amalar of Metz (c.775–850) thought that the Gospel canticle excluded the Responsory.[41] Medieval books witness to the survival of some Vespers responsories, but these were Long Responsories like those at Nocturns: for example, the Sarum Breviary provided responsories for Vespers on many feasts.[42]

Although the inclusion of hymns in the Roman office was resisted for a long time, the *place* of their inclusion in the Benedictine office may be significant in determining which part of Roman Vespers was of cathedral origin. The Responsory may have been a psalm with response that was part of the cathedral rite and perhaps part of a light ritual. It has been suggested that this cathedral service could have commenced with a blessing drawn from 2 Corinthians 1 (see below), while the monastic psalmody preceding it, opened with the versicle from psalm 69: 'Deus in adjutorium meum intende'. The latter being the sort of phrase a lay led group would use to commence prayer (not having priests to greet them or bless the beginning of the office). After the lamp-lighting, a theme adumbrated by the hymn, if the versicle stands for psalm 140, then we have the evening sacrifice of praise, with an incense ceremony from an early date. Finally, before the intercessions, we have the *Magnificat*.

The Psalms and other Scriptural Elements

The evening psalmody is begun on Sundays with psalm 109, the first psalm of the 16th *kathisma* in the Palestinian arrangement of the Psalter.[43] About a third of the current Psalter was recited at Vespers of the old Roman Breviary:

Sunday 109–13	Monday 114–16, 119–20
Tuesday 121–5	Wednesday 126–30
Thursday 131–2, 134–6	Friday 137–41
Saturday 143–7	

The gradual psalms, for which we suggested a vesperal function in Jerusalem, are found at Roman Vespers, Monday to Thursday, and the classical evening psalm, 140 (together with 141) is appointed for Friday. When Benedict re-ordered the psalms, spreading 118 over Sunday and Monday

[40] See *RB xvii*, p. 212.

[41] J.M. Hanssens, SJ (ed.), *Amalarii Episcopi Opera Liturgica Omnia* (*Studi e Testi* 138–140, Rome: Vatican Polyglot Press, 1948–50), p. 434.

[42] E.g. 'Reges Tharsis', 1st Vespers of Epiphany, *Sarum I*, cccxviii.

[43] Callewaert, 'Vesperae antiquae', op. cit., 111.

Minor Hours and Tuesday Prime, the Minor Hours of the rest of the week employed psalms 119–27, except Prime which used psalms displaced from Matins.[44] Vespers was reduced to four psalms, and Vigils to two Nocturns of six each, even on Sundays.[45] Down to Vatican II, Roman Vespers had festal variations in the psalmody of particular days (e.g., 2nd Vespers of Christmas started with 109–11 and then 129 and 131 replaced 112 and 113). In this way the principle of discretely selected psalms was still observed to some extent.[46]

After the psalms (and the later hymn), the versicle and response for all days of the week, except Saturday, was:

V. Dirigatur, Domine, oratio mea.
R. Sicut incensum in conspectu tuo.[47]

The Saturday versicle and response being:

V. Vespertina oratio ascendat ad te Domine.
R. Et descendat super nos misericordia tua.[48]

The first is an almost exact quote of psalm 140.2a: 'Let my prayer come before you, O Lord – Like incense in your sight.' The second paraphrases the rest of the verse: 'Our evening prayer ascends to you, O Lord: And your mercy descends upon us.'

Gabriele Winkler maintains that this is the fundamental surviving element of the Roman cathedral Vespers.[49] She cites Amalar, who says of the versicle: '. . . At this verse incense is offered, the offering that the Lord commands.' For Amalar, Sunday started on Saturday night, and the incensing now associated with the canticle *Magnificat* was associated with psalm 140. The canticle clearly followed the offering of incense.[50] Either the versicle was chanted rather more elaborately than in the form which survived to modern times, or elaborate chant had reduced a full psalm to just a single verse.

The short responsory, a form also found in the Day Hours of the Roman Breviary, is best illustrated by quoting an example, that for Sunday evening:[51]

---

44 *RB 18*, pp. 213–15.

45 See *Breviarium Monasticum.*

46 J. Pascher, 'De Psalmodia Vesperarum', *EL*, **79** (1965), 318–26.

47 See e.g., *Breviarium Romanum*, 149.

48 E.g., ibid., 161.

49 Winkler, 'Über die Kathedralvesper', 97–101.

50 Op. cit., 'Post hic sequitur ymnus Sanctae Mariae.'

51 *BM I*, 158.

R. How wonderful are * your works O Lord. How wonderful... (repeat).
V. In wisdom you have made them all.
R. Your works, O Lord.
V Glory to the Father...
R. How wonderful... (in full).

This is a quote from psalm 103.24, a psalm frequently seen at the beginning of Vespers. Hansjakob Becker has persuasively argued that this responsory is a shrivelled remnant of an opening *lucernarium* psalm.[52] Well suited to the end of the day, the psalm is also found in such Western monastic orders for Vespers as those of Caesarius and Aurelian.

Becker also makes the ingenious suggestion that the *capitulum* is not a lesson, but a blessing that once began cathedral Vespers. This would be analogous to the Byzantine 'Blessed is the Kingdom of the Father' now confined to the eucharistic liturgy, but in the Constantinopolitan cathedral office used to begin Vespers and Matins as well.[53] It is certainly interesting that the same *capitulum* was used on each day of the week except Saturday (festal *capitula* are clearly short selected readings).[54] The same was true of the Roman Breviary.[55] The passage, from 2 Cor. 1.3–4, reads:

> Blessed be the God and Father of our Lord Jesus Christ, the Father of mercies and the God of all consolation, who consoles us in all our tribulation.

At Vespers it is appropriate to bless God who is merciful and who offers consoling love to his people in their tribulations.

Becker suggests that the Vespers of the rule of St Benedict may be summarized as follows:

I. Monastic Office (Psalms, perhaps with silence and collects)
II. Cathedral Office
i) Opening: – Blessing and Evening Psalm (103?)
ii) Light ceremony: – Office Hymn
iii) Incense: – Psalm 140 and *Magnificat*
iv) Intercession: – Litany and Lord's Prayer.[56]

[52] Hansjakob Beker, 'Zur Struktur der 'Vespertina Sinaxis' in der Regula Benedicti', in *ALW 29* (1987) 177–88, 183–4.

[53] Borgia, op. cit., 235.

[54] *BM I*, 158, passim.

[55] *BR autumnalis*, 140 and passim.

[56] Becker, 184.

After the monastic psalmody follow the three basic components of evening prayer, the lighting of the lamp as a symbol of Christ, the evening psalm 140 and prayer.[57] Relics of these appear to be also visible in the Roman/Benedictine office of Vespers.

The *Magnificat* is so widely identified with evening prayer in Western Christianity that nobody seems to question its total lack of suitability as an evening canticle. From what we have seen of the East, most ancient forms of daily prayer confined all canticles to the morning, the New Testament ones taking the last place, so following biblical order. Unlike the *Benedictus* which refers to 'when the day shall dawn upon us from on high',[58] Luke 1.46–55 has no obvious connection with the evening hour, and in fact, in praising God for 'raising up the lowly' and 'scattering the proud of heart', has more in common with classical morning canticles such as the Exodus Song of the Sea.[59]

RM calls for readings from the Epistles and Gospels at each Hour of the Divine Office.[60] Thus: 'At Vespers in winter six psalms are to be said, always in the sequence of the Psalter, one responsory, a verse, a reading from the Apostle, and the Gospel, which the abbot must always say, and after this the prayer to God.'[61] Was the Gospel actually a canticle?

The rule of St Benedict is quite clear that there should be a Gospel canticle, we may presume that the *Magnificat* was intended.[62] Did the evening use of the *Magnificat* come from the monastic/cathedral office of the Roman basilicas? There is no way of answering that question that puts the matter beyond doubt. However, if the cryptic remarks of Amalar (see above) do indicate the possibility of forms of Vespers that had a responsory and no *Magnificat*, then the latter may have been a monastic import into whatever primitive cathedral rite existed in Rome. Perhaps it was imported by the monks who served the great urban basilicas.[63]

---

[57] Winkler, op. cit., 101.

[58] Luke 1.78 (RSV).

[59] Aurelian of Arles' rule (mid sixth cent.) appointed *Magnificat* for Sunday and festal cathedral Matins, see *PL* 68, 393, and Taft, *Liturgy of the Hours*, pp. 111–12.

[60] *RM XXXV* (p. 199).

[61] Ibid., *XXXVI*.

[62] *RB xvii* (212) – 'canticum de Evangelia'.

[63] Weekday *Magnificat* antiphons were normally verses of the canticle taken in turn – see *BR autumnalis*, 143–61 and *BM I*, 162–75.

Hymnody and Prayer

The common Western style of hymn appears to have originated with Ambrose of Milan, Benedict even calls the hymn 'ambrosian'.[64] It is highly probable that the Benedictines were influential in popularizing their use, but whereas in the Milanese Vespers the hymn is part of the opening rite, Benedict places it after the psalmody in close relationship to the versicle and canticle.

The Vespers hymns of the later Roman/Benedictine breviaries include many seasonal and festal compositions; we shall examine only those given for days of the week. They are believed to be quite ancient and are found in the same order in both Roman and Benedictine books. The Latin of the Roman Breviary hymns was altered to suit sixteenth-century humanist taste,[65] so we shall refer to the unaltered versions found in *BM* and *Sarum*.[66] The hymns have been translated into English and many are readily available, for example, in older editions of the *English Hymnal*.[67]

The hymns of Sunday–Friday meditate upon creation, like psalm 103, and on the idea of Christ the new creation, represented by the light of the lamp/candle. Sunday's 'O blest Creator of the light' celebrates the calling of order out of chaos, 'And o'er the forming world didst call/ the light from chaos first of all.' 'O boundless Wisdom, God most High', on Monday, sings of the creation of land and sea.' On Tuesday, 'Earth's mighty maker' speaks of the creation of seed-bearing plants, while Wednesday's 'Caeli Deus sanctissime' celebrates the creation of day and night. Thursday's refers to the flood and baptism: 'Be none submerged in sin's distress'. On Friday the creation of animal life commences: 'Maker of man, who from thy throne'. These hymns date from the fifth to seventh centuries and form a coherent group, but Saturday's, 'O Lux beata Trinitas', also attributed to Ambrose, is somewhat different:

> O Trinity of blessed light,
> O unity of princely might,
> The fiery sun now goes his way;
> Shed thou within our hearts thy ray
> To thee our morning song of praise,
> To thee our evening prayer we raise;
> Thy glory suppliant we adore
> For ever and for evermore.[68]

---

[64] E.g., Vespers in *RB xvii* (p. 212).

[65] See e.g., Taft, *Liturgy of the Hours*, p. 310, and Batiffol, op. cit., 214–20.

[66] *BM I*, p. 158–75, and *Sarum*, pp. 195–221.

[67] *The English Hymnal* (London: Oxford University Press and A.R. Mowbray, 1933, 15th imp., 1965), see nos. 51, 59, 61 and 62, herafter *EH*.

[68] *EH* 164 (Translation by J.M. Neale).

This simple and stately evening hymn does not have anything to do with the theme of creation, but it is well suited to the time of the lamp-lighting. Clearly not of the same series as the other weekday hymns, it might well be older and we may note (a) it is preserved on Saturday, that is, the first Vespers of Sunday, (b) it could well have been intended as a Western *lucernarium* hymn like *Phos hilaron*.

Like most forms of evening and morning office, the old Roman and Benedictine offices concluded with prayer. *RB* speaks of a 'litany' and the recitation, *by the superior*, of the Lord's Prayer.[69] *RM* refers only to the 'prayer to God'. The later Monastic Breviary provided, after the *Magnificat*, 'Kyrie eleison, Christe eleison, Kyrie eleison', the Lord's Prayer (by the Abbot alone) and the collect.[70] There is no mention of the collect in *RB*, while the Roman Breviaries had no Lord's Prayer, but a collect.[71] If the Lord's Prayer was an exemplar rather than a formula,[72] then it may well have *replaced* the collect because there were few priests in the early Benedictine monasteries.[73] By contrast, the secular office used the collect alone, but on certain days had the *preces feriales*, preceded by the Lord's Prayer. This form, identical in the evening and the morning,[74] was a *capitellum*, a series of scriptural verses arranged in versicle and response form which originated around the sixth century.[75]

The collect at the developed Roman and Benedictine offices was that of the feast or other liturgical day. If there was no particular observance, then the collect of the previous Sunday was used by default.[76] However, we have seen that there were evening collects in the older liturgical books, such as the Verona *Libellus*. Such collects are also found in later sacramentaries. The so-called Old Gelasian Sacramentary, copied c.750,[77] provides a set of eight 'Orationes ad Vesperum',[78] which do not seem to have any relationship to those of the Verona *Libellus* but do appear in other sacramentaries. The first prays to God

---

[69] *RB xiii* (208).

[70] See e.g., *BM I*, 159.

[71] See e.g., *BR autumnalis*, 141.

[72] Matthew 6.9: 'Pray then *like* this: ...'.

[73] Bradshaw, op. cit., p. 120.

[74] *BR autumnalis*, 63–4, 143–5.

[75] P. DeClerck, *La prière universelle dans les liturgies latines anciennes* (Münster: Aschendorff, 1977), pp. 269–73.

[76] *BM I*, 163.

[77] Vogel et al., *Medieval Liturgy*, op. cit., pp. 65, 69, 70.

[78] H.A. Wilson, *The Gelasian Sacramentary* (Oxford: Clarendon, 1894), pp. 292–3, and C. Mohlberg, et. al. (eds), *Liber Sacramentorum Romanae Aecclesiae Ordinis Anni Circuli* (*RED 4*, Rome: Herder, 1960), pp. 230–1, #1587, 1588, 1594.

who is worshipped at morning, noon and night, that the darkness of sin may be banished from our hearts, that we may come to the true light, which is Christ. The second prays that God who illuminates the night, and gives light after darkness, may bring us to worship him in the morning. The remainder employ similar themes: protection from the power of evil and darkness by the true light, Christ, whose full glory is to be celebrated in the morning, which, of course, can have eschatological overtones. For example:

> We give you thanks, O Lord, who has kept us through this day: we thank you for freeing us and guarding us by night: Lord we beseech you, hasten our coming to the morning hour safe and sound, so that at all times you may have us praising you. Through...

Several of these prayers are found in later collections such as the Frankish Gelasian sacramentary of Gellone.[79] This has three sets of evening prayers, one of them is particularly rich in associations with psalm 140:

> We give you thanks, Lord God almighty, who have granted us to live through the course of this day and come to the evening hour; praying to you we beseech that the lifting of our hands to you, may be an acceptable evening sacrifice in your sight. Through our Lord Jesus Christ.

These prayers probably fell into desuetude with the multiplication of saints' days. However they reflect a very similar theological approach to evening prayer to what we have seen elsewhere. The evening advances and darkness falls, but the light of Christ is a sign of the unquenchable light that protects us through the night until the morning, itself a symbol of God's eternal day.

Further Evidence for Old Roman Vespers

Some other fragmentary clues to an older form of Roman Vespers do exist. *Ordo Romanus XII* (possibly a late-seventh-century urban source)[80] describes a form of Easter week Vespers that appears to have only three psalms: 'Ad vesperum tres psalmos usque in sabbato et per singulos psalmos *Alleluia*'.[81] Van Dijk mentions this when describing the interesting Easter Vespers held in

---

[79] *Liber Sacramentorum Gellonensis*, (eds) A. Dumas and J. Deshusses (Corpus Christianorum: series Latina 159 & 159A, Turnhout: Brepols, 1981), vol. I, pp. 303–7, # 2132.

[80] S.J.P. van Dijk, 'The Medieval Easter Vespers of the Roman Clergy', *Sacris Erudiri*, **19** (1969–70), 261–363, 327.

[81] M. Andrieu (ed.), *Les Ordines Romani du haut moyen âge* (Louvain: *Spicilegium Sacrum Lovaniense 11, 23, 24, 28, 29*, 1931–61), vol. 2, p. 464.

the Lateran basilica by the clergy of Rome on Easter Sunday, after which they returned to their churches for the three-psalm form.[82] The solemn Vespers at the Lateran was at the Ninth Hour, and of the five psalms, only three were sung in church, while many other pieces of this unusual service did not correspond to the normal monastic Vespers.

Van Dijk concluded that the service was the result of combining the five psalm monastic Vespers with the older cathedral form, represented by the great Alleluiatic chants: 'The Lord has reigned', 'Pascha Nostrum', and psalm 94, 'Venite exultemus'. He goes so far as to suggest that the original three psalms were 129, 'Out of the depths', 140, and 11, 'Help us, O Lord, for good men have vanished... I myself will arise... I will grant them the salvation for which they thirst.'[83]

From Night to Morning in the Roman/Benedictine Tradition

For centuries it has been common to see the Night (Nocturns) and Morning (Lauds) offices of the Roman/Benedictine tradition as two offices normally joined together.[84] Depending whether it was summer or winter rising times could vary, but Lauds was always at daybreak.[85] A pause between the offices was possible, but the Rule of the Master expected no break between the two in summer.[86]

The distinction between the two offices was formalized by the use of the introductory phrase from psalm 69, 'O God, make haste to my rescue', and the *Gloria Patri* at the beginning of Lauds.[87] Since all introductory versicles and responses were omitted in the last three days of Holy Week,[88] and following Baumstark's rule that 'primitive conditions are maintained with greater tenacity in the more sacred seasons of the Liturgical Year',[89] the versicles may not be ancient, and the break between the two services becomes less obvious.

---

[82] Van Dijk, 330–31, and *Ordo XXVII* (paragraph 79), Andrieu, vol. 3, p. 362.

[83] Van Dijk, op. cit., 330–32.

[84] E.g., entries for Mattins and Lauds in F.L. Cross and E.A. Livingstone (eds), *Oxford Dictionary of the Christian Church* (2nd ed.), (Oxford: Oxford University Press, 1974), pp. 892, 804.

[85] *RB viii*, 'mox matutini, qui incipiente luce agendi sunt, subsequantur' (Fry, 202).

[86] *RM XXXIII*, 195: 'We have prescribed that the nocturns in these short nights are to begin after cockcrow and are to be joined to Matins so that the brothers do not go back to bed after the nocturns'.

[87] *BR autumnalis*, 19; *BM I*, 36.

[88] *BR verna*, 269; *BM I*, 522.

[89] *Comparative Liturgy*, p. 27.

If in the East, monastic vigils were added to 'cathedral Morning Prayer' (as in Egeria), then in the West, monastic usage absorbed cathedral elements or a distinct cathedral Morning Prayer duplicated the monastic one. It is possible that the monastic night vigil and the cathedral Morning Prayer were distinct but not always celebrated separately.

The perception of Matins and Lauds as separate services may have been influenced by the custom of enumerating the offices so as to fulfil literally the prayer of the psalmist 'Seven times a day have I praised you' (psalm 118.164). Benedict identified the seven times with Lauds, Prime, Terce, Sext, None, Vespers and Compline – the Nocturns were an extra, fulfilling psalm 118.62, 'At midnight I will rise and thank you'.[90]

Later tendencies worked against any break:[91] for example, the summer horarium of Lanfranc's *Consuetudines* for Canterbury (tenth century) left virtually no gap between Matins at about 2 a.m. and Lauds at around 3.30.[92] The rather later- founded Carthusians appear to have combined Matins and Lauds for centuries, starting at about 11.45 p.m., and lasting two to three hours;[93] so finishing well before light. In English medieval cathedrals the secular canons always combined Matins and Lauds, in Lincoln this was celebrated at midnight in the winter until 1548, and in the summer the service began at about 5 a.m. It was known as 'night matins', even when celebrated early in the morning.[94]

A later development again, was to anticipate Matins *and* Lauds the night before – thus emptying Lauds of its real meaning. This was particularly characteristic of the last three days of Holy Week down to 1955, when the combined service was known as *Tenebrae* (darkness) – a complete reversal of its original purpose.[95]

As we turn to examine particular details of this form of Matins, we should bear in mind the following points:

---

[90] *RB xvi* (Fry, 210).

[91] Many scholars treated the two offices as *one*, e.g. J.A. Jungmann, *Public Worship* (London: Challoner, 1957), p. 170.

[92] Laurance Goulder, *Church Life in Medieval England: The Monasteries* (London: Guild of Our Lady of Ransom, 1967), pp. 90–91. For winter, see D. Knowles OSB, *The Monastic Order in England* (Cambridge: University Press, 1949), p. 450.

[93] Goulder, op. cit., p. 89.

[94] Kathleen Edwards, *The English Secular Cathedrals in the Middle Ages* (Manchester: Manchester University Press, 1967), p. 56.

[95] A.J. MacGregor, *Fire and Light in the Western Triduum* (Collegeville, MN: Alcuin Club/ Liturgical Press, 1992), pp. 31–3.

1 The characteristic monastic recitation of the Psalter in course is confined to the specifically nocturnal part of the office, or vigil before dawn, as found elsewhere.
2 Scriptural reading is also nocturnal.
3 Where the texts at Nocturns refer to the Hour they speak of rising from sleep. Where there is a gap between Nocturns and Lauds, that gap is (a) not used for sleep, and (b) can disappear altogether, even though Lauds may then take place before dawn or sunrise.
4 It will be suggested that there is a structural progression from the beginning of Nocturns to the climax at Lauds.

The Shape of the Service

The Nocturns of the last three days of Holy Week began directly with the antiphon to the first psalm; the opening versicles, the invitatory psalm and the hymn being omitted. While this might reflect the primitive form of this office, it may also mean that early editors would not have thought it worthwhile to include frequently used formulae. In monastic use psalm 3, sung without an antiphon, was followed by psalm 94 with the Invitatory, and then the hymn.[96] All of this is found in *RB*;[97] the Rule of the Master makes no mention of psalm 3.[98] The Roman Breviary began with psalm 94 and the hymn.

The greater part of the Nocturnal offices was taken up by the recitation of the Psalter in course, and the reading of scripture punctuated by Responsories. Most of these features do not bear upon the time of day (or night), but were rather a continuous meditation upon the psalms and the scriptures. The scriptural readings were originally continuous or semi-continuous over the year.[99] Their later abbreviation caused a loss of continuity.[100] They are followed by responsories, forms whose origin is still not clear. Perhaps beginning as a form of 'responsorial psalm', they function as extended meditations upon the readings, though the oldest, those for Epiphany and Septuagesima, rely on the psalms of the previous nocturn for their texts.[101]

---

[96] *BM I*, 17–19.

[97] Op. cit., *ix* (Fry, 202).

[98] *RM XXXII*, p. 194.

[99] See e.g., *Ordo Romanus XIII* (Vogel et al., p. 166), which gives the order in which the books of the Bible are to be read.

[100] See e.g., S.J.P. van Dijk and J. Hazelden Walker, *The Origins of the Modern Roman Liturgy* (London: Darton, Longman and Todd, 1960), p. 127.

[101] Joseph Dyer, 'The Singing of Psalms in the Early-Medieval Office', *Speculum*, **64** (1989), 535–78, 545.

The content of Roman/Benedictine Lauds is far more fixed than that of the Nocturns or Vespers. While Benedict made some alterations, the basic shape remained intact. There were fixed morning psalms, including psalm 50, together with one or two morning psalms for each day of the week; a canticle (*Benedicite* on Sundays); the praise psalms (148–50); then *capitulum*, morning hymn, versicle, New Testament canticle *Benedictus* and prayer. This fundamentally simple morning office most easily stands on its own on weekdays. Comprising confession, prayer for the new day, and praise of God's glory, it makes a logical and consistent whole. However, just as in Egeria's Jerusalem a longer vigil preceded the main morning service, so the devout might await the morning in a nocturnal watch that climaxed with Lauds.

For Callewaert the night ended, and the service moved directly from Nocturns to the morning praises.[102] Jungmann concurred,[103] following Hanssens who saw Lauds as the sunrise climax to the dawn and pre-dawn morning vigil, which had extended back into the night through monastic influence.[104] The core of this morning praise was the 'Laudes', psalms 148–50 as in the East, the praises that gave this part of the office its name of Lauds, and which only lost their central place in the Roman liturgy in 1912.

Mateos and Taft are less sure that the two services, Nocturns and Lauds, have always been united. However, the provision for a break between the two in *RM* and *RB* may itself be a development. *RB*'s abbreviation of Nocturns, in comparison to the old Roman office, means a shorter office that allowed time for spiritual reading or bodily needs.[105] If meditative reading was done during the interval, then a too clear distinction between the night and first light parts of the vigil is anachronistic. Where a distinction does appear to be made, for example, Jerusalem as described by Egeria, it is never a complete one. The two services are so closely related that they can still be seen as two parts of a whole.

The Scriptures from Night to Morning

Psalm 3 with its references to rising after rest is a widely used morning psalm; psalm 94 is less common and may have been a particularly Roman tradition. The Invitatory antiphons are general, except on feasts, that for Sunday in Roman and Benedictine books being 'Adoremus Dominum, qui fecit nos'.[106]

---

[102] 'de Laudibus Matutinis', in *Sacris Erudiri*, op. cit., 53–89, 53–60.

[103] 'The Morning Hour in the Roman Liturgy', in *Pastoral Liturgy* (op. cit.), pp. 151–7, 153.

[104] J.M. Hanssens, *Nature et genèse de l'Office des Matines* (*Analecta Gregoriana* 57, Rome: 1952), pp. 96ff., 58.

[105] *RB viii* (Fry, 202).

[106] *BR autumnalis*, ibid.; *BM I*, 18.

The ordinary weekday Invitatoria are quite joyful: for example, Jubilemus Deo, salutari nostro' on Tuesday and 'Dominum qui fecit nos, venite adoremus' on Thursday. If there is a common theme it is creation/new creation in redemption.[107]

The psalms of the first nocturn in *BR* are grouped in sets of four under a single, simple antiphon, usually taken from the first psalm of the set. At the second and third, there is a single antiphon for each psalm.[108] On weekdays the twelve psalms had an antiphon for each pair.[109] On feasts when there were only nine psalms, specially selected antiphons were used for each psalm, but it does not seem that those antiphons were chosen to bring out some salient feature of the psalm.

The ordinary antiphons appear to have originally been refrains that punctuated the solo reading of the psalms:[110] for example, 'Serve the Lord with awe and trembling, pay him your homage'.[111] The versicle in both forms of Sunday Nocturns, however, is illuminating:

V. Memor fui nocte nominis tui Domine.
R. Et custodivi legem tuam.[112]

The night, or time before dawn, is the time to meditate on God's deeds and integrate them into one's life.

The scripture readings appointed for the Vigil were originally continuous or semi-continuous. *BM*, following *RB*, had only a brief reading at the end of the second Nocturn on weekdays[113] and no patristic reading. The short chapter for ordinary days was from 1 Corinthians 16.13–14,[114] 'Be watchful, stand firm in your faith, be courageous, be strong. Let all that you do be done in love', eminently suited to the vigil theme. Others are seasonal yet appropriate, such as 'Wash yourselves, make yourselves clean' (Isaiah 1.16) and 'We were buried therefore with him' (Romans 6.4), for Lent and Eastertide respectively.[115]

In the third Nocturn of *BR* the readings were from patristic homilies on the Gospel of the Sunday and, instead of the third Responsory, the hymn *Te Deum*

---

[107] *BR aut.*, 64 and 88; *BM I*, 65 and 92.

[108] Op. cit., 4–18.

[109] E.g., ibid., 48–59.

[110] See Joseph Dyer, 'Monastic Psalmody of the Middle Ages', *Révue Bénédictine*, **99** (1989), 41–74, 43 and 50.

[111] *BR*, ibid., 5.

[112] *BR aut.*, 11 and *BM I*, 23.

[113] *RB ix* (Fry, 204).

[114] *BM I*, 56.

[115] Ibid., 57.

was sung.[116] *RB* instead required three canticles chosen by the Abbot, New Testament readings and responsories, and then, *after* a responsory, *Te Deum*, the Gospel of the day read by the Abbot and the short hymn *Te decet laus*.[117] This remained the form of Benedictine nocturns until Vatican II, except that the readings were patristic homilies on the Gospel. This part of the Benedictine office may have been influenced by the cathedral vigil. There is no mention of whether the Gospel is to be one of the resurrection pericopes (*BM* simply duplicates that of the Sunday Eucharist),[118] though Caesarius and Aurelian certainly expected it to be so.[119]

The canticles in *BM* are appointed rather than left to the abbot's discretion. On ordinary days there was first, Isaiah 33.2–10 (see vv. 2 and 10, 'be our arm every morning' and 'Now I will arise, says the Lord'). Then Isaiah 33.13–18 (the righteous may have confidence in God); and finally Ecclesiasticus 36.12–19 (Joy in the heavenly Jerusalem).[120] The ordinary Sunday canticles dwell on the morning themes of God's protection and look forward to the coming light. Seasonal canticles always include these themes: for example, the alternative Advent canticle from Isaiah 42.10–16, verse 16: 'I will turn the darkness before them into light'.[121]

We can assume the praise psalms are central to the dawn 'Laudes' (sung under one antiphon, 'Alleluia'),[122] but what precedes them? On Sundays and feasts they were preceded by the Daniel 3 canticle *Benedicite*,[123] which we also associate with the Paschal vigil, and which often occurs elsewhere as a prelude to the praises. This and the Song of the Sea of Exodus may once have been used together in the Roman cathedral tradition.[124] The Sunday antiphons refer to the three children in the furnace as a type of the resurrection, especially that in *BM I*:

> Surrexit Christus de sepulcro, qui liberavit tres pueros de camino ignis ardentis, alleluia.[125]

---

116 *BR aut*, 18–19.

117 *RB xi* (Fry, 206).

118 E.g., *BM*, op. cit., 451–3 (2nd Sunday of Lent).

119 Bradshaw, op. cit., p. 146.

120 *BM*, 30–31.

121 Ibid., 28–34.

122 *BR aut.*, 22–3; *BM I*, 40–41.

123 *BR aut*, 21; *BM I*, 39.

124 Baumstark, op. cit., pp. 35–7.

125 Ibid., p. 39.

For the rest of the week there was a different canticle each day, in *BR* these were as follows:

Monday	Isaiah 12.1–6, 'I will give thanks to thee, O Lord'
Tuesday	Isaiah 38.10–20, 'The prayer of Hezekiah'
Wednesday	1 Samuel 2.2–10, 'Canticle of Hannah'
Thursday	Exodus 15.1–19, 'The Song of the Sea'
Friday	Habakkuk 3.2–19, 'O Lord, I have heard the report...'
Saturday	Deuteronomy 32.1–43, 'Give ear, O heavens, ...'[126]

The only one of the above not found elsewhere as a morning canticle is the first, Isaiah 12. It is, however, appropriate to the role with words like: 'Behold, God is my salvation; I will trust and will not be afraid; for the Lord God is my strength and my song, and he has become my salvation' (v. 2). *RB* presumes the same system of canticles,[127] but later Benedictine offices added a second 'festal' canticle as an alternative to each of the above. All are suited to the resurrection/new creation themes: for example, Tuesday – Tobit 13.1–10, especially 13.2 'he leads down to Hades, and brings up again'.[128]

In the old Roman use the canticle itself was preceded daily by psalms 62 and 66 under one antiphon.[129] Psalm 66, 'O God be gracious and bless us and let your face shed its light upon us', is described as a sunrise psalm by Callewaert.[130] Psalm 99, 'Cry out with joy to the Lord all the earth', may be seen as the variable psalm for Sunday, especially as it is to do with creation.[131] Psalm 92 at the beginning of Lauds, 'The Lord is King, with majesty enrobed... holiness is fitting to your house, O Lord, until the end of time' echoes East Syrian use and appears to have taken the place of psalm 50 on Sundays.[132] This may be seen as an extended burst of praise to the creator God, followed by the vigil psalm 62 leading to sunrise, and then the canticle as the praise of all creation finding its climax in the 'laudes'.

On weekdays we find the ancient custom of beginning Morning Prayer with psalm 50, followed by a selected daily psalm. For example, 5 ('It is you whom I invoke, O Lord. In the morning you hear me'), 42 ('O send forth your light and

[126] *BR*, 62–136.

[127] *BR*, *xiii* (Fry, 208).

[128] *BM I*, 61–140.

[129] See table of psalm orders at Lauds in Taft, *Liturgy of the Hours*, pp. 136–7.

[130] Callewaert, de Laudibus, 70.

[131] Ibid., 117.

[132] Ibid., 71, who concludes that this is pre–Benedict use.

your truth'), or 142 ('In the morning let me know your love'). All breathe a spirit of prayer for the light that brings God's grace, having first confessed sin in psalm 50.

St Benedict somewhat altered this simple arrangement by having two variable psalms per weekday, except on Saturday when the canticle was much longer, and changing the position of some of them. Psalm 62 was reserved for Sunday. Psalm 50 was used every day, even Sunday (which could be a more primitive practice), preceded by psalm 66 without antiphon as a 'gathering' psalm like psalm 3 at Nocturns. Also, on Sundays, psalm 117 was to follow psalm 50, a very appropriate choice, 'This day was made by the Lord, we rejoice and are glad'. *BM* also adds psalms 92 and 99, not mentioned by Benedict.[133]

As the praise psalms are at the centre of the morning office, then the rest of that central core could be said to include the *capitulum* (the Benedictine Responsory) the morning hymn, and the canticle *Benedictus*. Forming a New Testament conclusion to the canticles and psalms that have preceded it, the canticle recognizes the present light, but in an eschatological spirit looks forward to its consummation in the everlasting day.

The *capitulum* for Sunday: 'Blessing and glory and wisdom and thanksgiving and honour and power and might be to our God for ever and ever! Amen' (Revelation 7.12), again seems more a blessing than a reading. However, the weekday *capitulum* from Romans 13.12–13, 'The night is far gone, the day is at hand', is a simple and appropriate reading for the time.

The Morning Hymnody and Prayers

The winter hymn for Sunday sings of the resurrection: 'This day the first of days was made,/ When God in light the world arrayed', and exhorts, 'Slumber and sloth drive far away;/ earlier arise to greet the day.'[134] The shorter summer hymn praises the Father '*now the night is over*', and looks to the eternal day, 'Bring us to heaven, where thy Saints united/ Joy without ending.'[135] In Monday's 'Somno refectis artubus' we rise from refreshing sleep,[136] and day replaces the passing night:

> As shades at morning flee away,
> And night before the Star of day,

[133] *BM I*, 38.

[134] *EH* 50, vv. 1 and 2; *BM I*, 18.

[135] *EH* 165, vv. 1 and 2; *BM I*, 19.

[136] *BM I*, 45.

So each transgression of the night
Be purg'd by Thee, celestial Light![137]

Light overthrowing night and the scattering of the spirits of darkness are found in other hymns, e.g., 'Consors paterni luminis,/ Lux ipse lucis, et dies, . . .' on Tuesday.[138] Although hymns are latecomers to pure Roman Nocturns, their presence in the Benedictine books, and elsewhere, demonstrates the liturgical/ theological presuppositions behind this time for prayer. Those redeemed by Christ rise in the night and pray to overcome evil and temptation, so that they may await the coming of the true light that overcomes the darkness of death, the light of God in Christ.

The final element of hymnody in the nocturnal vigil on Sundays and feasts was the hymn *Te Deum*. Of a composite nature, with 'capitellum' type intercessions attached to the hymn of praise, some have argued that its origin was perhaps in the Paschal vigil, and others have suggested that it might be a eucharistic prayer. Baumstark noted that the hymn had the same content and structure as a set of chants from early sixth-century Palestine,[139] from whence came also *Te decet laus* (attested to in the Apostolic Constitutions)[140] which Benedict added after the Gospel. The structurally similar Great Doxology was more popular in the East for concluding Matins.

The *Te Deum* is very much a morning hymn. There is an opening praise to God's holiness, and the enumeration of the praises of the saints, 'Te gloriosus Apostolorum chorus', etc. Then the hymn turns to the Spirit ('Sanctum quoque, Paraclitum Spiritum'), and finally then to Christ ('Tu Rex gloriae, Christe'), to the liberation he brings through his incarnation, passion and just judgement. The intercessory material prays that God will save his people (as in the Great Doxology), that we may bless the Lord all the days of our life, and, again echoing the Great Doxology, prays that the day may be free from sin. Clearly we are entering upon the morning part of the office, this hymn is the harbinger of Lauds.

In *BM* there are Sunday hymns at Lauds, for winter and for summer:[141] 'Aeterne rerum Conditor' and 'Ecce jam noctis tenuatur umbra'. The first is more suited to cockcrow (where it is found in Milan). The second sings of the light of dawn scattering the shadows of the night. Monday's hymn, Ambrose's well-known 'Splendor paternae gloriae', is a paean to the new day:

---

[137] Neale's translation in *Collected Hymns of John Mason Neale DD*, ed. Mary Sackville Lawson (London: 1914), p. 85.

[138] Ibid., p. 65.

[139] Baumstark, op. cit., pp. 105–6.

[140] Ibid., 87.

[141] *BM I*, 41–2, 63.

O Splendour of God's glory bright,
O thou that bringest light from light,
O Light of light, light's living spring,
O Day, all days illumining.[142]

It is also a prayer for the day: 'Our mind be in his keeping placed'. On Wednesday darkness and sin are banished by Christ's light:

Ye clouds and darkness, hosts of night,
That breed confusion and afright.
Begone! o'erhead the dawn shines clear,
The light breaks in and Christ is here.[143]

The beautiful 'Aurora jam spargit polum' on Saturday has a fine verse looking forward to the eternal day:

So, Lord, when that last morning breaks,
Looking to which we sigh and pray,
O may it to thy minstrels prove
The dawning of a better day.[144]

The hymns then reflect the same morning themes identified in other elements of this tradition.

The concluding intercessory material is the same as at Vespers in both *BR* and *BM*, and the printed books again know only collects for Sundays and feasts. However the sacramentaries again provide examples of morning collects. The first in the Gelasian Sacramentary thanks God's for guidance from night to morning, and that the day may be without sin.[145] The fourth greets God as true light and author of light, and prays for entry into light, and the fifth for increase of faith and the light of the Spirit. An excellent example is the ninth collect:

> We give you thanks for your inexpressible mercies, almighty God, who, having dispelled the gloom of night and the mean blindness of ignorance, has led us to the beginning of this day, calling us back to the worship and knowledge of your name: illumine our senses, almighty Father, so that walking always in the light of your precepts, we may follow you as our leader and guide. Through . . .

---

[142] *EH* 52.

[143] *EH* 54.

[144] *EH* 57.

[145] Mohlberg et al., op. cit., #1576, 1579, 1580, 1584.

> All these collects have the general theme of emerging from threatening darkness into the light of God's day. God is praised for protection, and entrusted with the new day, a symbol for the whole of the Christian life.

The Sacramentary of Gellone provides a series of sixteen prayers *ad matutinas*.[146] The last three, all short, are found in other Frankish Gelasians, and also in the eighth-century Roman Hadrianum.[147] They again emphasize the passage from darkness to light, and the short prayers are good examples of the genre. For example:

> You, O Lord, are the truth that enlightens us, and from every deformity you defend us. Through...

> Hear us, almighty merciful God and shed the light of your grace into our minds. Through...

The Minor Hours and Compline

We have already seen that the Day Hours largely comprised the same psalms each day. The Hours in *RB* were mostly made up of sections of psalm 118. The Benedictine system roughly halved the pensum of psalmody, confining psalm 118 to Sunday and Monday and for the rest of week using psalms 119–27. In both cases the reasoning behind the systems seems to be the idea of the services being recited from memory. This agrees with the fixity we find elsewhere in Minor Hours.

The psalms used, especially 118 and the gradual psalms, could be seen as representing the following of God's law through the pilgrimage of life. The short chapters also take us through the day. At Prime, 'Love truth and peace, says the lord' (Zechariah 8); Terce, 'Heal me O Lord, and I shall be healed' (Jeremiah 17); 'Prove all things, hold fast that which is good...' (1 Thessalonians 5); and None, 'Bear ye one another's burdens' (Galatians 6). There is no reflection in all this of the long-standing tendency to identify these Hours with moments in Christ's passion, or in the case of Terce with the coming of the Holy Spirit.

The hymns associated with these Hours were also normally fixed, and therefore able to be committed to memory:

> *Prime*: Now that daylight fills the sky
> *Terce*: Come Holy Ghost, with God the Son

---

[146] *Liber Secra. Gell.*, op. cit., 300–302, #2116, 2118.

[147] Vogel et al., op. cit., p. 81.

Sext: O God of truth, O Lord of might
None: O God, creation's secret force

Only that at Terce associates the Hour with a particular devotion. The fact that all of the above offices but Prime were concluded by proper prayers means that there was no room there either for devotional contemplation of the passion. The collect at Prime, 'O Lord God almighty, who have brought us safely to the beginning of this day', was one of the few fixed features that had a clear temporal reference.

Compline was, if anything, simpler. After a Confessional rite came psalms 4, 30, 90 and 133, under one antiphon (4, 90 and 133 with no antiphon in *BM*). These were all well chosen for last thing at night. The hymn 'Before the ending of the day' was followed by the *capitulum*,'Thou O Lord, art in the midst of us' (Jeremiah 14), the Benedictine version finishing with a versicle, *Kyrie eleison*, Lord's Prayer and fixed collect. *BR* included a short responsory and the canticle *Nunc Dimittis*. In both cases the collect was 'Visit, we beseech Thee, O Lord this dwelling' but the Sarum Breviary used 'Lighten our darkness, we beseech Thee, O Lord'.[148] Additional material, such as Marian anthems, was clearly a devotional addition of the Middle Ages. Some Benedictines still celebrate Compline from memory in the darkness.

Conclusions

I From the structures

1 There are early indications (Jerome and Arnobius) of a lamp-lighting tradition at evening and the use of psalm 140.
2 When the developed service of Vespers appears in the Roman office it has continuous psalmody before the central core.
3 If the Roman monastic psalmody was followed by the cathedral office, Benedict may have placed the hymn where the two joined, not at the beginning.[149]
4 The Roman Psalter included the gradual psalms in the evening psalmody.
5 There are hints that the *Magnificat* is not original to this office.

[148] Fasciculus II, 240–1.

[149] The position of the hymn after the short reading has implications ignored in the reformed Roman offices, see. S. Campbell, FSC, *From Breviary to Liturgy of the Hours* (Collegeville, MN: Liturgical Press, 1995), p. 182.

6 There is evidence, in *Ordo Romanus XII* and in the Paschal Vespers described by Van Dijk, of a three-psalm cathedral Vespers.
7 The night to morning offices, though described as separate, are often to be recited without any break, and are always a vigil culminating in morning praise.
8 The Night office comprises psalmody and scripture for meditation, climaxed by the dawn praises.
9 The office of Lauds, especially on weekdays followed the shape of confession, prayer for new day, and praise. It has Paschal vigil type canticles, (e.g., Benedicite on Sundays), and exhibits a similar overall shape to that found in Milan, Old Spain and in the Bangor Antiphonary (see Chapters 12 and 13).

II. The textual evidence

1 The references to the evening light and offering in the Benedictine psalm 103 Responsory, and in the versicle 'Dirigatur', show a similar understanding of Vespers to that found elsewhere.
2 Hymn texts at Vespers sing of creation, but Saturday's 'O lux beata Trinitas' has overtones of a *lucernarium*.
3 Evening collects seek light after darkness. In the morning, day replaces night in the hymns, and the collects also speak of light banishing darkness.
4 Much has been said about Vespers because there is so little evidence that it is necessary to tease out what there is. However the night to morning thrust of Nocturns and Lauds, is well borne out in hymn and collect texts, culminating in hailing the true light which God's people are called to walk in.
5 Most importantly, it seems possible to say that although the Roman and Benedictine offices were both descendants of the monastic offices of the Roman basilicas, they still reflected a similar theology of daily prayer to that which we have identified elsewhere.

CHAPTER 12

The Old Spanish Offices

There are a number of discrepancies between the majority of the remaining Old Spanish manuscripts,[1] such as the Antiphoner of Leon[2] (hereafter AL) and the printed Mozarabic Breviary[3] (hereafter *Br*). Ortiz is believed to have drawn upon a manuscript tradition now represented by only a few documents associated with Toledo Cathedral. The first group is referred to as Tradition A, and the Breviary and related manuscripts as Tradition B. There is dispute over questions of dating and authenticity, but this author is of the opinion that the best case has been made for saying that Tradition A is a developed cathedral/monastic one, and Tradition B the tradition of certain parishes in Toledo that retained relics of older practice.

Old Spanish Vespers

This service at first sight appears to lack any ordered psalmody. Psalm verses and antiphons only occasionally require the whole of a psalm – and then usually just the one; there are neither readings nor New Testament canticle. The hymn follows the 'psalmody' and immediately precedes the intercessory section, which includes the Lord's Prayer. The offices begin with a presidential greeting.

Early evidence for the structure is found in two ordos, that of Bobadilla, probably older than the eleventh-century manuscript in which it is found, and the *Regula Monachorum* of St Isidore (seventh century). We compare them to the ordo of the later liturgical books:

Bobadilla	**Isidore**	**Cathedral Ordo**
		Oblatio luminis
Psalmus	*Lucernarium*	*Vespertinum* (*Lucernarium*)
		[*Sono*]
Psalmus	Psalmus	Antiphona
Psalmus	Psalmus	Alleluiaticum (*Laudes*)

[1] Based on G.W.Woolfenden, *Daily Prayer in Christian Spain* (London: Alcuin/SPCK, 2000).

[2] L. Brou and J. Vives (eds), *Antifonario Visigotico Mozarabe de la Catedral de Leon* (Madrid: *Monumenta Hispaniae Sacrae*, ser. Lit. V, 1959).

[3] A. Ortiz (ed.), *Breviarium secundum Regulam Beati Isidori* (Toledo: 1502), and more easily available in F. A. Lorenzana (ed.), *Breviarium Gothicum* (Paris: *PL* 86, 1862) – we shall refer to the column numbers of the latter.

Responsorium	Responsorium	
Laudes	*Laudes*	
	Hymnus	Hymnus
		Versus (Trad. A only)
		Supplicatio
Completuria	Oratio	*Completuria*
		Lord's Prayer
		Petitio (i.e., embolism)
		[*Psallendum*]
		Benedictio[4]

Isidore appears to describe an office of three psalms, how does this relates to that of the printed books?

In *Br* all offices begin: 'In nomine Domini nostri Jesu Christi lumen cum pace' (In the name of our Lord Jesus Christ, light with peace), with the response: 'Deo gratias'. After a salutation the *vespertinum* or *lucernarium* follows, which usually comprises a very few psalm verses referring to light in the evening. Originally it may have been a complete psalm chosen because of its reference to light, and perhaps reduced because of the increasing complexity of the chant.[5]

Between the *lucernarium* and the hymn there are a number of pieces usually composed of psalm verses and having a variety of titles. The first, found only on Sundays and Feasts, is the *sono*; then follow one or more entitled *antiphona* and finally the *laudes* or *alleluiaticum*. On weekdays there is either, one *antiphona* and one *laudes*, or a psalm with antiphon and the *laudes*. On some great feasts the *antiphonae* are multiplied. After the First Sunday of Lent there is no *sono*, so the office has a more ferial aspect. Some offices, mostly in Eastertide, have more than one *laudes*.

The *sono* does not really fit in with the other units, often making no reference to the hour of the day.[6] It may at first have been a festal addition to Vespers and at a later period came to be repeated at Matins. The second unit, the *antiphona*, bears a resemblance to the Antiphons found also at Matins (see pp. 238–9) and the cathedral Hours, being made up of an antiphon, a psalm verse and 'Gloria' (usually). The antiphon may once have accompanied a whole psalm or substantial parts of psalms.[7] The *antiphona* at Vespers appears

[4] J. Pinell, 'El Oficio Hipano-Visigotico', *Hispania Sacra*, **10** (1957), 385–427, 386 and 401.

[5] Pinell, 'El Oficio', 401 and 'Vestigis del Lucernari a Occident', *Liturgica I – Scripta et Documenta*, 7 (Monserrat) (1956), 91–149, 110, 117.

[6] Pinell, 'El Oficio', 402.

[7] Ibid., 419.

to have been selected to harmonize with the season or feast, and may have replaced an evening psalm with the theme of God as the refuge and protector of his people (as in the first three weeks of Lent).

In *de Officiis*, Isidore described *laudes* as an alleluiatic chant.[8] In the monastic hours it follows a reading; at mass it follows the Gospel. The pieces used in the cathedral office with this title are sometimes entitled *alleluiaticum* as for instance in *AL*,[9] the number of the psalm is often cited, usually psalm 118.[10] This psalm was often associated with daytime in the West, whereas elsewhere it was used at night.

Isidore's rule says of Vespers: '... In vespertinis autem officiis primo lucernarium, deinde psalmi duo, responsorius unus, et laudes, hymnus atque oratio dicenda est'.[11] Did this mean a *lucernarium*, two psalms and then a responsory and the *laudes*? It is possible that Isidore may have intended *responsorius* and *laudes* in this context to refer to the manner of performing the two psalms that followed the *lucernarium*. If this were the case, the Vespers he knew may have comprised a *lucernarium* psalm, then a responsorial psalm and one with alleluia, followed by hymn and prayer.

Primitive Spanish Vespers may have comprised a *lucernarium* (a lamp-lighting psalm), a psalm expressing confidence in God's protection, and a psalm (usually psalm 118) asking God to teach his people and keep them faithful to that teaching. This simple rite has a progression, it may be seen as a miniature vigil of light ritual, song of rescue, and song concerning God's will. Thus God would be praised every night as the God who frees and saves his people, who shines his light upon them, brings them powerful aid, and leads them into the right way.

In this tradition hymns were always included after psalmody and any readings, and before the concluding prayers. This is as true of the monastic style of day hours (cols. 939–60) as it is of the cathedral Hours. Hymns were prohibited prior to Toledo IV (633), and later were largely imported from elsewhere. There was a particular vogue for composing hymns for the feasts of martyrs, and two found only in *Br* are for St Justa, with St Rufina, patron of the parish in Toledo that remained most faithful to the ancient rite (see cols. 1153 and 1157). These late compositions often have poor grammar, and uneven metre and, in some cases, refer to contemporary events such as persecution of Christians by the Moslems.[12]

---

[8] *PL* 83, 749, 'de laudibus'.

[9] Pinell, 'El Oficio', 405 and J.M. Martin Patino, 'El Breviarium Mozarabe de Ortiz...', in *Miscellanea 40 Comillas*,1963, 217–69, 276.

[10] J. Janini, *Liber Misticus de Cuaresma y Pascua* (Toledo: Istituto de Estudios Visigotico–Mozarabes, 1979), p. 54.

[11] *PL* 83, 876.

[12] J. Perez de Urbel, 'Origen de los Himnos Mozarabes', *Bulletin Hispanique*, **28** (1926), 5–21, 113–39, 209–45, 305–20, 124.

The concluding prayers follow the hymn. First there is the *supplicatio*, a variable prefatory unit with response and *Kyrie eleison*. Next is the *completuria*, the concluding prayer of the service, which leads into the distinctive version of the Lord's Prayer with *Amen* after each petition.[13] This is followed by an embolism, the *petitio*. A blessing was common from at least the fifth century, but did not become securely established throughout Spain. There is a further Salutation, further variable *laudes* or *psallenda* and the Dismissal:

> In nomine domini nostri Jesu Christi perficiamus cum pace.
> (col. 50)

The *psallendum* is a simple antiphon with one or more psalm verses followed by a prayer. Some texts in the Breviary are entitled *Lauda ad fontes* or *Lauda de fonte* (cols. 201 and 198/205), implying a procession to the baptistery, so these pieces may have originated as a processional appendix to the service. Psalm 118, stressing the doing of God's will, would be a suitable reminder of baptismal commitment, and the martyrs would be seen as examples of the cost of following the Christian call.[14]

In Lent (according to *Br*) the *psallenda* are followed by psalm 50, some *preces* and penitential prayer. These seem to be much later additions turning a now redundant procession to the baptistery into a penitential exercise for Lent. After the *psallendum* and an invariable 'commemoration' (col. 50) comprising psalm 54.17, 'At evening, morn and midday, we will praise you Lord', there was a collect and the dismissal was repeated. There was something similar at the end of Matins (col. 58). The *psallenda* were treated as of secondary importance, being recited not sung, even on feasts.[15]

The Psalms at Vespers

(NB In what follows the term 'Antiphona' will refer to that unit of the Old Spanish office and 'antiphon' to the verse from the psalm used as a refrain or response.)

The chants of the *lucernaria* usually express the theme of light, even in seasonal pieces. The archetypal evening psalm, 140, is quoted in 'Elevatio manuum' (col. 185), only appointed for First Vespers of the First Sunday after Epiphany octave, while the remaining ordinary Sundays make up a kind of

---

[13] See *Daily Prayer in Chrisitian Spain*, op. cit., p. 43.

[14] See also Martin Patino, op. cit., pp. 280, 83–4.

[15] Lorenzana and Fabian y Fuero, *Missa Gotica seu Mozarabica* ... (Pueblo de los Angeles: 1770), pp. 189ff.

cycle for First Vespers employing appropriate verses from psalms 41, 12, 133, 29 and 35. The weekday cycle, beginning on Sunday evening, employed psalms 103, 17, 26, 54, 26, 103 and 133. Some prayers seem to indicate that psalm 140 was once more frequently used in Spain, and it is of more frequent occurrence in Tradition A manuscripts.

The weekday cycle is particularly clearly marked in Lent but the more important celebration, with the greater variety of texts, is the Saturday night, the 1st Vespers of Sunday. The importance of the celebration on the Saturday night is further emphasized by the fact that the texts for the Sundays of Lent rarely lose the light theme, even when texts are selected for a particular day, such as Palm Sunday.

A good example of a Spanish *lucernarium* from *Br* is the unique text drawn from psalm 140:

> The lifting of my hands like an evening sacrifice.
> *V*. Let my prayer arise Lord, like incense in your sight.

Another for the 4th Sunday after the Epiphany octave (col. 2240) and several other Sundays, is from psalm 133:

> Lift up your hands in the holy place and bless the Lord in the night.
> *V*. Who stand in the house of the Lord, in the courts of the house of our God.
> *P*. Bless the Lord in the night.

This is also found in the Leon Antiphoner amongst the collection of texts for an ordinary Sunday (fol. 281v). Weekday *lucernaria* comprise a single verse or part of a verse. For example, for Tuesday:

> The Lord is my light and my salvation.
> (psalm 27.1)

Psalm 140 may have been displaced as the light emphasis became more important. The Tradition A Antiphoner of Leon drew a basic repertoire of *lucernaria* from psalms 4, 133, 41, 135, 103, 112, 138 and 29.

Advent *soni* are good examples of festal texts. Typical psalms being 94 ('Come let us sing unto the Lord'), and 95 ('all the trees of the wood exult in the presence of the Lord for he comes'), redolent of joy at the Lord's promised coming celebrated in the season of Advent. The Christmas *sono*, in both Traditions A and B, is from the Messianic Psalm 109:

> In the splendour of the holy ones; from the womb I begot you before the dawn. Alleluia.
> *V*. The Lord has sworn, and does not change: you are a priest for ever according to the order of Melchisedech.

> *V*. The Lord at your right hand breaks the kings in the day of his wrath. He will judge the nations, he shall heap up the corpses, He shall crush the heads of many on the earth. He shall drink of the spring on the way: therefore shall he lift up his head.

The great majority of *soni* in the Sanctoral and Common of saints are independent of the time of day. By contrast, 1st Vespers *soni* for Sundays after Epiphany comprise a rough cycle of psalms expressing trust in God the healer and protector. As an example from psalm 138 (6th Sunday after Epiphany, col. 232):

> Darkness does not hide us from you,
> *P*. And the night is lit up like the day: Alleluia.
> *V*. Your eyes see my imperfection, and all my days you have seen and written in your book: Alleluia.
> *P*. And the night ...

We shall see that Milanese Vespers possesses a possible parallel to the *sono*, the *antiphona in choro* following the *lucernarium* and preceding the hymn on Sundays and feasts. Similar psalms, emphasizing trust in God, are used. The Milanese *antiphona in choro* and the Spanish sono appear to be chants added to the *lucernarium*, to give a festal flavour and later, extended to Sundays as well.

Amongst the *antiphonae* are those that cite psalm numbers: for example, the fragmentary weekday cycle in *Br* for Monday, Tuesday and Wednesday, employing psalms 8, 13 and 14 (cols. 194–203). The Lenten ferias of the Breviary appear to have no system at all, and in Leon the Vespers psalm is always selected from the gradual psalms (119–33) or a section of psalm 118. In the last three weeks of Lent the psalms and other texts are clearly selected to reflect the betrayal and abandonment of Christ. For example, psalm 21, 'My God, my God ... why have you forsaken me?' (col. 568).

The 1st Vespers *antiphonae* often reflect themes from the Sunday readings. For example, the *antiphona* for 1st Vespers of the Second Sunday of Lent, in which the antiphon is from Deuteronomy 10.17–19 and the verse from psalm 81.1 (col. 322). The Gospel of the day is of the man born blind, John 9.1ff., *PL* 85, col. 319, more importantly, the epistle is James 2.14–23 that calls into question the faith profession of those who do not succour the needy:

> The God of gods and Lord of lords, the great, strong and terrible King, who is not partial and takes no bribe; he gives justice to the orphan and widow and loves the sojourner,
> *P*. giving him food and clothing: therefore love the sojourner.
> *V*. God stands in the assembly of the holy ones: in the midst of them he judges.
> *P*. giving him food and clothing: therefore love the sojourner.

The *antiphonae* for 1st Vespers of Sunday exhibit a similar structure and use appropriate evening psalms. These include 103 and 144 thanking God for creation, 79 praying that God's face may shine upon his people, and 112 for the line: 'From the rising of the sun to its setting' (v. 3). The antiphons refer to the power of God in creation and to the vigil nature of the celebration. Two examples, one from after Epiphany and one from after Pentecost, will illustrate differences in style between two types:

a 1st Sunday after Epiphany octave (col. 186, verse from psalm 103):

> Who is this, in whose keeping the stars shine and rejoice in his calling of them? They are brightened by the joy of him who made them.
> *V*. *He* made the moon for its season, the sun knows the time of its setting.
> *P*. And rejoice ...

b 2nd Antiphon of 3rd Sunday after Pentecost (col. 702, verse from psalm 144.1):

> I will praise the Lord upon my bed:
> *P*. Day and night I will cleave to him and not desert him.
> *V*. I will praise you O Lord my God and King; and bless your name for ever and to endless ages.
> *P*. Day and night ...

Leon has a large number of similar texts for ordinary Sundays that are not allotted to any particular day.[16] They are linked with the corresponding *laudes*.

The *laudes* in *Br* for Lent make much use of psalm 118 and the choice of this psalm with its emphasis on instruction may be primitive. In the Leon Antiphoner *laudes* are also mostly from psalm 118.[17] An example of the Sunday *laudes*, for 1st Vespers of the 4th Sunday after the Epiphany octave (col. 224), again employs psalm 118 (vv. 25, 26):

> My soul lies in the dust, O Lord:
> *P*. Revive me according to your word. Alleluia, Alleluia, Alleluia.
> *V*. I declared my words and you heard me: teach me your righteousness.
> *P*. Revive me ...
> *V*. Glory ...
> *P*. Revive me ...

---

[16] Ff 284–7.

[17] Passim. *Laudes* entitled *Alleluiaticum* even when lacking 'Alleluia' in Lent.

The *laudes* for seasons such as Advent and Eastertide are purely festal, and the growing use of other scriptural texts with the psalm verses as antiphons rendered the *laudes* progressively more indistinguishable from the preceding *antiphona* except for the large number of Alleluia responses.

Prayers and Hymns

The *lucernaria* prayers often reflect the theme of evening light. For example:

> O God, whose name is praised from the rising of the sun to its setting; just as in your sight our prayer may come before you like incense; so to you may the raising of our hands, the evening sacrifice, be the fulfilment of our accustomed duty. (col. 185, 1st Sunday after Epiphany)

Or the more general themes of entering the presence of God at evening:

> In the night we lift our hands to you O Lord, taking our place standing before you; ... (col. 224, 4th Sunday after Epiphany)

On the other hand, only 14 of 21 hymns listed for Vespers are really *evening* hymns and of these, four are also seasonal. Purely evening hymns are largely found after Epiphany or Pentecost.

The first concluding prayer, the *completuria*, is a collect to conclude the office, summing up evening or morning office as appropriate. Evening prayers were often for protection and prayers in the morning sought God's blessing on the day. Many seasonal or festal *completuriae* allude to the time of day (especially if the morning *completuria* is a psalm collect to accompany the *matutinarium* or morning psalm). Vespers *completuriae* are, as a rule, prayers for protection during the coming night.

Some *completuriae* introduce the Lord's Prayer but also suit the time of day. For example, 1st Vespers of the 3rd Sunday after Pentecost (col. 703), quoting from psalm 140:

> O Lord our God, sacrificing to you an offering of evening praise on this day of holy solemnity, we pray that you may turn your ears to the cry of your suppliant people. Let this prayer of supplication be in your sight as the savour of incense; the lifting up of my hands as the evening sacrifice. Lord, help your people with your firm protection; so that in every hour and season, by the gift of your mercy towards us, we may be protected in our daily acts and guarded in sleep at night.

Prayers at Vespers often stress forgiveness of sins and protection for the night, and another example is that for the 3rd and 4th Thursdays of Lent (col. 421):

> O God, who at this approaching eventide grants the gift of repose to frail humanity: permit, we pray that we may take these good things and use them well, these benefits of which we know you as the author.

Prayers alluding the time of day contribute to our understanding of the theology of daily worship that pervaded the Old Spanish office. The approach of night symbolizes life-threatening darkness, the darkness of sin that can only be overcome by God. God is acclaimed as creator of the darkness as well as the hoped for day.

An appropriate evening blessing, recalling psalm 140, is that for 2nd Vespers of the 4th Sunday after the Epiphany octave (col. 228):

> May the prayers you pour out in petition ascend to the Lord.
> *R*. Amen. May that which you have earnestly entreated be given by the most merciful Pastor.
> *R*. Amen. May he guide your minds to an understanding of salvation, and let not your souls fall into temptation.
> *R*. Amen.

On ordinary Sundays and in Lent the *psallenda* were usually taken from psalm 118 but in no particular order.[18] There was little connection between the chant and the prayer. As an example, the *psallendum* and part of the prayer for 1st Vespers of the 4th Sunday after the Epiphany octave (col. 225), (psalm 118.4, 20):

> You have commanded your commandments. Alleluia.
> *P*. To be kept with care. Alleluia, Alleluia.
> *V*. My soul desires eagerly your decrees, at all times
> *P*. To be kept ...
> *V*. Glory and honour to the Father ...
> *P* To be kept ...
> O God our refuge and strength, be to us a helper in time of distress, ... may the waters of the river give joy to the city, the place where the most high dwells: ... allow your people to reap abundant grace.

The theme of Matins and Mass on this day is to do with the new Covenant in which God inspires his people to goodness.

The Lenten *psallenda* are often the best examples, as we may see in one for 1st Vespers of the Fifth Sunday (col. 501):

> See my affliction and save me, O Lord: for I do not forget your law.
> *V*. Uphold my cause and defend me; by your promise give me life.
> (psalm 118.153–4)

[18] Martin Patino, op. cit., pp. 277–9.

> *Prayer*
> Lord, see our affliction and save us; lift us up and restore us even as we are thrown down; for with you sustaining us we are not ruined but rescued.
> *R.* Amen.

The 1st Vespers, 2nd *psallenda* collect of Palm Sunday is entirely baptismal:

> Build Lord, upon the waters of refreshment, a people formed from the baptismal water ...
>
> (col. 565)

In Old Spanish Vespers the light of Christ's presence was welcomed and the Creator God thanked and praised for his redeeming work amongst his faithful people, who prayed confidently for protection and new life. The light of Christ was greeted as the light that conquers the darkness of sin and death.

Old Spanish Matins

Old Spanish Matins in *Br* has rather more familiar landmarks than Vespers. The Sunday order starts with a hymn and prayer. The three canonical psalms follow and a further prayer. Next, the *missa*, a unit comprising three *antiphonae* and a Responsory with prayers, takes us back to unfamiliar territory, though the fragmentary weekday cycle expects whole psalms to be part of these a*ntiphonae*. Under the heading *in laudibus* (at Lauds) there is an Old Testament canticle at full length, followed by an abbreviated version of the canticle from Daniel 3. The traditional Lauds psalms, 148–50, are followed by a reading and hymn, and then prayers and concluding material similar to that already seen at Vespers (see cols. 50–58). The division into Matins and Lauds is not ancient, we will treat the whole service as a unified whole.

The monastic rules of Isidore and of Fructuosus of Braga, together with the Bobadilla ordo, refer to 'three psalms' to begin the morning celebration that followed the monastic nocturnal vigils. The documents also speak of groups of three psalms known as *missae*, and Isidore and Bobadilla speak of a *missa* of three canticles. The morning part of the service is three psalms (according to Fructuosus and Bobadilla), or a fifth *missa* (Isidore). Bobadilla also stipulates a hymn and the Lord's Prayer.[19]

Schematically, the three patterns look like this:

Isidore	**Fructuosus**	**Bobadilla**
	VIGILIAE	
Psalmi Canonici		*Psalmi Canonici*

[19] Pinell, 'El Oficio', 385–9 and Taft, *Liturgy of the Hours*, pp. 158–9.

Missae Psalmorum	*Responsoria sub ternorum psalmorum divisione*	*Missae de Psalterio*
Missa Canticorum		*Missa de Canticis*
	MATUTINIS	
Quinta missa matutinarium officiorum	*Tres Psalmi*	*Psalmi matutinari tres*
		Responsum Laudes
	cum laude et benedictione sua	
		Hymnus Dominica Oratione

This shape is very similar to what we find in *Br*, especially if the three morning psalms spoken of are psalms 148–50, as seems most likely.

After an invocation and greeting, the introductory material includes, *either* the hymn *Aeterne rerum conditor* with a collect, and, on Sundays psalms 3, 50 and 56 with antiphons and another collect, *or* psalm 3 alone with an antiphon and collect in Eastertide and on most weekdays, *or* psalm 50 with an antiphon and a collect (psalm 56 on certain weekdays of Advent) on other weekdays, and on all the feasts of saints. Monastic vigils also opened with the 'canonical psalms' replaced on Sunday by psalms 46, 99 and 116, perhaps to avoid duplication.

The hymn *Aeterne rerum conditor*, first mentioned in the ninth/tenth century and used in more or less the same place in Milan, was also found in the developed Roman and Benedictine offices at Lauds on winter mornings. Psalms 3, 50 and 56 are 'canonical' in the sense that they are according to rule. The Leon Antiphoner gives a large set of undifferentiated antiphons for these psalms, arranged in sets of three, and comprising texts from each of the psalms in turn.[20] Usually the prayers quote all three psalms.

Psalm 50 was possibly the original first element of Matins each day, later perhaps replaced by psalm 3 in Eastertide. Increasing use of a cathedral vigil of psalms with prayers and later, Antiphons with prayers (see below) on Sundays and Saints' days, pushes psalm 50 back to before these vigil elements. However on some days psalm 50 precedes the canticles: that is, it remains at the beginning of the ancient cathedral morning office.

[20] Ff 287–8v.

The *missa* of three Antiphons ('Antiphon' again referring to the complex of antiphon, psalm verse(s) and doxology, 'antiphon' to the response itself) or three psalms with antiphons may have originated as a cathedral vigil of three psalms with prayers and a Responsory. This three-psalm unit could simply be multiplied on feasts.[21]

Unlike the Roman tradition, scriptural canticles in the Old Spanish rite were confined to Matins, and canticles from the New Testament appear to be a later addition used only very sparingly. While the canticles that originated in the paschal vigil, such as *Cantate* and *Benedicite* maintained their pre-eminence, in Spain they were spread over several Sundays, and not weekdays. Other canticles replaced and supplemented the original ones in order to reflect the liturgical seasons. The Old Spanish books contain a large number of canticles, 43 are found in *Br*, together with the short form of the Daniel 3 canticle, used daily, the *Benedictiones*.

After the canticle or canticles, came the *matutinarium*, or, on Sunday, *sono*. This was normally an antiphon with psalm verse, usually from a psalm referring to light or morning. On many days the concluding prayer or *completuria* of Matins in the Breviary, although separated from the psalm by psalms 148–50, Reading(s), hymn and *supplicatio*, is the psalm collect of the *matutinarium* psalm.

According to *Br*, psalms 148, 149 and 150 are to be used on all Sundays and feasts. They are grouped together under one antiphon, with *Gloria* at the end of all three. On certain weekdays, however, psalm 150 is appointed to be used alone, something not found outside of Spain until modern times. The Old Spanish office here appears to have undergone very little alteration, at least in tradition B sources. At the earliest stages prayers no doubt followed these psalms that were the climax of the morning office, the praise of God who restores life after the darkness of the night that signifies death.

If Old Spanish Vespers never acquired reading of scripture, Matins did. The most complete arrangement is found in Lent, a series of lengthy readings in course from the 'Law and the former Prophets'. These lengthy Lenten readings follow the *laudate* psalms and precede the hymn, a position for a lengthy reading in course not found anywhere else. The course is also spread over the cathedral Minor Hours of Terce and None and the Masses of Sunday, Wednesday and Friday. The early sources do not give any hint of readings: for example, the Bobadilla ordo: 'In Matins are said three morning psalms, then the responsory and the *laudes*, followed by a hymn and the Lord's Prayer'.[22]

[21] Pinell, *Liber Orationum Psalmographus* (Barcelona–Madrid: 1972), [87], [88] & 'Las *Missae* Grupos de Cantos ...', *Archivos Leoneses*, **8** (1954), 145–85, 154, 184–5.

[22] Quoted in Pinell, 'El Oficio', 420.

Fructuosus in the seventh century made no mention of readings at this point, though Isidore expected there to be reading in the monastic office.[23]

The hymns at Vespers and at Matins were probably first added to reflect festal and seasonal themes rather than the hour of the day. The introduction of hymns still further disrupted the unitary theme of the morning celebration, for together with the praise psalms, they isolated the *completuria* from the morning psalm.

Psalmody and Scripture

Psalm 3 is always found as an invitatory in Tradition A, whereas in the Tradition B cycle of weekdays, and on many feasts, psalm 50 takes its place. The antiphons and collects connected with psalm 50 at the beginning of the office are often the same as those used when the psalm precedes the canticle.[24] There seems to be a parallel to ancient and contemporary Byzantine use of psalm 3 as a pre-dawn vigil element, and psalm 50 to mark the passage from night to morning.

The antiphons with the canonical psalm are often short: for example, 'O God of salvation, bless your people', an ordinary Sunday antiphon in both the Breviary (col. 80) and Leon.[25] All the antiphons maintain this theme of confidence in the face of adversity. This invitatory is a call for God's people to rise in the night and take up their stand against evil in the power of God's protection.

As at Vespers, there is an almost total absence of complete psalms at Matins. On certain days there are indications of psalm numbers between an antiphon and a collect, on other days there is the 'Antiphon', with a collect that probably draws its theme from the antiphon. After three Antiphons or three antiphons with psalm numbers, there is a Responsory which may also have a prayer. On feasts, the whole complex of three Antiphons with prayers and a Responsory (the *missa*) may be repeated several times. If the psalm verse of the Antiphon stood for a whole psalm, then the *missa psalmorum* originally comprised three psalms and a Responsory, as in Isidore's description of the *missa* as a series of psalms sung by a soloist to which the congregation or choir responded.

Both Leon and the Breviary provide offices for the first half of Lent that include complete psalms in each Antiphon of Matins, Terce, Sext and None. The Leon arrangement is an irregular reading of the whole Psalter, with a few omissions, spread over the three weeks.[26] While the Breviary appears to have

---

[23] See *PL* 83, 876–7 – Chapter 6 of *Regula Monachorum.*

[24] See e.g., cols. 191, 459; 294, 449.

[25] 288v.

[26] See *Daily Prayer in Christian Spain*, op. cit., pp. 74–5.

no order, there is often a linking word or theme that might run through the *missa*, and the multiplied *missae* of great feasts all recall different aspects of the feast.[27] This thematic use may have developed from something once more spontaneous, and there may never have been an ordered *psalmodia currens*.

Spanish monks probably recited four offices in the course of the night: *ad Medium Noctis, Peculiaris Vigilia, Nocturnos* and *post Nocturnos*.[28] These could have accounted for thirty psalms and finished in time for cathedral Matins. With psalm 118 used at the Day Hours and inter-Hours, there would be ample opportunity for the monks to cover the entire Psalter in a week. Since Synodal legislation in Spain had kept the cathedral and monastic offices strictly distinct, the monastic night psalmody was probably not adopted by the Spanish cathedral office. In that case, the three-week arrangement discernible in Leon may be a later cathedral modification of the monastic Psalter in course, and so a form of cathedral vigil added before Matins. The psalms cited in the *missae* of the fragmentary Weekday cycle of *Br* may be an unfinished attempt at a coherent current Psalter.[29]

The psalms and psalm collects of the first three weeks of Lent in *Br*, spread over Matins, Terce, Sext, None and Vespers, are neither an orderly recitation of the Psalter nor related to the hour of the day. However, on the Wednesday of the first week of Lent, for example, we find psalms 15, 68 and 69 at Matins, all psalms of hope and confidence in God. The prayer for psalm 15, *Conserve nos, Domine in timore*, is a prayer for forgiveness with phrases such as 'keep us from the contagion of sin'. The other two prayers seek the Lord's protection for his people: 'Lord, impart life to the souls of those who seek you' and 'Come to our aid Lord and quickly increase your assistance to us'.

Terce the same day cites psalms 59, 71 and 72 with a very similar emphasis on placing hope in God, also found at Sext with psalms 122, 128 and 129; for example, the antiphons: 'To you have we lifted up our eyes, you who dwell in the heavens, have mercy on us' and 'The blessing of the Lord be upon you, we have blessed you in the name of the Lord. With the Lord there is mercy; and plenteous redemption' (col. 294).

The Eucharist replaced None, and at Vespers, we find psalm 66 with the antiphon: 'The Lord our God has blessed us. May God still give us his blessing till the ends of the earth revere him' (cols. 294–5) bringing the office of the day to an end. The progression from confidence in God's mercy and protection to a song of confident joy fits well with a day when the Eucharist Gospel is the account of Jesus' temptation in the wilderness, Matthew 4.1–12.

27 Pinell, 'Las *Missae*', 146ff.

28 Pinell, 'Las Horas Vigiliares del Oficio Monacal Hispanico', *Liturgica 3 –Scripta et Documenta*, **17** (1966), 197–340.

29 For the author's thoughts on this see chapter 10 of *Daily Prayer in Christian Spain*, op. cit.

It is possible that appropriate psalms, antiphons and prayers from a large, general repertoire were selected in order to express themes suited to Lent. If the Toledo manuscript T2 was typical of a parish liturgy at the church of Sts. Justa and Rufina in Toledo,[30] then this may have been the pattern of the Old Spanish parish office, in which a *psalmodia currens* was regarded as inappropriate.

The Sunday cycles also suggest an attempt to impose order on a set of undifferentiated psalm Antiphons. The *missa* for the Second Sunday after Epiphany will serve as an example:

Antiphon I (psalm 9)
The Lord has heard the desire of the poor: your ear has inclined to the preparation of their heart; to plead for the orphan and afflicted that man may no more boast on the earth.
V. Arise, O Lord God; let not man prevail: may the heathen be judged before you.

Prayer

Be greatly pleased to hear the prayer of your poor, O Lord, and grant us a copious flow of the gifts of heaven. Keep from us the passing commotion of earthly matters: Turn your ears to us who offer you prayer as *the humbled orphan seeking justice*, lavish on us your paternal forgiveness; and in place of our present lowliness, grant us an eternal reward.

Antiphon II (psalm 11)
Because of the misery of the poor and the sighing of the needy, now I will arise says the Lord.
V. The words of the Lord are pure words, as silver tried in the fire, proved in a furnace of earth, purified seven times.

Prayer

O God who the proud resist, destroy all lying lips, the tongue that speaks high-sounding words; *make our words to be pure words, that they may be tried even as silver is tried in the fire*; so that all arrogant ferment be thrown down, exposing the contagion of our corruption, and that as greatness and majesty be given to you, we be raised up, renewed by you who renew all things.

Antiphon III (psalm 12)
How long, O Lord, will you forget us? How long will you hide your face from us? Look on us, hear us, O Lord our God!
V How long shall I take counsel in my soul, these sorrows in my heart every day? How long shall my enemy be exalted over me?[31]

---

[30] Janini, op. cit., pp. xxiv–xxvi.

[31] Changes from the biblical singular to the plural are in the original liturgical texts, and are common in this rite.

Prayer

Look upon us, answer us, O Lord our God; help us who you know to be fearful to be pleasing to you, grant the end of the work, you who willed its beginning: grant, as we complete what you have wrought in us, that it may be brought to completion.

Responsory (Verse from psalm 101)
Lord you know the final end of our sins; strike out injustice and invest us with your holy righteousness, that Jerusalem may rejoice in it.
V. You will arise and have mercy on Zion: for the time for mercy has come.

The italicized phrases indicate points where the collects most reflect the psalms they accompany. The theme at Mass for this day is Jesus' synagogue proclamation of the fulfilment of Isaiah's prophecy (Luke 4.14–22; *PL* 85, 247).

We can find similar patterns, for example on the First Sunday of Lent (psalms 48, 61 and 84), when the Gospel is that of the Samaritan woman from John 4.3–42 (*PL* 85, 299). Also the Third Sunday's account of the raising of Lazarus (John 11.1–52; *PL* 85, 337), when the Antiphons call upon God that he might act: 'Revive us now, God our helper! Put an end to your grievance against us' (psalm 84).

We venture the hypothesis that these Antiphons and psalm collects *were* chosen to reflect on, or prepare for, the proclamation of that particular day's Gospel. It is likely that the eucharistic lectionary would have been established early on in the history of the Old Spanish liturgy,[32] and it may well be that appropriate psalms and prayers were selected to accompany those readings. The Sunday morning service was then preceded by a short vigil reflecting on the day's lectionary theme.

Missae antiphonarum of a more developed type might combine verses from the psalms and antiphons from elsewhere in scripture, with the collects based on the latter. For example the Sunday before the Epiphany (cols. 147–8),[33] a reflection on the themes of Christmas and Epiphany, employing for example, Proverbs 8.22a and 26 in Antiphon 1 and Isaiah 9.2 in Antiphon 2, and psalm 44, often associated with Christmas because of its bridal imagery. At a later stage other scriptural texts were combined with the psalm verses, and the themes of the collects drawn from them. There is again, some degree of consonance between the day's reading and the Antiphons of Matins.

[32] The two Sundays mentioned are found in the ninth-century *Liber Commicus* (lectionary) edited by Urbel and Ruiz-Zorilla (Madrid: 1950), pp. 142–4, 210–12.

[33] See W.C. Bishop, *The Mozarabic and Ambrosian Rites* (London: Alcuin/Mowbrays, 1924), pp. 78–80.

Beside the *Benedictiones*, nine canticles, all Old Testament, are used on Sundays:

1. *Give ear, O heavens* Deuteronomy 32.1–43 (Advent especially)
2. *My soul yearns for thee in the night* Isaiah 26.9–20 (Lent)
3. *Let us sing to the Lord* Exodus 15.1–19 (Easter)
4. *My heart exults in the Lord* 1 Samuel 2.1–10 (after Epiphany)
5. *O Lord, I have heard the report of thee* Habbakak 3.2–19 (Advent)
6. *O Lord who inhabitest eternity* IV Esdras 8.20–36 (before fasts)
7. *I said, in the noontide of my days I must depart* Isaiah 38.10–20
8. *I will greatly rejoice in the Lord* Isaiah 61.10 – 62.7 (6th Sunday of Advent)
9. *Then Jacob called his sons* Genesis 49.2–27 (The Sunday before the Epiphany)

The Deuteronomy canticle *Attende* occurs on ten Sundays of the year; in Advent, Lent and ordinary time, and outside of Lent the antiphons are simply verses taken from the canticle in order. A universally used canticle, *Cantemus* from Exodus 15, is found on all Sundays of Eastertide (col. 616). The other Sunday canticles are used much less often.

The variable canticle on Sundays is always followed by the *Benedictiones* from Daniel 3, except on Palm Sunday. The canticle is recited in a shortened form, part of which is given here (col. 55):

> Blessed are you, Lord God of our Fathers and praised and glorified for ever. And blessed be the glory of your name, which is holy and praised and glorified for ever ... All virtues, the sun and the moon, the shower and the dew, every spirit, fire and cold, ice and snow, lightning and cloud. Earth, mountains and hills, and all that comes from the earth; ... Priests, servants of the Lord, spirits and souls of the just, holy and humble of heart. Ananias, Azarias and Misael, sing a hymn to the Lord, and exalt him above all for ever. Amen.
> *P.* Bless the Lord. Glory and honour to the Father ...
> *P.* Bless the Lord.

The eighteen festal canticles are a later development and include eight of those that also have a Sunday use. The song of Hannah, *Confirmatum est*, is used on many feasts, after Christmas, in August and September and also on Ascension Day. *De nocte vigilat* from Isaiah is used for the Circumcision and the Purification and the antiphon used on these feasts stresses the theme of light, hence the selection of that canticle. There are no less than forty-one canticles appointed for use on weekdays.[34]

[34] See appendix to ch. 11 of my *Daily Prayer in Christian Spain.*

A feature that very much contradicts the standard expectations of daily offices in the West is the very limited use of New Testament canticles. *Benedictus* only twice, on Epiphany with an Old Testament canticle and on 24 June on its own. *Magnificat* is used at Christmas with an Old Testament canticle and on the Annunciation (18 December) on its own. It is also used in the Lady office of Saturday (col. 214). The older tradition would appear to have known only Old Testament canticles.

Most ancient morning liturgies have one or more specific morning psalms. The Old Spanish tradition had a large number of such psalms employed less systematically and, eventually, the Sunday version, the *sono*, was reduced to a single verse. Of the morning psalms used in Spain, the most frequently used for the *matutinarium* and *sono* were 5, 35, 42, 62, 66 and 89. All of these are in the Benedictine office and only 35 is not in the old Roman office, so it is possible, that the oldest strata of morning psalms in Spain was a very similar repertoire to that of Rome: 5, 42, 62, 64, 66, 89 and 142.

The structure of the Sunday morning *sono* is simple. For example, that for the First Sunday after Epiphany:

> Give ear to my words O Lord, Alleluia.

The antiphon is from verse 1 of psalm 5 and the verse is:

> Listen to the sound of my cries, my King and my God, it is you whom I invoke. Alleluia

Originally psalm 5 may have been sung in full with the response 'Alleluia'. It is possible that earlier versions of the weekday *matutinaria* were corrected and amplified in later use. As an example, this *matutinarium* from psalm 5:

> In the morning you hear me Lord, I stand before you and worship you. [Tuesday after Epiphany octave (col. 197) and 1st Monday of Lent (col. 265) – citing the first verse of the psalm after this antiphon].

There is only a very small repertoire of antiphons of the *laudate*. For example, on Sundays:

> Praise the Lord from the heavens, Alleluia, Alleluia. Praise him in the highest. Alleluia, Alleluia.
>
> (col. 55)

This basic form re-appears with slight variations, sometimes being extended into the next verse. The antiphon is simply the first verse of the set and may be a relic of singing these psalms right through with Alleluia as a refrain.

On weekdays there is also a generally common pattern to the use of psalm 150.

The first verse introduces the psalm:

> Praise the Lord in his saints. Alleluia. Alleluia. Praise him in the firmament of his power. Alleluia.
> *Psalm 150*
> *P*. Praise the Lord ...
> *V*. Glory and honour to the Father and the Son, etc.
> *P*. Praise him in ...
>
> (col. 61)

The Lent lessons at Matins, and the cathedral Minor Hours, begin as a semi-continuous reading of Genesis, Exodus, Numbers, Deuteronomy, Joshua, Judges and Ruth. The books of Samuel and Kings are followed in Holy Week by Lamentations and Isaiah. Commencing with the creation and first sin of mankind, we pass on to Cain and Abel and the Tower of Babel. The Abraham, Isaac, Jacob and Joseph cycles are all covered. After Moses and the Exodus, there are the accounts of Gideon, Samson and Ruth. Continuing with the stories of Samuel, Saul and David, the cycle concludes with a few of the Elijah stories and his succession by Elisha.[35] In all this there is a theme of oscillation between obedience and disobedience to God's will.

The truth that men and women do sin and are sinful is constantly reiterated. Some of the most heinous crimes that people can commit are related in detail and at length. But there are also plenty of examples of repentance and sorrow and, in general one could say that while humanity's depravity is taken very seriously indeed, so is the fact of God's forgiveness of sinners and his continued faithfulness. The lessons, complemented at Terce and None by readings from the sapiential books, may have formed a series of catechumenal lectures followed (at the Hours) by three Antiphons, except on Wednesdays and Fridays when the Eucharist followed.[36] Tradition A used a similar system to order the same material.[37] This catechumenal instruction was probably inserted into the morning service as a result of Roman and Benedictine influence. This whole system of readings contrasts starkly with those of the old Roman and Benedictine systems of *lectio continua* and the Little Chapter.

---

[35] For details see ibid., ch. 14.

[36] Bishop, op. cit., pp. 87–9.

[37] V. Martin Pintado, 'Las Lecturaes Cuaresmales de Antiguo Testamento en la Liturgia Hispanica. Estudio de Liturgia Comparada', *Salmanticensis XXII.2* (1975), pp. 217–69, esp. 218–19.

Hymnody and Prayer

Placing *Aeterne rerum* at the very beginning of Matins shows that the morning office, Matins, was, like that of Milan, a single service starting at cockcrow. The prayers composed to accompany the hymn keep closely to its themes: the dawn as the end of the night watch, the identity of darkness with sin. Both are banished by the new light of resurrection hope that gives God's people renewed strength and knowledge of his forgiveness. For example:

> Now that the paean of cockcrow had driven forth the silence of the night; before you O Lord the elder night gives birth to day heralded by the cockerel's flourish. As they give voice to a jubilant morning hymn; so Lord to you in heaven be given praise; you who command the dissolution of darkness by the incoming rays of the sun. Almighty Father these wonders are yours alone, we can bring only the pledge of ourselves, offering to your holy name this morning sacrifice; that we may be acquitted of and escape our sins, made worthy to be freed from the danger that threatens. Amen. (col. 240)

The prayers of the canonical psalms are also general morning texts. As an example:

> Lord our upholder, our glory and the lifter up of our heads, who enrich us in your mercy: cleanse our innermost hearts from guilt and purify us of polluting sins; send from heaven and save us from those who oppress us; so that hastening back to this your altar; we may offer to you a morning sacrifice in the temple. Amen. (6th Sunday after Epiphany octave (col. 233) and Lent V.)

The prayer quotes from psalm 3.3 and psalm 56.3 and echoes psalm 50. The Easter prayer associated with psalm 3, – 'Lord Jesus Christ, who for us undertook the sleep of death . . . ' (col. 615) – takes the theme of waking found in the psalm and applies it to the resurrection.

Antiphons and prayers connected with Psalm 50 tend to be penitential in tone. Some festal texts balance joy with penitence. For example, an antiphon: 'Give to us the joy of your help: with a spirit of fervour sustain us Lord.' And a prayer:

> Give us again the joy of your help, Lord; that we be let go of the iniquity we bear and our neglects passed over; so that you may call us to the joy restored to us; and with sins driven forth, righteousness may enter in, unfaithfulness repulsed, and eternal joy made present . . .

The Canticle prayers often cite the canticles and many are not particularly matinal. A good example of a vigil canticle is *De nocte vigilat* of Isaiah 26, the collect most often used with it begins:

> Our souls yearn for you in the night, O God, the beauty of your commands shines out and in the tempest of our expectancy, we watch for you; the light that comes at midday ...
>
> (col. 238)

Of two prayers given for the *Benedictiones*, one quotes the canticle, while the other only does so indirectly.

Most morning hymns are not Spanish in origin, one is *Splendor paternae gloriae* (col. 148), attributed to St Ambrose, and without doubt a very suitable for the morning. Festal hymns are not necessarily connected with morning themes, but *Noctis tempus jam praeterit* ('Now the time of night is come') (col. 446), used on mornings of the second half of Lent, makes reference to the cockcrow of Peter's betrayal. The main theme is the passion and betrayal of Jesus Christ. Similarly Ambrose's *Hic est dies verus Dei* ('Here truly is the day of God') for Easter (col. 618) for Sunday Matins in Eastertide is not a specifically morning hymn.

The *completuria* was originally the psalm collect of the *matutinarium*, summing up the morning service as expressed in that psalm. The prayers often develop the ideas of emerging from the night as if awaking from the dead and being restored to new life at the break of day. The following is a weekday collect for Psalm 5:

> O our King and our God, remove from our hearts the errors and ignorance of the night, so that, renewed in the new man, in the morning you hear our voices and make us to stand before you at the break of day in good works; as we look upon you, grant us to share in the earnest of your Resurrection.

The *completuriae* on Sundays are Morning Prayers. For example, the 3rd Sunday of Lent, which is also a prayer on Psalm 5 (col. 384):

> Standing here in the shining presence of eternal light to offer our morning vow to you, who receive the cries of our prayers: that daily the lustre of the eternal may shine upon us, and vanquish the foul darkness of the night and the encroaching mist of error; may we be kept in the shining rays of his true Son.

This is probably a survival of an older use in which psalm prayers served to conclude Sunday as well as weekday offices. Another example is this for the 6th Sunday after the octave of the Epiphany (col. 235):

> Now the east brightens, now the day hastens, now darkness flees, dawn blushes with most pure light: the heavens are brightened by the sun whose rays enlighten the world; all hasten, all hurry, to rejoice in the Lord's favour, he who is ever known as creator and defender.

Once again the theme of resurrection light in the morning appears to be the dominant idea. It can be said that the morning office is the time of rejoicing in the gift of a new day, as a rising to new life brought about by the power of God who raised Jesus Christ from the dead.

The Minor Hours in Spain

We have mentioned the so-called cathedral Hours in passing. Their shape can be seen in the schemata of the services that we have in this case appended to the chapter. The Terce, Sext and None of the cathedral office all seem to be integrated into the system of psalm Antiphons and catechetical readings that we have described above. None is omitted on days when the Eucharist was celebrated, no doubt at the Ninth Hour. These offices are characteristic of Lent and a few other days, their themes are inextricably linked with the seasons in which they occur.

The monastic hours, found in the Lorenzana version of *Br* (*PL* 86, 939–71) are short and similar in shape to the Roman/Benedictine offices, but with four psalms or parts of psalms. The orders of *aurora* (before Prime), 'Before Compline' and Compline are of the same family. As will be apparent from the schema, psalm 118 is the main psalm used, but it is started at *aurora*, and then continued through Prime and Terce. There is then a considerable gap between Terce and Sext, and the end of the psalm is missing as None begins with psalm 145 and then has psalms 121–3. It seems likely that there were inter-hours between Terce and Sext and probably between Sext and None. These would be short services punctuating the day at each hour, and one can well understand that they would soon disappear.

Conclusions

The Old Spanish cathedral office is of a shape that we will also see reflected in Milan and Ireland, and which has some similarities with what we have discovered about the Roman tradition. The offices of Vespers and Matins were relatively short and originally largely fixed, but acquired festal material over time. Minor Hours were only added in Lent and a few other days, and then only at Terce, Sext and None.

There is no evidence that the Psalter was ever completely recited in course in the cathedral rite, instead there was a highly developed principle of selecting psalms primarily for their suitability to the time of day, and secondarily for the season. The monastic office, on the other hand, appears to have had many services at night and morning, and possibly accomplished the entire Psalter daily.

Many canticles were used in this office, but ancient Spanish custom appears to have been to employ New Testament canticles very sparingly, and probably only from a relatively late date. The structure of canticle followed by the praise psalms and prayer again appears to reflect the form of a miniature Paschal vigil. Like the Paschal vigil, only Old Testament texts were used, the readings at the Eucharist 'fulfilling', as it were, that which the prophecies of the canticles had looked forward to in the progress from night to morning.

Table 1 The Schemes of Vespers ***(brackets indicate units not always present)***

Sundays and Feasts	**Weekdays**
Opening Service of Light	
Opening Formula	Opening Formula
Vespertinum/Lucernarium	*Vespertinum/Laudes*
Prayer (on most Sundays and Feasts)	
Sono (usually omitted in Lent)	(*Sono* only in Eastertide)
Variable Psalmody	
Antiphon	Antiphon and Psalm (most weekdays)
(More ants. on Feast and some Suns.)	
(Prayer on great feasts)	
Laudes/Alleluiaticum	*Laudes/Alleluiaticum*
Hymn	Hymn
Prayer and Conclusion	
Supplicatio and *Kyrie*	*Supplicatio* and *Kyrie*
Completuria	*Completuria*
Lord's Prayer and Embolism	Lord's Prayer and Embolism
Benedictio	*Benedictio*
Appendices	
Variable *Psallenda* and prayer (several in Lent, sometimes *Preces*)	Variable *Psallenda* and prayer
Concluding formula	Concluding formula
Fixed *Psallendum* and prayer	Fixed *Psallendum* and prayer
Concluding formula	Concluding formula

Table 2 The Schemes of Matins

Sunday	Feasts	Weekdays
Opening at Night		
Aeterne rerum and prayer		
Antiphon and psalm 3	Antiphon and psalm 3	Antiphon and psalm 3
Antiphon and psalm 50		(or psalms 50 or 56)
Antiphon and psalm 56		
Prayer	Prayer	Prayer
Variable Psalmody – 'Missa'		
Antiphon 1 – prayer	Antiphon 1 – prayer	Ant. – Psalm – prayer
Antiphon 2 – prayer	Antiphon 2 – prayer	Ant. – Psalm – prayer
Antiphon 3 – prayer	Antiphon 3 – prayer	Ant. – Psalm – prayer
Responsory (prayer)	Responsory – Prayer (Whole unit may be repeated)	Responsory (prayer)
Morning Praises		
	(Ant. – psalm 50 – prayer)	Ant. – psalm 50 – prayer
Ant. – OT canticle	Ant. – OT canticle	Ant. – OT canticle
Prayer (usually)	Prayer (on some feasts)	Prayer
Ant. – *Benedictiones*	Ant. – *Benedictiones*	
Prayer (ordinary Sundays)		
		Matutinarium
Sono (not Lent)	*Sono*	
Ant. – psalms 148–50	Ant. – psalms 148–50	Ant. – psalm 150 (148–50)
Lesson	Lesson	Lesson
Hymn	Hymn	Hymn
Prayer and Conclusion		
Supplicatio and *Kyrie*	*Supplicatio* and *Kyrie*	*Supplicatio* and *Kyrie*
Completuria	*Completuria*	*Completuria*
Lord's Prayer and Embolism	Lord's Prayer and Embolism	Lord's Prayer and Embolism
Psallendum and prayer	(*Psallendum* – prayer)	(*Psallendum*)
Benedictio	*Benedictio*	*Benedictio*
Appendices		
Psallendum – prayer	(*Psallendum* – prayer)	*Psallendum* – prayer
Concluding formula	Concluding formula	Concluding formula

Table 3 The Hours of Terce, Sext and None

Cathedral Ordo	**Monastic Ordo**
Opening	
Deus in adjutorium	
Readings	
Wisdom (only one given on weekdays)	
Old Testament (Only one at Sext)	
New Testament (Occasionally at Terce and None)	
Psalmody	
Antiphon	
Antiphon – psalm – prayer	Psalm (T 94, S 53, N 145)
Antiphon – psalm – prayer	Psalm (T 118, S 118, N 121)
Antiphon – psalm	Psalm (T 118, S 118, N 122)
(Complete psalms omitted in second half of Lent)	Psalm (T 118, S 118, N 123)
	Antiphon
Responsory (not at None)	Responsory
Readings, etc.	
	Short OT lesson
	Short NT lesson
Laudes (weekdays)	*Laudes* (1 or 2)
Prayer and other material	
Preces	
(Hymn)	Hymn
	(Versicle at Easter Terce)
	Clamores
(*Supplicatio*)	*Supplicatio* and *Kyrie*
Completuria	*Completuria*
Lord's Prayer (and Embolism)	Lord's Prayer and Embolism
Conclusion	
(*Benedictio*)	*Benedictio*
Concluding formula	Concluding formula

NB The verses of psalm 118 used at the monastic pattern hours are not given above.

CHAPTER 13

The Ambrosian and other non-Roman Western Traditions

Outside of Spain, non-Roman Western evidence is either monastic or virtually non-existent. However, Milan has had a continuous ritual history since at least the time of Ambrose. The rite was revised in the 1970s according to the same principles as those of the modern Roman rite, so we shall concentrate on this office as it was before those revisions.[1]

The most important surviving document for the offices is the *Manuale*, an eleventh-century compendium for the choir at mass and the offices, edited by Marco Magistretti[2] who also edited a twelfth-century description of the services of the Cathedral, *Beroldus, sive Ecclesiae Ambrosianae Mediolanensis Kalendarium et Ordines*.[3] These provide the earliest written information on the daily offices of this tradition. Printed books first appeared in 1475 and 1482. The Minor Hours and Compline prior to recent reform were more or less Roman, they may only have been required of the secular clergy from the ninth/tenth centuries.[4] The orders of Vespers, Matins and Lauds, prior to recent reform, were as follows:

Table 1 Schemes of Milanese Vespers

Feast days	**Holy Week**
<u>Light Service</u>	
Lucernarium	*Lucernarium*
(*Antiphona in Choro* – Sunday)	
Hymn	Hymn
<u>Psalmody</u>	
Responsory in Choro	*Responsory in Choro*
Proper psalm and psalms 133 and 116	Proper psalm

[1] A new Missal was promulgated in Advent 1976, and the first volume of a new Breviary emerged the following year.

[2] M. Magistretti (ed.), *Manuale Ambrosianum*, 2 vols. (Milan: 1905), hereafter *Manuale*.

[3] Marco Magistretti (ed.), *Beroldus, sive Ecclesiae Ambrosianae Mediolanesis Kalendarium et Ordines* (Milan: 1894, repr. Farnborough: Gregg International, 1968), hereafter *Beroldus*.

[4] Enrico Cattaneo, *Il Breviario Ambrosiano* (Milan, 1943), p. 212.

Prayer I	Prayer
Proper psalm	
Prayer II	
Magnificat	
Prayer III	12 x *Kyrie eleison*
Appendices	
Psallendum	
2 *Complenda*	
Prayer IV	
Conclusion	
As above	As above

Sunday	**Weekday**
Light Service	
Greeting	Greeting
Lucernarium	*Lucernarium*
Antiphona in Choro	
Hymn	Hymn
Psalmody	
Responsory in Choro	*Responsory in Choro*
Psalms 109–13 and Prayer I	5 psalms and Prayer I
Magnificat and Prayer II	*Magnificat* and Prayer II
Appendices	
Psallenda I/Resp. in Bapt.	*Resp. in Bapt.*
2 *Complenda*	
Prayer III	Prayer III
4 verse psalm	4 verse psalm
	Complenda
Prayer IV	Prayer IV
Psallenda II	
2 *Complenda*	
Oratio Ultima	
Conclusion	
Dismissal formulae	Dismissal formulae
Lord's Prayer	Lord's Prayer
Concluding formula	Concluding formula

Table 2 Schemes of Milanese Matins

Sunday	**Weekdays**
<u>Opening</u>	
Introduction	Introduction
Aeterne rerum	*Aeterne rerum*
Responsory	Responsory
Benedictus es (Dan. 3)	*Benedictus es*
'<u>Psalmody</u>'	
3 Canticles with antiphons*	Psalter in course in three parts
3 Readings and 2 Responsories	3 Readings and 3 Responsories
Te Deum	
(Prayer)	
<u>Morning praises</u>	
(*Benedictus*)	*Benedictus*
Antiphona ad Crucem	
Secret Collect I	Secret Collect
Cantemus (Exodus 15)	Psalm 50 (117 on Saturday)
Secret Collect II	*Benedicite* (Daniel 3)
Prayer I	Prayer I
Psalms 148–50 and 116	Psalms 148–50 and 116
Capitulum	*Capitulum*
Psalmus Directus	*Psalmus Directus*
(Laus Angelorum Magna)	
Hymn: *Splendor paternae*	Hymn: *Splendor paternae*
<u>Prayer</u>	
12 *Kyries*	*12 Kyries*
<u>Appendices</u>	
Psallendum I	*Responsorium in Bapt.*
Complenda I	
Prayer II	Prayer II
Psallenda II	4 verse psalm
Complenda II	*Complenda*
Prayer III	Prayer III
<u>Conclusion</u>	
As above	As above

* On feasts there were selected psalms, canticles, and 9 readings.

The Ambrosian Vespers

Prior to the eleventh/twelfth centuries, we have only tantalizing glimpses of the original rite.[5] The Vespers we know from *Beroldus*, the *Manuale* and the later Breviaries had several forms.[6] In the most common, that of Sundays and weekdays, after the salutation *Dominus vobiscum*, there was a lamp-lighting ceremony during the singing of the *lucernarium*, followed on Sundays by the *antiphona in choro*. Then came the office hymn and the *responsory in choro*. After this were sung the five psalms of the Roman cursus (see Chapter 10). The psalms were followed by a prayer, then the *Magnificat*, another prayer and finally, responsories, etc. in procession to the baptisteries.[7]

On certain feasts, instead of the five psalms, there was a selected psalm with psalms 133 and 116 and then a prayer; another selected psalm and a prayer, and then the *Magnificat*. This appears to be a relic of the night vigil once used, which involved the clergy singing the entire Psalter over night.[8]

On the first three days of Holy Week, the order was even simpler: *lucernarium, responsory in choro*, selected psalm and its prayer, and the twelve *Kyries* (The Office Hymn may not have been used on these days at the time of Beroldus).[9] Holy Week Vespers also shows its antique structure by not having the usual processional appendix.

The *Manuale* envisaged two baptisteries in Milan, one for the winter church of Santa Maria, and one for the summer church of St Thecla.[10] Vespers proper finished with twelve *Kyries* (found in the Holy Week office, and probably the remains of a litany), and then there was a procession singing the pieces known as *psallenda* or *responsorium in baptisterio*. Two further pieces, *complendae* or *completuria*, were followed by a collect. Four verses of a psalm originally covered the move to the second baptistery, and after a collect there, a *psallenda* and two more *complendae*

---

[5] M. Magistretti, *La Liturgia della Chiesa Milanese Secolo IV* (Milan, 1899), pp. 119–86; P. Borella, *Il Rito Ambrosiano* (Brescia, Marcelliana, 1964), pp. 225–71; Cattaneo, op. cit., pp. 11–46; Alzati, op. cit., vol. I.

[6] W.C. Bishop (ed. C.L. Feltoe), *The Mozarabic and Ambrosian Rites* (London: Alcuin/ Mowbrays, 1924), pp. 98–134: 'The Breviary at Milan'.

[7] See e.g. *Manuale*, p. 94 for 1st Sunday after Epiphany, pp. 411–13 for common of Sundays, and description in *Beroldus*, pp. 55–7.

[8] Ibid., p. 118, and see Alzati, vol. II, pp. 28–9.

[9] See *Beroldus*, p. 101.

[10] King, *Liturgies of the Primatial Sees*, op. cit., pp. 318–19. The present Cathedral replacing both was begun in 1386.

accompanied the procession back to church for the final collect and usual conclusion.[11]

The Vesperal psalmody

The five psalms of the Roman cursus, as they appear in the *Manuale*, cannot be original.[12] The festal form of two proper psalms, the first linked with psalms 133 and 116, is seen as the more primitive by many writers.[13] Winkler, however, points out that 116 may simply be a doxology, and 133 is, in almost all other rites, proper to the Midnight office. She concludes, contra Cattaneo and Borella, that this form is proper to feasts that had an all night vigil, and is nothing to do with ordinary Vespers.[14] If the five psalms of the Roman course cannot be regarded as original, it seems likely that the *Magnificat* was imported as well, for the latter was absent from Vespers in the first three days of Holy Week, and was omitted on all other Friday in Lent.[15]

The beginning of Vespers betrays a 'cathedral' origin by starting with the greeting 'The Lord be with you', rather than with 'Deus in adjutorium'. The *lucernarium* is made up of select verses of a psalm, usually with the theme of light. The common Sunday one, sung to an elaborate chant,[16] was:

> You, O Lord, are my lamp, my God who lightens my darkness.
> *V*. For you deliver me from the attack against me, O Lord, my God.
> (psalm 17.29–30a)[17]

The *Manuale* gives first place to psalm 117.1a and 2a, 'O give thanks to the Lord: for he is good. Give thanks to the God of gods, for he is good',[18] more a thanksgiving for the day past in a similar way to psalm 103. The ordinary weekday *lucernarium* is:

---

[11] Outlined in Bishop, op. cit., pp. 126–7 and Azati, vol. II, pp. 26–7. *Manuale* describes one set as *Psallendae in baptisterio*, and another as *Psallendae de baptisterio in aliud*, p. 412; ceremonial in *Beroldus*, pp. 56–7.

[12] Alzati, vol. II, p. 26.

[13] E.g. Borella, 'Il Breviario Ambrosiano', in M. Righetti, *Storia Liturgica* (Milan: Ancora, 1946), 603–41, 631.

[14] Winkler, 'Uber die Kathedralvesper', op. cit., 95–7.

[15] *Brev. Ambr. pars Hiem. II*, op. cit., p. 37; *Manuale*, vol. I, p. 133.

[16] *Liber Vesperalis juxta ritum Sanctae Ecclesiae Mediolanensis* (Rome: Desclée, 1939), pp. 1–2.

[17] *Manuale*, p. 411.

[18] Ibid.

The Lord is my light and my help; whom shall I fear?
V. The Lord is the stronghold of my life; before whom shall I shrink?
(psalm 26)[19]

The Fridays of Lent, rather interestingly, employed psalm 140 as a *lucernarium*, referring more to the evening offering of incense than to evening light as such:

Dirigatur oratio mea sicut incensum in conspectu tuo; elevatio manuum mearum: sacrificium vespertinum.
V. Domine, clamavi ad te, exaudi me, intende voci deprecationis meae: sacrificium ...
V. Pone, Domine, custodiam ori meo: sacrificium.[20]

This is thought by many to be the original form, and it is clear that in earlier times the light offering *and* the evening incense were closely linked.[21]

Support for the theory that the celebration of the evening light was the original theme of the Milanese *lucernarium* is found in the *antiphona in choro*, a Sunday addition to the *lucernarium*.[22] This antiphon maintained the theme of light or of the evening. For example, 'O God be gracious and bless us and let your face shed its light upon us' (psalm 66), 'At night there are tears, but joy comes with dawn' (psalm 29).[23] Not only is there a reference to the evening but often to preparation for the coming night.

The *responsories in choro* are also drawn from a repertoire of fairly general texts, and we find that those for ordinary Sundays reflect the theme of God the Saviour forming and teaching his people:

Let your love come upon me, Lord, and I shall live: for your law is my delight.
V. It was your hands that made me and shaped me: help me to learn your commands.
(psalm 118.77 and 73)
I am lost like a sheep; seek your servant, O Lord.
V. Leave me, you who do evil; I will keep God's command
(psalm 118.176 and 115).[24]

Weekday responsories were similar, but often more obviously vesperal; that for Monday having a verse from psalm 103, while Friday's is from psalm 140:

---

[19] Ibid., p. 432.

[20] *Manuale*,vol. I, pp. 132–3.

[21] Winkler, op. cit.; Borella, 'Il Brevario', 629–30.

[22] *Antiphona in choro* for feasts falling on Sundays; see e.g. *Breviarium Ambrosianum, Pars Hiemalis I* (Milan: 1944), p. 170.

[23] *Manuale*, vol. II, p. 411.

[24] Ibid.

> Let our prayer come before you, O Lord:
> *V.* Like incense in your sight.

We need not discuss the psalms of the Roman cursus and the *Magnificat*. A typical *psallenda* at the end of the office is: 'Salva nos, Domine, Deus noster: salva nos, et congrega nos de nationibus'.[25] Similar again is 'Inclina ad me aurem tuam, et salva me: esto mihi in Deum protectorem'.[26] The second set are less tied to the psalms but are biblically inspired, 'My sin Lord, is like an arrow piercing me ... save me by the medicine of penitence'.[27] Perhaps a renewal of baptismal 'healing'? This second set seem to reflect baptismal themes and are somewhat more optimistic; the final one is a good example: 'Brethren, let there be in us one heart in God, and one soul: O author of peace, king eternal, from all evil defend us'.[28] The texts of the *complendae* are very general and add little to the discussion.[29] If there is a principle of selection for the four-versed psalms on weekdays, perhaps it is praise by those who know themselves guarded by God's goodness, in other words, the baptized![30]

Vesperal Hymnody and Prayer

The hymn *Deus creator omnium* also establishes the light theme at the beginning of Vespers:

> Day sinks; we thank thee for thy gift;
> Night comes; and once again we lift
> Our prayer and vows and hymns that we
> Against all ills may shielded be.
> That when black darkness closes day,
> And shadows thicken round our way,
> Faith may no darkness know, and night
> From faith's clear beam may borrow light.[31]

Two prayers, one after the psalms, and one following the *Magnificat* are similar in theme. That after the psalms on Sundays:

---

[25] Psalm 105.47; *Manuale*, p. 412.

[26] Psalm 30.3; *Manuale*, ibid.

[27] *Manuale*, pp. 412–13.

[28] Ibid.

[29] E.g., ibid., p. 412: 'Benedictus es, Domine, Deus patrum nostrorum, et laudabilis, et gloriosus in saecula.'

[30] For texts, *Liber Vesperalis*, op. cit., pp. 18–47.

[31] *English Hymnal* 49; *Brev. Ambr.*, op. cit., 176*.

> Look down, Lord from your seat of majesty upon high,
> and enlighten with the rays of your splendour the dread
> darkness of the night: wipe from each sense the dulling
> torpor of sleep, and from the sons of light remove the ills of darkness.[32]

The references to light and protection at night are taken up even more explicitly in the prayer after the *Magnificat*:[33]

> O God, who are the worker of salvation in the whole earth; to whom the darkness is not darkening, and the night is as light as the day, lighten our darkness, we beseech you; that being led through a calm and peaceful night, we may rise up in Your praises at the morning hour.

These prayers would actually be better placed if the former followed the *lucernarium* and the latter, the *responsory in choro*. The first introduces the terror of night, the second looks beyond it in the power of God's light. The same is true in the week. On Tuesday the course of the day is said to be finished, and this is an occasion to offer thanks and prayer for mercy; while the second prayer is one for protection.[34] On Wednesday the first prays that our hearts may shine out at the time of evening incense, and the second that we may brave the dangers of night and rise safely in the morning.[35]

Vespers in Milan may anciently have comprised at least two psalms with prayers: the light psalm and one seeking God's protection at night. There may also have been a third psalm, proper to the day, which would then give us the same shape as the Vespers of the first three days of Holy Week before recent changes: *lucernarium, responsory in choro*, proper psalm and prayer. The latter prayer was the only one in Milanese Vespers of Holy Week, and appears to be a kind of psalm collect; for example, on Tuesday, psalm 17.49, 'You set me above my assailants, you save me from violent men', and praying that Christ's condemnation may be propitiation for all.[36]

The final prayers, which in *Manuale* accompany the baptistery processions, often pray for forgiveness of sins, and also for light and joy:

> O God, strength of the faithful, life and resurrection of the dead; grant constancy to your faithful and restore to us the gift of your salvation. Hear us, merciful God: and enlighten our minds with your grace.

---

[32] *Manuale*, p. 418.

[33] Ibid.

[34] Ibid. p. 435.

[35] Ibid., p. 437.

[36] Ibid., p. 178: 'ut, sicut in condempnatione Filii tui salus omnium fuit piaculum perfidorum'.

> Lord, may our mouth be filled with joy, and may we ever rejoice in your mercy.[37]

There are very similar themes during the week. The Saturday prayers are good illustrations; the first, which we give, is an evening prayer for the coming light of Christ, and the second is a simple prayer that God will be with his people to free them:

> At evening, morning and at noon we make our supplications to your majesty, almighty God: that the darkness of sin being driven out from us, you might bid us come to the true light that is Christ.

Thus was baptism daily renewed in the lives of the people of Milan.

The concluding texts, which were the same evening and morning, include a dismissal formula, followed by the silent recitation of the Lord's Prayer.[38] The Lord's Prayer was probably a later addition, and the conclusion was simply:

> *V*. Procedamus cum pace: *R*. In nomine Christi.

The Ambrosian Matins

Festal Matins commenced with the *Deus in adjutorium*, etc., the daily hymn *Aeterne rerum conditor*, a responsory (that on summer Sundays included verses from psalm 94, 'Come ring out our joy to the Lord'),[39] and *Benedictus es*, the first part of the song of the three children from Daniel 3. On Sundays three Old Testament canticles were followed by *Kyrie eleison* three times: three readings with responsories after the first two and *Te Deum* after the third. Thc Ncw Testament canticle of Zechariah, *Benedictus Dominus Deus Israel* was now sung, followed in Beroldus by a complex procession during the singing of the *antiphona ad crucem*.[40] Prayers introduced the canticles *Cantemus* (the Exodus 15 Song of the Sea) and *Benedicite*; then were sung the *laudate* psalms (148–50 and 116) with incensation.[41] A *capitulum* was followed by the *Psalmus in Directus* (psalm 92, 'The Lord is King'), and then, originally, a long form of the *Gloria in Excelsis*, the *Laus Angelorum Magna* and the hymn *Splendor Paternae*

---

[37] *Manuale*, p. 418.

[38] See e.g. *Breviarium Ambrosianum, par hiemalis I*, 182*.

[39] *Manuale*, vol. II, p. 400.

[40] See *Beroldus*, pp. 4–43; it involved summer and winter churches, and their baptisteries (see King, op. cit., pp. 318–19).

[41] *Beroldus*, p. 44.

Gloriae. The office concluded with twelve *Kyries* and a processional appendix like that of Vespers.

Monday to Friday, instead of the three canticles, there were sung ten or so psalms of psalms 1–108 (divided rather arbitrarily into three Nocturns) over a two- week period. On Saturday, the first 'Nocturn' was *Cantemus*, in both weeks, and then half of psalm 118 one week and the other half the next.[42] Readings and responsories were as above, but after *Benedictus* a prayer introduced psalm 50 (117 on Saturday), and another, the *laudate* psalms. After the *capitulum* there was a different *Psalmus in Directus* each day, the *Laus Angelorum Magna*, hymn, *Kyries* and processional appendix. Originally no division was made between the night part of the office and Lauds; *Te Deum* was introduced after the third reading in 1440, and *Deus in adiutorium* was inserted before the *Benedictus* in 1625.[43] The ancient *Laus Angelorum Magna* was suppressed as from the 1582 edition of the Breviary.[44]

To the end of the *laudate* psalms, the service follows a logical progression: the Sunday canticles with overtones of Paschal vigil, and psalm 50 on weekdays with its theme of repentance, are followed by the psalms of praise. The *Psalmus in Directus* is more problematic, see below. The cosmic praise of the *Laus Angelorum Magna* and then the twelve *Kyries* brought the office proper to an end. The appendices, with procession to the baptisteries, are of a similar kind to those already described above for Vespers.

The Psalms and Other Scriptures at Matins

Leaving aside momentarily the responsory after the hymn and the song of the three children we turn first to the Psalter. Psalms 1–108 were divided into ten units entitled *decuriae*. This system took no account of psalms used elsewhere, and did not fit with the Roman system used at Vespers, which omitted duplications.[45] Either it came from elsewhere, or it is the remains of an older Milanese system. Prior to the Carolingian period, whatever older monastic communities might have done,[46] it seems unlikely that the secular clergy of Milan ever recited the whole Psalter in the course, except when following the festal custom of reciting the entire Psalter in one night. This custom survived into the Middle Ages in an altered form, anticipated on the day before rather

[42] See Bishop, op. cit., pp. 98–133, esp. 114–15.

[43] Borella, op. cit., p. 240.

[44] Cattaneo, op. cit., pp. 186–7, Alzati, vol. II, pp. 33–5.

[45] Bishop, op. cit., pp. 114–15.

[46] E.g., the basilica of Sant'Ambrogio, until it became Benedictine in 789; King, op. cit., p. 321.

than being sung at night, and by then it was additional to the normal daily course.[47]

The Psalter in course was only used Monday to Friday; on Saturday, psalm 118 made up the Psalter, together with the Exodus 15 canticle. This psalm is also used as the nocturnal psalmody for Saturday in the Byzantine and Palestinian monastic rites,[48] emphasizing the festal character of the Milanese Saturday service.[49] On Sunday were sung the canticles Isaiah 26.9–20, 'My soul yearns for thee in the night'; 1 Samuel 2.1–10, the canticle of Hannah; and Habakkuk 3.2–19, 'O Lord, I have heard the report of thee'.[50] These canticles indicate the Paschal vigil nature of the service, proclaiming the power of God, whose light overcomes darkness.

The readings at Matins were an adaptation of the Roman scheme of the time,[51] but the responsories seem to be from Milanese sources. These responsories, one after the hymn and the two between the readings, are almost always from the psalms, and although the summer Sunday ones after the hymn are from psalm 94, there is nothing specifically invitatory about them. The Sunday ones praise God as creator. For example:

> O ruler, Lord of the heavens and the earth, creator of the waters: king over all your creatures, hear the prayers of your servants.
> *V.* (Psalm 101.1) O Lord, listen to my prayer and let my cry for help reach you. King ...[52]

The weekday ones mostly pray God as protector and Saviour to have mercy on his people.[53]

The responsories between the readings are much the same, none have any but the most coincidental contact with the readings, and seem to have been drawn from a general repertoire. 'At night I mused within my heart ... Does God forget his mercy ?';[54] 'I will bless the Lord at all times';[55] 'The Lord set my feet upon a rock ... I waited, I waited for the Lord';[56] all in all, a varied

---

[47] Alzati, vol. II, p. 28.

[48] See above.

[49] Cattaneo, op. cit., p. 147.

[50] Respectively the 5th, 3rd and 4th odes of the Greek canon, see *Horologion*, pp. 99–106.

[51] Righetti, *Storia Liturgica*, op. cit., pp. 615–16.

[52] *Manuale*, pp. 399–400.

[53] *Manuale*, vol II, pp. 430–46; e.g. p. 430, summer Mondays: 'Deus in te speravi: Domine, and p. 433, summer Tuesdays: 'Miserere nobis, Domine: misere nobis. *V.* Ad te levavi ...'.

[54] Ibid., p. 401 (psalm 76).

[55] Ibid., pp. 401–2 (psalm 33).

[56] Ibid., p. 402.

collection of what may be relics of responsorial psalms with a broad vigil theme. This is again borne out by those for Wednesday:

> In every place of his dominion, bless the Lord, O my soul.
> *V.* Bless the Lord O my soul, and all that is within me bless his holy name: bless ...[57]
> In the morning I think of you: for you have been my help, O Lord.
> *V.* In the shadow of your wings I rejoice: for ...[58]

It is interesting that these two responsories are drawn from psalms (102 and 62) that are part of the six that commence Palestinian/Byzantine Matins. They are well suited to a vigil before dawn and may indicate early Eastern influences at work in Milan.

In the arbitrary system by which each *decuria* was divided into Nocturns, each group of psalms under one antiphon was followed by *Kyrie eleison* three times and V. *Benedictus es Deus*, R. *Amen*. The same formulae followed *each* Sunday canticle.[59] As Jungmann once pointed out, sets of *Kyries* often indicate a period of intercessory prayer.[60] We may suggest that the daily vigil part of the morning service was a simpler form of the Sunday version, comprising perhaps three psalms and three prayers.

Turning to the strictly matinal parts of the office, we note immediately that *Benedictus Dominus* sits very uneasily at this point. If on a weekday there was a vigil of *selected* psalms and then psalm 50 (an ancient beginning of the morning part of an office), it is hard to see *Benedictus Dominus* as being in its original position.[61] Sunday Matins too, with the Paschal canticles *Benedicite* and *Cantemus*, seems to be interrupted by a New Testament interloper. An additional piece of evidence that might tell against *Benedictus* at this point, is the fact that on Sundays in Advent, and on the feasts of Christmas, Circumcision and Epiphany, Deuteronomy 32, 'Give ear, O heavens',[62] was appointed to be used instead.[63] On the other hand, the Irish Antiphonary of Bangor (see below) lists 'Give ear, O heavens' at the very beginning of the document, and then, after some hymns, *Benedictus, Cantemus* and *Benedicite*, so the use of a New Testament canticle at this point may in fact be ancient.

---

[57] Psalm 102.22 and 1–2.

[58] *Manuale*, p. 436, psalm 62.7–8.

[59] E.g., *Breviarium Ambrosianum, Pars Hyemalis II* (Milan, 1944), 45*–47*, 4*–6*.

[60] 'The Kyrie eleison of the Preces' in *Pastoral Liturgy* (London, Challoner, 1962), pp. 180–91.

[61] Though Alzati does not appear to doubt it, vol. II, pp. 33–5.

[62] 2nd in Greek canon, *Horologion*, pp. 94–9.

[63] *Breviarium Ambrosianum, pars hiemalis I*, 8*–11*.

The *capitulum* after the praise psalms also fits the theme of morning praise, much more so than is the case in the Roman/Benedictine traditions (see pp. 205–7). For example, that for Sunday:

> Cantate Domino canticum novum: laudatio ejus in Ecclesia sanctorum.[64]
> (psalm 149.1)

Psalm verses provide those for the rest of the week, for example, Monday: 'Caeli enarrent gloriam Dei: et opera manuum eius annutiat firmamentum' [65] (psalm 18.1). If *capitula* were traditionally defined as abbreviated lessons, the Milanese versions (except some festal ones) cannot be explained this way. These psalm verses seem more like antiphons, or other morning songs of praise to God the creator.

Most writers see the *Psalmus in Directus* as the ancient morning psalm.[66] The Sunday psalm, 92, is not strictly a *morning* psalm while psalm 142 on Fridays was one of the few that were classically used as morning psalms elsewhere.[67] The following phrases establish a different theme in these psalms: 'But I have God for my help, the Lord upholds my life' (psalm 53); 'May God still give us his blessing' (psalm 66)'; 'You are my rescuer, my help, O Lord, do not delay' (psalm 69); 'May the name of the Lord be blessed both now and for evermore' (psalm 112); 'For your names sake, Lord, save my life' (psalm 142); and 'Let the favour of the Lord be upon us' (psalm 89). They may have originally been intended as psalms of dismissal, praying for God's continued blessing throughout the day.

Morning Hymns and Prayers

The interpretation of the ancient Matins may be found in the hymns at the beginning and end of the office. *Aeterne rerum conditor* – 'Maker of all, eternal King' – is thought to be Ambrosian.[68] A cockcrow hymn, at rising in the night before it is light:

> Roused at the note, the morning star
> Heaven's dusky veil uplifts afar;
> Night's vagrant bands no longer roam,
> But from their dark ways hie them home.
> O let us then like men arise;

[64] *Manuale*, p. 404.

[65] Ibid., p. 431.

[66] E.g., Cattaneo, op. cit., p. 185.

[67] Bishop lists the psalms, op. cit., p. 116.

[68] Cf. Borella, op. cit., p. 56.

The cock rebukes our slumbering eyes,
Bestirs who still in sleep would lie,
And shames who would their Lord deny.[69]

The hymn at the end, *Splendor paternae gloriae*, is also widely thought to be one of Ambrose's.[70] The hymn salutes the rising sun, signifying Christ the true sun, and, in verse eight, it looks for the eternal day of the 'perfect morn':

O Splendour of God's glory bright,
O thou that bringest light from light,
O Light of light, light's living spring,
O Day, all days illumining.
(verse 8)
Morn in her rosy car is borne;
Let him come forth our perfect morn,
The Word in God the Father one,
The Father perfect in the Son.[71]

Clearly what comes between the two hymns is an office that took place between cockcrow and sunrise, not a night office but a night to morning one.

The Sunday and festal *antiphona ad crucem* was anciently accompanied by a complex procession which might connect us with a Sunday vigil of the Resurrection.[72] The antiphon was repeated a number of times for the procession,[73] and the texts reflect a laudatory style:

> We do not remember the multitude of his mercies; deliver us according to your name, that we may know your power.[74]

> It is good to trust in the Lord, rather than to trust in men; it is good to hope in the Lord, rather than to hope in princes: I will confess you, O God, because you have heard me, and made to save me.[75]

An analysis of some of the present Easter texts by Marco Navoni[76] emphasized the festal 'excess' of the procession, with its strong resurrection

---

[69] Trans. J.W. Copeland; Bishop, op. cit. 76, *Breviarium Ambrosianum, Pars Hiemalis I*, 1*.

[70] Cattaneo, op. cit., p. 24.

[71] *EH 52, Brev.Amb.*, 17*.

[72] Borella, pp. 241–2.

[73] *Beroldus*, pp. 40–43.

[74] *Manuale*, p. 402.

[75] Ibid.

[76] 'Le Antifone 'ad Crucem' dell'Ufficiatura Ambrosiana del Tempo Pasquale', *EL*, **99** (1985), 239–71.

content, especially as the procession was led by a triumphal cross decked with candles.

The prayers associated with the canticles *Cantemus* and *Benedicite*, like the canticles themselves, continue the themes of emergence from darkness into God's protection, symbolized by delivery from slavery in Egypt, or from the fiery furnace:

> O God, you made Moses worthy to be the one who led your family to freedom from the darkness of Egypt with many mighty works: may we too who also are your people, be freed from the affliction of this present age, and permitted to enter into the rest promised to our fathers. Through ...
>
> O God, who sent a fourth to be with the three children in midst of the fire, one to ease the nature of fire and put out the attacking flames: in the same way, O Lord, extend your strength to protect and deliver our souls.[77]

This combination of *antiphona ad crucem* and two paschal canticles could indicate that this part of Matins was indeed the Milanese cathedral vigil, the morning praises being simply the praise psalms, *Laus Angelorum Magna* and morning hymn. On weekdays, psalm 50 was used (but Psalm 117 on Saturday, again a resurrection psalm), and the prayers to accompany psalm 50 pray for mercy and light.[78]

The prayer before the Sunday *laudate* psalms praises God's light after the night,[79] and looks forward to the everlasting day of God's undimmed glory.[80] The weekday ones pray that the light may be an earnest of blessing for the day – which suggests that they once concluded the office.[81] The same themes are found in the Saturday offices.

The *Laus Angelorum Magna* was the *Gloria in Excelsis*, the Great Doxology, with variations. After the phrase 'Qui sedes ad dexteram Patris, miserere nobis' was inserted:

> subveni nobis, dirige nos, conserva nos, munda nos, pacifica nos. Libera nos ab inimicis, a tentationibus, ab haereticis, ab arrianis, a schismaticis, a barbaris: quia tu solus sanctus ...[82]

---

[77] *Manuale*, p. 414.

[78] e.g. ibid., p. 431; 'Have mercy on us, almighty God: and grant your light to us always.' – 'O Lord, who are light and truth to us, make our presence here shine with your holiness.'

[79] Ibid., p. 415.

[80] Ibid., 'et sempiternum diem jubeas pervenire'.

[81] E.g.; ibid., p. 431, 'O God, author of light, creator of brightness, enlighten, we beseech you, the darkness of our souls: that we your family may be upheld by your morning benediction.'

[82] Ibid., p. 415.

The reference to Arians may argue an early date. The next part quotes passages found in the Greek version:[83]

> ... Every day I will bless thee ... Vouchsafe, O Lord, to keep us this day without sin. Blessed art thou, O Lord teach me thy statutes.[84]

The final section employs intercessory psalm verses, and finishes in a way reminiscent of the *Benedicite*:

> ... Blessed are thou, O Lord; teach me O God of our Fathers, praised and glorified for ever and ever. Amen. Glory and honour be to the Father, and to the Son, ...[85]

This hymn was probably the result of early Eastern influence.

The prayers of the processional appendix, usually of a general nature, seem concerned with renewing, or continuing, baptismal grace. For example: (Monday) 'Stretch out your right hand to us, O God, and in your goodness overshadow us with your aid from on high'; (Thursday) 'O God, be pleased to hear our crying unto you: that we may be rescued from the depths of sin'; one of those for Friday looks forward to the eternal day: 'Lord, bless us with your grace, and lead us to eternal life',[86] thus returning to one of the constant matinal themes which we have identified, both here and elsewhere.

There is no documentary evidence for Minor Hours and Compline at Milan until the *Manuale*. A time of midday psalmody may have been known, and the office hymn of Terce, *Iam surgit hora tertia* was composed by Ambrose – but perhaps not originally for that role, it is after all a passion hymn.[87] The material appears to have been taken over wholesale from the Roman rite, though Compline exhibits some peculiarities.

The Gallican Evidence

What can be said about the Gallican traditions has been summarized by Robert Taft[88] and Paul Bradshaw,[89] so we shall content ourselves here by

---

[83] *Horologion*, pp. 126–7.

[84] *Manuale*, p. 416.

[85] Ibid.

[86] *Manuale*, vol. II, pp. 432–42.

[87] See Alzati, vol. II, pp. 35–6.

[88] Taft, *Liturgy of the Hours*, pp. 93–163.

[89] Bradshaw, *Daily Prayer in the Early Church*, pp. 111–49.

drawing out any structural and internal similarities to what we have found elsewhere.

A monastic use, the fourth-century *Ordo Monasterii*, a North African document but employed by Caesarius of Arles, provided psalms 62, 5 and 89 for the morning. It speaks of a *lucernarium* service of one responsorial, four antiphonal and another responsorial psalm; and, depending on the length of the nights, up to twelve antiphonal and 6 responsorial psalms at Nocturns.[90] Of the few psalms mentioned, 62 is commonly found and the other two less so. The seeming absence of psalms 148–50 or any mention of canticles may imply a deliberate distancing from the cathedral office. The totals of psalms at evening and at night; 6 and 18, are vaguely reminiscent of early Italian arrangements.[91]

Cassian expected a lengthy nocturnal vigil followed, after a pause, by the morning office of sunrise, and comprising psalms 62, 118.147–8 (I rise before dawn and cry for help), and 148–50. Vespers was largely characterized by continuous psalmody and reading.[92] In Caesarius, *duodecima* and Nocturns both largely comprise psalmody, probably in course.[93] *Duodecima* was preceded by the public, cathedral *lucernarium*, and the Nocturnal/Vigil psalmody was followed by the public morning office.[94]

The cathedral evening service comprised an invitatory, three antiphonal psalms, and the intercessory *capitellum*. At Matins, after an invitatory psalm, 117 (which we saw as a morning psalm in Milan), were possibly psalms 42 and 62;[95] then *Cantemus* and *Benedicite*, with psalms 145–7 between them and 148–50 after them; *Te Deum, Gloria*, and a hymn are mentioned, and the *capitellum*. Most of this was used on weekdays as well, though not the canticles.[96] The basic structure is very similar to what we have seen of the Milanese Matins of Sunday and Saturday, except for psalms 145–7 between the canticles. This use of all six psalms of the *pesukai d'zimra*, the verses of song, was defended by W. Jardine Grisbrooke in a recent article.[97]

---

90 Taft, *Liturgy of the Hours*, pp. 94–6.

91 A. De Vogüé and L.Eberle (eds), *The Rule of the Master* (Kalamazoo: Cistercian Publications, 1977), pp. 26–8.

92 Taft, *Liturgy of the Hours*, pp. 96–100, and *PL* 49, 77ff.

93 Taft, *Liturgy of the Hours*, pp. 107–9.

94 Combining of cathedral and monastic offices is also found in Aurelian, *PL* 68, 391–3, 402–3; monastic *duodecima* follows cathedral *lucernarium*.

95 Taft's hypothesis, *Liturgy of the Hours*, p. 111.

96 Ibid., pp. 112–13.

97 'The Laudate Psalms: A Footnote', *SL*, **20** (1990), 162–84, 175–6.

From the middle of the sixth century we have evidence of the content of cathedral Matins in Gregory of Tours' description of the death of his uncle, St Gall of Clermont. The service mentioned appears to comprise:

Psalm 50
Benedicite
Psalms 148–50
Capitellum.[98]

There may have been more material, but we still have an exactly similar structure to what we found in Caesarius and Aurelian, and in Milan and Spain.

The Offices of the *Antiphonary of Bangor*

The *Antiphonary of Bangor* is an Irish monastic work, dated by F.E. Warren to between 680 and 691.[99] Michael Curran has analysed this work,[100] comparing it with other evidence such as the *Navigatio Sancti Brendani* (a ninth-century work), and has been able to suggest what the content of the offices might be.[101]

The following scriptural texts formed the offices. At Vespers, psalms 64, 'To you our praise is due in Sion, O God', 103 and 112 (with the words 'from the rising of the sun to its setting'), all appropriate, not only because of references to the evening, but because they have 'a special concentration on such favourite evening themes as the work of God and man in creation and praise of God for all his wisdom and bountiful goodness, as manifested in his creation'.[102] These themes fit in well with what we have seen elsewhere, and may well indicate a natural development from psalm 103 alone to a group including it with two others.

The greater part of the psalmody appears to have been fulfilled at the Nightfall and Midnight offices, both of which have twelve psalms, and there are collects that pray to God the source of light who overcomes the works of darkness. Once again Curran puts it well: 'The Church's daily struggle with the

[98] Taft, *Liturgy of the Hours*, p. 146 and *PL* 71, 1034; the service begins in the early 'white' light before sunrise, 'Albescente jam coelo ...'.

[99] F.E. Warren (ed.), *The Antiphonary of Bangor* (London: Henry Bradshaw Society, 1893), Part I, p. x; hereafter Warren.

[100] M. Curran, *The Antiphonary of Bangor* (Dublin: Irish Academic Press, 1984), hereafter Curran.

[101] Ibid., pp. 169–71.

[102] Ibid., p. 171.

works of darkness is one of the great evening themes, a struggle that is carried on in the awareness of the presence of Christ, the light of the world, in our time, even at night.'[103]

The Morning office was divided into two parts, the first was a further lengthy monastic psalmody, and the second, a more or less cathedral Matins, the material for which forms the greater part of the Antiphonary.[104] The canticles *Cantemus* and *Benedicite* are immediately preceded by *Benedictus*, and the Deuteronomy canticle *Audite coeli* is found at the beginning of the Antiphonary; so these last two named canticles may have had a similar place in this office to the one they had at Milan.[105]

The psalms chosen for the day hours reflect what has become the traditional commemoration of the passion and death of Christ. Could Irish monasticism be the origin of this tendency to identify the day hours with the salient moments Christ's suffering and death?

An oddity of this rite was the *Gloria in Excelsis* employed at Vespers as well as at Matins, possibly after the psalms.[106] There were also collects for the services. For example, at Vespers:

> At the time of evening we invoke you, o Lord. Our prayer is always that you pardon our sins.[107]

> Let our evening prayer ascend into the hearing of your divine majesty, and may your blessing descend, Lord upon us, as we have placed our hope in you.[108]

The second prayer has clear overtones of psalm 140 as Curran admits. There is a formula of intercession at this point intended for all the day hours, and with which Vespers are grouped.[109]

Collects at the Midnight office see it as the hour when Christ comes, so vigilance must be exercised: 'Jesu, clementer visita/ Nocte orantes media'[110] and 'At the middle of the night there is a cry, grant that we may prepare to meet the bridegroom'.[111] The morning collects contain references to cockcrow,

---

[103] Ibid., p. 179.

[104] Ibid., p. 183.

[105] Warren, pp. 1–8.

[106] Curran, 173.

[107] Warren *II* (1895), p. 20, #21.

[108] Ibid., p. 21, #31.

[109] Ibid., p. 31, #117.

[110] Warren, p. 20, #23.

[111] Ibid., p. 24, #57.

'Gallorum, Christe, cantibus';[112] the coming of the day that expels the darkness, 'Deus, qui pulsis tenebris diei lucem tribuis, Adventum veri luminis tuis effunde famulis';[113] and waiting for the morning light, 'ad te de luce vigilare debemus, et tu excita de gravi somno'.[114] This last appears to have overtones of psalm 62.

The antiphonary also gives sets of collects for the canticles, the praise psalms and so on, as above. A collect for the Exodus canticle sums up baptismal faith very well indeed:

> O God, who every day lift up the yoke of Egyptian slavery from your people, and by washing in a spiritual stream lead them by conquering evil, into a promised land; grant us victory over hostile attacks of enemies, that defeating our darknesses we may be led to our inheritance in the sanctuary prepared by your hands, O Saviour of the world.[115]

A prayer from the *Benedicite* speaks of the faith of the three children cooling the furnace,[116] another sees their delivery as a type of the resurrection.[117] The collects for the praise psalms are general prayers of praise:

> O God whose hosts in heaven sing, whom saints praise in the Church, who is hymned by all in spirit, Have mercy, we entreat, upon us all, Who . . .[118]

Curran suggests the following basic structure of the morning praises:

1. (*Benedictus* or *Audite Coeli* ?)
2. *Cantemus* and collect
3. *Benedicite* and collect
4. Psalms 148–50 and collect
5. Gospel reading and collect
6. Hymn and collect
7. Commemoration of the Martyrs

The *Gloria* is given as a hymn for Matins, so is *Te Deum* for Sundays.[119]

---

[112] Ibid., p. 20, #25.
[113] Ibid., #26.
[114] Ibid., p. 24, #58.
[115] Ibid., p. 25, #68.
[116] Ibid., #72.
[117] Ibid., 26, #82.
[118] Ibid., 27, #90.
[119] Curran, p. 184.

This again provides a striking similarity to the form of office that we found in Milan; in fact, if the *Gloria* and hymn were both used, then we have almost exact correspondence, as Curran points out.[120] He is of the opinion that in this tradition, the same basic shape, though probably without the Gospel, was used on weekdays as well.[121]

Again we have an ancient form of Morning Prayer following on from the night watches to a paschal celebration of Christ the new light, the risen Lord, who has delivered, and continues to deliver his people from their sins and from their spiritual enemies.

Conclusions

I *Structural comparison*

1 One of the striking features of these non-Roman Western rites is their similarity of structure, especially at Matins. Evidence for Gallican Vespers is very slight but when we examine the Ambrosian form, our preferred original type (that of Holy Week comprising little more than three psalms and prayer) is very similar to the old Spanish form of three psalms and prayer. The psalms also seem to be selected on the basis of the light that overcomes darkness.

2 Milan and Spain also had visits to baptisteries after Vespers. Milan's occasional all night vigil of psalmody has some parallel in the old Spanish monastic vigils edited by Pinell that appear to expect the current Psalter to be done overnight.

3 Leaving aside the probably later *decuriae*, we can suggest a daily vigil in Milan of three select psalms, and a Sunday one of three canticles. These are paralleled by the Spanish three antiphons. The Morning Office of Paschal canticles, such as *Cantemus* and *Benedicite*, with psalm 50 perhaps only on weekdays, reaching a climax in the praise psalms and the Great Doxology (until 1582 in Milan), is also reflected both in Gregory of Tours and in the Bangor Antiphonary, as well as in the Spanish books.

II *The texts*

1 The texts that comprise these structures reflect much of what we have seen elsewhere. Milanese prayers and texts on light at Vespers are followed by

[120] Ibid., p. 186.

[121] Ibid., pp. 190–91.

prayer for protection, but also for light in the night, that the night may be as light as day.

2 The baptismal focus of the post-vesperal additions is also reflected in prayer and chant texts.

3 The Milanese night to morning office is begun with Ambrose's *Aeterne rerum* praying to drive away darkness, and at the end, his *Splendor paternae* sings of the light of the new day foreshadowing the everlasting light.

4 Prayers with the canticles *Cantemus* and *Benedicite*, show their importance of at the hinge of night and morning, as reminiscences of Easter delivery from slavery and danger.

III *Other considerations*

1 The Western offices have interesting parallels with Eastern traditions, such as the candle-decked cross in the procession at the Milanese *antiphona ad crucem*. These appear to show a common concern for what Michael Curran described as the Church struggling daily with works of darkness, but confident of its eventual triumph in the power of the risen Lord Jesus Christ.

2 Once again, the Paschal thrust running through from Vespers to Matins is obvious. From light in the darkness, through the night watch to praise at sunrise, the Paschal Mystery is celebrated.

CHAPTER 14

The Shape and Theology of the Office

Drawing to a close, we must ask what we may have learnt from the overview of the early and medieval offices. More importantly we may perhaps be able to say whether there may or may not be a single theology of daily prayer that can help us with the problems perceived in the offices of the present-day.

The Ritual Shape of Daily Prayer

One of the peculiarities of liturgical books is the way in which they differ in their arrangements of the daily offices. The pre-1912 Roman Breviary opened with the title, 'The Psalter disposed for the week with the ordinary of the Office of the Time'.[1] After the introductory prayers that preceded all the offices came the order of Matins and of Lauds for Sunday, without seasonal or festal propers. Now followed Prime, Terce, Sext and None, and then the order of Matins and Lauds for each day of the week in turn. After Saturday Lauds was found Sunday Vespers, Vespers for each weekday and daily Compline. The page that followed the order of Compline began the temporal with the *Magnificat* antiphon for the 1st Vespers of the First Sunday of Advent.[2] In other words the order in ordinary offices reckoned the day from Matins to Compline, while both seasonal and festal propers, and the common orders for saints, began at Vespers.

We find a strikingly similar thing when we examine the liturgical books of the other most widespread liturgical tradition, that of Byzantine Orthodoxy. The tenth-century Typikon of the Great Church starts the cycle of the months with Vespers on the eve of 1 September,[3] and a modern *Menaion* also starts the feasts of August with Vespers on the eve of Procession of the Cross.[4] On the other hand the standard *Great Horologion*[5] begins with the order of the Midnight Office, the *orthros* or Matins, the Hours and Inter-Hours with the

[1] 'Psalterium dispositum per Hebdomada cum Ordinario Officii de Tempore', *Breviarium Romanum, pars Autumnalis*, op. cit., 1.

[2] Ibid., 169.

[3] Mateos, *Le Typicon*, op. cit., p. 2.

[4] Μηναιογ Αυγουστου (Athens: Φως, 1970), p. 8.

[5] Ωρολογιον το Μεγα (Athens: της Αποστολικης Διακονιας. 1993), p. 3.

Typika,[6] then Vespers, Great and Little Compline. In both traditions one set of liturgical ordos reckons the day from midnight to midnight and the other from evening to evening. This little-remarked discrepancy is found in other liturgical traditions as well. Since a very large number of the oldest surviving liturgical books (as opposed to books of the Bible, such as the Psalter) are compilations of festal or seasonal material, the reckoning of the day from Vespers may argue for antiquity. After all, it is likely that the fixed parts of the offices were originally supplied from simple Psalters or even from memory.

It is doubtful whether any conclusive proof that one reckoning is more ancient than the other will ever be obtained. However, we will suggest that both the evidence of the ancient documents and the theology of the offices we have tried to tease out in all that has gone before make it easier and clearer in what follows to continue to reckon the liturgical day from evening to evening.

Throughout this work we have concentrated on the offices of Vespers and Matins, including in the latter the service often known in the West as Vigils or Nocturns. It is widely agreed by scholars that we have clear indication of services at the Third, Sixth and Ninth Hours of the day from a very early stage. However for reasons of clarity some further reflection on Day Hours will follow our conclusions about the evening and morning offices. As the euchological and hymnic material inevitably varies greatly from rite to rite, we shall concentrate most of our concluding remarks on the shape of the services and their use of scripture.

The Overall Shape of the Evening Office

We propose that there is a more or less common shape of the evening office that can be described schematically as follows:

> Introductory material, often concluding the day
> Current psalmody (when present, always in the first part)
> The 'Core' of the evening office – lights and incense
> (Readings not usually present)
> Intercession, Prayer in preparation for the night, other prayers
> Originally processional appendices (Not always present)

We could say that this structure concludes the day, perhaps allows space for meditative praying of the Psalter, celebrates the evening light and offers prayer and praise in thanksgiving, signified by the use of incense. There may then be a vigil reading, but in most cases prayer is offered both for the church and the

[6] This service is related to or replaces the Liturgy and is not discussed here.

world, and for protection through the coming night, that we may come to the new day. The service may conclude with devotional appendices that might, for example, provide a remembrance of baptism. In other words, the day ends and Christ the light of the world guides his people, washed in the waters of baptism, into the night from which they will arise the next morning.

The ways in which the offices begin are themselves interesting. Byzantine offices always start by blessing God, either simply in the presumed Palestinian form 'Blessed is our God, always, now and ever . . . ', or with the more elaborate Trinitarian form 'Blessed is the kingdom of the Father, the Son and the Holy Spirit . . . ' which in Constantinople began the services of the cathedral office as well as the Divine Liturgy, and which still commences Vespers when combined with either the ordinary or Presanctified Liturgies. East Syrian Vespers begins by ascribing glory to God in the Highest, and a kiss of peace,[7] in Milan and in the Old Spanish rite the service begins with the priestly greeting, 'The Lord be with you'. The traditions that retained a blessing or salutation continued to give witness to the public and ecclesial nature of the services.

All West Syrian offices begin by invoking the triune name. The Roman and Benedictine offices begin with the verses of psalm 69, 'O God make haste to help me', the Armenian Vespers with verses from psalm 54, Coptic offices with the Lord's Prayer. The Coptic and Roman traditions have been heavily influenced by monastic practices, and it may be that those rites that begin with psalm verses and other similar prayers may here show their close connection with the lay-led services of early monasticism.

Almost all traditions have preparatory prayers, which may be said silently before the formal beginning as in most Western traditions,[8] or aloud after the opening blessing or psalm verses, as in contemporary Byzantine offices. These are all much later developments as are penitential rites that are usually found at the First Hour and Compline, and which may come at the end or at the beginning of the service.[9] Many ancient vesperal offices are intended to be services of confession and forgiveness in themselves.[10]

An opening psalm such as psalms 85 or 103 of the Armenian / Byzantine traditions may serve to draw the day to a close. By contrast the Roman, Benedictine and Coptic monastic rites, together with the East Syrian rite, begin the Psalter in course almost immediately after the opening verses. West Syrian

---

[7] Maclean, op. cit., p. 1.

[8] The Lord's Prayer is a common component of these prayers.

[9] E.g., In the old Roman (*Pars Verna*, 167) and Monastic (I, 176) Breviaries, the confession and absolution are at the beginning of the service, in the Sarum Use (Sarum Brev. Psalterium, 239) they come towards the end, as does the rite of forgiveness in Byzantine Great Compline (Great Horologion, 181).

[10] See Winkler, 'L'aspect pénitential dans les Offices du soir en Orient et en Occident', op. cit.

Vespers draws the day to a close in prayer that mentions rest from the labours of the day and release from worldly thoughts.[11] Prayer at this point is not uncommon. For example, the Byzantine Great Litany has moved to this point. The Old Spanish and Milanese Vespers began with a light ritual, but the Old Spanish rite lacks current psalmody, and such psalmody at Vespers may not be original to Milanese tradition. Ethiopian *wazema* appears to be the only traditional rite that commences with a hymn, though it also has supplication at this point.

Rites that lack current psalmody proceed directly to the unchanging core: the West Syrian, Old Spanish, Ethiopian and Armenian services. Current psalmody dominated the first part of the Roman and Benedictine rites of Vespers, also the cathedral rite of Constantinople and East Syrian *ramsha*. Although now often abbreviated, the current Psalter is also found here in the contemporary Byzantine office of Palestinian origin. A form of semi-current psalmody made up much of the Coptic monastic Vespers.

A major difference between the rites is the way in which the Psalter is discharged. The cathedral rite of Constantinople chanted the psalms with simple responses, whilst the monastic custom of one voice reading *recto tono* was adopted from Palestine into the contemporary rite. East Syrian practice was to read the psalms without responses on weekdays and supply such responses on Sundays and feasts.[12] Early Western monastic practice appears to have been a mixture of meditative reading by one voice together with the responsorial method.[13] By the high Middle Ages this had become choral chanting of the psalms by all in choir, usually side to side. This practice probably contributed to the idea common by the sixteenth century and still heard today, that the recitation of the psalms in course was the *raison d'être* of the Divine Office.

What we have called the core of the evening office is broadly characterized by select psalmody, especially the use of psalm 140, and ritual than might involve lights and / or incense. The Armenian group of psalms 139–41, prayer for the blessing of light, and the hymn *Phos hilaron*, is closely paralleled by the Palestinian / Byzantine group of psalms 140–1, 129 and 116 with poetic *stichera*, procession with lights and incense, and the same hymn. The West and East Syrians used the same group of psalms 140–1, 118.105–12 and 116. The former has an incense rite, the latter once had a procession with lights and incense to the Bema on which the core service was celebrated, and still has incensation introducing that core. The old Byzantine office had a procession into church with lights and incense at psalm 140, and the core continued with

[11] Griffiths, op. cit., p. 4.

[12] Maclean, op. cit., p. 2, n. 3.

[13] See *RB 1980*, op. cit., 402–3.

the 'Little Antiphons' at the Ambo. We have suggested that the Coptic raising of incense may have had a connection with psalm 140, which is one of the psalms that make up Ethiopian *wazema*.

Is this core so readily identifiable in Western rites? We have suggested that the Milanese complex of *lucernarium, antiphona in coro* and Responsory *in coro*, may be that core. This is a complete service which appears to be very similar to the Old Spanish order of *lucernarium*, antiphon and *alleluiaticum*. The Roman and Benedictine offices seemingly had a vestigial core that included a scriptural blessing, and the versicle and response from psalm 140, also the incensation that comes to be associated with the *Magnificat*. It may be that the growing emphasis on choral chanting of the current Psalter contributed to the withering of the core.

This core is vital to understanding the theology of the Vespers. The light was sometimes brought in from outside of the church, as in Milan. Sometimes it was simply shown to the people, as was presumably the case in Spain and the Constantinopolitan cathedral rite, and sometimes it has left vestiges in the candle or candles carried in procession in the contemporary Orthodox rite[14] and in older East Syrian practice. Original practice must have been to begin the light ceremony when it became dark enough for artificial lighting to be necessary, just as the modern Jewish synagogue service to begin the Sabbath starts at sunset on Friday, at whatever hour that might occur. In Spain and possibly ancient Milan, in Armenia, Ethiopia and Western Syria where the current Psalter was largely carried out at night / early morning, this light ritual seems to have come near the beginning of a relatively short service. Where the custom was to have psalmody in course before the *lucernarium*, in Byzantine Orthodoxy, East Syria and possibly in Rome, that psalmody could be seen as a form of 'gathering rite' whilst waiting for the sunset. In either case the light appears to have functioned in the same way as that lit at the beginning of the Western Easter Vigil, as a symbol of Christ the light who conquers the darkness of sin and death. This light may well have been left throughout the night as in the Temple light mentioned on pp. 9–10 above.

An exception to the above which cannot simply be explained away is Egeria's account of the light ceremony taking place at four in the afternoon, the light being brought from the sepulchre and, one would presume, well before sunset. The order was the lighting of the lamps, psalmody, the entrance of the bishop, more psalmody and prayer. This pattern does not appear to be replicated by what we know of later Palestinian practice, nor do we see it reflected elsewhere, unless our proposals about the ancient Milanese office are

[14] It was ancient Russian practice for the candle bearers to push open the holy doors of the iconostasis with their candlesticks (Uspensky, *Evening Worship*, op. cit., p. 98), thus light might be seen to open the doors to the altar that can represent Christ's tomb.

completely wrong. Perhaps the pattern simply changed to combine the light ritual with the entrance of the bishop, which would form a blueprint for the present rite.

The Roman and Benedictine traditions appear to have had a core of *capitulum*, (Responsory), Hymn, Versicle and *Magnificat* with festal incensation. Any light ceremony has disappeared and incense is associated with the canticle and represents the prayers of the saints. Although the hymn was a later addition to this core in the Roman rite, it is interesting that it was added here and not at the beginning of the office as in the modern rite.

The other ritual act of the core was that of incensation, a rite that seems to have survived even when the light ritual had disappeared or shrunk to insignificance. Obviously taking inspiration from the words of psalm 140, the evening sacrifice of incense has usually involved the incensing the altar as a symbolic offering of prayer and praise in the evening sacrifice, but also the incensing of the people as a rite of cleansing and forgiveness of sins.[15] Even on weekdays in the contemporary Byzantine Vespers when there is no entrance, the censing still takes place, and the prayer of the entrance with its reference to the evening sacrifice is always prayed. The West Syrian rites give great importance to the purificatory aspect, which in the East Syrian was probably also originally associated with the procession to the Bema. Incense as an evening sacrifice for forgiveness of sins is central to the Coptic rite of Evening Incense.[16] Armenian usage seems to be connected with the prayer section of the core.[17]

As already stated, the Western use of incense at Vespers seems to have become associated with the prayers of the saints, although Amalarius commented on the ritual in conjunction with the versicle from psalm 140. There is no ancient evidence for a standing censer placed on or near the altar. The censer with chains traditional to East and West, and even the hand-held *katzion* of Greek use, witness to a traditional Christian view of incensation as an action rather than as an object of contemplation. This raises some interesting questions that are too complex to enter into here.

It should not be forgotten that this proposed central core of Vespers must also include the intercessions and other prayers. In the old Roman and Benedictine rites this element immediately followed the *Magnificat* with its incensation, and was later reduced to the collect of the day (preceded by the Lord's Prayer in the Benedictine rite) except when the so-called *Preces Feriales* were used. The core of the Constantinople Vespers taken in the nave included a

---

[15] See especially, Winkler, 'Über die Kathedralvesper', op. cit.

[16] E.g., *Coptic Liturgies and Hymns* (Hayward, CA: Jonathan Center, 1995), pp. 12–13.

[17] In St Sarkis, London (November 2001), incensing took place during the singing of the Trisagion.

whole range of litanies and prayers, and this shape has survived at the Sunday and Festal Great Vespers of the present rite. *Phos hilaron* and the acclamatory *prokeimenon* are followed by two litanies with the ancient prayer 'Vouchsafe, O Lord, to keep us this night without sin'. In the East Syrian *Ramsha* the same lengthy set of intercessions that are also used at the Eucharist and baptisms follow hard upon the evening psalms and variable material of the core. Moreover this is often the only point at which a minister, the deacon, is vested. We have seen that the Armenians also have litanic prayer at this point, and the West Syrian tradition has the variable, poetic form of intercession, the *b'outho*. Intercessory prayer is very much part of the Coptic raising of incense, and the Old Spanish tradition shows relics of an intercessory section which includes the Lord's Prayer.

We have emphasized several times the lack of readings from most orders of Vespers. Where they exist they are often, as in the modern Byzantine rite, a first part of the vigil observance of a feast, distinct from the evening service proper. In the same rite in Lent, they appear to be a displaced catechumenal instruction. The adding of a Gospel reading to the West Syrian festal Vespers and to a recent celebration of the Armenian vespers seems to be the result of later influences. The Old Spanish and even the Romanized Milanese rite prior to Vatican II had no readings at all, just like the East Syrian and the Constantinople sung office on most days. We have also suggested that the short chapters of the Roman and Benedictine offices are not vestigial readings that may now be lengthened into full ones, but have entirely different ritual origins. Ancient evening rituals were not vehicles for reading scripture but scripture-based celebrations of the saving death of Christ. Systematic reading of scripture had its place, but not there. The only strictly edificatory scriptural material in ancient Vespers appears to have been the reading of the Psalter in course.

Finally we have seen that most rites of Vespers seem to have concluded, at some time in their history, with devotional appendices of a once processional nature. The Roman Breviary commemorations often included processions in the Middle Ages, and revival has been encouraged of those that survived at Milan, which are similar to Old Spanish forms. The modern Byzantine Vespers has relics of such processions, which actually take place when a festal *litia* is appointed.[18] The East Syrian forms are no longer processional and the Armenian ones may be very reduced. Nothing of this kind seems to have survived in the West Syrian or Coptic rites. As later rites, these appendices often vary very considerably, but some recall visits to the baptistery, to a place

[18] This is a penitential procession that is part of the vigil of a feast (every Saturday in some books and Russian Old Ritualist practice) – the rubrics expect there to be simplified vesture and the holy doors of the altar remain closed.

of the cross, or to the martyrs. In all cases one may see these processions as further reinforcing the ideas celebrated in the core of Vespers, that entering upon the night in the light of Christ is also accepting for oneself a commitment to die to sin and rise to new life in Christ.

The Psalms of Vespers

Although psalm 140 is frequently cited as the most common psalm anciently used at Vespers, it is not the only one. There are relatively few psalms obviously appropriate to Vespers and so the same ones regularly appear in different places, quite possibly without any direct influence of one centre upon another. We have already said something about psalms 85 and 103 in their role as introducing the office by concluding the day. Psalm 140 on its own in the Byzantine cathedral rite, and possibly elsewhere, partially employed in Spanish *lucernaria* and Roman versicles, and grouped with two or three other psalms is certainly very widespread. The groups in which it occurs make a three-psalm unit, psalm 116 in Byzantine, West and East Syrian use being almost certainly to serve as a doxology. As we have discussed above, these psalms often dwell on themes of protection against enemies. The Ethiopian *wazema* has psalm 140 preceded by psalms 23 and 92 which sing of God's grandeur and probably reflect the festal nature of this particular service in which the psalms are each accompanied by other poetic and euchological material.

Psalm 140 and those associated with it do not exhaust the psalms we find at Vespers. We have noted the frequent employment of the gradual psalms (119–33), the themes of which can be said to move from prayer at going up to the heavenly Jerusalem to praying through the night in the holy house. At certain times of the year (in winter and in Lent) these psalms are the 'current' psalmody at weekday Byzantine Vespers, while they also characterized much of Monday to Thursday in the old Roman rite, and the psalmody of Coptic monastic Vespers. There is no exact fit here and we cannot make too much of this, except to note that these psalms certainly did strike some people as suitable evening psalms.

A thoroughgoing current psalmody is less common in ancient rites of Vespers than one might think. It is only found in contemporary Orthodox practice in the summer months, though it was once common in the old Constantinople cathedral office. The East Syrian *marmitha* was, as we have seen, a semi-continuous reading that appears to show signs of selectivity, as well as being seemingly unconnected with the overnight recitation of the Psalter at *lelya*. The old Roman and Benedictine systems were selective in that psalms 109–50 were always used in the evening (always excepting those used in other offices), to the extent that festal psalms for Vespers were also drawn from this part of the Psalter.[19] As has been said above, the major part of the recitation of the Psalter in course appears to have been more characteristic of the nocturnal part of Matins than of Vespers.

The use of a canticle, usually *Magnificat*, at Vespers is not found in the East,[20] and was not as universally used in the West as popularly supposed. The Old Spanish vespers had no canticle, Milan probably did not have one originally, and there is evidence to suggest that it may not have been part of the original Roman tradition. The *Magnificat* is regarded as the evening canticle *par excellence* by Western Christians, Catholic, Anglican and Protestant, whereas it is the morning canticle *par exellence* for modern Orthodox!

The Shape and Psalmody of Matins

It is relatively easy to demonstrate a common shape of Matins in traditional rites, though at the cost of great simplification:

Pre-dawn Vigil	Introductory material
	Current psalmody
	(Readings – not everywhere)
Dawn to Sunrise	Psalm 50 (not everywhere)
	Canticles and / or Morning Psalms
Morning Praise	Psalms 149–50
	Morning Hymn / Doxology / Canticle
	Intercession and Prayer
	Concluding material (incl. appendices)

We have not included in this the cathedral vigil, which in the contemporary Orthodox and East Syrian rites is placed more or less between the pre-dawn and dawn sections, and after the canticles in the Armenian Matins. This plan could apply to the Old Spanish office as well, but that was a cathedral vigil with Morning Prayer that may have been intended to be preceded by monastic pre-dawn psalmody.

The sheer amount of material involved in this, the longest of the ancient offices in their full development, means that while the above scheme is very over-simplified, it yet reflects something of a common progression of prayer and praise from darkness into light. Vespers may have developed around a

[19] See e.g., Louis Van Tongeren, *Exaltation of the Cross* (Leuven: Peeters, 2001), pp. 203–4.

[20] Contemporary Byzantine use of *Nunc Dimittis* as part of what we have identified as the processional / devotional appendix, and the fact that it is normally read rather than sung, would argue a later development.

central core, often approached quite slowly, and then rather more quickly drew to a devotional and ceremonial close. Matins, on the other hand, appears to move from darkness into increasing light, and finally reaches its ritual climax in the sunrise praise of and prayer to the risen Christ. For example, the contemporary Byzantine rite on feasts climaxes in the Praise psalms and Great Doxology. The service is then concluded with two litanies and the dismissal rite, or in Greek parochial use leads directly into the eucharistic liturgy.

Some kind of invitatory rite is much more universal in Matins than at Vespers. Psalm 3 began the Benedictine rite, it also commonly occurred at this point is Spain, and was part of the introductory groups of three or six psalms found in the ancient and modern Byzantine rites and the Armenian and West Syrian rites as well. Even the Midnight psalmody in the Coptic cathedral rite begins with psalm 3. Milan began with the cockcrow hymn *Aeterne rerum* and the East Syrian rite with introductory prayers in the night and then immediately the current psalmody. Other psalms used at this point included psalm 62 (Byzantine, Armenian, Ethiopian) which Western rites tend to reserve to the beginning of the sunrise section, Lauds. The Roman tradition employed psalm 94 as an invitatory for the night office, in Benedictine use it was preceded by psalm 3.

This point of the service was traditionally seen as a time of prayer in the darkness, waiting in vigil for the light and acknowledging one's sinfulness and the need for God's saving grace. In fact the whole night part of the ancient offices seems to have been a vigil before dawn for which the recitation of the Psalter in course was particularly appropriate. The East Syrian, ancient West Syrian, Armenian and probably the Old Spanish monastic rites all regarded this time as the most suited to current psalmody. As we have seen, this is also largely true of the contemporary Byzantine rite at certain seasons, and pre-Carolingian Milan may have had current psalmody only when there was an overnight vigil praying the whole Psalter. We have also noted that psalms 1–108 (with the exceptions of those used as fixed psalms elsewhere) were substantially the base of Roman and Benedictine Matins / Nocturns. The Ethiopian morning service *Sebhata Nagh* in Lent appears to be the only time that that tradition has recitation of the whole Psalter. Although a morning office, the recitation would have to start before light.

In the ancient and early medieval world it would appear that only in the cathedral rite of Constantinople could the current psalmody ever be equal in length at both Matins and Vespers, and that only around the spring and autumn equinoxes! Only in the sixteenth century will we begin to find movements to equalize the morning and evening psalmody.

Most of the forms of Matins that have been examined in this book do more than simply recite the psalms before dawn. The simply structured East Syrian rite intersperses suitable vigil prayers, as did the Constantinople cathedral office. The Roman and Benedictine traditions interspersed biblical, patristic and Hagiographic readings.[21] Many traditions used poetic chants to reinforce the vigil themes, such as the Sessional hymns of the Palestinian / Byzantine weekday *otoechos* with their insistence on penance. As far as we can tell from the evidence of the use of Tikrit, the West Syrian tradition, like the Armenian, interspersed canticles with the psalmody.

Although most Eastern rites of daily prayer do not have lengthy biblical readings at Matins, it should be remembered that, for example in the Sabaite *typikon* which is the basis of modern Byzantine practice, biblical or patristic reading was often inserted between Vespers and Matins when vigil was kept. There are also directions for readings between odes of the Canon. The difference between this practice and what one might call the later interpretation of the Western offices was that the Eastern custom continued to see current psalmody and reading as material to nurture one's prayer through lengthy nocturnal vigils. The more obviously ceremonial parts of the daily ritual at evening and morning were liturgical celebrations of the light of day as a symbol of the redemption wrought by Christ.

We have seen that there is a clear moment when the morning office takes over from the night, often marked by the penitential psalm 50. The modern Byzantine office has its cathedral vigil with resurrection gospel on Sunday inserted at the end of the nocturnal psalmody, then psalm 50 and the canon – we move from the night part of the office to the morning. Something similar was true of the old Roman office on weekdays, psalm 50 always began the morning psalms. The Benedictine office also began the morning part of the office, Lauds, with psalm 50 on weekdays. On Sundays, however, it concluded Matins with a series of canticles, a gospel reading by the Abbot and the hymn *Te Deum*. This structure is similar in some ways to the Byzantine cathedral vigil. The Armenian morning office inserts a vigil at a later point in the morning praises, perhaps similar to the inclusion on Sunday of the Constantinople resurrection gospel at the end of Matins. The East Syrian festal vigil has no Gospel and is simply inserted between the night and morning parts of the office, the latter starts straight away with the morning psalms. The Old Spanish office appears to be a daily cathedral vigil with morning praise and the same may also once have been true in Milan and elsewhere in the West.

We shall say little more about this vigil except that as a celebration of the resurrection in the night, preferably whilst still dark, it maintained the tradition that it was at such a time that Christ rose. Obviously Sundays as the weekly commemoration of the resurrection would attract such a festal insertion, but the very fact of prayer before the light on weekdays would show that some,

[21] Psalm prayers were known but do not seem to have become widespread, see Van Tongeren, op. cit., p. 206.

especially monastics, wished to watch and pray in the hope of resurrection every night.

The morning praises seem, from a very early stage, to have been organized around a canticle or canticles and the praise psalms, 149–50. We have suggested that the Ambrosian office demonstrates a very clear and primitive version of this: the Exodus 15 canticle and the *Benedicite* were followed by the praise psalms on Sunday, the weekday version having psalm 50 and the praise psalms alone. The Celtic rite of the Bangor Antiphonary is very similar in shape, and both are close to the early description from the account of the death of St Gall. The Old Spanish service had a variable canticle instead of only Exodus 15, but preceded by Psalm 50 as probably implied in the account of St Gall, and then the abbreviated *Benedicite*, a variable morning psalm and the praise psalms.

The mutual similarity of the Western non-Roman shapes is striking, and we may also propose a very considerable similarity between them and the Roman and Benedictine Lauds. In these latter offices the *Benedicite* was the Sunday canticle, followed by the praise psalms. On weekdays there was a canticle for each day of the week, Exodus 15 being appointed for Thursday. In both cases there was a series of morning psalms preceding the canticle, of which the first on weekdays was always psalm 50 (92 on Sundays). The first morning psalm in the Roman rite was proper to the day, the next two, psalms 62 and 66, were to be used daily. The Benedictine form varied this but retained the same fundamental shape, which we can see was more or less the same throughout late antique, early medieval Western Europe.

When we turn to the Eastern morning liturgies we find first that the proposed reconstruction of the Coptic *Psalmodia* of the night has Exodus 15 and *Benedicite* (separated by psalm 135), and the praise psalms after intervening poetic and intercessory material. The Ethiopian *sebhata nagh* has more canticles, but with psalms 62, 91 and 5 (all appropriate morning psalms) preceding those canticles, which normally include *Benedicite*, and finally bringing in the praise psalms, this office also reflects the same shape. The modern Byzantine office has replaced the canticle on most occasions with poetry, but the suggestion has been made that three Sunday canticles was once normal, and they could have been Exodus 15, *Benedicite* and the *Magnificat* and *Benedictus* together. These then being followed by the praises. The Constantinople cathedral rite marked the shift from the pre-dawn vigil to the morning office by a procession of entry from narthex to nave with incensation, at the canticle *Benedicite*. The ensuing core of the service at the Ambo was the praise psalms, this time preceded by psalm 50. In the contemporary rite a relic of this may be in the fact that the daily Matins incensation is begun during the eighth ode which replaces *Benedicite*.

The Armenian morning office also has *Benedicite* followed by New Testament canticles and psalm 50, and then the praises. The West Syrian rites seem to have a duplicated morning office, but the normal order of this ritual core includes psalm 50, canticle (often *Benedicite*) and praises. The East Syrian *sapra* alone has a series of morning psalms, including 99, 90 and 92 immediately followed by the praise psalms. The *Benedicite* comes a little later on Sundays, psalm 50 replacing it on weekdays. The Chaldean use of *Benedicite* here may supply for the lack of the Great Doxology that immediately follows the praises in both cathedral and contemporary Byzantine tradition, and also the Armenian. The Great Doxology, 'Glory to God in the Highest', is found in the form of the *turuhat* of the Coptic *psalmodia* which follows an incense rite introduced by the praises. The Ethiopians seem not to use this ancient Christian hymn, while the West Syrian rites use it before the morning praise.[22] Western use of this hymn was usually limited to the Eucharist except in Milan where the Great Doxology, or *Laus Angelorum Magna*, followed the praises and the *psalmus directus* until the sixteenth century.

The continuation of the cosmic praise after psalms 148–50 seems in the Roman and Benedictine traditions to have been represented by the Lucan canticle *Benedictus*, a most appropriate choice for the morning. There is a real ritual cohesion in this whole outburst of praise in the old Roman rite of Sundays, beginning with the *Benedicite*, continuing through psalms 148–50 and the *Benedictus*, to the doxological capitulum: 'Blessing, and glory and wisdom ... to our God for ever and ever'.[23] The morning hymn, versicle and the *Benedictus* then further extended this praise of God the creator of all things.[24] In Constantinople, *Benedictus* appears to have once come immediately before the Great Doxology, but in the contemporary office it finishes the canon and immediately precedes the praises.

We have so far said little of ceremonial enactment of the morning service of praise. As a progress towards the light, the morning offices needed no light ritual. However incense and processions often characterized this part of the rite. We have already noted the existence of incensation and procession in the Byzantine tradition, and the cathedral rite on Sundays had a further movement to the altar for the resurrection gospel reading. Milan, and perhaps old Spain, may have associated incensation with the praise psalms; it is possible that a Roman and Benedictine tradition of incensation at the *Benedictus* derived from this.[25] The raising of incense may also have been seen as an entirely suitable introduction to the intercessory and concluding prayers, which bring most of

---

[22] See e.g., Griffiths, op. cit., pp. 20–1.

[23] Revelation 7.12.

[24] One of the hymns used was *Aeterne rerum conditor*, see *Brev. Rom.*, op. cit., 24.

[25] It was rare to have a solemn Lauds except at Christmas, see Adrian Fortescue, *Ceremonies of the Roman Rite Described* (London: Burns & Oates, 1918), pp. 236–7.

these rites to a close. Their structure is much the same as at Vespers and we will say nothing more about them here.

The Psalms of Matins

Before concluding these reflections on Matins, a few words should be said about the psalms and canticles employed. The praise psalms, 148–50, seem to have most usually been used as an unbroken and unchanging group of three, except for the addition in some places, for example, Milan, of psalm 116, almost certainly as a primitive doxology. There are indications that the last *six* psalms of the Psalter may once have been used and not just these three. Other psalms appear to have been chosen for their morning themes, and certainly there are more to choose from than there are evening psalms. Any psalm with a theme of the reign of God is an appropriate psalm for a morning service envisaged as a celebration of the new day, itself an earnest of the eternal day; psalms 92, 96 and 99 are frequently found. Psalm 5's statement that in the morning we offer prayer is sufficient to justify its frequent occurrence, for example in the rites of Tikrit, Spain, Rome and the Benedictines.

As many scholars have pointed out, early offices seem to have either employed psalms appropriate to the time of day, or simply read the whole Psalter in course. Egeria is an early witness, especially in her description of Holy Week, to the selection of both psalms and other scriptural readings to suit particular celebrations. Seasonal psalmody is found in various places, and is often in the form of verses selected from psalms rather than whole psalms, for example the Byzantine *prokeimenon*, many of the Roman and Benedictine Responsories, the Old Spanish *antiphonae*, and the East Syrian *shuraye*. Most rites signified seasons and feasts by adding poetic material to the fixed psalmody or using scriptural verses as antiphons, which were originally responses, with a largely fixed psalmody. Festal psalms in the Roman rite were always drawn from those used normally at that time of day.

Canticles could, of course, be drawn from a wide variety of other Old Testament texts, as the Old Spanish tradition certainly proved. However, most rites confined themselves to a relatively small number of such texts; the nine odes of the Byzantine canon containing some of those most often used. We have already mentioned *Cantate* from Exodus 15 and *Benedicite* from Daniel 3, other frequently found examples were the canticle from the last chapter of Deuteronomy and the Isaiah 26.9 canticle, 'My soul yearns for thee in the night'. Much more has been said of these in the foregoing chapters, we may summarize by noting that they can mostly be connected with typical Paschal vigil themes. If the canticles were first connected with the Paschal vigil readings that lead into them (which is the case with *Cantate* and *Benedicite* in the contemporary Byzantine vigil, and with the former in the contemporary Roman vigil) then it seems that all were chosen for their appropriately resurrection themes. Only the Old Spanish tradition, until modern times, seems to have exploited texts suited to other festal or sanctoral themes.

Even the Old Spanish tradition made use of only three New Testament canticles, *Magnificat, Benedictus* and *Nunc Dimittis*, and that only sparingly and always in the morning. These canticles seem to have their original setting in the morning office, as fulfilment of the promises made in the Old Testament canticles. The numerous other New Testament texts, thought by modern New Testament scholars to be early Christian songs, and thus widely used in modern offices, have no discernible history as liturgical canticles.

Vespers and Matins, and Prayer at Other Times of the Day

We have largely concentrated on the offices at the beginning and end of the day, or the end and beginning of the night. What might be the place in the overall scheme for a series of Day Hours, or for prayer late at night? The East Syrian rite is famous for having no surviving Day Hours or Compline, except some possible relics in Lent. The West Syrian Day Hours have lost their psalmody, though *soutoro* (Compline) retains psalms 90 and 120, and been reduced to additions to the main Hours of Vespers and Matins. The Ethiopian cathedral office only has a form of Day Hours on certain solemn days, and the monastic provisions are too varied and too recent to supply us with a clear, historical pattern. The Armenian Day Hours seem to exhibit signs of have been abbreviated, except for Compline which has no less than nine psalms.

The ritual traditions that retained an accessible and analysable series of Day Hours until modern times, are the contemporary Byzantine Orthodox, the Roman (in which we shall include the Roman-derived Milanese Hours), the Coptic, the Benedictine and the Old Spanish. The Byzantine Hours are made up of three psalms chosen for the time of day, always the same except when Royal Hours are celebrated. For example, psalm 5 at the First; psalm 50 at the Third (verses 12 and 13 are associated with prayer for the Spirit); psalm 90 at the Sixth (protection at noon) and psalm 85 at the Ninth. Most of the remaining material, except the short Troparion and *kontakion* of the day, is the same each day and every day. The Roman Breviary until 1912 supplied a similar, largely unchanging diet, mostly of psalm 118. The Benedictine office had already re-distributed the Psalter and as a consequence had slightly more variety and shorter offices. The Coptic and Old Spanish monastic Hours are also always the same each day, though in the former case, that is true of the evening and morning offices as well, and all the offices of this tradition have at least 12 psalms. Where Inter-Hours exist (Byzantine

Orthodoxy and ancient Spanish monasteries), they are as fixed, and even simpler.

It is not only the fixed nature of the psalmody in most of the above cases that is of interest, but the fact that hymns and prayers also tended to be largely unchanging. In Lent the Byzantine offices acquire readings from the current Psalter, and Isaiah at the Sixth Hour, but the Troparia and *kontakia* are the same each day and do not vary as they do at other times. This fixity is ancient and means that these short services can be read in a simple monotone in about ten to fifteen minutes, just as the short Benedictine Hours could be sung to chant in about ten minutes. It is likely that these services were originally committed to memory and prayed without ceremony, alone or in small groups, wherever a monk's work happened to take him. Their brevity seems to have contributed to the later tendency to group them together, so that they did not disrupt a busy day.[26]

The lack of variable material, the fixity, and the absence of ceremonial, may all suggest that the Day Hours (and Compline) originally belonged to structures of private devotion rather than to the ancient fully ecclesial rites of evening and night-morning. As many scholars have pointed out, the Fathers and many early church documents speak of prayer at the Third, Sixth and Ninth Hours of the day and seemed to regard them as periods of private prayer, at least in the beginning. Since they developed liturgical forms they should be regarded as part of the historic Liturgy of the Hours together with Vespers and Matins. However, if these latter principal services emerged from the context of public daily worship in the fourth century, and were, as we have suggested, derivatives of the Paschal vigil that celebrated the Christian mystery of Redemption, then they must be our principal source for the theology of daily prayer.

Baptism and the Sacramentality of the Daily Offices

Having noted the importance that many New Testament texts give to the idea of staying awake to pray at night, we should also note some of the many texts that have baptismal themes. If baptism is entry into resurrection life (2 Cor. 5.17), a walking in newness of life (Romans 6.4), and a participation by all in the gift of the Spirit (1 Cor. 12.13), then that once-for-all baptism must

[26] The Trinity-St Sergius Podvorie in Moscow groups Ninth Hour, Vespers, Compline, Matins and First Hour in the evening, and Midnight, Third and Sixth Hours before Liturgy in the morning (July 1999). The Benedictines of Prinknash, near Gloucester, in the 1980s had Terce at 8.20, Sext combined with Mass before lunch, and None at 2 – in all cases leaving a lengthy morning and evening work period.

continue to have central importance to the Christian life. 'For as many of you as are baptized into Christ have put on Christ' (Gal. 3.27).

That continued importance of the themes of new birth on the one hand, and death and resurrection on the other,[27] seem to us to have powerfully influenced the Christian tradition of prayer. We read of the symbolism of night and day, death and resurrection in Clement of Rome, of the sun's daily baptism in Melito, and of the light and darkness symbolism in the accounts of baptism in the Acts of Judas Thomas. For Basil the Great, baptism is a passage from darkness to light, and for Ambrose morning light shines in the darkness. The evidence of baptismal and other vigils at night culminating in the morning celebration of the Eucharist, appear to be strong signs of the importance of daily common prayer, when it emerges fully, as a daily or at least weekly, renewal of baptism.

Among the Church Orders, *Apostolic Tradition* expects nocturnal baptism and seems to know of meal vigils, perhaps with the Hallel psalms supplying reminiscences of the Red Sea. The *Testamentum Domini* has strong echoes of baptismal imagery in is treatment of darkness and light. There is a strong connection of baptism and the dawn celebration of the resurrection. We arc not just recalling baptism but seeing it as having opened up to us the kingdom which is to come.

The strong connection of the Paschal vigil canticles with Morning Prayer, and the common connection of the vigils themselves with baptism show how the same themes of enlightenment and entry into new life undergird the daily life of the community of the baptized. The Old Byzantine office, with its progressive entry into the church building, may be seen as a daily catechumenal procession. The often remarked similarity between the cores of Vespers and Matins and the first part of the eucharistic Liturgy are not accidental and seem to be a part of a continuing sanctification of the whole of the Christian's life. The similar structures of the Chaldean offices are reinforced by that tradition's use of the same set of intercessory litanies at Vespers, baptism and the Eucharist. These rites are all intimately related to one another. In the West Syrian tradition the idea of incense as a cleansing rite may be a recollection of baptism and the *sedro* at the lighting of thc lamps quoted on p. 162, could be minimally altered to make it suitable for a baptismal rite.

The Roman and other Western daily offices are not so obviously similar to the liturgies of baptism. However the widespread use of processions to the baptistery, especially in ancient Rome and medieval and modern Milan, show a similar pastoral concern to continue and deepen the life of the baptized as they move ever closer towards the *eschaton*.

---

[27] The biblical themes identified by Maxwell Johnson in his *The Rites of Christian Initiation* (Collegeville: Liturgical Press, 1999), p. 31.

Concluding Reflection

The sixteenth-century theologian Dominicus Soto objected to the proposed reforms of the Franciscan Cardinal Quignones because the Divine Office was not just about learning psalms and studying scripture, but about praise of and prayer to God. From the late Middle Ages at least there have been two fundamental theologies of daily prayer or Divine Office. The first, more characteristic of earlier periods even in the monastic rites, emphasizes the contrasts of darkness and light, night and of day, to both enact and express the Christian mystery of Redemption, thus to inspire the faithful caught up in that enactment to praise and prayer as the sons and daughters of God.

The second theology is more characteristic of the Renaissance and the Reformation periods, powerfully influencing Roman Catholic attitudes to daily prayer as much as those of Anglicans and Protestants. This theology has dominated Western offices up until the present time. This may be seen as a theology of the divine office as inculcating of scripture so as to support a powerful and formative spirituality, most especially for the clergy. Having attempted to explicate the first theology in this book, the second will need more extended treatment, and we hope to return to that theme in a future volume.

Many efforts at reform are being undertaken today, but a really effective reform must return to first principles, and we have tried to enunciate what those principles might entail. To return to first principles will not mean that we try to reconstruct an ancient cathedral office, but that we try and learn from the ancient and medieval sources the principles and the theology that might allow for a fresh start. For those of us who use an un-revised, traditional rite, such as that of Byzantine Orthodoxy, the return to first principles must begin with recovery of the original meaning of these rites. Then they may be celebrated in a way that reflects their integral meaning, rather than formalistically going through inadequately abbreviated versions.

Daily prayer services need to be recognized as having been conceived and developed as public, ceremonial and participatory acts of the church gathered in prayer. Bishop Hilarion (Alfeyev) says: ‘Orthodox theology regards the sacraments as sacred actions through which an encounter takes place between us and God.’[28] Throughout this book we have argued that the ancient and medieval rites of daily prayer were just such ‘sacred actions’. To confine sacramentality too narrowly to the seven rites identified by the later scholastics, or even to the clearly biblical ordinances of the Reformation, is to risk marginalizing daily prayer. If, as we have suggested, the underlying rationale

[28] *The Mystery of Faith*, op. cit., p. 130.

that lies beneath the huge variety of rites of daily prayer is to recall us to and renew us in our baptismal entry into the coming kingdom of God, then they too are sacred actions in which there is indeed an encounter between us and God.

Bibliography

Abbreviations

ANCL	*Ante-Micene Christian Liturgy*
CSCO	Corpus scriptorum christianorum orientalium
DOP	*Dumbarton Oaks Papers*
EL	*Ephemerides Liturgicae*
PG	J.P. Migne (ed.), *Patrologiae Cursus Completus*, Series Graeca
PL	J.P. Migne (ed.), *Patrologiae Cursus Completus*, Series Latina
PO	F. Graffin (ed.), *Patrologia Orientalis* (Paris)
OCA	*Orientalia Christiana Analecta* (Pontifical Oriental Institute, Rome)
OCP	*Orientalia Christiana Periodica* (Pontifical Oriental Institute, Rome)
SL	*Studia Liturgica*

a Sources

Acoluthia Triplicis Festis ex Typico, Menaeis, aliisque Ritualibus Graecis impressis, interprete Nicolao Rayaeo societatis Jesu, in *PG* 29, CCCXXVI–CCCLXV.

Amalarii Episcopi Opera Liturgica Omnia, ed. J.M. Hanssens, SJ (*Studi e Testi* 138–40, Rome, Vatican Polyglot Press: 1948–50).

M. Andrieu (ed.), *Les ordines Romani du haut moyen âge* (*Spicilegium Sacrum Lovaniense* 11, 23, 24, 28, 29, Louvain: 1931–61).

Antifonario Mozarabe de la Catedral de Leon, ed. L. Brou and J. Vives (Madrid: 1959).

Antiphonarium Mozarabicum, ed. Benedictines of Silos (Leon: 1928).

The Antiphonary of Bangor, ed. F.E. Warren (London: Henry Bradshaw Society, 1893).

The Apostolic Tradition: A Commentary, ed. Paul E. Bradshaw, Maxwell E. Johnson and J. Edward Phillips (*Hermeneia*, Minneapolis: Fortress, 2002).

Aurelian of Arles, *PL* 68.

Basil the Great, *Hexaemeron*, trans. B. Jackson (Oxford: 1895).

Beroldus, sive Ecclesiae Ambrosianae Mediolanesis Kalendarium et Ordines, ed. Marco Magistretti (Milan: 1894; repr. Farnborough: Gregg, 1968).

M. Black (ed.), *A Christian Palestinian Syriac Horologion (Berlin MS Or.Oct. 1019)* (Texts and Studies I, Cambridge: Cambridge University Press, 1954).

Book of Common Prayer of the Syrian Church, ed. Bede Griffiths (Vagamon, Kerala: Kurisumula Ashram, n.d.).

Breviarium Ambrosianum [4 vols] (Milan: 1944).

Breviarium ad usum Insignis Ecclesiae Sarum [3 vols], ed. F. Proctor and C. Wordsworth (Cambridge: 1879–86).

Breviarium Gothicum, PL 86.

Breviarium Secundam Regulam Beati Isidori, ed. A. Ortiz (Toledo: 1502).

Breviarum Monasticum...pro omnibus sub regula S.Patris Benedicti militantibus [2 vols] (Bruges: Desclée de Brouwer, 1930).

Breviarum Romanum ex decreto SS. Concilii Tridentini restitutum... [4 vols] (Tournai: 1894).

Breviarium Romanum (Rome: Vatican Polyglot Press, 1961).

The Canons of Hippolytus, ed. R. Coquin in *PO* 31.2 (1966).

T.K. Carroll and T. Halton (eds), *Liturgical Practice in the Fathers* (Wilmington, DE: Michael Glazier, 1988).

Chasoslov (Zhovkva: 1910).

Clement, *PG* 8 & 9.

Coptic Liturgies and Hymns (Hayward, CA: Jonathan Center, 1995).

The Coptic Morning Service of the Lord's Day, trans. and ed. John, Marquess of Bute (London: 1882).

Didascalia Apostolorum et Constitutiones Apostolicae, ed. F.X. Funk (Paderborn: 1906).

The Didascalia Apostolorum in Syriac, 2 vols, ed. A. Vööbus (CSCO 175, 176, 179, 180, Louvain: 1979).

Didascalia Apostolorum: The Syriac Version Translated and Accompanied by the Verona Latin Fragments, ed. R. Hugh Connolly, OSB (Oxford: Clarendon Press, 1929).

Diurna Laus (Milan: Centro Ambrosiano, 1990).

William Durandus *Rationale Divinorum Officiorum* (Venice: 1599).

East Syrian Daily Offices, trans. and ed. A.J. Maclean (London: Rivington, Percival, 1894).

Égérie: Journal du Voyage, ed. Pierre Maraval (*Sources Chrétiennes* 296, Paris: Cerf, 1952).

L'Eucologio Barbarini gr. 336 (eds S. Parenti and E. Velkovska) (Rome: OLV-Edizioni Liturgiche, 1995).

Ευχολογιον *sive Rituale Graecorum*, ed. J. Goar, OP (Paris: 1647; Venice: 1730; repr. Graz: 1960).

Euchologe de la Grande Église (MS Coislin 213), ed. J. Duncan (Rome: Pontifical Oriental Institute, 1978).

The Festal Menaion, ed. Mother Mary and Archimandrite Kallistos Ware (London: Faber & Faber, 1969).

Gelasian Sacramentary, ed. H.A. Wilson (Oxford: Clarendon Press, 1894).

D. Guillaume (ed.), *Horologe des Veilleurs: Les 24 Heures des Acémètes* (Rome: Diaconie Apostolique, 1990).

Gregory Nazianzen, *Oration on the Holy Lights*, trans. B. Swallow (Oxford: 1894).

Hermas, *The Shepherd* (Ante-Nicene Christian Library I, Edinburgh: 1867).

Horologion (Rome: Vatican Polyglot Press, 1937).

IEPATIKON (Αθηναι: Αποστολικη Διακονια, 4th edn, 1992).

IEPATIKON [3 vols] (Αγιον Οροζ: Ιεραζ Μονηζ Σιμονοζ πειραζ, 1992).

Ignatius of Antioch, *PG* 5.

Jerome, *Letters*, trans. W.H. Fremantle (Oxford: 1893).

Jerome, *PL* 22.

John Chrysostom, *PG* 62.

Las Horas Vigiliares del Oficio Monacal Hispanico, ed. J. Pinell, OSB (*Liturgica* 3 – *Scripta et Documenta* 17, Monserrat: 1966), pp. 197–340.

Le Lectionnaire de Jérusalem en Arménerie, ed. C. Renoux, in *PO* 35 Fase 3 (Turnhout Bofors, 1989).

The Lenten Triodion, ed. Mother Mary and Archimandrite Kallistos Ware (London: Faber & Faber, 1978).

Liber Commicus seu Lectionarium Missae, ed. G. Morin, OSB (*Anecdota Maredsolana* I, Maredsous: 1893).

Liber Misticus de Cuaresma, ed. J. Janini (Toledo: Instituto de Estudios Visigotico-Mozarabes, 1979).

Liber Misticus de Cuaresma y Pascua, ed. J. Janini (Toledo: Instituto de Estudios Visigotico-Mozarabes, 1980).

Liber Mozarabicus Sacramentorum, ed. M. Ferotin (*Monumenta Ecclesiastica Liturgica*, Paris: 1912).

Liber Orationum Psalmographus ed. J. Pinell, OSB (*Monumenta Hispaniae Sacra* IX, Barcelona / Madrid: 1972).

Le Liber Ordinum en usage dans l'Eglise Wisigothique et Mozarabe de Espagne du V a X siecle, ed. M. Ferotin (*Monumenta Ecclesiastica Liturgica*, Paris: 1904).

Liber Sacramentorum Gellonensis, ed. A. Dumas and J. Deshusses (Corpus Christianorum: series Latina 159, 159a, Turnhout: Brepols, 1981).

Liber Vesperalis juxta ritum Sanctae Ecclesiae Mediolanensis (Rome: Desclée de Brouwer, 1939).

Liturgies Eastern and Western, ed. F.E. Brightman (Oxford: Clarendon Press, 1896; repr. 1967).

The Liturgikon (Englewood Cliffs, NJ: Antiochian Orthodox Christian Archdiocese, 1981).

A. Longo (ed.), 'Il testo integrale della "Narrazione degli abati Giovanni e Sofronio" attraverso le "Hermineiai" di Nicone', *Rivista degli Studi Bizantini e Neoellenici*, ns **23** (1965–6), 233–67.

Manuale Ambrosianum [2 vols] ed. Marco Magistretti (Milan: 1905).

J. Mateos, SJ (ed.), 'Un Horologion inédit de Saint-Sabas', *Studi e Testi*, **233** (Rome: Vatican Polyglot Press, 1964).
Melito of Sardis, *On Pascha*, ed. S.G. Hall (Oxford: Oxford University Press, 1979).
Μηναιογ Ανγονστον (Athens: Φωζ, 1970).
The Mishnah, trans. Herbert Danby (Oxford: Oxford University Press, 1933, repr. 1991).
Molitvoslov (Rome: 1950).
The Mozarabic Psalter ed. J.P. Gilson (London: Henry Bradshaw Society, 1905).
The Office of Vespers for Sundays and Feasts trans. Archimandrite Ephrem (Lash), (Manchester: St Andrew's Press, 2000).
Oracional Visigotico ed. J. Vives and G. Claveras (*Monumenta Hispaniae Sacra* I, Barcelona: 1946).
New Testament Apocrypha, eds W. Schneemelcher and E. Hennecke (London: Lutterworth, 1967).
'The New Testament Foundations for Common Prayer', *SL* 10, (1974), 88–105.
Origen, *PG* 11, 12.
Παρακλητηκη (Athens: Φωζ, 1991).
Paulinus of Nola, *PL* 53.
Prayer with the Harp of the Spirit [A version of the West Syrian office, 4 vols.] ed. Francis Acharya (Vagamon, Kerala: Kurisumula Ashram, 1983–6).
A Prayerbook (Cambridge and New York: New Skete, 1976).
Pseudo-Dionysius, *The Complete Works*, trans. and ed. C. Luibheid and P. Rorem (The Classics of Western Spirituality, New York / Mahwah: Paulist Press; 1987).
Rituale Armenorum, ed. F.C. Conybeare and A.J. Maclean (Oxford: 1905).
The Rule of the Master, ed. A. de Vogüé, trans. Luke Eberle (Kalamazoo, MI: Cistercian Publications, 1977).
RB 1980: The Rule of St Benedict in Latin and English with Notes, ed. T. Fry et al. (Collegeville, MN: Liturgical Press, 1981).
Sacramentarium Veronense, ed. L.C. Mohlberg et al. (RED Series maior I, Rome: 1956).
Severus of Antioch, *PO* 4, 8, 12, 16, 20, 22, 23, 25, 26, 29, 35–8 (Paris: 1908–).
Singer, S. (ed.), *The Authorised Daily Prayer Book* (London: Eyre & Spottiswoode, 1962).
Symeon of Thessaloniki, *PG* 155.
M. Tarchnischvili (ed.), *Le Grand Lectionnaire de l'Église de Jerusalem (V^e–VIIIe siècles)* (CSCO 188, Louvain: 1959–60).
Tertullian, *PL* 1.
The Testamentum Domini: A Text for Student.... ed. Grant Sperry-White (Alcuin / GROW 19, Bramcote: 1991).

The Testament of the Lord, ed. J. Cooper and A.J. Maclean (Edinburgh: T. & T. Clark, 1902).
Tipikon (repr. Moscow: Patriarchal Publishing House, 1997)
La Tradition Apostolique de Saint Hippolyte, ed. B. Botte, OSB (Münster: Aschendorff, 1963).
ΤΡΙΩΔΙΟΝ (Athens: Εκδοσειζ Φωζ, 1992).
Le Typicon de la Grande Église, [2 vols] ed. J. Mateos, SJ (OCA 166, Rome: 1966).
Le Typicon du Monastère de Saint-Sauveur à Messine, ed. M. Arranz, SJ (*OCA* 185, Rome: 1969).
The Typicon of the Patriarch Alexei the Studite: Novgorod-St Sophia 1136, ed. D.M. Petras (Cleveland, OH: 1991).
Bernard Velat (ed.), *Études sur le Me'eraf* (*PO* 33, Paris: 1966).
Vespers and Matins (Oxford: St Stephen's Press, 2001)

b Secondary Literature

Arranz, Miguel, SJ, 'Les prières sacerdotales des vêpres byzantines', *OCP*, **37** (1971), 85–124.
——, 'Les prières prebytérales des matines byzantines', *OCP*, **37** (1971), 406–36; *OCP*, **38** (1972), 64–115.
——, 'Les prières presbytérales des Petites Heures dans l'ancien Euchologe byzantin', *OCP*, **39** (1973), 29–82.
——, 'Les prières presbytérales de la "Pannychis" de l'ancien Euchologe byzantin et la "Panikhida" des défunts', *OCP*, **40** (1974), 314–43; *OCP*, **41** (1975), 119–39.
——, 'Les étapes de la liturgie Byzantine', *Liturgie de l'église particulière et liturgie de l'église universelle* [= Conférences Saint Serge 22] (Rome: Edizioni Liturgiche, 1976), pp. 43–72.
——, 'Les prières prebytérales de la Tritoekti de l'ancien Euchologe byzantin', *OCP*, **43** (1977), 7–93, 335–54.
——, 'L'office de l'Asmatikos Hesperinos ("vêpres chantées") de l'ancien Euchologe byzantin', *OCP*, **44** (1978), 107–30, 391–419.
——, *Kak molilis' Bogu drevnie bizantitsy* (Leningrad: Theological Academy, 1979).
——, 'La liturgie des heures selon l'ancien Euchologe byzantin', *Eulogia: Miscellanea liturgica in onore de P. Burkhard Neunheuser* (*Studia Anselmiana* 68, *Analecta Liturgica* 1, Rome: Editrice Anselmiana, 1979), pp. 1–19.
——, 'N.D. Uspensky: The Office of the All-Night Vigil in the Greek Church and in the Russian Church', *St Vladimir's Seminary Quarterly*, **24** (1980), 83–113, 169–95.

——, 'La Liturgie des Présanctifiés de l'ancien Euchologe byzantin', *OCP*, **47** (1981), 332–88.
——, 'L'office de l'Asmatikos Orthros ("matines chantées") de l'ancien Euchologe byzantin', *OCP*, **47** (1981), 122–57.
——, 'Les prières de la Gonyklisia ou Génuflexion', *OCP*, **48** (1982), 92–123.
Badger, G.P., *The Nestorians and their Rituals* (London: 1862).
Baldovin, J., SJ, *The Urban Character of Christian Worship* (*OCA* 228, Rome: 1987).
Batiffol, Pierre, *Histoire du Bréviaire* (Paris: 1893; Eng. trans. A. Baylay, London: 1898).
Baudot, Jules, OSB, *The Roman Breviary: its Sources and History* (Eng. trans., London: 1909).
Bäumer, Suitbert, OSB, *Histoire du Bréviaire* [2 vols] (Paris: 1905).
Baumstark, Anton, *Festbrevier und Kirchenjahr der syrischen Jakobiten* (Paderborn: Schöningh, 1910).
——, *Liturgie Comparée* (Chevetogne Abbey: Éditions de Chevetogne, 1940) translated as *Comparative Liturgy* (London: Mowbrays, 1958).
——, *Nocturna Laus* (Münster: Aschendorff, 1967).
Becker, Hansjakob, 'Zur Struktur der "Vespertina Synaxis" in der Regula Benedicti', *Archiv für Liturgiewissenschaft*, **29** (1987), 177–88.
Bertonière, Gabriel, *The Historical Development of the Easter Vigil and Related Services in the Greek Church* (*OCA* 193, Rome, 1972).
Bishop, W.C. (ed. C.L. Feltoe), *The Mozarabic and Ambrosian Rites* (London: Alcuin / Mowbrays, 1924).
Borella, P., 'Il Breviario Ambrosiano', in Mario Righetti (ed.), *Storia Liturgica* (Milan: Ancora, 1946), pp. 603–41.
——, *Il Rito Ambrosiano* (Brescia: Macelliana, 1964).
Borgia, Nilo (Ieromonaco), ΩΡΟΛΟΓΙΟΝ: *'Diurno' delle Chiese di Rito Bizantino* (*Orientalia Christiana* xvi–2, Rome: Pontifical Oriental Institute, 1929).
Bradshaw, Paul F., 'Other Acts of Worship', in G. Cuming (ed.), *Essays on Hippolytus* (Grove Liturgical Study 15, Bramcote: 1978), pp. 61–3.
——, *Daily Prayer in the Early Church* (London: Alcuin / SPCK, 1981).
——, *The Canons of Hippolytus* (Alcuin / GROW 2, Bramcote: 1987).
——, 'Cathedral vs. Monastery: The Only Alternative for the Liturgy of the Hours?', in J. Neil Alexander (ed.), *Time and Community* (Washington, DC: Pastoral Press, 1990), pp. 123–36.
——, 'Ancient Church Orders: A Continuing Enigma', in G. Austen (ed.), *The Fountain of Life* (Washington, DC: Pastoral Press, 1991), pp. 3–22.
——, *The Search for the Origins of Christian Worship* (London: SPCK, 2002).
Bradshaw, Paul F. and Hoffman, L.A. (eds), *The Making of Jewish and Christian Worship* (Notre Dame: University of Notre Dame Press, 1991).

Brock, S. and Vasey, M. (eds), *The Liturgical Portions of the Didascalia Apostolorum* (Grove Liturgical Study 29, Bramcote: 1982).

Brogi, M., *La Santa Salmodia Annuale della Chiesa Copta* (Cairo: Edizioni del Centro Francescano di Studi Orientali Cristiani, 1962).

Brou, L., 'Le Psautier Wisigothique et les Editions Critiques des Psautiers Latins', *Hispania Sacra*, **8** (1954), 37–60.

Brovelli, F. and Maggiani, S. (eds) *Liturgia delle Ore: tempo e rito* (*BEL subsidia* 75, Rome: Edizioni Liturgiche, 1994).

Burmester, O.H.E., 'The Canonical Hours of the Coptic Church', *OCP*, **2** (1936), 78–100.

——, 'The Turuhat of the Coptic Year', *OCP*, **3** (1937), 78–109, 505– 49.

——, *The Egyptian or Coptic Church: A Detailed Description of her Liturgical Services*... (Cairo: Société d'Archéologie Copte, 1967).

Callewaert, C., 'de Laudibus Matutinis', *Sacris Erudiri* (Steenbrugge: Abbatia S. Petri 1940), pp. 53–89.

——, 'Vesperae antiquae in officio praesertim Romano', ibid., pp. 91–117.

——, 'de Capitulis in officium Romanum', ibid., pp. 131–3.

——, 'de Matutino in antiquo officio Romano', ibid., pp. 145–8.

Campbell, S., FSC, *From Breviary to Liturgy of the Hours* (Collegeville, MN: Liturgical Press, 1995).

Cassuto, U., *Commentary on Genesis* (Jerusalem: Hebrew University; Eng. trans. 1961).

Cattaneo, E., *Il Breviario Ambrosiano* (Milan: 1943).

Coakley, J.F., *The Church of the East and the Church of England* (Oxford: Clarendon Press, 1992).

Cody, Aelred, OSB, 'L'office divin chez les Syrien Jacobites... ', *Proche Orient Chrétien*, **19** (1969), 293–319.

——, 'The Early History of the Octoechos in Syria', in N.G. Garsoïan, T.F. Matthews and R.W. Thomson (eds), *East of Byzantium: Syria and Armenia in the Formative Period* (Washington, DC: Dumbarton Oaks, 1982), pp. 89–113.

Cuming, Geoffrey, *Hippolytus: A Text for Students* (Grove Liturgical Study 8, Bramcote: 1976).

——, 'The Liturgy of Antioch at the time of Severus (513–518)', in J. Neil Alexander (ed.), *Time and Community* (Washington, DC: Pastoral Press, 1990), pp. 83–103.

Curran, Michael, *The Antiphonary of Bangor* (Dublin: Irish Academic Press, 1984).

Cuva, Armando, 'I Vespri Pasquali Battesimali della Liturgia Romana', *EL*, **35** (1973), 101–18.

Dagron, G., 'Les moines et la ville: la monachisme à Constantinople jusqu'au concile de Chalcedoine (451)', *Travaux et Mémoires*, **4** (1970), 229–76.

Daoud, M., appendix to *The Liturgy of the Ethiopian Church* (Cairo: Egyptian Book Press, 1959).

DeClerck, P., *La prière universelle dans les liturgies latines anciennes* (Münster: Aschendorff, 1977).

De Vogüé, A., OSB, *La règle de St Benoit* (*Sources Chrétiennes* 184–6, Paris: 1979).

Dölger, F., 'Lumen Christi. Der christliche Abendhymnus "Φωζιλαρον,"', *Antike und Christentum*, **5** (1936), 1–43.

Donaldson, James, *The Apostolic Constitutions* (Edinburgh: T. & T. Clark, 1870).

Duchesne, L., *Christian Worship: Its Origin and Evolution* (London: SPCK, 1927).

Dyer, Joseph, 'Monastic Psalmody of the Middle Ages', *Révue Bénédictine*, **99** (1989), 41–74.

——, 'The Singing of Psalms in the Early-Medieval Office', *Speculum*, **64** (1989), 535–78.

Edwards, K., *The English Secular Cathedrals in the Middle Ages* (Manchester: Manchester University Press, 1967).

Eliade, Mircea, *Rites and Symbols of Initiation* (New York: Harper & Row, 1958).

Fassler, Margot E. and Balytzer, Rebecca A. (eds), *The Divine Office in the Latin Middle Ages* (New York: Oxford University Press, 2000).

Fortescue, A., *The Lesser Eastern Churches* (London: Catholic Truth Society, 1913).

——, *Ceremonies of the Roman Rite Described* (London: Burns & Oates, 1918).

Gamber, K., *Codices Liturgici Latini Antiquiores* [2 vols] (*Spicilegii Friburgensis Subsidia I*, Fribourg: 1968); and *Supplementum* of 1988.

——, *Sacrificium Vespertinum* (*Studia Patristica et Liturgica* 12, Regensburg: Pustet, 1983).

Gemayel, P.E., 'La structure des Vêpres Maronites', *Orient Syrien*, **9** (1964), 105–34.

Goulder, L., *Church Life in Medieval England: the Monasteries* (London: Guild of Our Lady of Ransom, 1967).

G. Guiver, CR, *Company of Voices* (London: SPCK, 1988).

Hannick, C., 'Étude sur L'Ακολουθια', *Jahrbuch der Österreichischen Byzantinistik* 19 (1970), pp. 243–60.

Hanssens, J.M., SJ, *Nature et genèse de l'Office des Matines* (*Analecta Gregoriana* 57, Rome: 1952).

Hermiz Jammo, Sarhad, 'L'office du soir Chaldéen au temps de Gabriel Qatraya', *L'Orient Syrien*, **12** (1967), 187–210.

——, *La Structure de la Messe Chaldéenne* (*OCA* 207, Rome: 1979).

Hill, D., *The Gospel of Matthew* (New Century Bible Commentary, Grand Rapids: Eerdmans / London: Marshall, Morgan & Scott, 1972).

Hill, H. (ed.), *Light from the East* (Toronto: Anglican Book Centre, 1988).

Hoffman, Lawrence A., *The Canonization of the Synagogue Service* (Notre Dame: University of Notre Dame Press, 1979).

Janeras, S., *Le Vendredi-Saint dans la tradition liturgique Byzantine* (*Studia Anselmiana* 99, Rome: 1988).

Janeras, V., 'La partie vespérale de la liturgie byzantine des Présanctifiés', *OCP*, **30** (1964), 193–222.

Janini, J., 'Cuaresma Visigoda y carnes tollendas', in *Anthologica Annua 9* (Rome: Santa Maria di Monserrato, 1961), pp. 11–83.

——, 'Las Collectas Psalmicas del *Liber Ordinum*', *Hispania Sacra*, **28** (1975), 103–24.

——, 'El Oficio de Pentecostes del Oracional Visigotico y el Breviario de Cisneros', *Analecta Sacra Tarraconensia*, **57–8** (1984–5), 101–10.

Jardine Grisbrooke, W., 'A Contemporary Liturgical Problem: The Divine Office and Public Worship', *SL* (1970–3), **8**, 129–168; **9**, 3–18, 81–106.

——, 'The Laudate Psalms: A Footnote', *SL*, **20** (1990), 162–84.

——, *The Liturgical Portions of the Apostolic Constitutions: A Text for Students* (Alcuin / GROW 13–14, Bramcote: 1990).

Jeffery, Peter, 'The Sunday Office of Seventh-Century Jerusalem in the Georgian Chantbook (Iadgari): A Preliminary Report', *SL*, **21** (1991), 52–71.

Joncas, J.M., 'Daily Prayer in the Apostolic Constitutions', *EL*, **107** (1993), 113–35.

Jungmann, J.A., *Public Worship* (London: Challoner, 1957).

——, 'The Origin of Matins', in *Pastoral Liturgy* (London: Challoner, 1962), pp. 105–22.

——, 'The Pre-Monastic Morning Hour in the Gallo-Spanish Region in the 6th Century', ibid., pp. 122–57.

——, 'Psalmody as the Introduction to the Hours', ibid., pp. 157–62.

——, 'The Kyrie eleison of the Preces', ibid., pp. 180–91.

——, 'Why was Cardinal Quinonez' Reformed Breviary a Failure?', ibid., pp. 200–214.

Kidane, Habtemichael, *L'Ufficio Divino della Chiesa Etiopica* (*OCA* 257, Rome: 1998).

King, Archdale A., *The Rites of Eastern Christendom II* (London: Burns & Oates, 1947).

——, *Liturgies of the Primatial Sees* (London: Longmans, 1957).

——, *Liturgies of the Religious Orders* (London: Longmans, 1955).

Kniazeff, A., 'La lecture de l'Ancien et du Nouveau Testament dans le Rite Byzantin', in Msgr Cassien and B. Botte (eds), *La prière des heures* (*Lex Orandi* 35, Paris: 1963), pp. 201–51.

Korolevsky, C., 'Chez les Starovères de Bucovine', *Stoudion*, **IV** (1927), 123–37.

Larson-Miller, L., 'A Return to the Liturgical Architecture of Northern Syria', *SL*, **24** (1994), 71–83.

(Lash), Archimandrite Ephrem, review of Taft's *Liturgy of the Hour...*, *Sobornost*, **11** (1989), 102–105.

Lauterbach, J.Z., *Rabbinic Essays* (Cincinnati: Hebrew Union College Press, 1951).

Lazor, Paul (ed.), *Great and Holy Saturday: Vespers and Divine Liturgy of St Basil the Great* (Latham, NY: Department of Religious Education, Orthodox Church of America, 1986).

Lorenzana, F.A. and Fabian y Fuero, F., *Missa Gotica seu Mozarabica et officium itidem, Gothicum, diligenter ac dilucide explanata* (Puebla de los Angeles: 1770).

Louth, A., *Denys the Areopagite* (London: Chapman, 1989).

MacGregor, A.J., *Fire and Light in the Western Tradition* (Collegeville, MN: Alcuin Club / Liturgical Press, 1992).

McKay, H., *Sabbath and Synagogue* (Leiden: E.J. Brill, 1994).

McKinnon, W., 'On the Question of Psalmody in the Ancient Synagogue', *Early Music History*, **VI** (Cambridge: 1986), 159–91.

——, *Music in Early Christian Literature* (Cambridge: Cambridge University Press, 1987).

Magistretti, M., *La Liturgia della Chiesa Milanese Secolo* IV (Milan: 1899).

Marcora, C., *La Vigilia nella Liturgia* (*Archivio Ambrosiano* VI, Milan: 1954).

Martin Patino, J.M., 'El Breviarium Mozarabe de Ortiz, su valor documental para la Historia del Oficio Catedralicio Hispanico' *Miscellanea 40 Comillas* (1963), 207–97.

Martin Pintado, V., 'Las Lecturas Cuaresmales de Antiguo Testamento en la Antigua Liturgia Hispanica. Estudio de Liturgia Comparada', *Salmanticensis XXII.2* (1975), pp. 217–69.

Mateos, Juan, SJ, *Lelya-Sapra: Les Offices Chaldéens de la Nuit et du Matin* (*OCA* 156, Rome: 1959, repr. 1972).

——, 'Un office de minuit chez les Chaldéens?' *OCP*, **25** (1959), 101–13.

——, 'Les matines chaldéennes, maronites et syriennes', *OCP*, **26** (1960), 51–73.

——, 'Les différentes espèces de vigiles dans le rite Chaldéen', *OCP*, **27** (1961), 46–63.

——, 'La vigile cathédrale chez Égérie', *OCP*, **27** (1961), 281–312.

——, 'Quelques problèmes de l'orthros byzantin', *Proche Orient Chrétien*, **11** (1961), 17–35, 201–20.

——, 'Office de minuit et office du matin chez S. Athanase', *OCP*, **28** (1962), 173–80.

——, '*Sedres* et prières connexes dans quelques anciennes collections', *OCP*, **28** (1962), 239–87.

——, 'L'office divin chez les Chaldéens', in Msgr Cassian and B. Botte (eds), *La prière des heures* (*Lex Orandi* 35, Paris: 1963), pp. 253–81.
——, 'L'office monastique à la fin de IVe siècle: Antioche, Palestine, Cappadoce', *Oriens Christianus*, **47** (1963), 53–88.
——, 'La psalmodie variable dans l'office Byzantin', *Acta Philosophica et Theologica II* (Rome: Societas Academica Dacroromana, 1964), pp. 327–39.
——, 'Une collection syrienne de "prières entre les marmyata"', *OCP*, **31** (1965), 53–75, 305–35.
——, 'The Origins of the Divine Office', *Worship*, **41** (1967), 477–85.
——, 'Trois recueils anciens de Prooemia syriens', *OCP*, **33** (1967), 457–82.
——, 'The Morning and Evening Office', *Worship*, **42** (1968), 31–47.
——, 'Quelques anciens documents sur l'office du soir', *OCP*, **35** (1969), 347–74.
——, 'La synaxe monastique des vêpres byzantines', *OCP*, **36** (1970), 248–72.
——, *La Célébration de la Parole dans la Liturgie Byzantine* (*OCA* 191, Rome: 1971).
Mearns, James, *The Canticles of the Christian Church Eastern and Western in Early and Medieval Times* (Cambridge: Cambridge University Press, 1914).
Navoni, M., 'Le Antifone "ad Crucem" del'Ufficiatura Ambrosiana del Tempo Pasquale', *EL*, **99** (1985), 239–71.
O'Leary, De Lacey, *The Daily Office and Theotokia of the Coptic Church* (London: 1911).
——, *The Difnar (Antiphonarium) of the Coptic Church* (3 vols, London: Luzac, 1926, 1928, 1930).
Pascher, J., 'De Psalmodia Vesperarum', *EL*, **79** (1965), 317–26.
Perez de Urbel, J., 'Origen de los Himnos Mozarabes', *Bulletin Hispanique*, **28** (Bordeaux: 1926), 5–21, 113–39, 209–45, 305–20.
Phillips, L. Edward, 'Daily Prayer in the Apostolic Tradition of Hippolytus', *Journal of Theological Studies*, ns **40** (1989), 389–400.
Pinell, J., OSB, 'Las *Missae*, Grupos de Cantos y Oraciones en el Oficio de la Antigua Liturgia Hispana', *Archivos Leoneses*, **8** (1954), 145–85.
——, 'El Liber Horarum y el Misticus entre los Libros de la Antigua Liturgia Hispana', *Hispania Sacra*, **8** (1955), 85–107.
——, 'El *Matutinarium* en la Liturgia Hispana', *Hispania Sacra*, **9** (1956), 61–85.
——, 'El Oficio Hispano-Visigotico', *Hispania Sacra*, **10** (1957), 385–427.
——, 'Vestigis del Lucernari a Occident', *Liturgica I – Scripta et Documenta*, **7** (1957), 91–149.
——, *De Liturgiis Occidentalibus, cum speciali tractatione de Liturgia Hispanica* (pro manuscripto, Rome: Istituto di Sant'Anselmo, 1967).
——, 'Los Canticos del Oficio en el Antiguo Rito Hispanico', *Hispania Sacra*, **27** (1974), 5–54.

——, 'Las Oraciones "de Cantico" del Antiguo Rito Hispanico', *Didaskalia VIII* (Lisbon: 1978), pp. 197–329.

——, *La Liturgia delle Ore* (Rome: Pontificio Istituto Liturgico, 3rd edn, 1983).

Porter, A.W.S., 'Early Spanish Monasticism', *Laudate* (Nashdom Abbey), **X 37–39** (1932), 2–15, 66–79, 156–67; **XI 44** (1933), 199–207; **XII 45** (1934), 31–52.

——, 'Studies in the Mozarabic Office', *Journal of Theological Studies*, ns **35** (1934), 266–86.

——, 'Cantica Mozarabici Offici', *EL*, **49** (1935), 126–45.

Power, D.N., OMI, *Unsearchable Riches: The Symbolic Nature of Liturgy* (New York: Pueblo, 1984).

——, *Sacrament: The Language of God's Giving* (New York: Crossroad, 1999).

Pudichery, S., 'Composition interne de l'office Syrien', *Orient Syrien*, **2** (1957), 77–92; *Orient Syrien*, **3** (1958), 25–62.

——, 'Les Heures Canoniales Syriennes et leur Composition', *Orient Syrien*, **3** (1958), 401–28.

——, *Ramsha: An Analysis and Interpretation of the Chaldean Vespers* (Dhamaram College Studies 9, Bangalore: 1972).

Raes, A., SJ, *Introductio in Liturgiam Orientalem* (Rome: Pontifical Oriental Institute, 1947).

——, 'Les complies dans les rites orientaux', *OCP*, **17** (1951), 133–45.

——, 'Note sur les anciens matines, byzantines et arméniennes', *OCP*, **19** (1953), 205–10.

Renoux, C., 'A propos de G. Winkler "The Armenian Night Office II", *Révue des études Arméniennes* ns. t.XVII (1983), p. 471–551', *Révue des études Arméniennes*, **18** (1984), 593–8.

——, 'Les commentaires liturgiques arméniens', in A.M. Triacca and A. Pistoia (eds), *Mystagogie: pensée liturgique d'aujourd'hui et liturgie ancienne* (Rome: Edizioni Liturgiche, 1993) pp. 277–308.

Roberson, R., *The Eastern Christian Churches* (Rome: Pontifical Oriental Institute, 1990).

Salaville, S., 'La Prière de Toutes Heures dans la Littérature Éthiopienne', in *Studia Orientalia Liturgico-Theologico* (Rome: Ephemerides Liturgicae, 1940), pp.17–185.

Salmon, P., OSB, *L'Office Divin: Histoire de la Formation du Bréviaire* (Paris: Cerf, 1959).

Sanders, J.N. and Mastin, B.A., *The Gospel according to John* (London: A. & C. Black, 1968).

Schmemann, Alexander, *Introduction to Liturgical Theology* (London: Faith Press, 1966).

Schneider, H., 'Die Biblischen Oden im Christlichen Altertum', *Biblica*, **30** (1949), 28–65, 239–72, 433–52, 479–500.

Senn, Frank, *Christian Liturgy, Catholic and Evangelical* (Minneapolis: Fortress, 1997).

Skaballonovich, M., *Tolkovy Tipikon* (repr. Moscow: Palomnik, 1995).

Sperber, D., *Rethinking Symbolism* (Cambridge: Cambridge University Press, 1974).

Storey, William G., 'Public Worship: The Liturgy of the Hours', *Worship*, **49** (1975), 2–12.

——, 'The Liturgy of the Hours: Cathedral versus Monastery', *Worship*, **50** (1976), 50–70.

Stroes, H.R., 'Does the Day begin in the Evening or the Morning?', *Vetus Testamentum*, **16** (1966), 460–75.

Strunk, Oliver, 'The Byzantine Office at Hagia Sophia', *DOP*, **9/10** (1955–6), 177–202; repr. in Oliver Strunk, *Essays on Music in the Byzantine World* (New York: Norton, 1977).

——, 'The Antiphons of the Oktoechos', *Journal of the American Musicological Society*, **13** (1960), 50–67.

Stuhlman, Byron D., 'The Morning Offices of the Byzantine Rite: Mateos Revisited', *SL*, **19** (1989), 162–78.

Tabet, J., *L'Office Commun Maronite* (Kaslik, Lebanon: Bibliothèque de l'Université Saint-Esprit, 1972).

Taft, R.F., SJ, *The Great Entrance* (*OCA* 200, Rome: 1975).

——, *Beyond East and West: Problems in Liturgical Understanding* (Washington, DC: Pastoral Press, 1984).

——, *The Liturgy of the Hours in East and West* (Collegeville, MN: Liturgical Press, 1986).

——, *The Byzantine Rite: A Short History* (American Essays in Liturgy, Collegeville, MN: Liturgical Press, 1992).

——, 'On the Use of the Bema in the East Syrian Liturgy', *Eastern Churches Review*, **3** (1970), 30–39.

——, 'The Byzantine Office in *The Prayerbook* of New Skete: Evaluation of a Proposed Reform' , *OCP*, **48** (1982), 336–70.

——, 'Praise in the Desert: The Coptic Monastic Office Yesterday and Today', *Worship*, **56** (1982), 513–36.

——, 'Mount Athos: A Late Chapter in the History of the Byzantine Rite', *DOP*, **42** (1988), pp. 179–94.

Talley, T., 'Word and Sacrament in the Primitive Eucharist' in E. Carr, S. Parenti, A.-A. Thielmayer and E. Velkovska (eds), ΕΥΛΟΓΗΜΑ: *Studies in Honour of Robert Taft SJ* (*Studia Anselmiana* 110, *Analecta Liturgica* 17, Rome: 1993), pp. 497–510.

Touliatos-Banker, Diane, 'The 'Chanted' Vespers Service', *κληρονομια*, **8** (Thessaloniki: Moni Vlatadon, 1976), 107–18.

——, 'The Byzantine Orthros', *Byzantina*, **9** (1977), 323–83.

——, *The Byzantine Amomos Chant of the 14th and 15th Centuries* (*Analecta Vlatadon* 46, Thessaloniki: 1984).

Tripolitis, Antonia, 'Φωζ ιλαρον – Ancient Hymn and Modern Enigma', *Vigiliae Christianae*, **24** (1970), 189–96.

Turaev, B., *Chasoslov Efiopski Tserkvi* (St Petersburg: Imperial Academy of Sciences, 1897).

Uspensky, Nikolai, trans. P. Lazor, *Evening Worship in the Orthodox Church* (Crestwood, NY: St Vladimir's Seminary Press, 1985).

Van Dijk, S.J.P., 'The Medieval Easter Vespers of the Roman Clergy', *Sacris Erudiri*, **19** (1969–70), 261–363.

Van der Paverd, F. *Zur Geschichte der Messliturgie in Antiocheia und Konstantinopel gegen Ende der vierten Jahrhunderts* (*OCA* 187, Rome: 1970).

Van Tongeren, Louis *Exaltation of the Cross* (Leuven: Peeters, 2001).

Vellian, Jacob, *East Syrian Evening Services* (Kottayam: Indian Institute for Eastern Churches, 1971).

Vives, J., 'El Oracional mozarabe de Silos', *Analecta Sacra Tarraconensia*, **18** (1945), 1–25.

Vogel, C. (ed.); Storey, W. and Rasmussen, N. (ed. and trans.), *Medieval Liturgy: An Introduction to the Sources* (Washington, DC: Pastoral Press, 1986).

von Rad, G., *Genesis: A Commentary* (London: SCM Press, rev. edn, 1972).

Weiser, Arthur, *The Psalms* (London: SCM Press, 1962).

Wilkinson, J., *Egeria's Travels* (London: SPCK, 1971; new edn Warminster: Aris & Phillips, 1999).

Winkler, Gabriele, 'Das Offizium am Ende des 4. Jahrhunderts und das heutige Chaldäische Offizium, ihre strukturellen Zusammenhänge', *Ostkirchliche Studien*, **19** (1970), 289–311.

——, 'Der Geshchichtliche Hintergrund der Präsanktifikatenvesper', *Oriens Christianus*, **56** (1972), pp. 184–206.

——, 'Über die Kathedralvesper in der verschiedenen Riten des Ostens und Westens', *Archiv für Liturgiewissenschaft*, **16** (1974), 53–102.

——, 'L'aspect pénitentiel dans les offices du soir en Orient et en Occident', in *Liturgie et Rémission des Péchés* [= Conférences Saint Serge 1973] (Rome: Edizioni Liturgiche 1975), pp. 273–93.

——, 'New Study of the Early Development of the Office', *Worship*, **56** (1982), 27–35 (and also **56**, 264–7).

——, 'The Armenian Night Office I', *Journal of the Society for Armenian Studies*, **1** (1984), 93–112; 'The Armenian Night Office II', *Révue des études Arméniennes*, **17** (1983), 471–551.

——, 'Nochmals des Armenische Nachtoffizium und weitere Anmerkungen zum Myrophorien offizium', *Révue des études Arméniennes*, **21** (1988–9), 501–19.

Woolfenden, G.W., 'The Use of the Psalter by Early Monastic Communities', *Studia Patristica*, **26** (Leuven: 1993), 88–94.

——, 'Daily Prayer: Its Origin in its Function', *Studia Patristica*, **30** (Leuven: 1997), 364–88.

——, *Daily Prayer in Christian Spain* (London: Alcuin / SPCK, 2000).

——, *Joyful Light* (Witney: St Stephen's Press, 2001).

Zanetti, Ugo, SJ, 'Horologion Copte et Vêpres Byzantines', *le Muséon*, **102** (1989), 236–54.

——, 'La distribution des psaumes dans l'horologion copte', *OCP*, **56** (1990), 323–69.

Index of Persons

Index of Scriptures referred to or cited

General Index